THE RASHOMON TEA
AND SAKE SHOP

The Rashomon Tea and Sake Shop

旅 館

A PHILOSOPHICAL NOVEL ABOUT THE NATURE AND EXISTENCE OF GOD AND THE AFTERLIFE

Carol V.A. Quinn, Kyle Cottengim and Kait Cottengim

Rock's Mills Press
Oakville, Ontario

PUBLISHED BY
Rock's Mills Press

The epigraph on page 3 is from "A Prayer to Spring" by Robert Frost, which was published in the author's collection *A Boy's Will* in 1913. The poem is in the public domain in the United States and Canada.

This is a work of fiction. Apart from references to actual historical figures, including the philosophers and religious figures discussed herein, the characters, events, and locations depicted in the novel are fictitious. No resemblance to actual individuals, events, or locations is intended and any that exists is coincidental.

Cover image: Carol V.A. Quinn
Title page image: Kait Cottengim

Library and Archives Canada Cataloguing in Publication data is available from the publisher. Email us at customer.service@rocksmillspress.com or visit us online at www.rocksmillspress.com.

ISBN-13: 978-1-77244-025-6

DEDICATIONS AND ACKNOWLEDGMENTS

In memory of Renee Woodruff-Krumpholz and Ralph Woodruff

This book could never have happened without the loving support of my parents, Michael and Judy, and my husband, Bogdan. I dedicate this book to them and to the rest of my family, including the Chlebus clan in Bristol. I want to especially thank my nephew, Jordan, who is a terrific writer in his own right, and my stepdaughter, Maria, for helpful input. Thanks to my longstanding dear friend since graduate school, Sean McAleer, and my good friend Randall Sunshine. Thanks to my former student, Carrol Miller, and to anonymous reviewers of earlier drafts. Finally, this book would not have been possible without Mason "Thorne" Cassidy who started this project with Kyle and me before life got in the way, and our editor David Stover. Love to all of you.

—*Carol Quinn*

I would like to thank my many friends for the years of listening to my existential musings. To my parents for supporting my wandering-leaf spirit, and to my mom for the many late-night discussions from politics to religion—a heartfelt thank you. A big thank you to all of the philosophy professors and students from PLNC to MSU Denver—some who are very near and dear to me even today—for their guidance and input over the years. Finally, to my family, my son Galen, and Kait—my wife and best friend—for encouraging, helping and participating in seeing this project through to the end, massive thanks.

—*Kyle Cottengim*

A big thanks to our son, Galen, for his patience and tolerance when we could not go out because we were writing, and for making dinner on more than one occasion when the muse was especially insistent. For reading and suggestions, our family and friends were invaluable—thank you. For being there and being such a great partner in life in this and many more writing projects, a huge hug of appreciation to my phenomenal hubby and co-writer, Kyle. Finally, an immense shout of gratitude to Carol for inviting me to be a part of this work and for her inexhaustible knowledge, humor, and creative collaboration.

—*Kait Cottengim*

AN ANNOTATED TABLE OF CONTENTS
OF PHILOSOPHICAL AND THEOLOGICAL TOPICS

§

A Glossary of Japanese Terms Used in the Novel, Notes and References, and an Index of Philosophers, Theologians, Writers, and Other Thinkers cited in the text are included at the end of the book, beginning on pages 319, 321, and 327 respectively.

THE RASHOMON TEA
AND SAKE SHOP

PROLOGUE

It was just about time. Phil looked around the room, his eyes and mind wandering. He finally settled on a single photograph in a simple black frame. Three people stood arm-in-arm on the deck of a vintage yacht, mugging for the camera. The white of *The Gloria's* wheelhouse was a perfect contrast to the canvas of color clinging to those three young, tanned bodies. Phil smiled, remembering Michal's electric-blue string bikini, his red-hibiscus island shirt, and Max's size-thirteen boat shoes that would end up as fish bait following a tragic suntan-lotion accident.

Unbidden, specters from the past haunted his reverie. It was becoming a habit. He shook his head to cast out the inky water, the smoke, and the chaos invading his mind. He ran his hands through his hair, so much thinner than the younger man's in the picture. He stared into the mirror. He was drinking more and it showed. He was sleeping less too. Stepping into his slippers—the ones that stubbornly refused to look like proper footwear—he slid the *shōji* to the left and walked through, leaving the phantoms behind.

He went down the hall to the room where Max would be staying. As he approached the opened door, he looked critically at the floor's hardwood perfection. He paused and then made two long marks with the heel of his worn slipper. With a satisfied harrumph, he surveyed the room, noting the custom-length futon unrolled and ready for inspection. Given his size, Max was disappointed with most beds. Phil laughed at the thought of the bill for the eight-foot mattress. Closing the door, he continued down the hall, down the stairs, and exited the main building.

He opened the door to the new cabin, then closed and opened it several more times to ensure its smooth operation. Inside the simple room, he tidied the shelves, adjusting and readjusting the position of Michal's favorite book, until it was arranged just the way she would find pleasing to the eye, without seeming deliberate. He winked at the statue standing on the shelf. He imagined feeling a few drops of her healing water. Smiling, he reached into his robe pocket and walked to the desk. Closing the little hidden drawer, he moved to the rolled-up *shikibuton*, placed his face into the organic cotton covering and inhaled deeply. Finding no evidence of the new mattress smell, he folded the *kakebuton* and placed it to one side. Then he fluffed Michal's prized buckwheat *makura*. He laughed, remembering how she swore up and down that it was the best thing since her fishbone corset. He walked to the alcove and gazed out the window at the garden. He looked cockeyed at the scene outside. She should like this, he tried to reassure himself for the hundredth time in two days.

He walked across the gravel path and opened the door to a small shed in the garden. Grabbing a set of shears, he approached the well-manicured hedges. He snipped at the branches, finally lopping off a big hank. It looked far less perfect now. Satisfied, he put the shears away and walked down the path to the bar.

Once inside, he lit the fire and made sure that at least three chairs were not tucked neatly under the nearly dozen tables. He walked behind the bar, checked that several bottles of Michal's favorite wine were on hand, then moved two bottles of middling wines in front to obscure them. He walked to the kitchen.

He made sure the fridge was stocked full for their two-week visit. He walked over to the pantry and found several handpicked tins of Max's favorite teas. He placed them behind the seaweed paper so that they would be visible but not obvious.

Surfing fiascos and pub-crawls merrily crowded Phil's mind. But then the clamoring voices of ghosts past drowned out his nostalgia—ghosts that now threatened his peace and beckoned him to abandon himself to their design. He shook his head and walked out of the kitchen, through the main room, out the front double doors, and onto the circular drive. He looked at the garden with its splash of reds, yellows, and blues, and the mindless trickle of the water feature.

He looked up at the sky, the beginnings of rain clouds gathering overhead. He glanced at his watch again—the one he had checked five times in as many minutes. Judging by the hour, he guessed that his two friends were right about . . . .

SPRING

OH, give us pleasure in the flowers to-day;
And give us not to think so far away
As the uncertain harvest; keep us here
All simply in the springing of the year.

ROBERT FROST

§

ONE

*If you would be a real seeker after truth, it is necessary that at least once in your life
you doubt, as far as possible, all things.*
RENÉ DESCARTES

MAY 23, 2014. *Somewhere over the Pacific Ocean, approaching Japan*
One more bump and Max was going to puke all over the pretty flight attendant.
He stared at the water glass sitting on the tray. The ice cubes chattered quietly as
the plane rose and fell imperceptibly. Imperceptibly to most, but not to Max. Like
the ice cubes, he was keenly aware of each change in altitude. The knowledge that
the ice cubes could predict the turbulence was only moderately useful, as it
afforded awareness of the change only moments before it happened. Right now
the ice cubes sat relatively undisturbed.

Max learned the fine art of ice cube divination when he was ten years old. It was
on his first flight—Dallas to L.A. His daddy put him on the plane to stay the summer at Uncle Ethan's wild-pig-hunting ranch. He sat next to a mastiff from Burbank who was an extra in the movies.

"They always call me when they want a big-boned woman," she drooled.
"Here, want a Chiclet?"

Max smiled and grabbed one from the pack.

Miss Mastiff slapped his hand. "Not the red one. Red's my lucky color," she
barked. "I always chew a red one before my audition. . . . . Did you see me in
Total Recall? . . . Choose the orange. I've got plenty of orange here—see? You can
have two."

She pulled out a statuette from her oversized red purse. "Red. . . ." She raised
her bag and smiled.

3

Max opened his mouth to speak, but Miss Mastiff continued to drool on. "Look at this." She lifted the little statue. "This is Mary, the Mother of God, with little baby Jesus. See, little baby Jesus is sucking her teat. Isn't that just so darling? I got it in Naples. Ever been to Naples? Not Naples, Florida—in Italy, I mean. They've got no problem showing Mary's boob on a statue in Italy. After all, the Son of God's got to eat."

Max picked up the statuette and studied it. She grabbed it from him and set it next to her Diet Coke.

"Mary and Jesus help me tell turbulence. . . . Once they glowed golden and a minute later the plane started getting bumpy, but usually they just start to shake when the turbulence is coming. They'll tip themselves right over shaking. —If you can't go to Naples to get one of these little statues, then the ice cubes can tell you too. Now you can't buy a Mary statue in one of those Catholic shops because they don't sell the right kind. You've got to have the one with the little Jesus *here*—just like this."

Max finally got a word in. "I've got a Coca-Cola just like you. . . . Show me how to tell the turb'lence too. I doubt my mama will let me have one of those Mary statues."

The mastiff explained that he had to look very carefully at the ice cubes for any sign of movement. "Of course it's easier to see them in a 7-Up, but it works all the same."

Just then the ice cubes started to chatter in little Max's Coca-Cola.

"Why do you suppose he wants to meet now? Don't get me wrong. I enjoy the visits, but he's early. Weren't we just there a couple of months ago?" Max looked at his companion.

Michal gazed at the heavy cloud cover over Japan, rain tapping at her window. The captain announced that they had just descended to twenty thousand feet. She turned back to see the wing, imagining that she might just discover the little devil creature from *The Twilight Zone* pulling at the metal.

"Who knows? Maybe a thought came into his head and he just had to get it out. Why not just be happy for the pleasant travel?" She smiled. "I'm certainly happy for the companionship. We three see each other far too infrequently anyway." Michal stared at Max, wondering why he was focusing so intently on his water glass. She thought about Aunt Chloe. Aunt Chloe was always dressed in trashy retro-style animal-print jumpsuits, which showed off her so obviously fake double D's. Every time Michal would visit her (right up till the night Chloe drove her car into the lake, having taken a turn too fast after drinking way too much at Uncle Harold's birthday party) Chloe would be shoving a glass of water in Michal's face. "It's good for your skin, Michal. Keeps you young. Look at me. Never had a facelift. Seventy years old and never had a facelift. Take your auntie's advice and drink, drink, drink. Chew on that ice, too. It helps with sexual frustration. . . . Now, where are those flowers for my funeral?" Aunt Chloe was as batty as could be ever since her mother died. She was convinced that they would come for her next. Every time Michal visited, Chloe would sneak in the comment about the flowers and her funeral.

Michal shook Aunt Chloe out of her head and smiled at her good friend.

Max was a big man. Stood six-foot-six, with dark hair and eyes. Most people were afraid of Max because of the look of him. But he was more Gummy Bear than rough-and-tumble. He had an accent from the Great State of Texas, which he could turn on and off like the dial of a radio depending on the company he kept. But it would often betray him when he got hornet-mad.

"You're right about not seeing each other enough. However, I'm going to have to disagree with Buddha and say that I don't relish the journey, I just wish for the destination." Max reached for his glass and took a sip of water. One of the nice things about first class was that he got a real glass. He set the glass down on the tray and watched the ice cubes as they lay motionless. He began to relax. The ice cubes announced that his Steak Diane and mashed potatoes would stay down until they landed. It was such a good meal, airplane food or not. He was just growing comfortable when the ice cubes jumped clean out of the glass. He clenched his teeth as he felt the plane suddenly drop several hundred feet.

Michal was not quite so aware of the impending change. It felt more like a calamity than something to be borne. She found herself entering into a tired old dialogue, seemingly with herself. Max caught fragments, which drew his attention:

"I am not afraid to die."

Yes you are.

"I am not afraid to die!" To ease her anxiety, she offered a petition to her god: "I know you are the pilot of my soul. . . ." She smiled at her wit and pulled herself together.

Maybe next time. You can't escape me forever. I'm very patient.

The familiar voice slid across her mind like hot paraffin wax. It coated every nook and cranny, finally finding its way into her darkest fears, activating them and leaving a raw nerve. Michal looked around the plane surreptitiously. She knew she wouldn't see anyone belonging to the voice. The old man across the aisle, the one in the green baseball cap, was absorbed in a *Times* crossword.

Max gritted his teeth and looked at Michal. The change in her face was concerning. He had heard her speak of this "issue" before, but this was the first time he had witnessed it. He slid his hand over to hers as she continued to look around the cabin. What was she looking for? No matter, he would offer some solace.

Michal felt something touch her left hand. The skin was like that of a snake, its rough scales slithering over her flesh as it moved slowly up her forearm. Suddenly it moved back down to her hand, the scales abrading her skin. She let out a small cry and pulled away, only to find Max's hand pulling back, palm out, in a sign of peace. She looked at him, eyes wild. Glancing at her arm, she expected to find furrows where the scales removed flesh, but found only her own delicate skin—thanks to the apple blossom scrub she used regularly and the three liters of water she made a habit of drinking daily. Thank you, Aunt Chloe.

Max made no advances, talking only quietly. The curvy flight attendant, with the Marilyn Monroe face, approached with a warm towel and a glass of ice water. Michal marveled at the poise this woman showed toward what must seem to be two crazy people. The attendant was so reassuring and friendly she could make a Frill-necked lizard fall in love with her. First class definitely had its perks.

"Is there anything I can get for you, miss? Another Cabernet, perhaps?" She extended the glass of water and towel, the latter held between metal tongs. Michal watched the blue and green light play off the textures on the implements. She could barely hear Max or the attendant over the sound of the engines.

Then Michal realized that it wasn't the engines at all, but the rushing of blood through her ears. She whispered her mantra once again: "You are the pilot of my soul." She focused on their lips moving, noticed the glass and reached for it, trying not to shake as she did so. Forcing away the phantom pain, she paid closer attention, watching the attendant's lips, and then Max's. As Max's lips moved, he began making sense to her.

"And I thought I was the one who had a problem with flying." Max smiled, his own problems with motion banished by his need to help.

"Are you OK, miss? We should be landing shortly. Can I get you anything else?" the attendant asked.

"I'm fine, thank you." Michal took another look around the cabin. "Another Cab would be nice, please." She hoped she sounded less broken than she felt. She smiled at Max in an effort to fool everyone into believing just that.

"I'm fine, really. I *will* blame you for raising my fears. If you didn't panic so often over a bit of turbulence, I might get through these flights a lit— a little better." Her smile belied her mental state, but it was convincing enough.

"Oh sure, blame me." He smiled.

Marilyn Monroe, with the same sweet demeanor, approached again. She had already put on her landing lips. "The captain has just turned on the fasten-seatbelt sign, so you hang onto that glass of water and try to relax. I'll get that wine for you, but then we'll be on the ground soon enough. You just hang onto those, and we won't tell anyone you have them." She smiled and then turned to attend to the other passengers, collecting glasses and trash.

Max looked at Michal one more time, then resumed staring at the seatback in front of him. Michal sipped at her water, crunching the ice. Each crunch brought back some clarity. She stopped herself from looking around the cabin one last time. "Foolishness. . . ." she said under her breath. She knew the truth. I do, she told herself, almost believing it.

Despite the bumpy air, the plane landed smoothly and our two friends made their way to the terminal to wait for the commuter plane. This was Max's least favorite part of the trip. *Why can't we just take the express train like everybody else?*

They looked across the tarmac at the Boeing 777-300ER that had just flown them to the Kansai International Airport. It was a huge plane, able to carry several hundred people across the ocean at hundreds of miles an hour in relative comfort. It even offered lie-flat luxury for those who could afford it. Or who had friends who could. The 777 taxied out and passed behind several commuter planes. Then it passed behind a single-engine prop that had just pulled up to the hub. The pilot exited the little plane and strode over to Michal and Max.

Maybe there was some kind of pilot agreement, a secret handshake or some such thing, that all the pilots agreed upon every year at some cleverly disguised convention. Whatever the reason, every time that Max and Michal flew to the Rashomon Tea and Sake Shop, their pilot—always someone different—wore a garish floral shirt. Once Max asked the pilot whether these shirts were the standard airline uniform. The only answer he got was a smile, a "nope," and "please fasten your seatbelt," which annoyed Max, since the pilot could reach across him and do it himself, on this size of plane.

The pilot, sporting pink flamingos and palm trees, put their luggage in the back seat, although he made a point of letting them know that he had "stowed" their luggage. Michal smiled at this. She imagined that their luggage had snuck on board and was hiding like some kind of one-shoed vagabond. "Stowaways. . . ." She laughed. She sat down in one of the three seats and buckled up.

Max stepped out of the plane after they landed at Phil's private airstrip. While the term "deplaning" was the proper way to describe it, all he could think about was the "de-lunching" he had just experienced.

"Sorry, I was really hoping I would keep it down." Max presented the bag to the pilot.

"No worries, mate. We can't all be born with one leg in the air." The pilot patted him on the back before helping Michal out of the plane.

The final leg of their journey was by off-road vehicle. This time it was a Lexus LX—a bit fancier than what they were used to. Usually conditions were not so bad they needed to go off-road, but there was always that chance. A road could be washed out by a heavy downpour or blocked unexpectedly. Last time it was an overturned cabbage truck and a couple of cages of squawking chickens that required them to travel, if only briefly, "off-road." That said, Max was happy to be back on terra firma, whether off-road or on, and so more inclined to talk.

The forest all but covered the road with the grabbing branches of the deciduous trees that lined their route. Drops of water fell onto the windshield from leaves drenched by the recent rain. Max looked out the window at the maples and pines and tall skinny trees that were altogether bare except for lollipop tops. Pure in a way, he thought. As if to punctuate this point, a flock of cranes flew overhead. He could just make out their loud rattling calls. The canopy obscured his view as they passed into more dense forest. "Cranes," he said absent-mindedly.

"What's that?" Michal asked.

"Cranes," he said again, motioning out the window. "There was a small flock of them flying overhead. Must be heading to the marsh at the other end of the valley."

"Did you know that in Japan they are considered to be mystical or holy? The dragon, too, and the tortoise," Michal said.

"I didn't know that," Max said. Michal looked past Max into the dark underbrush. The shadows hid many things there—things she could not see but were there nonetheless. Max sensed that she was distracted. What was on her mind? He saw her look nervously at the Filipino driver dressed in proper chauffeur's garb. Why Phil insisted on this get-up was anybody's guess. The driver seemed to be far more interested in their conversation than on the road.

"The cranes are quite something. —I used to make origami cranes when I was a girl," Michal said somewhat distractedly.

Max heard the hushed tone in Michal's voice and saw her glance at the driver again. Here, now? He knew the answer, especially since she had told him that it had happened again.

"Um, well, y'know, I. . . ." Max felt like an idiot. *Great comeback, you dumb ass. Isn't a deacon supposed to be better at this sort of thing?*

"You know better than anyone, Max, I never was the religious sort before..." Michal caught the driver's glance in the rearview. Max tilted his head and nodded in the direction of the road, making sure that the driver was paying attention. His lips stretched in an overly polite smile—the one that he borrowed from some of his church's blue-haired busybodies. That combination of confidence and Texan charm inspired their driver to look back toward the roadway. Max returned his attention to where it belonged. His friend.

And then he felt it happening again. He saw, in the dimness of the SUV's backseat, a meager haven. It reminded him of rehab.

FOUR YEARS EARLIER

Max stared at the computer screen. The Saving Grace You're Looking For, it read. His hands shook as he rubbed his achy thighs. His eyes went to the 1920s Waterbury clock his memaw had given him, lit green by the vacancy sign of the Bluebonnet weekly motel at which he was staying. The sound of it ticking his life away was unmistakable. He was dying. He knew it. At least it felt like it. He had already emptied the contents of his stomach several times over. He felt he had vomited out his soul along with everything else. Not wanting to sit still any longer, he backed away from the tiny wooden desk, so small that his knees could barely fit under it, and paced around the room. It was nine paces wide, eight paces across, with nothing to block his path. In one corner stood a mattress on a metal frame, draped with a brown crocheted blanket that he got at the Good Will. And in the other corner stood that damned desk. He made another lap around the room. He looked out the rain-tapped window wondering, for the tenth time in fifteen minutes, how long it would take him to get to Gary's place a few blocks away. He sneezed, again.

Drywall dented in as Max's fist hit the wall. Chips of bone-white paint flew off and caught in his matted hair. He was so tired. The room tilted and he collapsed on the floor, pain coursing through his head and limbs. He grabbed his skull, willing it to stop hurting, but the pain had no mercy. Mercy. . . Someone had to have mercy. Calm washed over his body, enabling him to crawl across the floor, barely avoiding the trashcan still filled with his stomach contents. He eyed the phone as the pain returned, and with shaky hands he picked up the receiver. Silence. Darkness.

"So I told the guy, if you want her phone number, let me have a crack at her first. After I'm done with her, she'll practically beg you to take her number. . . . "

Laughter broke out and Phil grinned at his own joke. He was enjoying his "research." Opening a bar, as he was planning, was the best idea he'd had in ages. Still playing the charming patron, he downed his drink and signaled the bartender to pour him another. Before it arrived, his phone rang.

"Your dime, start talking." Phil nodded at the bartender who was holding the bottle of Jameson's, eyebrow raised in question. He poured the drink as Phil tried to listen. "Who is this? I can't hear you." He looked at the bartender again, pointed to the phone at his ear and then at the door. The bartender smiled. He placed Phil's glass behind the bar and put a "Reserved" sign in front of his stool.

"Hello?" Phil looked at the number on the display. He did not recognize it, only the area code. He knew only two people in Texas who were still speaking to him.

"Max, is that you?" He hadn't heard from Max in months. His grip on the phone tightened when he only heard the sound of breathing on the other end. "Max—?" His voice cracked.

"Haaay . . . Phil . . . Jeshme. . . ."

"Are you OK, Max?"

"OK? Hmmm. Okaaay. . . . No. I don't thank I'm OK. I almosh kill mama yeshterd'y . . . and . . . I'm not feelin' jesh right. Shick. I'm shick, and the fire's on body, and the world, I think, ish not spinnin' like it should. . . . Maybe God kicked it?" There was a thump on the other end. Phil could barely make out the words as Max rambled on. "I jesh can't sheem to make my hands do the right thing. . . . Shakin' too mush. . . . You were my besht friend, Phil. Know that?" Max sneezed several times followed by an exaggerated sniffle.

"Max, talk to me. What do you mean you almost killed your mom?" Phil reached into his pocket and pulled out his earbuds so that he could talk and text at the same time. He listened to Max go on about skipped classes, yelling at his mom, getting caught stealing money from her purse. He texted a message to the other person he knew in Texas, who wasn't *really* speaking to him.

"That sounds harsh. Is she OK?" Phil's fingers flew over the touchscreen, his texting frenetic. The PI he had on retainer, the one at the other end of the text, informed Phil that it would be extra since it was such short notice and Phil would owe him big. "Of course I owe you, you stupid prick," Phil said under his breath. "Just get there."

"Whaat?" Max's voice was drifting.

"Hey! Stay with me. Sounds like you need a doctor. Let me get you a doctor." Phil walked back into the bar, waved at the bartender, and put a fifty on the counter. The bartender waved back. Phil continued to stab at his phone, connecting to a travel website as he walked to his car.

"I don't thank I desherve a doctor, Phil. Maybe a crem—crim—cramitor—a mortician."

"Now who's being the drama queen, Max?" Phil finished typing in his credit card information and saved the ticket invoice to present at the terminal. Then he sent an email to the treatment facility. He started his car and drove off.

Phil kept talking to Max, waiting until he heard a knock. David, the PI, had made good time getting to Max's door. Phil could hear the door shut before the line went dead. He dialed back the number, but only got the annoying recording about it not being in service. Then his phone buzzed. David's mobile number flashed on his screen.

"Yeah, David. You there?" Phil ran his fingers through his hair before laying on the horn for the asshole who had just cut him off. Light rain began to fall. The sound of the wipers made his shoulders and neck tense. He snarled at his reflection in the rearview. The streetlights flashing by cast his face into an almost demonic visage.

"Of course. I've got all the arrangements made. I'll meet you at his room and take it from there. Make sure he stays clean until then. . . . What? Never mind. And for the tenth time, yes, I know I owe you." Phil jerked the wheel of his carnelian-red Jaguar to the right, cutting across two lanes of traffic to take the airport exit. It would be an almost four-hour flight. He opened his contact list and hit the all-too-familiar entry.

"Yeah, I just emailed you the details. I'm bringing in my friend. No, I'm financially responsible. I've already paid the deposit. Patient's last name is Cardin. Maxwell Cardin. Yes, I'll hold." He listened to the woman's Southern drawl and tried not to mind. "Excellent. Thank you. No, I'm not absolutely sure, but I think heroin. He had some kind of trigger yesterday. When can I visit him?" He waited impatiently for her reply. "Well, I guess that'll have to work. Thank you." Phil ended the call. His flight to Dallas left in just over an hour.

PRESENT DAY. *Our two friends, still on their way to the Rashomon Tea and Sake Shop*
"You know," Max said to Michal, "how I found myself doubting my own sanity. Remember? I was desperate, addicted to heroin, life out of control. I was in debt and stealing from the people I loved. I realized that I was starting to slip in my role as a son and a decent human being. I thought I could revisit these roles, to allow myself to overlook all the rest. This thought was a sort of touchstone for me of all that was normal. Despite living in the grip of addiction, I was proud of being part of a good family, proud of my academics, though the rest of my life was completely out of control. But then I started to fail in these areas as well."

Max glanced at the driver, who was eyeing the rearview. He secretly hoped that he had a new ear to bend, but the driver gave the impression that he'd understood Max's earlier, less-than-good-natured hint to butt out. Max knew that Michal had heard his story before. When he looked at her, he found her politely waiting for the familiar tale to run its course. He knew this, but liked telling the story anyway. "So I panicked and ran to a group meeting. . . ."

Michal raised her hands in mock terror to assist Max in telling the story. A smile crept out from under her previously conflicted countenance. "Church was the last place I wanted to go. . . ."

"What about God in the first three steps?" She played along while keeping with the oratorical pace. Max took such playfulness as encouragement and continued.

"Well, the folks there assured me that it wouldn't be a problem. One guy even said that he was a 'dirt-worshipping' pagan and the program worked for him." Max laughed for dramatic effect as he did every time he shared his story. "I remember sitting in on one meeting where this woman had messed her brain up so bad from using crack, or meth, or whatever, that she couldn't even put sentences together—" Then with less drama, but in good faith, Max whispered, "But I could understand her."

He stopped for a few seconds, hoping that it might make more sense to her than it did to him. He saw something in her eyes that he hadn't seen before when he had shared his testimony.

"Though the woman seemed to ramble incoherently at first, I could hear her saying that she knew that we couldn't understand her, but she wanted to share anyway. . . ." Then in the howling dramatic tone of a lewd punch line, Max said, "There I was 'interpreting.'" He raised his hands heavenward only to scratch the air with quoting fingers. "They were speaking in tongues and testifying, though they just called it 'sharing.' All the while, the Holy Spirit in the form of their 'Group Consciousness' made me see—" Max hesitated as if he hadn't shared these inexpressibly wondrous acts of God's grace with her at least a dozen times. He slowed down. "—Made me see what it might have been like in the early church. Like Jonah, I ran to the other side of the world, only to find myself in the belly of the whale and on my way back to where God wanted me to go."

"Yes," Michal said, recognizing the conclusion of the story, "but I'm not speaking figuratively."

Max started to object, gesturing with an upturned palm, which she mimicked, causing them both to laugh.

"But your female addict friend had something to add to the conversation this time." Michal smiled. "She was interacting with her reality, and it was just as real to her as your experience was to you. However, without a translator, she just kept wearing the crown of Descartes' madman. She only *thought* that she was king." And then in earnest, albeit faux-pleading, she suggested, "Can we talk about Descartes?"

Max extended his arm in a chivalrous manner as if he had been urging her to pass in front all along.

"Remember when Descartes is writing in his pajamas, sitting by the fire, maybe drinking some brandy?" Michal breathed out the words, as if she had just sipped from the same drink. "Descartes says that he cannot deny these experiences, as they are immediately present to him." She focused her attention on the seat that cradled her, centering herself in the real world before continuing. "But at the same time he was shaken by the possibility that he might be a madman who thinks himself a king when he's only a pauper."[1]

Looking out Michal's window, they watched another flock of cranes fly overhead. Michal seemed to be addressing them: "This is how I feel—you know what I mean—a little conflicted about you-know-what." She glanced at the driver. He no longer seemed interested in his passengers. "Maybe I just need a translator." She patted Max's knee.

Max didn't follow her eyes this time. Instead, he was heartened by this new debate. The world afforded too few opportunities like this. This shared sentiment was a cornerstone, buttressing a great friendship. It was why they kept coming for visits, why they kept in touch though separated by geography.

"Do you think he's right? —Descartes, I mean. For my part, I'm not so sure that we can all be so deluded. At least not those of us who are paying attention, those of us who are examining our lives," Max baited. "I honestly think that Descartes' argument was largely just theatre for the Catholic Church, which was breathing heavily on the back of his neck even as he wrote." Max paused to consider what he would offer next. "Descartes wanted the Church to regard the methods of science and philosophy as harmless and irrelevant"—he returned to his niggling habit of scratching at the air—"to the spiritual 'truth' and the confessions that the Church ripped from his fellows." Looking down at his now-clenched fist, Max relaxed his hand and gestured lazily toward Michal.

"And yet Descartes got into a lot of trouble with the Church. He regarded the evil demon as *summe potens*, but only God can be *summe potens*." She stabbed her finger upward and outward. "Max, I think you know better than to argue that our senses are anything but notoriously unreliable. And I'm not just talking about optical illusions, rainbows, or phantom pains. Science itself tells us that the common-sense axioms that our perceptions afford us disperse like fog in the light of reason. That a flat earth's horizon opens up to yet another horizon on an endlessly round world. And we know conclusively that the seemingly solid is nothing more than energy arranged in a particular way. We may experience a solid cushioned seat here, when really there is little more than space between atoms and even within them." Pleased with her argument, Michal sank back into her seat just as the SUV hit a rut in the road. She slammed against the door and winced.

"Sorry, the road is rutted out from the rain. Are you all right?" the driver asked.

"We seem to be. Thanks for asking," Max said, borrowing his manners again from those all-too-proper church ladies. He returned to Michal and smiled. "Actually there's been common-sense evidence of a round earth since ancient times. People just ignored it. When a ship sails away, for example, the top of the mast remains visible longer than the rest of the ship, as it follows the curve of the earth. And ever since physicists split the atomic nucleus over a century ago we've known that it's composed of smaller particles—protons and neutrons. We now know through even more powerful particle accelerators that they in turn are made up of quarks. . . . And if we go with superstring theory, the smallest particles are not point-like at all but more like tiny strings vibrating in eleven-dimensional space, and. . . ."

"I see you've been reading your *Scientific American*," Michal said with a smirk.

Max smiled and then put on a matter-of-fact face that he hoped to pass off as an argument. "I'm still convinced that we are actually sitting here in this fancy Lexus, on this road, in Japan, heading to meet up with Phil, our flesh-and-blood friend." Michal's raised eyebrow let him know that he would have to try a little harder.

Max pointed at her shoulder. "How're you doing?" She grimaced. He thumped his satchel that held, among other things, three different Bibles. "Revelation trumps reason every time." He smiled as if to suggest that was enough, but he had more. He started again a little more carefully, "You don't ignore the talking, ever-burning bush just because you can't explain it."

"But I think it's fair to doubt your senses in such a situation even as you remove your shoes on holy ground. —I'm not ignoring *anything*. That's the problem, Max, I *can't*. You really need to open your ears," Michal said with a swaying, tsk-tsk finger. "I believe, as I am certain you do, that one can be reverential and awed, yet still have doubts. . . . All I'm saying is that maybe the 'burning bush' you always bring up 'seems'. . . ." She smiled, noting that she didn't share Max's habit of scratching at the air with quotes. "Maybe the burning bush isn't always what it seems to be at first."

"Like a mirage?" Max asked. "Or a rainbow?" He gestured toward Michal's window at the faintest hint of a rainbow beyond the cranes.

"If we stay with Descartes, we could talk about dreams. Descartes says that we can't be certain that we aren't just dreaming all of this."

"I'm not sure I agree this is all just a dream." Max paused to make sure that he wasn't speaking out of turn. "First, there are far too many details that are consistent with everything else. No major gaps—and trust me, I'm paying attention. Second, we did not just appear here, talking in this SUV, but we can both recall our long flight and our fixed, so-far-complete, history of a very long friendship. And the only thing morphing before our eyes here are our arguments." Max laughed, thinking he was pretty clever. Having seen *Inception* on the flight over, he trusted that she wouldn't call him out on borrowing his two points from it. They both practiced this sort of charity. "I think we'd realize it, if we were dreaming."

"I can fly in my dreams," the driver intruded, speaking into the rearview mirror, "and I saw that movie too. *Inception*, right?" His words startled them. Michal laughed when she noticed Max blushing. The driver continued, "Dreams within dreams. That was some movie, huh? Complicated as shit, but really something. . . . What do you call it when you know you're dreaming?"

"Lucid dreaming," Michal surrendered the words interspersed with her laughter. She addressed Max: "You know very well we could be dreaming all of this, even our history."

"If you insist on not letting this go. . . ."

"Have you ever heard about Zhuangzi's butterfly dream?[2] Zhuangzi dreamt that he was a butterfly. Being a butterfly, he didn't think that he was Zhuangzi. But when he woke up, there he was, Zhuangzi, as plain as the nose on your face." She tapped Max's nose and he smiled. "But then it struck him: he didn't know whether he was Zhuangzi who had dreamt he was a butterfly, or a butterfly dreaming he was Zhuangzi. . . . We think that the dream world is a fiction and that the real world exists. But Zhuangzi's butterfly dream shows us that we can't know for sure which is which. We can't, with any sort of certainty, distinguish between the existing and the dream worlds. Perhaps they are equally real, or there's a blurring between the two, or a bleeding of one into the other. Or perhaps only the dream world is real. . . ."

"You know, there's a modern day version of Descartes' argument: Gilbert Harman's brain in a vat.[3] Perhaps you are really only a brain hooked up by some mad scientist to some futuristic supercomputer that perfectly simulates the outside world. How do you know that you're not just a brain in a vat? If you can't rule out this possibility then all of your beliefs about the real world are thrown into doubt. . . . I'm not convinced though."

"Well, if Descartes' dream or madman arguments don't work for you, Max, we can turn to his evil demon. An evil demon could be responsible for cooking up our reality. The modern-day version of this would be, of course, dissociative identity disorder. Might the evil demon whispering into Descartes' ear be Descartes' alternate personality? Or maybe he has a brain tumor. —Hell, maybe God Himself is the evil demon. We can't rule any of this out."

"The butterfly dream reminds me of Shakespeare's *Taming of the Shrew*. Remember? A lord comes upon a drunken tinker, Christopher Sly, who's passed out in a field. He brings him to his home and convinces the guy that he is actually a lord, who has only been dreaming that he was a drunken tinker. 'Banish hence these abject lowly dreams. Look how thy servants do attend on thee. . . .'" He laughed.

Suddenly a raccoon dog ran across the road, barely escaping becoming road kill.

"Did you see that?" Michal asked. "Wasn't that a *tanuki*? Isn't that what Phil calls them?"

The driver looked at her through the rearview. "It was—and nearly a dead one."

As they continued down the road, they came upon a broken-down cargo van. It was sage green, and on the sides it had black-painted pictures of a buckboard wagon with signs above reading *Ryuu's Ragbag*. A large man with a round face, full grey beard, octagonal glasses, and a Roman nose sat on a stool on the side of the road. He was smoking a cigar and talking to a squirrel perched above him in a tree. The squirrel wasn't paying much attention.

The driver stopped the SUV, and the three of them walked over to the man. Max noticed a wheel lying on the other side of the road.

"Need some assistance?" Max asked. He looked into the van through the opened rear doors and noted a bunch of well-organized junk.

"You selling snake oil?" Max said and laughed.

The man was rubbing his knee. He looked up at Max.

"Oh no, sir. I am allergic to snakes." The man put out his cigar, stood up and walked to the back end of the van. He grabbed a couple of items. "I sell everything. Everything but the kitchen sink. But I sell the *faucets* for the kitchen sink. . . . Here's a pasta cooker. Genuine stainless steel for the pretty young lady. Makes the best spaghetti. You like spaghetti? Sure you do. Everybody likes spaghetti. I've also got a tablecloth here. Notice the pattern? Cactus and cowboy hats. And for the gentlemen I've got aftershave. I make it myself. It's my best selling item. I sold three just this month. I call it 'Tombstone.' The ingredients are secret, but I'll let you in on it, since I can see that you are very trustworthy. The secret is"—he looked around to make sure that the squirrel was no longer listening—"just the right mixture of cedar, oakmoss, sandalwood and sage. You'll smell like the Wild West.... I'm also selling elixirs, tinctures, ointments, liniments. I've got stuff that can cure anything. What's ailing you? Bad back? Sore throat?"

Max laughed. "That's—um—snake—oh, never mind."

Michal saw that the man had what appeared to be a tobacco-spit stain on his wrinkled-up suit jacket. The man noticed her looking.

"I assure you, I am a respectable salesman. I'm not like those disreputable types who end up tarred and feathered." He straightened his jacket.

Max looked at the driver and rolled up his shirtsleeves, motioning him to the runaway wheel. They got to work repairing the van.

The man plopped back down on his stool. He looked at Michal and smiled amicably.

"My back gets achy from the broken springs." He continued to smile at her and then stood up. "What am I thinking? How rude of me.... Please, sit down." He gestured at the seat. "I have another stool in the back." He walked to the back of the van and grabbed the stool and a bottle of what looked like peach-colored soda. He offered it to Michal. "Here, drink this. What a lovely day—well, except for the rain...." He sat back down.

Michal looked at the bottle. "What is it?"

"It keeps the spirits away." He looked over at Max and the driver who were reattaching the wheel. "Make sure you secure it really good. My wife wants me home for dinner. She's making blackened cod pizza. Recipe comes from my grandpappy's restaurant. Best pizza in the Old World...." He smiled. "I see that you're staring. You don't see many Italian travelling salesmen in Japan, you're probably thinking. My wife and I decided to retire here. Why don't you join us? She would love the company. I'm sure she gets tired of seeing only my old mug.... We live in the village just up the road."

Max smiled at the man. "Thank you kindly, sir, but we're on our way to see our good friend."

The man rubbed his knees some more. "Who is he? Perhaps I know him. There aren't many people around these parts."

"Phil Foster. He owns the Rashomon *ryokan*."

The man frowned and then looked at Michal. "You enjoying that, young lady?"

Michal smiled. "This is good." The fizz tickled her nose. "Drives away spirits, you say? ... I hope you're talking about *evil* spirits. I wouldn't want it to drive away the good kind." She smiled again.

Max and the driver approached. "We're done. You should be just fine now." Max smiled.

The man got up from the stool and walked to the van. He grabbed a leather pouch and handed it to Max.

"Oh, no, thank you." Max handed it back to him. Michal leaned into Max's ear and whispered, "C'mon, Max, where are your Texas manners?"

The man put it back in Max's hand. "It's not for you, young man. It's for your friend, Phil. I suspect he's needing it."

Max, Michal, and the driver waved the man off and got back into the SUV. After they were a safe distance away, Max extended the pouch to the driver.

"Want a magic pouch?" He laughed and then whispered to Michal, "Phil doesn't believe in that bunk."

"No, Max. . . . Don't. Give it to Phil. What's the harm, really, were you to give it to Phil?"

"OK, fine. I'll give it to Phil. . . . But you know I'll never hear the end of it." He stuffed it into his shirt pocket.

As they drove along, Michal looked at Max and said, "Who was that guy anyway? Seems like he came straight out of a Sergio Leone flick. . . ."

The SUV pulled off the main road and passed under a two-beam *torii*-style arch. It was simple, vermilion-painted wood with silver lettering. The upturned crescent of the *kasagi* kept watch over the name. The words *Rashomon Tea and Sake Shop* stretched across the straight beam below. In smaller though still readable letters underneath it read, *RTSS Ryokan*. The road ahead cut through denser forest. Blue-gray light seeped through the now-heavy rain. The Lexus suddenly swerved and the driver cursed.

"Potholes. . . . Sorry, friends. Maybe you can convince him to take better care of his road. He would get more customers." Max and Michal caught the driver frowning. The driver was well aware of the implications of the potholes. He shared his thoughts with our two friends: "It's bad enough that he's *gaijin*, but he doesn't fix his road as well? It's almost like he doesn't want business."

Michal and Max exchanged knowing glances. They had mentioned the potholes before—many times before—but Phil had only waved them off. *"If someone doesn't want to work around a few rough edges, I don't want 'em here."*

They drove through the forest a few minutes more. The branches reached out, at once inviting and foreboding. Michal cracked the window, welcoming the fresh scent of evergreen mixed with rain. She heard birds chirping. She hoped that meant the rain would stop soon.

Max leaned over toward the opened window and inhaled deeply. "We don't get this smell where I come from. . . .We get hot cement—and of course our famous 'tortilla breeze.'" He chuckled. But then he thought about the mission where he ministered to the homeless and the overpowering stench of unwashed men. He forced that memory out of his head and tried to enjoy the moment.

The SUV emerged into the open courtyard. In the center was a garden adorned with birds of paradise, other exotic flowers, and well-manicured shrubbery. Michal smiled at her favorite hand-carved granite bench—the one that looked like an ancient tiger warding off evil spirits.

On the other side of the road was a parking area, with a line of trees obscuring the vehicles from the simple buildings beyond. At least the trees *would have* obscured the vehicles, had there been any. There were none. No scooters, no wheeled conveyances of any kind.

"I see that Phil continues his economically self-destructive plan of not having any patrons," Max observed.

There was a reason folks tended to stay away, besides the shitty roads. Anyone who entered the Rashomon Tea and Sake Shop quickly became acquainted with Phil's jeering demeanor. And unless he was a total dimwit, anyone stepping foot inside the establishment would judge Phil a puffed-up narcissist with a penchant for conversations of the oddest type.

The Lexus passed the parking area and approached the main building.

It was a two-story affair with heavy square edges, except for the front left corner, which was cut diagonally from roof to ground. This curious feature was hard to miss. The shutters were opened, providing a glimpse into the building. They could only see the upstairs ceiling, but they had a waist-up view of the common area below. Phil stood inside, wearing his familiar tattered gray robe. He was holding a glass. He stared at the fireplace that burned in the middle of the room. Off to the side, they could make out the top of another man's head, likely sitting at one of the tables. They were both surprised that Phil had a customer. But even more of a surprise was that the customer didn't seem to have any transportation. No matter. Phil attracted strange types.

The grounds around the main building were bedecked with shrubberies and paths that meandered to various gardens and the structures behind the parking area. One could get lost in thought while on a stroll, contemplating the mysteries of the universe and getting drenched by the rain for the effort, since the trees offered scant coverage from the elements. The *Kuraokami* would often visit these parts.

The SUV pulled up to the large double doors and stopped. Michal reached for her bag and quietly pulled out a pair of bright yellow three-inch heels. They complemented her yellow- and red-hibiscus sundress. Her long hair, the color of dark chocolate tiramisu, was pulled up into a loose ponytail. She grabbed a tube of orange-red lipstick from her purse and quickly painted her lips. Max looked at her and grinned.

"What? A girl can't look nice?"

"Sure, when it will be appreciated. And I think you know that he won't care a whit about what you're wearing."

Michal knew that Max was right, and at first she considered leaving the heels in her bag, but she decided to put them on anyway.

"Well I'm not prettying up for him, I'm doing it for me. Isn't that what's important? Whether I'm a mind or a body, I still like to look nice." She deflected Max's playful accusations with philosophy.

Michal had a unique look about her and was considered a beauty by just about anybody's standard. Once a stranger told her that she looked Egyptian. She didn't understand the remark.

"You know," the stranger said. "Like Liz Taylor in *Cleopatra.*"

Max put up his hands in surrender while Michal put on her shoes. Their attention was drawn from each other to the driver who was getting out of the vehicle.

They watched with a certain bemusement as the driver, noticeably absent an umbrella, scampered around to Michal's door, the rain pelting him. The gesture was at once endearing and irksome. It was typical of Phil to make sure that his guests were well-cared-for but exposed to the "natural world." The driver stood there, hand extended for Michal.

She reached into her bag, pulled out a bright orange compact umbrella, and waved it at the driver like a magic wand. She opened it and stepped out into the rain. There was barely enough room under it for the driver too, but she was happy to share it with him. He held out his arm and she took it as they walked toward the building. He hesitated and looked back at Max. He lifted a finger, signaling that he would return just as soon as they were inside.

Max looked out at the rain, wondering whether it might let up just enough for him not to get thoroughly soaked. How would the driver, sans umbrella, help *him* to stay dry? He might get even wetter with a second pair of feet splashing in the puddles. These trifles dawdled about his mind. Sometimes being overly inquisitive was a curse. As if to answer his questions and inspire action, the rain pelted down even harder. Max smirked.

"Typical. . . . *Summe potens* indeed! Is that you or your deceiver friend? Think you could have it let up for just a minute?" The rain came down in sheets. "OK, OK, I hear ya. *'Ask and it shall be given to you'* —well, I didn't ask for the Flood." He put up his collar and calmly made his way through the rain to the door.

The door swung open just as Max was approaching. The driver looked at him approvingly, mumbled something about getting their luggage, and went back out to the SUV.

Phil had heard the Lexus pull up. He took another sip of his Blanton's whiskey sour, enjoying the burning, sweet sensation as it moved down his throat. He stared into the fire. The flames were seducing him with a private belly dance. Draining the drink, he peered through the glass at the blaze. He wondered at the reality of it all. The glass had been full only a few minutes ago, and now it was empty. Finally mumbling "just like wax," he threw the glass into the fire and watched with some small boyish delight as it shattered, the shards slipping into the flames. The front doors opened and he crossed his arms in thought.

Max squeezed out the water from his Western indigo chambray shirt. The air was warm inside. The scent of jasmine, sweet and peppery, was inviting. A table stood in front of them. Atop the table sat an aqua and bronze teacup with Max's favorite green tea, and warm sake for Michal.

The warmed cup felt comforting in Michal's hands. She closed her eyes, taking in the sensation. This was nothing like the time she tried coffee for the first time and spit it out all over her mother's new white plush carpet. She wasn't sure why she was remembering that just now. Daddy grounded her from going to the school dance, plus no allowance. It was the morning after Michal refused to clean her bedroom and snuck out her window to see an R-rated movie with her best friend, Makayla. The movie was *Pulp Fiction*. Daddy had enough. The next time she did it, he took her hamster and released it to fend for itself in the field behind the backyard. This was bound to happen sooner or later. Daddy hated the sound of the hamster wheel squeaking night after night, *all night long.* Michal tried to shake these thoughts out of her head.

The caramel aroma wafted past her nose as she brought the cup to her lips, savoring the liquid. She closed her eyes and heard a rustling from her old friend by the fire. *Ah, he must be ready to talk now.* She caught Max's eye as she tilted her head in Phil's direction. Max returned her look with a playful smile. It didn't really matter whether their host wanted to make an entrance; the tea was excellent and Max was intent on enjoying it. Propriety dictated that someone should say something, but history showed that their friend always had something to say, and so they waited.

Phil approached with a fresh drink in his hand and looked them directly in the eyes:

"Why do you believe?"

"You referring to our faith?" Max asked.

"Why do you believe?" Phil repeated.

Michal felt her heart pound at the thought of answering such a question. Yes, she believed. She considered herself a hard-core Jesus freak. But she tended to keep her reason to herself. Once she had told her pastor only to be met with a blank response. But hadn't her pastor heard it all? Michal's reason for believing wasn't *that* far out of the norm, was it? She looked at her dear friend and clutched her sake cup so tightly she thought it would break.

THREE YEARS EARLIER

The pastor sat at his massive mahogany desk. Ruddy and round, he looked a bit like Santa Claus, but without the beard. It was a blistering hot August day and his office lacked air conditioning. A small standing fan whirred noisily. Beads of sweat dripped off the pastor's head, and his mint-green button-down shirt was plastered wet to his skin. He grabbed his McDonald's strawberry shake, which sat next to his closed MacBook and his smartphone. He slurped through the straw and set it down. Behind him there was a bookshelf filled with the sort of books one would expect to find in a Lutheran pastor's office: C.S. Lewis' *Mere Christianity*, Augustine's *Confessions*, Bonhoeffer's *The Cost of Discipleship*, *The Lutheran Study Bible ESV*, and Martin Luther's *Basic Theological Writings*. Michal sat across from him, eyeing his books and mindlessly playing with his Martin Luther Bobble Head doll, which sat atop his desk. She spotted a Schefflera plant, droopy and brown, sitting on the floor in the corner. The pastor noticed her looking.

"My wife said that I couldn't kill it." He chuckled. "Well, welcome to our congregation, Michal." He smiled while picking up a napkin from a stack which he had clearly grabbed at the McDonald's. He dabbed his forehead and then wiped down the sweaty shake cup before tossing the napkin into a wicker trash basket beside him. "Were you raised Lutheran?"

"No, I wasn't," Michal said.

"You were Catholic, then? We get a lot of Catholics."

"No. I was raised atheist. Well, my mom dabbled in New Age stuff for a time. I was saved just a few months ago."

"Baaheeehem." The pastor cleared his throat. "We don't use that word here."

"What do you mean?"

"You don't become a Christian in an instant, as if by magic. It's not like drinking a magical potion." The pastor picked up his shake again, by way of demonstration, and took another slurp.

"It was for me." Michal wondered whether she would tell him how it really happened. "So if not by magic, as you say, how would you describe it?"

"We are all born children of God. But we are separated from Him because of the Fall. Baptism is the bridge that reconnects us to Him. We might fall off that bridge, now and again. Indeed, some of us choose to swim around with the man-eating piranhas." He laughed. "But we just need to find our way back onto that bridge and continue our walk towards our Father.... Were you baptized, Michal?"

"Yes I was. My mom's best friend insisted.... Do I need to be baptized again?"

The pastor laughed uproariously. "Nope. Once does the trick."

How is baptism any different from the so-called magic that he so vehemently rejects? I've got to tell somebody. Now is as good a time as any. And he's a pastor for crying out loud. Surely he's heard it all.

"Something on your mind?" The pastor noticed that Michal was deep in thought. She glanced at him. He seemed to be busy texting someone.

"I get a lot of messages," the pastor began, trying to explain himself. "Lucille is in the hospital right now, recovering from hip surgery. I hope you don't mind."

"Not at all. —I do have something on my mind. I don't want to come across as too crazy, though."

"You can't be any crazier than old Howard, who claims he eats breakfast with Jesus." The pastor laughed again.

"Well, maybe so." Michal decided that she was just going to do it. Just going to tell him everything, all at once:

"I had a spiritual battle with a demon a few months ago. Actually, I was drawn to him. I wasn't afraid of him at all. I walked toward him, he was so inviting, but then all of a sudden God intervened and He helped me break free. The next morning I laughed it off, of course. I didn't believe in demons, or angels, or God. I was an atheist. —I guess I did experience an angel when I was a little girl. Sat on my bed while I was trying to go to sleep. And then there were a couple of times when I just know, looking back now, that angels saved my life.... Do I sound crazy?" She said all of that without a breath.

"You're fine. Please continue," the pastor said with skinny lips. Michal couldn't read the expression on his face. She thought for a moment, listening to her own story replay itself in her head. She had never told it to anyone. Saying it out loud now made her wonder how it must have sounded. She had an instant of doubt. *Had I really?* ... Then just as quickly that thought was gone. She knew what she had experienced. She decided to continue. *Once more unto the breach, dear friends....*

"Two days after my demon encounter, I found myself crying out to God, out of the blue. Telling Him, 'I don't believe in you. I don't even know whom I should be praying to, if anyone at all. Jesus? My spirit guide?'" Michal paused and then explained. "You see, I had a spirit guide. Well, a friend got me hooked, but I never really took it seriously. ... Anyway, all of a sudden I experienced a flood of love. I can't explain it in any other way. A tremendous flood of love. And then I heard a voice, 'I am Jesus.' In an instant I fell in love with God and my life was transformed. I just can't explain it. I was flooded with God's love for something like three hours. Since then, God has blessed me with visions of heaven. . . ." Michal looked to the pastor for a response.

"You certainly had an experience of some sort." The pastor seemed to be scrambling for words. He paused longer than Michal liked. "Interesting, I must say." He picked up his phone again. "Sorry, another text."

He's probably calling the Funny Farm. She stood up. "Well, I have to make an appointment. I really must be going."

He quickly tapped in a few words then turned back to Michal. "You say you had visions of heaven and were flooded with love? That's the Good News of God's Word finding its way into the hearts of everyone. Even you, Michal." He put his phone into the drawer and gave her his full attention. "It happens to many people, though I don't usually hear such a, ahm, *direct version.*" He took a drink of his shake, put it down and got up from the desk. "I would like to hear more and I have time later this afternoon. Would you like some water before you leave?" He motioned to the water cooler. "I could offer you some coffee, but it's left over from last night's AA meeting. And you know what they say about church coffee." He smiled, looking like a jolly old elf. Michal half-expected him to offer her a candy cane. But his words just didn't feel genuine.

"Thank you." She sounded stilted even to herself. "I really do have an appointment to make." Her mind raced to her calendar. Something necessary. *Ah, the old standby.*

"A doctor's appointment—my gynecologist." She feigned embarrassment then realized that her embarrassment was all too real. She had seen how the pastor reacted to her story. She used that feeling to help her leave.

"Of course. I understand. Please do come by any time to talk." The pastor looked at the floor.

Michal grabbed her purse. "Thank you for your time." She turned to leave.

"I look forward to seeing you at service this Sunday." His words held no confidence.

Michal never went back to that church again.

Back at the RTSS

"Let's not get into why we believe right now, Phil. The far more interesting question is *what* we believe. And I'm as heretical as can go!" Michal smiled.

She felt her tension ease and her excitement heighten as she redirected Phil's question to something she could really get into. "But what about a few exchanges of pleasantries first? After all, we've been traveling some twenty hours to get here."

"True enough, the more interesting question just might be 'what?' That said, I am far more interested in the 'why.' Besides, the more interesting question is not always the best question." Phil looked up from his drink long enough to catch their angry eyes. He continued in an impatient huff:

"Oh, very well. Hello. How are you? Did the flight wear you out? What do you think of the weather? I am enjoying the extra rain. It's great for my ornamentals. Yes, I did add another house, and no, I still don't have many customers.

You will be the first to stay there, Michal." Phil sneered. "And now. . . . Shall we get to my question, or shall we dally about more?" He finished off his drink and walked over to the bar, his trademark bunny slippers making scuffing sounds as he went.

"You two have drinks and I need another." Phil leaned over the bar and reached for a bottle on the shelf.

"Do you have to be your usual asshole self already? I figured you'd warm up to that," Michal said half-jesting, half-serious.

Max frowned. "If I didn't know that you were doing this on purpose, I might have to teach you some manners. But since I know you won't be taught any, I won't waste my time."

"*Someone* has to be the asshole around here, otherwise the shit don't get dealt with." Phil pulled two glasses from the bar and set them down with a 'clink.'

"Show me to my room, Phil. I don't have patience for this. Maybe Max will indulge you, but I refuse."

Phil walked over to their luggage. "Well, then, let me get your bags." He picked up her suitcase. "Travelling light, I see. Very practical." He looked at Michal, or rather in her direction, since she was looking at the floor as she walked toward him. "You know what they say about people who carry light luggage? They are amazingly self-reliant and confident."

Michal stopped mid-step at his words. She dared to look at him. "Was that some kind of a compliment? Is that your best attempt at an apology?" She stood silently for a few seconds and then said, "Then I suppose I should apologize too. I'm just so wiped out. Good to see you, Phil." She extended her arms to give him a hug.

"*Feci quod potui, faciant meliora potentes.* Best I can do right now." He set down her luggage and straightened his robe before accepting her embrace. When he stepped away his demeanor had changed. His scowl was gone and replaced by the hint of a familiar smile. He picked up her suitcase and walked to the door that led to the outer buildings.

Max laugh-coughed as he reached for the pot of tea on the bar. "I guess I'll wait here until the lord of the manor sees fit to attend to me."

"Oh, don't you worry, once I get her settled in, I'll come back and we'll have a *man-talk*," Phil shot over his shoulder as he opened the door and stood to the side. Michal walked through, stepping onto the wooden planks of the back deck.

Her heels made a soft click-click sound as she walked over to the edge of the covering and stopped. She looked out at the rain. This time she didn't care about getting wet. Instead, she watched as the raindrops hit the petals of the cherry blossoms blooming on the trees that lined the path between the buildings. The foliage moved with each drop, performing entrechats in pinks and whites. She heard the scuffing of Phil's slippers as he approached from behind. A large umbrella opened above her head. He led her onto the path.

"Nothing will be kinder to your nice yellow shoes than this gravel path. Don't worry, there's compressed granite underneath, so those heels won't sink in."

Michal looked at Phil, who was smiling. The gravel made a crunching sound as she tested out the weight, but true to his word, the shoes only went down to the tight little pebbles. More confidently, she strode out onto the path as the rain pounded on the umbrella.

Phil opened the door to the new cabin. Once inside, Michal looked around, taking in the quaint surroundings. There was a black lacquer U-back armchair and a matching desk. A *shikibuton* was rolled up against the wall. Along the opposite wall were two South African Blackwood shelves. One held the 1876 edition of *Tales of Old Japan* and a small statuette of Kwan Yin. The other held a little bonsai and Michal's favorite book. Phil set down her suitcase, walked over to the desk, and opened the little hidden drawer, making a show of it as he did so. Then he moved to the mattress.

"You usually don't get so easily riled up by my asshole behavior. Have the past few months been enough to make you an easy target?" He knelt to unroll the mattress.

"At least you admit that you're being an asshole," Michal shot back with squinting eyes.

Phil put the pillow and comforter into place. He could feel her eyes boring into him. His job here was done, though he wasn't quite sure what that job was just yet.

Michal's mouth worked open and shut as she debated whether to prolong the conversation. "Phil, I—"

He waved her off. "Hey, it's OK. I know it's been a long trip. It takes it out of you. I should have gone a little easier on you. The bathroom is right there if you want to freshen up." He stepped out, closing the door behind him. As he was leaving, Michal could just hear him say: "By the way, darling, your fingernails shine like justice." She laughed and watched the shadows play on the screen as he walked back to the main building. She smiled when she noticed his umbrella sitting forgotten in a stand next to the door.

A mix of different alcohols from around the world was haphazardly arranged behind the bar. Noticeably absent was Phil's trademark twenty-three-year-old Evan Williams Bourbon, only available from the distillery. Max remembered when he'd gone with Phil to pick up a case. His mouth had dropped at the price. Phil had gotten a discount: $3600 for twelve bottles. Max was glad he no longer drank.

Not seeing the bottle, Max walked around the bar and began to scour the shelves underneath, on the off chance that Phil kept it hidden from his few patrons. He found Phil's stash behind the extra glasses. Surprisingly, there were seven empty bottles. He grabbed the half-empty one and a highball glass and returned to his barstool. He poured Phil a drink and waited for him to return.

Several minutes passed and the door opened. Phil walked in from the rain, his slippers making a squish-squish noise with each step. Max did his best to bite back his grin. Phil was drenched from head to bunny-slipper, water dripping all over the *tatami* mats. Max reached behind the bar, grabbed a towel, and walked over to Phil.

Silence filled the space, broken only by the drip of rainwater on the mats. Phil bent down and removed his footwear, squeezing them out and placing them on the shoe stand. He took off his sopping gray terrycloth robe to reveal a faded black tee with blue letters proclaiming Buckaroo Banzai Institute, and a pair of denim cut-offs. Both were damp. He hung the dripping robe on a hook. Without a word, he grabbed the towel that Max offered.

Phil dried his face and almost shoulder-length strands desperately in need of a haircut. Max remembered when Phil's hair was once sun-bleached to a much lighter blonde. Judging by his face, Phil hadn't shaved in about a week.

When Phil removed the towel from his head, he noticed Max's hands reaching forward, one empty and the other offering a glass filled with amber colored liquid. Phil thrust the towel into the empty hand and took the glass from the other. Max chuckled.

"So you finally replaced me with a new best friend," Max said and smiled at Phil's confusion.

"What?" Phil stopped mid sip and stared at Max.

"Either you have a new best friend worthy enough to drink the Williams with you, or you are drinking entirely too much alone. Seven empty bottles? At this rate, you'll go through all your money in no time."

Phil snickered. "Not likely. Besides I have a better distributor here in Japan. A case only costs me twelve hundred U.S." Phil tipped the glass and drained it before walking to the bar. He poured himself another drink and sat on the stool.

"Anyway, I'm not going to buy another case. When that's done, I'm going to try something else."

He took a sip and the bourbon first burned then mellowed to oaky goodness with hints of vanilla, chocolate, and cherry. He closed his eyes and enjoyed it as though it were the first time he'd ever tasted the EW 23.

Max's brow furrowed as he mulled over Phil's words. "You relish your new experiences, but this is a mainstay." He picked up his cup of tea. "Does this have anything to do with your cryptic, insistent question?"

"It might. So any answers, Faithful One?" Phil put his face down to the glass and let the nose of chocolates pass over him. "Hey, why didn't you put my drink in a snifter?"

Max smiled, "Honestly, I didn't think you would care, since it wasn't going to be in the glass long enough, judging by the mood you're in and what your liquor shelves imply." He smiled. "Here, Phil. I've got something for you." He reached into his shirt pocket and handed Phil the leather pouch the snake-oil salesman had given him.

"A present?" Phil gave a crooked smile. He opened the pouch and peeked inside. "You give me magic, medicine man? You want some land and irreplaceable resources in exchange?" He laughed. "Maybe I'll use it for a paperweight. It's all the respect it deserves. . . . C'mon, Max. Really? A magic leather bag?" He dropped it into his robe pocket.

"Comes from a traveling salesman we met on the road today. His van broke down. We helped him out," Max laughed at the nonsense of it.

"I know that guy. Came by to sell me herbs once. Never saw him again. He didn't seem to like my road. Fancy that."

"That's not a surprise. Of course, it could also be your not-so-pleasant disposition." Max chuckled.

"So how about that answer?" Phil asked flatly.

"If you really want to discuss this, I'll be happy to satisfy your curiosity." Max eyed him with suspicion. "Though the last time you asked anything like this about my faith, you were trying to get information for a date you were about to go on."

"Ah yes . . . Buxom Bailey. She was devout—for a while."

"You looking for another fling with a Jesus-type?"

"No, I'm legitimately interested."

"Well if you're going to be cryptic, I'll let you. But just because you left Michal with the umbrella. . . ."

"I'm surprised you noticed."

"It's the details that are important." Max poked Phil's chest. "Which is also why I believe, and why I almost didn't. . . ."

SEVENTEEN YEARS EARLIER. *Dallas*

Lee Wiley was promising that your essence is the quintessence of joy. It was actually some unnamed person that she was singing to, but Lee Wiley was singing Cole Porter's *Looking at You*. Max sat alone on his bed listening to the *LA Confidential* soundtrack. A Bible sat next to him. He had dozens of colored Post-it flags speckled throughout, like a veritable United Nations. Six were red, while the others were various colors: orange, yellow, violet, and pale green. He had it in his mind, when he laid them out, how the various colors would interact. The passages tagged by green Post-its contradicted those tagged by red. There were few green tags.

Max wasn't attending to the Bible right now, however. Instead, he was thinking about Guy Pearce as Detective Exley running down the hallway with a shotgun. Detective Exley's commanding presence, and his ability to make those hard decisions, passed over Max's mind. But Max was mostly consumed with thoughts *most unbiblical* about Exley's body.

He pressed 'stop' on the CD player, which drove his mind away from the titillation. Putting aside his graphic novel, *Preacher: Until the End of the World*, he picked up the Bible—*his* Bible—and opened to a tagged passage.

"*. . . He causes the sun to rise on both the good and the evil.*" That was enough to get him back to his project. He continued to pore over his Bible. He hoped that he could find a verse telling him that God loved gays despite their "condition." There were only six passages in the Bible that spoke about homosexuality. *Six passages.* Contrast that to the more than three hundred about our responsibility to care for the poor and work for justice. To make matters worse, Max knew that there was considerable dispute among scholars as to how many passages there really were. Many said there were six, but through Max's studies he discovered that the Sodom and Gomorrah story is actually about inhospitality, not homosexuality, which brought the total down to five: Leviticus 18:22 and 20:13, Romans 1:26-27, 1 Corinthians 6:9-10, and 1 Timothy 1:9-1.

But other scholars claimed Jude 7 referred to the sexual immorality and perversion of Sodom and Gomorrah, or to the 'mixing of strange flesh,' which suggested the Sodom-and-Gomorrah story was about homosexuality after all. That brought the number back up to seven.

So: Homosexuals were mentioned in the Bible in five, six, maybe seven places. He stopped and thought about the word. *Homosexual.* It sounded so clinical, descriptive, devoid of malice or venomous spirit.

"Fag, fairy, queer." He said the words to see if any of them fit. *Fag. That's what I am, a fag. And God hates me.* He cried quietly. Then he stopped crying and stared at his Bible. He came to a grim conclusion.

"If God hates me, *He can shove it.* I won't believe this crap any more. If God thinks I'm going along with this cowpat bullshit, then He must think I'm throwed down hard." Max got up and put on his tight blue jeans, cowboy boots, and *Push-monkey* tee. He looked at the Bible, now discarded on the floor. "I'll show you. I'm going down to the main drag and I'm gonna find that boy that keeps askin' me out and I keep sayin' no. You know what, God?" Max kicked his Bible across the room and it made a satisfying thump against the wall. A few Post-it flags broke free, escaping to the floor. Max smiled when he saw that one of them was red. "Piss on you, God!" He left the house, squeezing through his bedroom window. He snuck by the sliding glass door of the family room and saw his mom watching *ER* while his dad slept on the couch. His little sister, who was up way past her bedtime, was admiring her favorite Happy Meal Dumbo toy. Max got into his powder blue and Bondo gray '78 Chevy truck and headed toward town.

But Max could never bring himself to abandon God completely. After his anger subsided, he was left with even more questions and few reliable answers to take him through his senior year in high school and on to college.

Back at the RTSS

"I can't believe you used my words like that. I have failed as an atheist." Phil looked down at his half-empty glass and sighed.

"You and Professor Jackson were the ones who led me down this path of logic and debate."

"I haven't thought about him in years. 'It is better to debate a question without settling it'"—Phil started to quote and Max joined in—"'than to settle a question without debating it.'" They laughed.

"Joseph Joubert. I love that quote." Max lifted his cup and drank the last swallow of his now-cold tea. "Between Jackson's pushing for greater debating skills, and you pushing for the facts, I couldn't help but revisit the idea of God and the validity of the Bible from a different perspective. It was my settled question. So I began to look at the details. . . ." Max grabbed the electric kettle sitting on the bar, poured the steaming water into his cup, and inserted the loose-leaf tea infuser. "It was only when I began to look at who God really was, not who I or others thought He should be, that I heard God's voice. You started me down that path."

"Again, I say I have failed as an atheist. How the hell do you get God's voice from what I said to you?"

"It wasn't just you. . . . Egotistical much?" Max laughed. "You just started me on the path. It wasn't until Father M and rehab that I really began to understand just how messed up my understanding of God had become. Father M told me that God knows our hearts, and more importantly, that what many people value is highly detestable in God's sight. But it's not what you might think. When you look at the Bible, you see a lot of things that *man* esteems and believes. After looking at it for a good long time, I went back to the details. The details show you what *man* believes, and fears, and desires, and prescribes. God is not in the details, God is in the 'meta-.'"

"Wow, that's deep. Are you now one of the Seven Sages? So basically you follow a book that is supposed to give you genuine insight into God, but was written by men, and fallible men to boot. Is this what you're saying?" Phil looked legitimately confused.

"Phil, you kind of get it. But let me put it this way. I don't follow or read the Bible, I read the Word of God."

"And that inherent contradiction doesn't bother you?" Phil turned toward Max. His raised eyebrow disappeared beneath his shaggy bangs.

"The world is full of contradictions. What is it you like to say? *The truth is found in the extremes.*"

Phil smirked. "So at least you got something useful from me. Of course, you use that to prove that your God is real, so I'm still a little depressed."

"What you don't see is the one constant. Using the logic you love so dearly, think it through. What is the one verifiable feature of the Bible?"

Phil knew that he was being baited, so he held up a finger while he took a drink. A very long drink. Max tapped his fingers on the bar: thumb-forefinger-middle-ring-pinky. Five iterations later, he interrupted:

"You can't possibly still be drinking. Just say you don't know. It won't kill you."

"Fine. I would say the inherent contradictions, or maybe those ridiculous rules that people don't even follow, like not working on Sunday. But I'm pretty sure those aren't what you're going to say."

Max laughed while poking Phil's still-damp shoulder. "So you admit defeat? You're a smart cookie, Phil, but sometimes you miss the obvious, just like I do." He sipped his tea. After checking the rim for bits of stray leaves, he looked at Phil. "Oh—you want the answer, do you? The answer that you got, but didn't quite get? —All right, I'll tell you, and I even get to you use your knack for quoting movies: *'Nothing is ever what it seems, but everything is exactly what it is.'*"

"Cute. So my t-shirt gave you a bit of inspiration. Can you get on with it already?"

"You're right, of course. It *is* the contradictions. These contradictions are the result of man trying to understand and interpret his world over the course of many, many centuries. It's the *man* of the Bible who is the constant detail. And it is man who is the most incorrect. Of course we can't verify God with our five senses. He fails Popper's falsifiability test. But that also means that we can't dis-prove God."

Phil smiled. "But neither can we prove Him. . . ."

"Enough of that. I'm sure we'll get to that later, but for now let's just say that we agree that God fails falsifiability."

"You're willing to do that?" Phil looked at Max suspiciously.

"Of course. My faith would be dead if it were based on fact. I can't live that way. I know Michal would disagree, and we all find God in our own way. Even you, Phil. I still hold out hope for you. My point is that faith, by its very defini-tion, requires us to believe without any proof. Given that, I choose to see the Bible as fallible, full of contradictions, and flawed through and through. And that is the beauty of the Word of God. The truth tolls in spite of, and even in part because of, man's mistakes. As Father M likes to say, 'Don't miss the meaning for the words.' And that, Phil, is why I believe."

Phil looked at Max and held his tumbler up in toast. "As I said, it's good to see you." He opened his mouth to say more, then closed it and smiled.

FIFTEEN YEARS EARLIER. *Santa Barbara, California*

"People write books about these kinds of places." Phil held up his empty glass and waved it at the server. They were sitting in Grayson's Gastro Pub, famous for their beer-battered, fried, bleu cheese balls served with raspberry jam—and for accepting fake ID's. "I mean look at this place. We're sitting inside Billy Joel's *Piano Man*. People desperately trying to make sense of their lives. I guess I can't blame them for frantically trying to cling to the familiar." Phil chuckled at his own jibe.

"If that's the case, then what are *you* still clinging to?" Max stabbed at the slice of lemon in the bottom of his glass, trying to bring the stubborn piece of fruit to the top. It was impeding his alcohol consumption.

"I cling to nothing, my friend, save of course truth. And before you get that holier-than-thou bit going, yes, I believe that there is some truth to be had that doesn't revolve around anthropomorphized beings floating in the air." Phil went to take a drink of his whiskey and noticed again that it was empty. Max laughed. "Yep, right," Phil said. "I don't have whiskey, but I have hope and faith that it will be here shortly. I hear your same argument coming."

"Phil, I keep trying to educate you on the finer points of the English language and you keep ignoring me. . . . Hope and faith. It is neither hope nor faith that informs your prediction that your alcohol will arrive anon." Max finally pierced the lemon and fished it out of the glass. He finished off his drink. "'Anon' is Shakespearean for 'soon,' by the way."

"Yeah, Max, I know. . . ." Phil shook his head. "OK, so if not hope and faith, then how about *discipline and punishment?*" He smirked. "Foucault would high-five me for that one."

Max ignored him and continued. "It is a simple, informed, reasonable predic-tion, since the waitress not only wants your money, but she has been eyeing you all evening. I'm sure she will bring your alcohol, but as for hope and faith, I can't really say that they have anything to do with your current predicament. Now, whether you will go home alone—that could be something you might want to pray about, and *would* have more to do with hope or faith than getting your drink."

Max smirked as the server arrived almost on cue, her nametag proudly proclaiming her name *Staci* over the bounty straining to be kept in her tight white button-down shirt. She handed Phil another drink while Max's own sat forlornly empty.

Phil grinned at Max while he took the glass of whiskey from Staci. She held onto it for just a bit longer than necessary. He smiled.

"Maybe you can help us with a little discussion we're having. That *is* one of your skills as a service-industry professional, is it not? That of unwanted and unsolicited advice?" Phil gave her a wink.

"Sure is. But I need to make sure that my tip doesn't ride on my answer agreeing with whoever is paying the tab."

"Agreed," Phil began. "I'm paying and I definitely won't hold your opinions against you. In fact, I tend to keep company with those who blatantly disagree with me. Take Bill the Bard over here"—he stabbed a finger at Max—"who is constantly trying to remind me of things that I already know. . . . But that is neither here nor there. The question is. . . ." Phil took Staci's hand. "Is it faith or hope that leads us to believe in future events?" His eyes followed up her arms, pausing at her bounty, then finally settling on her inviting blue eyes. He dropped her hand and sat back, arms crossed.

Staci set her serving tray on the table and leaned against the chair. Her gaze drifted around the bar as she thought about the question. "Well, I would have to say hope is for the future and faith is more for the present. You have hope that something will happen, but you have faith that you are doing the right thing, right?"

Max tried to keep a straight face.

Phil smiled, "That is one way of looking at it. The temporal nature of the two words is important. You capture that distinction quite well. But as Kierkegaard said, 'We live forward but we understand backward.' Is that enough for us to make predictions? Does our understanding mandate that correlation becomes causation, and thus our hope for the future is nothing more than a self-fulfilling prophecy brought about by our own understanding of the ever-receding present?" He smiled and took a long pull on his drink, glancing again at her nametag. "What do you think, Staci?"

Max looked at her, waiting for her reply. His own response churned inside his head. "Yes, Staci, what do you think?" He grinned widely.

"I think that you are hoping for something other than an answer to your overly complex question. I'm guessing you have a bet going and you are trying to confuse me with a whole lot of fifty-dollar words." She looked at Phil. "And I think that you are trying to win that bet using phrases I don't quite understand." She turned to leave. "I have to tend to other tables."

Phil watched her walk away, all the way to the bar, in fact, as she made her way through the crowd, deftly moving aside at the right moments and twirling while keeping her serving tray level. She finally arrived at the bar and leaned on her elbows.

"I'll bet she's a dancer. . . ." Phil said.

"Back to it, you degenerate. As Hebrews 11:1 states, 'Faith is confidence in what we hope for and assurance about what we do not see.' I can plainly see the odds of you getting a drink and the odds of me not getting a refill. Faith is about trust, reasonable trust, not just a hope for something desired, or expected, even." Max raised his empty glass as another server walked by. He was careful to show the five-dollar bill extending just above the rim.

"Long Island?" The waiter took the glass, the five, and smiled suggestively.

"Yes, please. Can you make it a double? I have a feeling I'm going to need it."

The waiter nodded, his blonde hair sliding in front of his face in a practiced gesture. He flicked the bangs back with a tanned hand and made a beeline for the bar.

"You know," Phil leaned in toward Max, "if you flirted a bit more with the servers, you'd get your drinks much more quickly, not to mention several on the house."

"I'll leave the philandering to you, Phil. It's what you do best. I'm just an honest college student."

"True enough, but you make my point for me. In both circumstances, we did not have faith in anything. We made something happen. That's not faith, that's initiative and determination . . . or maybe even *determinism*. If this so-called God is looking down and manipulating our lives, then we could easily say that *He* has something to do with our fate, and therefore our faith should be in Him, our rock and our salvation. But then we could also say that our faith has something to do with the gray people of Stonehenge. There is as much physical proof for them as for your Übermensch in the sky."

"C'mon, Phil. I don't believe that God lives in the sky any more than you do. That would be ridiculous." Max took his drink from the server along with the piece of paper clandestinely placed under the glass. He eyed the number and stirred his drink with the straw before placing the paper in his shirt pocket.

"Would you rather I say 'Elysium,' 'Olympus,' 'the ether' . . . or maybe just 'heaven' will suffice? I mean we wouldn't want to be ridiculous about the dwelling place of the ultimate unicorn, now would we?"

"Ultimate unicorn—so now we're name-calling? Going to hell, I say. Nah, I'll be hopeful and say 'purgatory.'" Max made the sign of the cross and smiled at Phil.

"Stop that. You're not even Catholic."

"It's a good thing, too, because I would be trying to perform an exorcism on you right now, as you are clearly possessed and not of the greatest intellect."

Phil laughed. "Touché." He smiled widely at Staci's return, her nametag clutched in her hand. "Would you like to come to a bonfire and maybe explain that time and faith stuff a bit more?" she asked with a seductive grin.

Phil rose from his chair and offered his elbow to Staci. "Philosophy and fire? Now that's a great mix. Besides, my friend here has plans tonight, so I should free up his schedule." Phil eyed Max's pocket. "Don't be up too late, dear."

"Sure thing, honey." Max blew a kiss as Phil and Staci left arm-in-arm. He looked around the pub, considering Phil's question of faith. *What would Jesus do to help him on his way?* Then he spied the server whose number he held. He was pretty sure that Jesus wouldn't be contemplating hot guys in a bar, especially blonde surfer-types who gave out their phone numbers. *But I'm not Jesus,* he thought, as he walked across the bar toward the waiter.

TWO

When Adam ate the irrevocable apple . . .
C.S. LEWIS

PRESENT DAY. *Next morning at the RTSS*

Max looked at the little tea cookies that Phil presented on his Blue Onion china. Phil also set down a basket of freshly picked strawberries.

Freshly picked strawberries—such a sweet gesture, one would think, but in this very act Phil managed to rob a little field mouse of his breakfast, and not just any breakfast, but the very one that the mouse had been dreaming about. The evening before, the mouse had come upon the wild berries and set about to eat them, when he was disturbed by a raccoon dog running through the field. The raccoon dog, it turns out, had been roused from his nap by an old man carrying a walking stick, who was taking his evening stroll. This startled the raccoon dog, who took off in a mad dash. Of course, the mouse thought that the raccoon dog was chasing him for a snack, since it's not beyond a raccoon dog to take a mouse now and again. So the mouse went back home, determined to return to the delicious strawberries in the morning. He even dreamt about the strawberries, scrumptious as they were. He dreamt of a giant dancing strawberry, looking just like Fred Astaire, complete with top hat and cane. (Yes, he had seen the movie; hadn't everyone?) But Phil beat the mouse to the strawberry patch, and the poor mouse was denied this simple pleasure, having to settle instead for somewhat humdrum clover. The clover, as it turned out, gave him extreme indigestion.

Max picked up one of the cookies with the raspberry jam center and popped it into his mouth. "How's a big guy like me supposed to get full on these? Where's my *real* breakfast?" He poked Phil in the belly and gave a big smile.

"That'll be later, Maxie. I just picked these wild strawberries this morning, to make up a bit for last night." Phil smiled.

Phil smiled, of course, because he had no idea that he had denied a little mouse an indulgence. Instead, the clover gave the mouse a stomachache that would last for three days.

Michal was oblivious to their exchange. She looked pensively out the window. She grasped her teacup in two hands and brought it to her lips. The warmth, migrating to her chest and belly, made her smile. She noticed some activity in a nearby birch tree, which further distracted her thoughts. "A Japanese robin is feeding her young. Are robins harbingers of spring here, too? Do you know, Phil?"

"Well, even in North America that's not altogether true. Robins often stick around through the winter, even in the northern states. Here you'd be looking for the *uguisu,* or Japanese bush warbler. It's just a tiny little thing. If you look past the tree there you can make one out. It should be in the plum tree in back by this afternoon. He'll likely be looking for his hat."

Phil sipped at his drink while he stared out the window with Michal. He looked at her, wondering what she was looking at—so intent and yet so empty. *Very Zen,* he thought. He wondered if she was still thinking about the question he had asked, perhaps looking to nature for some answers. Then he noticed her neck and smiled.

"By the way, your garden is absolutely beautiful. It looks like Eden," Michal said.

"Ah yes, the Garden of Eden, the genesis of original sin. You know, I could never figure this out—have you seen David Davalos' play *Wittenberg?* Professor Martin Luther puts it well: a righteous God casts us down to hell because of our sins, sins we are damned to commit by Adam's original disobedience. So God damns us to sin, and then He damns us for sinning. . . ."[4] Phil smirked. "But you don't believe in original sin, do you?" He veritably chewed through the words. This was a topic he could really get into. Thoughts of *Zen* began to fade from his mind, as they so often did.

"You're right. I don't." Michal paused. "Paul completely misreads the second creation story. Remember what Paul says? 'Sin came into the world through one man, and death through sin, and death spread to all, because all have sinned.'"

Max piped in, "Paul's Letter to the Romans."

"Right," Michal confirmed. "Paul's Letter to the Romans. He makes a similar point in First Corinthians. But remember the second creation story? Adam and Eve are not kicked out of the Garden because they have sinned. Death is not a punishment for their sin. Remember, God fears that they will eat from the Tree of Life and live forever. They've already eaten the forbidden fruit, so now they know good from evil. If they were to become immortal too, they would be god-like. That's why God drives them out of the Garden. Divine jealousy, because they're trying to encroach on His prerogatives. *Not* because they have sinned. Many people miss this completely. . . . Paul evidently did." Michal took another sip of tea.

"But Michal," Max asked, "what about Genesis 2:17, where God says 'you must not eat from the tree of knowledge of good and evil for when you eat from it you will surely die'?"

"This just goes to show that the Bible is one big mess of contradictions," Phil put in. "One thing's for sure—as Denis Diderot famously said, 'The Christian God is a father who makes much of his apples, and very little of his children.'"

Michal smiled at Max. "I'd love to hear why *you* believe in original sin, Max. I know it's Christian teaching, but you're a thinking person."

Phil burst out laughing, blowing some of his drink from his mouth. He wiped his face, then turned to Max. "Yeah, Max—why?"

Max chuckled. "Are you suggesting that a thinking person might not necessarily swallow everything that Paul writes in his letters whole, without reservation or reflection? I'll concede that, but in the same breath, I'll side with Paul's interpretation. He got it right. Our world is fallen, and even our most basic nature is sodden thoroughly in this brokenness. . . . And to be clear, Michal, God did not 'fear'"—Max found himself air-quoting again—"that we would extend our hands and gain eternal life, because that was one of the options He laid before us from the beginning. We chose death. We just goofed up and were not ready for it."

So, dear reader. . . . Did you like that bit I added about the snake oil salesman at the beginning of my tale? I've always wanted to be in a Western. . . . I thought you might like that. I certainly liked it.

Henceforth we will assume that whenever Max is talking and says a word like 'this' that he is scratching the air with quoting fingers. We will also assume that Michal will steal a glance in the mirror at every opportunity, since she delights so in her image. Concerning Phil, well, except for that bit I disclosed about his poor choice of wardrobe and his disagreeable disposition, the rest of Phil's oddities will be revealed in the telling of my story.

By now you should be catching on to the fact that our three friends love to discuss all things philosophical and religious. Let me explain how this came about. They first met fifteen years ago in Dr. Alana Désiré's Knowledge and Reality class, and then again in Religion and Society. Phil and Max had known each other before, but hadn't been really close friends—just drinking buddies. One night, when they were pretty trashed on Coronas, Phil was trying to convince Max to take Dr. Désiré's class, because she was so hot. . . .

"Even the name sounds hot," Phil said. "Dr. *Desire*."

"Keep it in your pants, boy." Max laughed.

"I saw her once in a Mandarin Palace. She had a tattooed arm sleeve. You would not believe what she has. Eros, Dionysus, Aphrodite, and I swear a scene straight out of an illustrated *Kama Sutra*. This woman is HOT." Phil could barely contain his enthusiasm. "Her classes fill up fast, so let's register tomorrow, first thing."

"OK, fine. . . . I've always wanted to take a philosophy class anyway, but you know she's not going to do a darn thing for me."

"I hear she's a yoga instructor too. She can even do the Firefly Pose! Can you imagine lying under that?" Max rolled his eyes. Phil continued, "Well, Winston told me that last semester she invited Darius Jackson into her office and she gave him head right at her desk."

"Impossible. Darius is gay. Trust me, I know this one."

"But Darius is our tight end. How can he be gay?"

"You really have to ask?" Max shook his head.

The semester started, and Phil made sure to visit Dr. Désiré's office the first day, right after class. He looked at her office walls. Georgia O'Keefe everywhere and prints from Roman erotica in Pompeii. At that moment he vowed to make it to Italy one day, to see that erotica firsthand. Phil sat across Désiré's desk and fumbled every word. She asked him whether he had the books for the course and whether he was excited about the semester. He placed his backpack over his shorts to hide his infernal hard-on. He had no blood in his brain to think.

"I've gotta go," was all that Phil managed to say.

Dr. Désiré held Phil's sexual attention for a couple of weeks until he started to notice Michal. She sat in the front row—of course—and always had something interesting to say, often cutting other students off to make her point.

"I've gotta ask this girl out," Phil whispered to Max, loud enough for Dr. Désiré to hear. They were sitting one row from the back. "I'm gonna do it right after class. Why don't you come along?"

Dr. Désiré looked at them and shook her head disapprovingly.

Michal accepted Phil's invitation and the three of them quickly became inseparable.

They started a study group, and after Phil gathered enough followers he ran for Philosophy Club president, despite that he wasn't even a major. He slaughtered the current president: a smart kid with absolutely no charisma. Phil asked Michal to be the club secretary. He must not have realized how absolutely insulting that would be to Michal, a burgeoning feminist.

"Fuck you," Michal said to the offer. "Fuck off and fuck you." The result was a two-month-long silent treatment.

In the meantime, Max joined the Genders and Sexualities Alliance and the Intervarsity Christian Fellowship. Both organizations would end up kicking him out—the GSA because he believed in Jesus, and Intervarsity because he was a "practicing gay." So he ended up in the Philosophy Club, too—a group of misfits led by his best friend.

But now that we know how our three friends first met, let's get back to their discussion of original sin. . . .

Michal looked at Max incredulously. "You say that Paul got it right? First of all, Paul explicitly says that death entered the world *through sin*. I suppose that is *kind of* right. Adam and Eve ate the fruit, and God says, 'They are now *like us*, knowing good from evil.' So as I said earlier, God casts them out of the Garden because they could become immortal by eating from the Tree of Life. Notice, by the way, that God says 'like us.' God is being a polytheist here. I know, you'll say that He's talking to the angels—but back to my point. They are *not* cast out of the Garden as punishment for sin. —In any case, this is just a story, Max, and I would argue more a story about the hardships of life. You know, farming and childbirth. Oh, and sex. The Tree of Knowledge of Good and Evil is all about sex. I suppose we'll get there sooner or later." She eyed him with a smile.

"We can definitely jump right to sex, but considering that you think I'm an ass right now and I'm not Max's type, I think it might have to be a more academic discussion." Phil went to refill his glass. "Besides, I think Max is going somewhere with his discussion. Are you going to dig yourself a hole of direct interpretation as you usually do?"

"No, I won't. Just because I believe the Bible is the Word of God, and the truth comes through regardless of what humans attempt to distort, that doesn't make me wrong." Max continued: "You're right, Michal, God was talking to others, but not to the angels. This is a confirmation of the doctrine of the Trinity. Whether or not you believe as I do, or in some metaphorical, wishy-washy 'Progressive-Christian' way, makes little difference to the point of the story."

Phil nearly spilled his pour of Blanton's. "Max, you have to stop doing that. I won't be able to get a proper drink if you keep throwing out those ridiculous statements."

"What ridiculous statements? I know you don't believe, but calling it 'ridiculous' is nothing more than a modified *ad hominem*, and honestly it's beneath you."

"What I think he's referring to is your suggestion that you're not in the pool splashing around with those 'wishy-washy Progressive Christians.'" Michal returned his tsk-tsk. "You really shouldn't be so dismissive of those in your own group."

"I believe in the Bible. Now, if I can get back from your attempt to derail me?" Max looked down his nose at his two friends.

Phil turned to Michal, took her hand, and they curtseyed.

"Oh please, great maestro, fill us with your wisdom," Phil said. "Ah, but first, doesn't your point about the Trinity make God a schizophrenic? He's talking to himself. . . ."

"You mean 'multiple personality disorder'? That's what they call it these days. —No, Phil. . . . Can I get on with it now?"

"Hang on, Max," Michal cut in. "You know, I hadn't really thought about this before, but I've been looking at the Qur'an recently. Maybe the Genesis authors used the plural pronoun 'us' to reflect God's all-encompassing majesty. You find this throughout the Qur'an. . . . Anyway, to your point: the ancient Israelites would have had no way of knowing about the Trinity. —Hey! This just occurred to me: Fundamentalists don't believe in the Trinity. They've turned the Bible into a golden calf. God is *four* persons. . . ." She smirked.

"Heresy!" Phil declared.

"If I may?" Max pleaded. "It's impossible to get a word in with the two of you. . . . OK, in our modern world, many folks believe that the Bible is trying to speak to science and the origins of the material world, but that's not the point of Genesis. When I speak with some of the more militant atheists, I often have it triumphantly pointed out to me that the sun wasn't created until the fourth day, as if that had never occurred to the ancients that this was strange." Max feigned a confused face. "Curiously, the sun didn't merit a place within even the first three days, let alone the very first, which would have made more sense." Max extended one skyward-pointing hand above a downturned palm to gesture his argument. "God was making a point to show us the correct relationship between Himself— the Creator—and the much-worshipped, albeit merely-created, sun. Indeed God created the light on the *first* day with no need for a sun. —That said, Paul was a first-century man. . . ."

Phil jumped in: "If it's all metaphor then—"

"That's not what he said," Michal interrupted with a serious face that cracked with a smile. "You should let him squirm a little more first." Phil nodded.

"Adam stands in for all of us." Max raised his eyebrows and stared accusingly back-and-forth at his friends, and then because that still didn't feel direct enough, he sweepingly pointed. "I doubt very seriously that anyone at this table would have done differently. Forbidden fruit, after all, is more desirable. If someone tells you not to do something, that makes you all the more eager to try it. . . . Passed down through 'one man,' so to speak, we are all born into the same condition, the human condition."

Phil echoed Max's words to make his point. "So to speak. . . . 'So to speak' is filler for 'not exactly,' you know? It's sounding more and more like metaphor."

Max thumped his Bible, which conveniently sat at the table. "Philippians tells us that Jesus breaks this cycle as a 'new' man who, though He was in the likeness of God, didn't count equality with God as a thing to be grasped, but, rather, emptied Himself and took the form of a servant, born a man, humbling Himself by becoming obedient to the point of death, even death on a cross. So God exalts Him, giving Him a name that is above all names, so that at the name of Jesus every knee will bow. . . ."

Michal tried to redirect Max's sermon with a hand-wave, beckoning him back to the discussion. "Max, we're getting sidetracked. We were talking about original sin. So let me rein you back in. Mainstream Jews don't even believe in original sin. This is true of the Eastern Orthodox too, or so my Aunt Vi tells me. The notion didn't even come about until the second century. It was more fully developed by Augustine even later than that. If there is no original sin, then infant baptism, the magic water to free one from the power of this so-called 'original sin,' is completely unnecessary."

Phil gave a satisfied Cheshire cat grin and then added, "Too much green tea."

Suddenly Michal heard someone whisper from a nearby table in a heavy Russian accent: "Heretics go to hell." She tried to ignore the voice, but the words hit like a boulder to her gut. She dared to glimpse at the table and noted a professor-type, with full beard and little round glasses, wearing an avocado-and-brown tweed jacket. A fat black cat with piercing green eyes sat on his lap.

"What's with the cat?" Michal asked Phil.

"That guy's a regular here. Actually, my only regular, other than Tanaka, so I guess I have two regulars who come in somewhat regularly." He grinned. "Three—if you count the cat. —I tend not to get many customers, as you may recall. This guy usually keeps to himself unless someone stirs him up. The cat never seems to stray far from his lap."

Michal fixated on the cat, now atop the table, his fat paws sinking into a heaping plate of frankfurters. She could have sworn it gave her a mocking smile.

"Mysteries of the human psyche and condition. . . ." The professor-type said.

Michal shook her head to rattle out the words.

"To get back to our discussion—we baptize and share the Lord's Supper because He told us to. We do not do it to wash off original-sin cooties because we do not contract original sin at birth," Max said.

"As if spray painted out of the vagina!" Michal interrupted. She looked over at Phil who was trying to contain his laughter and not blow more drink from his mouth.

Max tried to ignore his two friends poking fun. "We are a broken creation that is fundamentally flawed through and through, from the beginning, or from the very first man. We must be re-made. We baptize and share the Lord's Supper to remember Him, while making a public confession of our need for His grace, as we ritually die with Him and are reborn as we eat the Bread of Life. We are broken and in need, just needy beggars asking for bread. There's no magic in the

wine or grape juice either, whether it is Catholic, Lutheran, or Episcopalian fla-
vored."

"You're right, Maxie," Michal began, "this is precisely why infant baptism is
unnecessary, and even more to the point, why there should only be an adult baptism, a believer's baptism, a public confession. Outing yourself to a community, if
you will. Babies can't do this." She paused before offering up some advice, "In any
case, you need to settle down, Max. You're not speaking from your pulpit, you
know. You're with your friends."

Max laughed. "Agreed on both counts. No point in sprinkling water on
babies, although I must admit this is my church's teaching."

"Then why stick with your church? You're beginning to sound like one of
those Cafeteria Catholics." Phil smirked.

"Because God led me to my church, and besides, *look at Michal—*" Max
extended his hand toward her. "She doesn't fit in *anywhere*."

"Thanks one hell of a lot, friend." She smiled.

"Pulpit or not, the idea of infant baptism is antithetical to the very belief system itself. Think about it. The idea is that we have free will so that we can make
the right choices and learn to be better believers and followers through the rein-
forcement of those actions. This is classic operant conditioning." Phil gestured
with his glass at nobody in particular, as if some disembodied audience were paying attention. "But how does making a decision for an infant, and washing away
the *vaginal paint of original sin,* square with the idea of free will?"

Max sighed, "Do we have to make 'vaginal paint' one of our working terms? I
prefer 'cooties.'"

Michal laughed. "Cooties" was an old fashioned word that reminded her of
Aunt Vi.

Growing up, Michal remembered the smell of Aunt Vi's living room. The
comfortable, yet very proper, maroon wingback chairs gave off an odor, not
unpleasant but distinctive. Perhaps it was from the years of use, or maybe, Michal
thought when she was much younger, old people just smell, well, *old.* The musty
scent, tinged with just a hint of camphor from the old-timey mothballs that Aunt
Vi insisted on using, permeated every bit of those cushioned seats—the only
furniture that wasn't dressed in plastic covers. That smell was the most distinctive
feature of her Aunt Vi.

This is not to say the visits were unwanted. Michal always made sure that her
chores were done on those days when she was to visit her favorite aunt. For
years, Michal would come over for tea. When she arrived, Aunt Vi would give
her a hug, first thing. The smell wasn't overpowering at this first contact, though
it was there, just at the edge of consciousness. They would then go to her aunt's
bedroom and get a sun hat or hairpin, white opera gloves, necklace, and a scarf
du jour to prepare Michal for teatime. Once properly adorned, they would retire
to the living room, the room with *the smell.*

Aunt Vi would add the tea to the Blue Willow teapot—the one with the
funny little oriental house—and let it steep. They would talk about what Michal's
week was like, or how school was going. All the secrets that a little girl might

keep from other adults. By then the tea would be ready and the ritual of teatime would officially begin. Aunt Vi would place the little metal strainer on top of Michal's cup and pour. When the cup was full, she would rotate the strainer one turn, lift, and then move it to her own cup. A second pour and both cups would be full. At the same time, Michal would take the little tea sandwiches of cucumber and butter and place two little triangles each on their plates.

Michal trusted Aunt Vi with her little-girl secrets. Her aunt listened with the calm attention that age exuded so effortlessly. In every respect, she was Michal's best friend and confidant, taking in her words and nodding with a smile. She made an occasional comment, but she would never exert her will.

—Except on one subject.

On the coffee table sat a big black book, the cover a worn, textured Nigerian goatskin. The gold letters of the title had aged as well, flecks of gold missing in a few spots. The title was still unmistakable: *The Holy Bible*. Michal would dread the end of her visit with Aunt Vi, as it always heralded *the testimony*. Aunt Vi would invariably talk about a doily or a bit of fabric that she delivered to the pastor's wife. Or her famous Balsamic Roast Beef cooked nine hours in the crockpot. And then she would add, "You don't go to church, do you, dear?" An innocent question smuggled in during a sip of tea. Michal would always answer the same "nope" and begin to take great interest in the floor. As she studied the loops and whorls of the clouds sewn into the scene on the rug, she could hear Aunt Vi reminding her that the decisions she made in this life would be all-important for the next.

Eternally important.

Michal didn't want to appear disrespectful, but she would rarely meet her aunt's eyes. Instead, she would continue to follow the lines of the cloud to the point where wind blew out and filled the sails of the mighty ship, forever sailing the high seas of Aunt Vi's living room. Eventually, around the point at which Michal had begun to stare at the captain forever ordering his men onward, Aunt Vi would end with her usual exhortation: "You'll see one day. I just hope that it's not too late for you, my sweet cupcake."

"With a cherry on top," Michal would smile.

"With a cherry on top," Aunt Vi would repeat.

With that, teatime would be over and Aunt Vi would get up and look at the clock on the wall. Antique French Provincial Style, Michal would learn when she was a bit older. The same clock that had been in plain view for the previous hour-and-a-half. Now, however, Aunt Vi would regard it with astonishment.

"Oh my, look at the time. We need to get you back to your mama and daddy." They would go to Aunt Vi's bedroom and return the adornments to their proper places, the last being the white-satin opera gloves. Michal loved the feel of the satin, as it all but flowed off her little arms. She would return them to the drawer after folding them "the proper way."

Many years later, Michal sat across from her Aunt Vi, who looked so tired. So tired, Michal imagined, from living so long. She still wore the same style of clothing, but it was a bit looser-fitting. Bits of frayed thread were unattended and showed at the edges of her blue chiffon dress. The eternal musty camphor smell of the living room offered comfort to Michal. It was the one constant in her life. Aunt Vi reached for the teapot, her hands guided by habit more than her now-diminished vision. Michal leaned forward and took the pot from her Aunt, who had shakily begun pouring their tea.

"Let me get that for you," Michal said.

"Oh thank you, dear. It's nice to see that my teaching has done some bit of good."

Michal gave a little laugh. "It's not surprising, since we did it so often. Even someone who is as stubborn as I am would have gotten it eventually."

Aunt Vi smiled.

"That's not all that your constant guidance influenced." Michal swallowed some tea to steel herself for what she was about to say.

"Oh, and what else has this old lady convinced you of?" Aunt Vi looked at Michal—or, rather, more in her direction.

Aunt Vi wasn't wearing her opera gloves, or any other accoutrements, except for her floppy straw sun hat with the overly big sunflower on the side. The opera gloves sat folded on the table between them, a bit of decoration that served as a reminder of days past.

"I'm a Christian now," Michal began. "I know you've been praying for me for a long time."

"Praise God!" exclaimed Vi, her tea sloshing a bit from the sudden movement. Her smile was large and genuine. "How did it happen?"

"Long story. Maybe another time." Michal was hesitant to share how it happened.

"Of course, of course. I—I don't want to pry too much. Have you found yourself a church-home yet?"

Michal sipped her tea. "No, not yet."

"You should try Greek Orthodox. You might like it. The women dress in very nice clothes. . . ." Aunt Vi stroked the gloves lying on the table. "But they're not high-society types. You know I don't like no high-society types." Aunt Vi tried to conceal her tenth-grade education, but sometimes it would come out in double negatives.

Michal smiled. "Why did you become Greek Orthodox? Weren't you Pentecostal?"

"For a long time. . . . But then I really began to fear God. I knew I just wasn't going to get to heaven unless I ate Jesus' body and blood. You know, I took John 6 very seriously. Pentecostals don't, but we Greek Orthodox do. Catholics do too, but I didn't want to go someplace that makes Mary a goddess. . . ."

"I'm not sure that Catholics make Mary a goddess, but I get what you're saying. About eating Jesus' body and blood, I mean. A couple weeks ago I popped into a church and took communion. I did feel nourished in a way, and by the end of the week I was craving it."

"I know the feeling," Aunt Vi said. "Jesus' body and blood were renewing your soul to help you face the trials of this world."

"But then I recently read a scholarly article which made a good case that the Gospel of John is actually a reactionary piece to the Gnostic Gospel of Thomas.

Of course this would date Thomas earlier than most scholars have. The author of John is showing that Jesus actually embraced the body and bodily desires. You see this in the Doubting Thomas story and the Wedding at Cana story too. Jesus—" Michal abruptly stopped her sentence, realizing that she could not take back any of her words.

"That's heretical!" Aunt Vi said. "Pray that God forgives you for saying that." She began to cry. "He will forgive you, but you should pray right now. You never know when your time will come or that trumpet will sound. Pray right now!"

"Don't cry, Aunt Vi. I don't believe it. Really. It's just something I read."

"You're a brand new Christian and Satan's already gotten hold of you. It's all those books you read. They sound reasonable enough, but the Serpent is very convincing. You can't let him get hold of your thoughts. Let's pray right now. Hold my hands."

Michal took her aunt's hands, immediately surprised by the ferocity of her grip. She understood her aunt's sudden outburst. She was now quite old and this bit of hope was more than she had ever considered possible. Maybe she was practicing some kind of transference or living vicariously through Michal. All of these theories danced around Michal's head as she felt her aunt's weathered old hands grip and grip and grip. As Aunt Vi prayed, Michal found herself thinking: *This is extremely fucked up. Do I have to be so utterly fucked up, now that I'm a Christian?* Then she apologized to God for her profanity and added an "Amen."

LATER IN THE DAY. *Back at the RTSS*

Phil sat in his bright red, overstuffed armchair—one of the few pieces of color in the RTSS. He kept most of the color outside. *Why is that?* He was sipping his Evan Williams, enjoying the oak, vanilla, and cherry notes. He had a stack of coffee-table books on his lap: *Monster Drawings from the Edo Period, Picasso,* and *Architecture from Around the World.*

The monster-drawings book was opened to Hokusai's *Kappa.* Phil read the caption below, which discussed the characteristics and behaviors of these *yōkai.* He read how the *kappa* would often lose an arm and then try to negotiate its return. He laughed. But then he frowned.

He looked at the Hokusai, the Picasso, and the world-famous architecture. All this beauty was trapped on the pages of books of places he'd been. *If only I could travel back in time. Maybe make a few changes. Set things right. Maybe Billy would still be alive. Maybe Michal and I would have a couple of little ones running at our knees. If I could, I'd move heaven and earth to make things different.* He thought of Spock with his dogmatic statements—"*Time travel is impossible, Captain*"—even though he'd then figure out how to travel through time. *How does that argument go? If I could travel back in time, I could kill my grandfather before my father was conceived. But then there'd be no me to do the travelling. . . . Now there's a paradox to wrestle down.*

Thoughts of twins travelling through space and Terminators coming back from the future rolled over Phil's imagination, eventually morphing into a strange conversation in a bar between the older and younger versions of Marty McFly, John Connor, some guy in an off-road motorcycle outfit, Bruce Willis

(*Twelve Monkeys* or *Looper*? He wasn't sure) and Rod Taylor in Victorian garb. They were all arguing about how lucky it was that they hadn't blinked themselves out of existence, followed by a discussion of circular and linear time. Phil smiled as he imagined them all blinking out, one by one, leaving an empty bar save for a rotund barkeep with a greasy white tee and gap-toothed smile, and a dapper English gentleman, donning a red bow tie, sitting in the corner.

How could they have existed there, when they had so obviously been "unmade," or whatever you call it when you get your timeline disturbed? They couldn't have been there to discuss how lucky they'd been, because they had already been erased. They couldn't have had that discussion in the first place, because there'd be no "them" to travel back there. . . .

My God, I'm living in the past, if the past even exists. If time even exists.

Phil often wondered about time.[5] He set his books down on the floor next to him and took another sip of his drink. *Was time even real?* J.M.E. McTaggart didn't think so.[6] There is no such thing as time. Our perception of time is mere illusion. He'd proven both the necessity and yet the utter incoherence of the 'A' series of time—of time as we ordinarily understand it, as past, present, and future. Phil knew about some of the other views on time: Plato, Aristotle, and Kant. Michal had even tried to explain Merleau-Ponty's conception of time once. But he had no settled opinion on time. You can't see time under a microscope or through a spyglass, which made it difficult to confirm its existence. *Kind of like that God-fellow that Max and Michal go on and on about.*

Phil tried to remember what Michal had said about Merleau-Ponty's conception.[7] *Time takes shape in the activity of consciousness. The present is what the subject now experiences explicitly. The past and future are co-present but implicit or hidden.* Phil held up his drink. *If I cover part of this glass with my hand, I explicitly see the parts that are not covered. But I am implicitly presented with the hidden parts. I experience the hidden parts as co-present with the parts I explicitly see. . . . The present, past, and future are like this.*[8]

Phil thought about Aristotle and Leibniz, how they said that time does not exist independently of the things and events that occur in time.[9] Time is nothing more than a system of relations among things and events, so time without change is incoherent. There is no empty time, and in any case, even if there were, we wouldn't know anything about it.

Plato and Newton, on the other hand, said that time is like an empty container, in which things and events may be placed, but that the container exists independently of what, if anything, is in it. So time can exist without change. *Hmmmm.*

Phil took a big swig of his drink. The temporal nature of the bourbon was disturbing. He reached for the bottle. *The Platonic notion of time has a lot of intuitive appeal. . . . Intuitive appeal? Since when have I relied on intuition? That's more Michal's thing. . . . Maybe time just froze, just now. And then unfroze. Sydney Shoemaker came up with that elaborate example of a possible world in which in a certain zone, time freezes and all change stops.*[10] *The people in the time-frozen zone don't notice it, of course, but people in other zones do. And what about Kant? Time is an* a priori *notion, which, along with space, another* a priori *notion, allows us to comprehend our sense experience.*[11] *'Space and time are the frameworks within which the mind is constrained to construct its experiences of reality.' Boy, I need another drink. One can't do Kant, or time, sober.*

Phil poured himself another drink. The various artistic representations throughout time of the Roman goddess Venus hopscotched around his brain like children at recess. They ranged from zaftig to stick-thin. Beauty throughout the ages. His thoughts traveled from time to beauty. He picked up the Picasso book and opened to a random page: *Le Rêve. The Dream.* Picasso's mistress, Marie-Thérèse Walter, was the model. He chuckled. It actually looked like a woman to him. The facing page was *Asleep.* Looked less like a woman's face and more like a landscape. He imagined a miniature mountain climber in Lederhosen and a Tyrolean hat scaling her nose. In any case, Walter again. *How many masterpieces of art, of architecture, of music, were inspired by love?* Phil sighed.

Too many ideas were bouncing around in his head. He really needed them to bounce off someone else, to see what trajectory they took after the impact. He started to do calculations of the angle of incidence and the angle of reflection. Were ideas like rays of light, bouncing around, changing their perspective, their reflective colors, depending on the surface? He looked up from his chair and saw Michal and Max entering with a platter of sushi.

Michal had been in the kitchen making *kappamaki* while sipping a glass of plum wine. She had found the bottle sitting forlornly in the cupboard. The *koshihikari* was in the rice cooker. She had already cut the cucumber strips. She laid the *nori* on the counter. While she waited for the rice to cook, she poured some soy sauce into little ceramic bowls. She smiled.

Max walked into the kitchen and opened the fridge. "Anything to eat?" He leaned against the door and put his head inside.

"I'm making *kappamaki.* Cucumber sushi. The rice is almost done. Why don't you help me?"

"I'm not very good at fancy cooking." He grabbed the carton of milk and took a slug. He was glad that Michal wasn't paying attention.

"Can you hold a fan?" Michal gave him a little handheld fan. "For the rice, while I mix."

Max fanned the rice while Michal mixed in the dressing of rice vinegar, sugar, and sweet rice wine. She covered the seaweed paper with a layer of rice and added the strips of cucumber. She rolled it into one long sushi roll and then cut it into smaller pieces. She arranged the rolls on a platter made of Blue Onion china. She garnished it with curled carrots and watercress. Max smiled while she was putting it all together.

"Beautiful," Max said.

"Thank you. . . . Now let's go find Phil."

Max and Michal found Phil looking up from his red chair, questions stamped all over his face. Michal put the platter on the little table in front of him.

"What a beautiful presentation," Phil said. "For me?" He smiled.

"For us," Michal said, smiling back. She pulled up a chair. Max did too.

Max noticed the monster-drawings book. "The Edo period. When was that?"

"From about 1600 to 1868. The period of time ruled by the shoguns of the Tokugawa family. There were some great artists then. Sawaki Suushi, who was a student of Hanabusa Itchō, Utagawa Kuniyoshi and, of course, my favorite, Hokusai."

"I love Hokusai's *Great Wave off Kanagawa*," Max said.

"I see you're in your napping-and-thinking chair," Michal said and smiled.

"Don't forget *drinking chair*," Phil said, lifting his glass.

"I drink therefore I am." Max laughed. "I can see by that half-empty bottle what you're drinking. But what are you thinking?"

Phil reached down and grabbed the Picasso book. He held it up like a sacred tome. "What do you think? Are there underlying characteristics across differing art forms—say Picasso's *The Dream*, the Taj Mahal, Tchaikovsky's *Pathétique* or Bach's *Goldberg Variations*, even Euler's formula—that allow us to call all of these very different things 'beautiful'? Are there innate properties or qualities that beautiful things possess, or is it just a matter of individual or cultural preference? *De gustibus non est disputandum.* There's no disputing taste."

"I like what Plato says about beauty.[12] The beauty of a painting, or a piece of music, or a flower, or a sunset, is an imperfect copy of Beauty itself. The form Beauty. Forms are the only things in Plato's ontology that are *really real*. Particular beautiful things partake in the form Beauty, and this is the reason we can say that beautiful things are beautiful," Max said. "Art is imitation. Art imitates things and events in this world, and so a work of art is a copy of a copy of the form. Wild."

"Plato is cool. He had a mind-blowing . . . mind." Phil smirked. "Of course the imitation theory fails. It might work for representational painting, drawing, or sculpture, but what about Joan Miró? His stuff is only vaguely representational. Or what about Jackson Pollock's drip painting? What does that represent? Emotions maybe? —And you, Michal? What do you say?"

"What? About the imitation theory? About Miró or Pollock? About shared characteristics across differing art forms? You lost me in your tangle of questions," Michal said.

"Thank you, Professor Keating."

Max raised an eyebrow.

"I meant my original question," Phil said. "Do you think that there are underlying characteristics across art forms?"

"Well, I'm not sure whether I can answer your question, Phil. Or at least that's what Kant would say. I'm a woman, after all, and women are limited in their comprehension of all matters of art and nature." Michal laughed. "Remember his *Observations on the Feeling of the Beautiful and Sublime*?"

"Right, Kant was a sexist asshole, and so were ninety-nine other philosophers before and after him. . . . So what do *you* think?" Phil said, rolling his eyes.

"You mentioned Euler's formula and the *Goldberg Variations*. I'd throw in the Pythagorean theorem and maybe even Bartók's music. I don't know about the Taj Mahal, but certainly the Parthenon and the Great Pyramid of Giza all seem to have something in common. It seems that all beautiful things have underlying mathematical properties, relationships, or structure," Michal said, pleased with her answer. "The Golden Ratio, at least in some of these cases."

Phil smiled. "I like that. You know Pythagoras made connections between musical intervals and mathematical ratios back in the sixth century BCE. Ratios relevant to the string length of a monochord. Pythagoras was a musician himself. The Pythagoreans saw beauty in numbers."

"So did that weird guy, Paul Erdős," Michal said. "Erdős blamed the god, in whom he did not believe, for his missing socks." She popped a sushi roll in her mouth. "Want one?"

"Socks? No thank you. I think I'll have one of your sushi though." Phil winked.

"Touché, Phil," Michal said.

"You mean Erdős, that *eccentric* Hungarian mathematician?" Phil asked. He grabbed a roll.

"Takes one to know one," Max said and smiled. He grabbed two rolls. "God is a mathematician, too. Ivan Panin discovered mysterious mathematical patterns throughout the Bible, which shows that it could not have been written by human hands alone. He scientifically proved God's existence by looking at mathematical patterns in the Bible."[13]

"I've read Panin. It's interesting, but I don't buy it. That would mean that God wrote all of that violent, intolerant stuff that we find in the Bible. Nope. You know, I dated a math prof once, and—" Michal began.

"Of course you did," Phil said, cutting her off. He smirked.

"She also once dated a one-balled man who looked like Nicolas Cage," Max said and laughed.

"True," Phil laughed along.

"Let's just keep that one to ourselves." Michal smiled. "As I was saying, I dated a math prof once, and he told me that whenever he is presented with two hypotheses, he always goes with the one that is most aesthetically pleasing. It also turns out to be the simplest, and as he says, it's also the one most likely to be true."

"That sounds a bit like Occam's Razor," Max said.

"So this seems to work in a lot of cases, but what about beautiful women? You know, those leggy beach girls," Phil said.

"What about leggy beach guys?" Max smiled.

"All right, leggy beach *people*. It seems that math might not work here. Standards of feminine—sorry, *human*—beauty have changed. Remember the Rubenesque women of the Baroque Period? And of course Marilyn Monroe and Twiggy couldn't be more different." Phil said.

"If we appeal to evolutionary aesthetics, we've got mathematical ratios again," Michal said. "Our aesthetic preferences have evolved in order to enhance our survival and reproductive success."

"I know a bit about evolutionary aesthetics," Max chimed in.

"Do tell, professor," Phil interjected.

"When people are presented with photos of different landscapes, young children have a strong preference for savannahs with lots of trees and water. This makes sense. Our evolutionary roots are supposedly in the East African savannahs,"[14] Max said. "Remind me about evolutionary aesthetics and female and male attractiveness."

"But wouldn't the attractiveness of a particular landscape be culturally bound? I'm pretty sure that the Inuit would not find that savannah all that appealing," Michal said. "And what about Pacific Islanders?"

"Maybe the study was not quite representative across cultures. Adults preferred landscapes with great water and food potential, and while the savannah provided that, it wasn't always their preference." Max shrugged.

"Which would make it suspect, and so not exactly the makings of a good theory," Phil chided. "But let's see if we have any better luck with body ratios. Waist-to-hip ratios are indicators of health and baby-making ability. What is it, point seven, right?"

"Point seven with slight variations across cultures. Point six to point eight. And this is true regardless of body size. It's the ratio that matters. You know, the Golden Ratio is found in female facial beauty, too, regardless of race. You're right, Max. God is a mathematician." Michal smiled.

"I've also read that in areas of the world where food is scarce, men prefer larger women, and in areas where food is plentiful, they prefer smaller women. . . . But what about *male* beauty?" Max asked.

"In this case, it's the chest- or shoulders-to-waist ratio. A man's waist-to-hip ratio is about point nine, which does away with the curves," Michal said.

"No wonder I like all curvy women, regardless of size." Phil grinned. "It's evolutionary science. But science also tells us that perfectly symmetrical humans are considered to be creepy, kinda like the *uncanny valley*, so we can't really capture beauty appeal through ratios. Beauty requires a certain amount of imperfection."

"The uncanny valley isn't really about symmetrical humans, is it? I thought it was about our revulsion to computer-generated or robotic humanoid figures, or even sculptures, that *almost* look and act like us, but are just enough 'off' to give us the creeps. Anyway, Phil, you're right. Evolutionary science doesn't explain everything. I dated a beautiful trans woman once, and obviously she didn't fit the female beauty ratios," Michal said. "Having been born with a male frame, she wasn't curvy, but she had a strikingly beautiful face and an even more striking mind. She had just transitioned about a year before I met her."

Phil shifted in his chair. Michal glared at him. "What, you're going to tell me that the master of relativism is uncomfortable with a trans woman?"

"No, nothing like that. I was just remembering an experience I had with a trans woman, or rather, man. Really attractive guy, Luke. He hit on me at a geology conference about five years ago. Just remembering how attracted to him I was, and what an enjoyable conversationalist he was—or *she* was—well, I'm an idiot, because I never really got comfortable with one or the other. . . . The pronouns, that is." Phil smiled. "That was actually one of the decisive moments of relativism for me. Really challenged my notions about beauty and attraction."

"*He*, Phil. It's simple: '*He* identifies as a *man.*' So you should respect that and refer to *him* as *he,*" Michal said.

Max tried to break the tension, as he so often did. "You can come over to my side any ol' time, Phil. Just not with me. Sorry, but you're not my type." His sentence dangled in the air. Laughter finally broke the silence.

"*If you even have a type*, Max," Phil grumbled, "since it's all choice anyway. Assuming 'choice' isn't just another elaborate illusion, which of course it is. . . ."

"Are you done talking to yourself, Mr. Eccentric?" Max looked at Phil. Phil hand-waved him to continue.

"You're not willing to kiss and tell on this one, eh, Phil?" Michal leered at him. He ignored her question while motioning more deliberately at Max.

Max turned to Michal. "What was her name?" He smiled.

"Katrina. . . . Kat. She was a veterinarian. That's how I met her. When I adopted Barney."

"Kat who treats cats," Max said. "And dogs."

"So many people have such a crazy limited notion of gender and attraction. I'm sure that created quite a stir," Phil said.

"People need to grow up, Phil. Most of Western society, I'm afraid, believes that our genitalia determine our gender, which determines our sexual orientation. But that's just not true. We live in a society that normalizes cisgender expression and heterosexual orientation," Michal said. "And shames everyone who doesn't conform."

"Sis-what?" Phil asked. "You are a veritable font of new vocabulary, Michal."

"Cisgender. Where a person's gender expression matches their biological sex," Max said.

"Like I said, *De gustibus non est disputandum*," Phil said. "Or how 'bout this instead: the ol' *Beauty is in the eye of the beholder?*"

"Let's talk about aesthetic judgment," Michal said. "We haven't done that yet. Seems appropriate here. Is beauty just a matter of sentimental reactions, as Hume would say?"[15]

"So long as we can get back to Kat the veterinarian," Phil said. "Kant said that judgments of beauty claim universal validity. The person who calls something 'beautiful' demands the same judgment from others. The person is not merely judging for himself but for everyone else. He takes beauty to be a property of a thing. He says that the *thing itself* is beautiful," Phil said. "And he blames others for having poor taste if they judge differently."[16]

"Right, Phil," said Michal. Kant has an example about someone enjoying Canary wine. I can say that Canary wine is pleasing *to me*, and nobody will judge me for my individual preference. If I enjoy drinking Canary wine, and you don't— well, neither one of us is going to accuse the other of being wrong. But judgments of beauty make a claim to correctness. We can be right or wrong about our aesthetic judgments. If you say that Picasso sucks, I say that you are wrong about your judgment."

"Despite all that cool stuff about underlying mathematical properties, the Golden Ratio, and all that, I'm still inclined to believe that at bottom, beauty is relative to individual taste, or to a culture. And of course a person's taste is informed by his culture. Beauty is part of the *Zeitgeist* of a particular culture or tradition. I'd be a bad relativist if I were merely a moral relativist, but denied relativism with respect to beauty," Phil added. "And I wouldn't have been nearly as attracted to Luke as I was."

"I'd have to disagree," Michal said. "It's not the case that if I *think* that something is beautiful, it *is* beautiful. It makes sense to say that Canary wine is agreeable to me, but not that Picasso is agreeable *to me*. Picasso *is* or *should be* agreeable, period. Judgment versus taste."

"But that is a ridiculous statement, Michal. That's like saying that Pollock *should be* agreeable, period, or Salvador Dali *should be* agreeable, or Andres Serrano. . . ."

"Serrano shouldn't be agreeable to anyone," Michal said in disgust.

Phil crossed his arms, "That's so limiting, Michal, and you're better than that. Should *everything* be agreeable, or just the things which *you* like?"

Michal glared at Phil. "Are you through with your smug pejoratives? If aesthetic judgment were entirely relative, then you'd have no problem torching a Picasso, if you didn't like or understand it. It'd be just as easy as destroying a paint-by-number made by an eight year old. But you never would. You defer to the experts and appreciate that even if *you* don't understand the Picasso, you recognize its value. This wouldn't be the case were aesthetic judgment entirely relative."

Phil glared back. "I can very easily imagine a possible world in which a paint-by-number is judged, *by the experts*, as being aesthetically superior to the Picasso, because they value staying in the lines or whatnot, Michal."

Max tried to interrupt: "Have you guys heard of Pierre Brassau? He was that chimpanzee who fooled the art critics. Remember the hoax? Back in 1964 a Swedish tabloid journalist exhibited a series of paintings done by the chimp, claiming that they were the work of some unknown French artist named Pierre Brassau. The journalist was trying to show that art critics couldn't tell the difference between avant-garde modern art and paintings done by a chimp." He smiled.

"But Max, after the hoax was revealed the critics still insisted that the chimpanzee's paintings were the best at the exhibit. They *still* recognized the value of the chimp's paintings. —In any case, the example doesn't seem to work because Pierre Brassau was supposedly an unknown artist, but everybody knows Picasso, and certainly critics recognize the value of a Picasso. It would be different had the hoax claimed the chimp's paintings were really done by a well-known artist like Picasso." Michal turned to Phil. "Why have we, by and large, appreciated the same works of art over the ages, Phil? You know, G.E. Moore makes an interesting observation in his *Principia Ethica.* He considers two possible worlds. One world is exceedingly beautiful. As beautiful as we can imagine. The other world is the ugliest that we can imagine. One big heap of filth, like Job's dung heap, containing everything that is most disgusting to us, without a single redeeming feature. Isn't it obvious that we would prefer the one over the other and even work to bring it about?"

"Not if you're a dung beetle."

"Michael Rosen asks us to imagine the end of life in our universe. He argues that it would be better were the ceiling of the Sistine Chapel to survive than it should crumble into dust, even if no one is left to appreciate it."[17]

Phil threw up his hands, "So mob-rule for art, with its much vaunted definition of quality? The gatekeepers of that definition are the very people who tend to profit from art's so-called intrinsic value. Or are you willing to accept that a Picasso doodle is no more intrinsically valuable than a Phil squiggle?" Michal opened her mouth to answer, but Phil held up his hand, got up, and walked out of the room. Michal and Max just stared at each other.

"I smell one of his brutishly amusing demonstrations coming on." Max crossed his arms, waiting for the inevitable sledgehammer object lesson to begin. Michal frowned.

Phil returned to the room holding two pieces of sketch paper, each with simple line drawings on them. One looked like a sideways W, or an epsilon, kissing a crooked M with a tail. Below it was a yellow Post-it note covering a portion of the paper. On the other there was a tipped-over letter D with legs and an eye. It too had a yellow Post-it covering a portion.

"Now, one of these is a Picasso. I bought it from a dealer to have around as a simple reminder of the subjective nature of beauty." Phil smiled. "I'm not joking. I promise, one of these is a Picasso."

"Fine Phil, we agree, you've got a Picasso. It's not exactly like you couldn't afford it," Michal huffed.

Max smiled.

Phil walked over to his desk and picked up a crystal lighter—the old-school kind that had no safety, so it could be left lit until the flint and ball overheated and exploded or the fuel ran out. He lit it and left it standing on his desk. He took a moment to play with the flame, his fingers dancing over it. Then he picked up the two pieces of paper with the line drawings.

"Michal, you choose. Which one should I put to the flame? If there is some intrinsic value to a Picasso, any Picasso, such that *I'd never torch it*, and since *I so obviously don't understand the greatness of a Picasso*, then why don't you tell me which one to burn?"

Michal made no reply to that. Instead, she gave Phil a venomous stare. She knew he would do it. But she couldn't really tell any difference. One was a Picasso. She recognized both of the line drawings. Obviously Phil had copied one. But she wasn't an expert to know which was the real deal. She trusted that Phil would burn it just to make his stupid point. That was Phil—stupid and stubborn. She watched him wave the papers over the flame, like some deranged magician.

"Which one, Michal? Where's that intrinsic value now?" Phil gave a smug smile.

Michal stared at the two line drawings. She thought she knew which one was the Picasso—pretty sure at least.

"You give? I'll put them both to the flame. I can squiggle out another Phil-original in a snap. It might take a bit of negotiating to get another Picasso, however." He put one of the papers closer to the flame but Michal stopped him.

"Fine, Phil, you're right. I can't tell the difference. But I never claimed to be an expert. I just don't want you burning either one." She held out her hand for the paper that Phil dangled over the flame. He thrust it at her. She removed the Post-it to reveal Phil's signature. She looked up and saw him admiring the other.

"It's OK, Michal. Even though I'm not an eight-year-old, you might think by my behavior that I act like one." Phil pulled the Post-it off the paper he was holding in his hand to reveal Picasso's classic signature. "The point is that beauty, art, anything, has no intrinsic value. The only value it has is what *we* place on it. If we decided not to care about it anymore, then it'd be worthless. As worthless as that Phil-scribble in your hand.... Well, my mother might treasure it." Phil smiled and then finished off his drink. "Kant was wrong, Michal ... and so are you."

Michal glared at Phil. Max, ever the peacemaker, tried to distract them with more philosophy. "You know, Hume used those archaic words—well, not to him—'approbation' and 'disapprobation.' Beauty invokes a feeling of approbation or delight. Ugliness, disapprobation."

"I like what Hume has to say here, and it relates to his ethics. The aesthetic and moral response is immediate." Michal took another moment to glare at Phil, then let it go. "A feeling or sentiment informs us that an object or an act is beautiful or ugly. Judgments of beauty, like judgments of action, involve our sentiments. This is the essence of our evaluations. Feelings, not thoughts. This was the way that Harriet Beecher Stowe stirred people up to sympathize with the plight of the enslaved Negro. She was clearly a big fan of both Hume and Adam Smith."

"So back to Kat," Phil said with a smile. "I'm genuinely intrigued."

"She committed suicide," Michal said blank-faced.

"What happened?" Max asked. "Was it because of all the crap she got for being trans?"

"Might have been. I remember we were at a restaurant once and we overheard a guy at a nearby table refer to her as an *it*. I was appalled, but she said that she was used to it. I guess to the extent that anyone can get used to it. But you know, vets have one of the highest suicide rates of any profession, if not the highest. Could have been that too."

"Why's that, I wonder?" Max asked.

"I'm sure they go into vet medicine because of their unconditional love of animals. Maybe they don't feel completely accepted by people, you know. I'm sure this was the case with Kat. Being trans, never feeling like she really fit in. I also imagine that vets become disheartened because of all of the abuse and neglect they see, day in and day out. And the stupid owners.... Or compassion-fatigue, maybe, and stress.... Plus, vets put animals down every day.[18] Kat said she'd euthanize a few animals a day, *every day*. It gives one a different perspective on death—a more *philosophical* perspective. And then you have access to the meds to do you in. It's really no surprise, I guess. —You know, we were going to celebrate our three-month anniversary, but she didn't show." Michal shook her head. "She didn't show. She wasn't answering her phone and so the next day I stopped by her clinic. They told me what happened." Tears welled up in her eyes.

"I'm sorry, Michal—I had no idea," Phil reached out and touched Michal's hand. Max hugged her.

Michal wiped her tears. "Hand me that bottle, Phil, I need a drink."

THREE

I don't know the question, but sex is definitely the answer.
WOODY ALLEN

EARLY EVENING. *At the RTSS*

Phil smiled as he looked at his friends, the melancholy of his existential wanderings of the last six months falling away. He stared into his glass, watching the liquid swirl lazily from his gesturing. *Why do I believe?*

"It's good to see you both again," Phil said. He let his mask of indifference slip. He opened his mouth to say more but then stopped. *Time enough to talk,* he thought. But he knew that statement was not defensible. *Time is a finite dimension.* He let the thought slip from his mind as he tried to direct their frenetic conversational energy to a single topic.

"It's good to see you, too." Michal gave a warm smile. "Let's get back to the Garden. I just love this topic. The Tree of Knowledge of Good and Evil. . . ." She paused to sip her drink. "It's so obviously about sex."

"Michal, you think that most things are about sex. Your monologues always lead in the same direction." Max pointed at her before gesturing toward Phil. "Both you and Phil do. It's one of the things you two have most in common."

"He might have something there, Michal," Phil said. "Both about your penchant for the titillating and your propensity to longwindedness."

Michal shook her head. "The Tree is definitely about sex," she reiterated. "First of all, 'knowing' is a common euphemism for sex. This is where our phrase 'carnal knowledge' comes from. After Adam and Eve are expelled from the Garden, Adam 'knew' his wife Eve, and she became pregnant and bore Cain. But 'eating' is also a euphemism for sex. In Proverbs 30, for example, we find the adulteress 'eating and wiping her mouth' and saying 'I have done nothing wrong.' And after Adam and Eve eat the forbidden fruit, they immediately recognize that they are naked. As scholars have pointed out, this is their first sexual experience in metaphor. What they now 'know' is their sexual nature. And to hide their shame, they cover themselves up with the proverbial fig leaves. What does God do after He punishes them? He makes clothes so they can cover themselves."[19]

"That seems like such a womanly gesture for a patriarchal God," Phil began. "Why didn't he order Eve to do it?"

Michal rolled her eyes. "That is a very *loving* gesture from God, and it comes right after He punishes them. Note that the punishment for Eve is that she will have difficulty in childbirth, but she will still sexually desire her husband. . . . It's all about sex, boys."

Michal pushed on either side of her breasts, lifting them up and forward, sloshing her third Gibson gin martini as she did. She laughed, looking at the liquid on her skin. "But I don't imagine you will agree, Max."

"Not me, I'm all over anything that has to do with sex," Phil said, making a show of getting on his tiptoes to ogle her spilled liquor.

"You pervert," Michal jabbed and smiled.

Phil gave his best smirk. "If we are to stick with the idea of the Bible being a book of advice from the establishment. . . ."

"If 'by the establishment' you mean of course the literate, privileged, male elite—those guys—you know, the writers of the Bible and the deciders of the canon. The ones who decided which books were divinely inspired, which of course turned out to be the ones that promoted their political and social agenda."

Phil grinned. "It makes sense that the establishment would be circumspect in their treatment of sex. After all this is *the* Bible, not a Tijuana Bible." Phil winked at Michal, clearly amused with himself for his clever connection. Michal rolled her eyes again, reminding him that his idea of clever wasn't always as clever as he thought.

"Further," Phil continued, "it makes sense that they would make that thing they most want to control the source of all the evil in the world. It's important for people to have sex and procreate, but it's even more important that they do so according to the edicts of the religious leaders, so that they don't add any more misery to their already perilous existence."

Max threw ice cubes at both of them. "Cool it, kids. You two may always have sex on the brain, but I don't think that was God's message to His people."

THIRTEEN YEARS EARLIER. *Rome*

"Mee-shel ma belle. . . ." Phil began in exaggerated, drunken serenade. "I love you, I love you, I love you. That's all I want to say. . . . I always forget the rest of the words."

Michal giggled. "If only *you* named me rather than my father."

"Right Mikel. *Je t'aime ma beauté . . .* and you've got brains too." Phil gave her a kiss. He picked up a second bottle of Vietti Villero and poured them another drink. "Let's get to our favorite topic. . . ."

"Sex!" Michal exclaimed.

"You've always got sex on the brain... I'm thinking something a bit more cerebral right now. I find it so difficult to deny you anything, so let's see if we can mix and match? Y'know, Sangiovese and Moscato? How 'bout that bit you were talking about with the Tree of Knowledge being all about sex? See—philosophy and sex?"

"Love it! We are just like Sartre and Beauvoir."

"Only cuter." Phil's voice softened, mirroring his emotions. He reached over and stroked her cheek with the back of his hand. At just that moment a breeze blew through the open shutters and past Michal's face, dancing through her hair.

Michal gazed into Phil's eyes. The span of several heartbeats flew by in the inimitable way that time refuses to allow lovers to have an eternal moment. Phil handed her the glass of wine.

You have to forgive me, dear reader, for this somewhat purple prose. Romance is not my genre. It's usually consigned to the more saccharine sorts. I'll do my best to keep such sentences to a minimum.

"To the topic at hand, Michal? Tree of Knowledge? Hey, I'm already moving into territory that makes me think of unicorns and the tooth fairy, but I'm willing to go there so we can mutually decimate the Jesus freaks."

Michal laughed. Phil rose from the leather loveseat, opened the sliding glass door, and walked out onto the balcony, a full moon behind him. The Coliseum could be seen just beyond some apartments. Night denizens, likely returning from some football match, sang bawdy songs that echoed through the winding streets. The cool breeze reminded Phil of purity, cleansing, innocence. He closed his eyes and basked in the sensation, then just as quickly pushed it aside and turned to Michal.

When he turned around, she was reclining on the loveseat, watching him. He considered that maybe he would talk philosophy later.

"You should join me over here. The view is spectacular." He knew that if he stayed there watching her any longer, the talk would revolve around the bedroom, rather than veiled allusions to the evils of Hebrew sex. He laughed at the irony.

"What? What's so funny?"

"The wonders and perils of irony in everyday life." Phil extended his hand to Michal.

She rose, grabbed her wine and walked over to Phil, who was standing by the railing. He encircled her waist, feeling the warmth of her skin through the sheer sundress, then stopped and held up his hands.

"You are too tempting. Must have been something like this for Eve. Eternal knowledge. Eternal life. All you have to do is disobey that God fellow. Don'tcha think?" Phil tried desperately and feebly to move the conversation back to the intellectual. Michal could be singleminded at times.

"I've always wanted to ask those nutty Christians why God would create the Tree of Knowledge of Good and Evil if He knew that they would disobey Him. Seems pretty fucked up. Makes God a sadist. And why would God tell His new creation that they must not eat from the Tree of Knowledge of Good and Evil, otherwise they will die? Why would God forbid knowledge, when He gave us such a thirst for knowledge? —Of course, that isn't about sex, but I just had to get that out there." Michal tried to be erudite, but her mind kept returning to Phil's carnality. "You know, if you insist I talk about sex—even sex in the Garden—I might just show you how hard it is to resist temptation." She licked her lips.

"Back, vile temptress. Back to the pit of hell from whence your luscious body sprang." Phil moved quickly back to the intellectual. "It does make sense that God would place temptation in the midst of these new humans. It all plays into His long-term plans."

"Do tell," Michal said. "Then I have a few words to say about sex and the Tree." She peered into his eyes.

"You first, so long as you can keep your mind on the latter." Phil waved his hand. "This is not the sex you are looking for," he stated in a quiet monotone. He hoped that the Jedi mind trick would work. He walked back into the apartment and made his way to the bedroom. He sat on the bed and tapped the comforter, inviting Michal to join him.

"Think about it, Phil. God plants a Tree of *Knowledge*. To 'know' is to fuck. . . ." Michal giggled at her words as she tossed a pillow into the air. "Carnal knowledge, y'know?"

"Indeed. So more metaphor from the Bible? Shocker! But surely you have more to back up your claim than that." Phil smiled and raised a single eyebrow.

Michal sipped her wine. "Serpents in the ancient world were symbols of wisdom, fertility, and immortality. It wasn't until much later that Christians interpreted the serpent that tempted Eve as the devil. Some scholars argue that the serpent represents Asherah, the Canaanite goddess of fertility. Did you know that the Israelites worshipped Asherah right alongside Yahweh *in the Temple*?[20] Up until the time of the Maccabees and the Hasmonean Dynasty in the second century BCE. Of course, their temple was destroyed by the Babylonians, and they were exiled for a time, but Cyrus the Great let them return and rebuild.

"Asherah was like Yahweh's *wife*," she continued. As scholars note, passages in the Bible against worshipping Asherah—like Jeremiah 7:18 where the Israelite women make cakes for the queen of heaven—can be seen as infighting about the proper way to worship. Archeologists have even found inscriptions that say 'Yahweh and Asherah.'[21] They were a team."

Michal paused to see whether Phil was following along. He smiled and clicked her glass with his, in approval.

"Go on. . . ."

"Of course, fertility concerns sex and reproduction. The second creation story is about women's sexual subordination to men and the difficulty of childbirth. The author of First Timothy, who was a real misogynistic bastard, even picked up on this: 'Adam was formed first, then Eve, and Adam was not deceived, but the woman was deceived and became a transgressor.' And get this: Right after that, the author says that women shall be saved *through childbearing!* Completely fucked up."

"Right out of First Timothy." Phil held up the Italian *Nuova Riveduta* Translation, which he had retrieved from the nightstand. "Catholics are scary. . . . It's like some kind of insidious propaganda ploy."

Affecting his best fake Italian accent, he began quoting 1 Timothy 2:15:

"*Tuttavia sarà salvata partorendo figli. . . .*"

Michal grimaced at Phil's overly dramatic reading. She glanced above the bed and saw the antiqued ceramic crucifix with the letters *INRI*. She grimaced some more. *Kinda puts one out of the mood.*

"Makes perfect sense. I frequently command an eternal pain process as a way to thank someone for their efforts in saving an entire species." Phil smirked. "Oh wait, that would be Mistress Melissa. Wrong person." Phil immediately regretted his comment as he watched Michal leer.

"Mistress Melissa? And who might that be?" She rose from the bed and moved toward the closet.

"Nobody. Uh, an old friend maybe. . . . Someone I made up?" Phil moved away from his jest. "But in Timothy, the writer is essentially saying that even though women will be saved *by making babies*, they still don't have any say-so in the church. . . . Yep, pretty fucked up." Phil looked up from the Bible to see Michal returning from the closet wearing nothing but a sheet wrapped loosely around her body. He stared appreciatively, and then attempted to get back on track.

"Keeping it on topic—" Phil moved toward the now-empty bottle expecting that by magic he could get more out of it. "Where is Jesus when we need him?"

"Huh?"

"You know . . . we're out of wine. Didn't Jesus work magic at that wedding in Cana?"

"Right. . . . But only because his mom didn't want to be embarrassed about not being a good hostess." Michal chuckled. "As you were saying, darling?"

Phil smiled. "Right. —So if the Tree was all about sex, then you have to say that the Judeo-Christian religion is all about control. But I don't think anyone in the fundie group is going to buy that. You might have to reinforce your claim with more Biblical references."

Michal gave a come-hither look. Control was not just a topic of religious thought right now.

"So we both agree that the Bible is bunk, at least as a deity-inspired empirical source of truth. I think that pretty much sums up most of our argument," Phil said. "It is a *great read*. It's packed full of sex, violence. Some people even say that it gives us evidence of an alien encounter, that Ezekiel's so-called vision of the wheeled chariot is actually a description of his encounter with an ancient astronaut." He laughed.

A serious expression suddenly crossed Phil's face. He looked at Michal and asked her point blank: "Then what *do* you believe?"

He had wondered this for a while. Surprisingly, he had never really talked with her about it. *I wonder why?*

Michal tilted her head slightly, musing on his words. Then she smiled, her inhibitions safely lubricated by the wine. "Well, I would say that I would have to take the route of Hume, or more specifically Philo—your namesake. You share his skepticism, too." She smiled.

She lifted her empty wine glass and twisted the stem between her fingers.

"In Hume's *Dialogues Concerning Natural Religion*, Cleanthes uses a *derviation* of the teleological argument to argue for God's existence. Philo ends up slam-dunking him."

"You mean of course 'derivation.'" Phil smiled as he watched her face flush. He wasn't sure whether it was anger or embarrassment.

"Quiet from the Peanut Gallery. You speak *drunkenese*, so follow along, Mister Soon-to-Be-MIT."

She looked at her empty glass and frowned. "You sure we're all out?"

"'Fraid so."

"Bummer. —Anyway, Cleanthes uses a *derivation* of the teleological argument—Paley's watchmaker, to be specific. He argues that we can infer the existence and nature of God by looking at the universe. The universe is like a house or a ship, so there must be a house-maker or a ship-builder, or, in this case, a universe-maker, God. . . . Assuming that the universe didn't just create itself, there must be an uncreated Creator. Mind you, this doesn't explain why God created the universe in the first place. Was it boredom? Loneliness? Maybe to satisfy His sadistic side? Michal laughed.

"The old demiurge rears its head again." Phil smiled.

"The argument may be old, but it's effective. It certainly was in the eighteenth century, when Hume was writing. But Philo argues that if we suppose that the universe is a house, or a ship, or whatever, there's nothing saying that there must be only *one* builder. And even more than that, we can't know the nature of this builder or builders. We certainly aren't entitled to jump right to Cleanthes' anthropomorphizing. Why should we suppose that there was only one universe-maker who looks and acts like we do, only perfect? At best, this argument allows us to say there *is* a demiurge, but we can't say anything about its *nature*.

"Indeed, the universe could have been created by one of the Supreme Being's fallible apprentices, like a toddler deity building an imperfect sandcastle. Imagine: his big brothers tease him, so in his embarrassment he stomps on it and moves to a different place in the sand to build a better sandcastle. Our universe could be the stomped-on sandcastle for all we know. . . . In his *Natural History of Religion*, Hume argues that monotheism, limiting the universe-maker to one being, essentially kills the self by advocating asceticism. Why would we want to kill the self while we are trying to find the eternal? Seems a pretty pointless, and even destructive or sadomasochistic, endeavor to me. So to your question: I would say that I'm a confirmed polytheist. I don't believe in a god, but only—perhaps—gods, and even then I'm pretty skeptical. Does that answer your question?"

Phil screwed up his eyes as he attempted to process what she had just said. "So you believe that *if* there is a god, then it would be one of many gods in a polytheistic system. But you don't believe in gods, or at the very least the jury's out? So, what, you're some kind of polytheistic agnostic?"

Michal stood triumphantly and placed her hands on her hips, striking her best superhero pose. "Yes! Exactly. The world's first agnostic polytheist!" she trumpeted.

Phil closed the Bible which was still open to 1 Timoteo 2:15 and placed it gently on the nightstand, never taking his eyes off Michal. She stood there with the sheet pooled at her feet, dressed only in her intellect. Phil walked over and knelt before her, gathering the sheet in his hands before showing it to her.

"Breezy in here, I think." He smiled.

"It is breezy, but you wouldn't know with all those clothes on." Michal walked over to the bed. She grabbed the crucifix from the wall and tossed it into the closet.

"We don't need him watching. . . ."

LATE EVENING. *Back at the RTSS*

Michal stared into the fireplace blazing in the middle of the bar. She looked around, taking in the surroundings. The ornamented woodwork was beautiful, intricate, and very exact. Something of a story played out as she followed the carved wood around the bar—a story about a couple and some devil taking items and then returning them.

"Interesting scrollwork, don't you think?" She didn't recognize the voice behind her. It wasn't Phil and it wasn't Max. She spent a moment and then turned around.

"What?"

An attractive Japanese man stood just behind her, almost uncomfortably close—so close that she could smell his cologne with its ginger-sudachi notes. He wore a green cotton jacket, faded denim jeans, and a white button-up shirt. A small snatch of green and white plaid kerchief peeked out of his shirt pocket.

"I said interesting scrollwork, don't you think? It's a very interesting story." He moved even closer to her, looking over her shoulder at the carving. She could feel his almost-sensual breath.

Michal shifted from one foot to the next, suddenly uncomfortable. "It's, ah, interesting, yes." The man stepped to her left and stood by her side.

"Touching story. . . . Involves a man—a woodcutter who is madly in love with a woman but is too afraid to speak with her. He eventually strikes a deal with an *oni*"—the man faced Michal and peered into her eyes—"that's the Japanese version of a demon, in case you weren't aware." Though his English was excellent, he had just enough of an accent to sound exotic to her. He smiled and turned back to his narrative.

"So the man strikes a deal with this *oni* to get the woman to love him. Well, as happens in these stories, magic comes into play, and the *oni* causes the woman to fall in love with the man, but for a price—that he never ask for the truth from the *oni*. Within months, the woodcutter and the woman are married. . . . See, that's the point where they marry, in that frame above the window there." A long finger pointed toward an intricate carving of a traditional Japanese wedding. "The bride is wearing a *tsunokakushi*. If the woodwork were painted, you'd see that she is also wearing heavy white makeup." The scent of patchouli and plum flowers wafted past her nose as he explained the scene.

"They were happy for many years, but then the man began to wonder whether she actually loved him. This consumed him to the point that he finally had to know, so he called to the *oni* and asked. The *oni* reminded him of his oath, but he is undaunted. See where he's begging the *oni* on his knees?"

Michal continued to feel uneasy. Whether it was the man's proximity, or perhaps his skill at storytelling, she couldn't tell. She managed to whisper a "yes" and he went on.

"The *oni* tells the man that, yes, she did actually love him, but that now she would know about the deal he had made with the *oni*. As often happens in these stories, the man then kills himself. . . . Rather lovely, though, don't you think?" He looked at her with piercing green eyes, which promised dark things. Michal turned away.

"It is interesting, yes," was all that she could manage to say.

"How rude of me. I'm getting so involved in the story that my manners fail me. My name is Yuwaku. I visit this place from time to time, though most of my friends tell me I'm dishonoring myself by doing so. I have heard the owner speak of you before. You are Michal, aren't you?" He extended his hand and gave a pleasing smile.

"Yes, my name is Michal. You say you know Phil?" Michal's voice rose just above a whisper. Mercifully, the effect of the story was passing. Yuwaku's hand was warm and comforting in her own.

"Phil, you say? I've not been formally introduced, but yes, I know of him. You have an interesting name, a man's name. . . . Very Western of you." He gave another smile. "I come here when I want to find peace. Since he has so few customers this place is frequently quite peaceful. But I must be off now. I'm needed at home." His smile continued through his words.

"Please stay for a little longer. . . . So what is your fascination with the story?" Michal was curious why this man had taken such an interest in her.

"It's a lovely tale of not knowing, and of doubting to the point that it imperils your own thoughts and sense of self. Has this ever happened to you Michal?"

"Actually it has—well, in a way. Once—fairly recently actually—I placed my watch on my dresser. I was sure of it. I saw it. I knew it was there. I took a shower and when I came out my watch was gone. I searched for an hour. I even asked my lover to help me look. He'd seen it on the dresser, too. " Michal pointed at an imaginary dresser across the room. "We looked under the dresser, behind the dresser, in the dresser, and in all of the other rooms." She smiled. "We even looked in the refrigerator." She laughed at the nonsense of it. "I hear that happens sometimes."

Yuwaku settled comfortably into a nearby chair. He was captivated by Michal's every word, his eyes lighting up at opportune moments as he leaned toward her.

"I had given up hope of finding my watch, but then a feeling came over me, almost a feeling of evil. I commanded the mischievous spirit. . . ." Michal's voice caught in her throat. *Why am I being so forthcoming with this man? Why do I feel so comfortable telling this very personal story?* She knew she should stop the story here, but she continued despite herself. "I commanded this mischievous little devil or demon to leave and return my watch."

She looked at Yuwaku, expecting him to start laughing, but he was as enthralled as ever. He looked at her expectantly, without the slightest hint of condemnation.

"Well, I left the room and retrieved a shirt from the dryer. When I returned, I noticed something at the foot of my dresser, and there was my watch in plain sight. —Now I know what you must be thinking. But I checked all around that dresser and even underneath. My lover and I checked that exact spot. How could we both have missed it? I was happy to have my watch back, so I put it on and went about the day." She looked away, staring at nothing in particular.

"That sounds like a wonderful story, Michal. What is the problem?"

"Did I miss the watch the first time? Did I overlook it? Did we both overlook it? Maybe my lover was just humoring me, but he swore up and down that he did not hide it. It didn't just grow legs and walk away. . . ." She rubbed her silver and gold Rolex watch—the one Phil had given her on their first anniversary. The feel was reassuring to her sanity.

"Does it matter? You got your watch back. I see it is still on your wrist. What is wrong with that?"

"I called it 'supernatural,' like an obedient demon or something, but I just don't know." Michal laughed softly. "I am the woodcutter. I want to be happy with the result, but I am also"—she hesitated—"I am also curious about what happened. I immediately called it 'supernatural,' and I still do. But there are questions."

"Surely this doesn't really bother you, does it? You didn't really think that it was a mischievous demon, as you say? You weren't a believer then, were you?" Yuwaku looked at her inquisitively.

"No, in fact I am a believer and I was then. Like I said, it wasn't that long ago. And I am even more of a believer now, thanks to the watch incident. You see, I'd been doubting my faith. . . . Actually, God and I had become like an old married couple." She laughed. "The honeymoon was over and I was taking Him for granted. Well, this little demon—or whatever it was—knew he couldn't take my soul, so he took my watch instead. But not for long. This renewed my faith."

"Oh, I see. I thought that since you were friends with Mr. Phil, you also didn't believe in all of this"—he crossed his arms and presented his best American accent—"*ghostly afterlife nonsense.*"

Michal laughed. "That sounds remarkably like him, but no, I do believe."

"But surely you didn't always. I'm not sure I can see Mr. Phil with a believer."

She thought back to Rome. "No, I didn't always believe. There was a time when I would have just dismissed it as missing the obvious." She smiled, thinking of those times.

"So what changed your mind?" Yuwaku stood and pulled a chair out from the table, inviting Michal to sit down.

"I really don't want to say, but it has to do with several experiences that I've had. These have all added to my belief. I have had these experiences where—" She wondered at her openness with this total stranger. She sat up straight and smoothed out her dress. "—Where, or rather, ah, *when* I have had experiences—um, these experiences were very vivid and. . . ." Michal could hear herself back-pedalling. "Let's just say that they made an extraordinary impression on me." She studied Yuwaku. He was still sitting in the chair. He hadn't run away laughing at this crazy person telling him a crazy story. His eyes were as intensely curious as ever.

"Please don't feel that I will be condemning of the mystical. I am syncretic. I'm a Buddhist who believes in Shinto. Seems like I'm just as conflicted as you are." He smiled that inviting smile again. She laughed.

"Well, it is a bit mystical, but yes, it also contradicts my earlier life." Michal said.

"Would your earlier self have thought that it was supernatural? Assuming of course that your earlier self wouldn't have banished the *oni*, or demon, or whatever you want to call it."

"No, I most certainly wouldn't have, nor would I have called it 'supernatural.'"

"So were you wrong then?"

"Well, yes, I mean I must have been. . . ."

"Of course, it only stands to reason right? The alternative has too many unpleasant implications. So you're not wrong now in your belief, correct?" His words were suddenly sharper, more direct. His accent seemed to have faded slightly. Or maybe it hadn't, and Michal was just uncomfortable with his incessant questioning. She stood up and backed away a couple of steps.

"Of course, I believe what I believe now, and when I didn't previously—well, that was a different time. A different me." She thought back to Rome again.

"You seem to posit some kind of discontinuity of personal identity. Maybe a reductionist account?"

"I don't remember exactly what that means."

"Reductionist accounts claim that we are not persons, or selves, but merely some collection of interrelated thoughts, or memories, or desires, or beliefs. And since these obviously change over time, this explains how you can say that you are a different person now."

"I see," Michal said. She shifted her weight from one foot to the other, arms crossed.

"So if you are a different 'you' now from the 'you' you were then, well, of course you could have dramatically different beliefs."

"I suppose so. " Michal began to wonder at her own beliefs. *Could I have been so different?*

"That being the case, you can get the point of the story of the woodcutter."

"Hmm, what? What's the point of the story?"

"That you should be happy for what you have, Michal. It doesn't matter where your watch came from, or whether a little mouse moved it, or a demon. You should be happy to have it back, right?"

Michal laughed nervously. At the time she *had* wondered if a mouse had moved the watch, perhaps a little mouse drawn to shiny objects. But then she had dismissed that idea. She hadn't said anything to anyone about any such mouse. She had tried to use Harman's "inference to the best explanation"—the hypothesis that made the most sense, compared to all the other alternatives. But had she *really* accepted the best hypothesis, given all the evidence? She could hear a hissing noise in the background that sounded like steam escaping from a pipe about to burst. It grew louder. Her vision began to blur. She dropped her head and began to murmur authoritatively, "I command you to leave in the name of—" Her words stopped abruptly when she heard the door open and Phil and Max enter, arguing loudly.

"You're a complete ass sometimes. Of course evil is not God's fault. It's not like that. God created evil, it's part of His design, yes, but He doesn't cause evil to happen to specific people, like it's a punishment on earth or something." Max pointed accusingly at Phil.

"Of course, how convenient! We need to have free will because a 'god'—oh, sorry, *God with* a *capital G*—doesn't want us to be puppets, but He's more than willing to hardwire us to act a certain way, and also more than willing to intervene when it serves His divine purpose! What a crock! He's little more than a capricious Greek pantheon god!"

"I see you're arguing again. Do you ever *not* argue?" Michal's head cleared as she addressed her friends.

"Of course not. *It's my nature to argue.*" Phil winked at Max. "Must be something about free will. . . . Can I get you a drink from the bar, Michal? I was just getting Max some tea. Of course, I'm having another whiskey." Phil reached behind the bar.

"Sure. I'll have a Red Zin. And what would you like, Mr. Yuwaku?" Michal turned to address her companion, but he was gone. She could hear the sound of the *shōji* closing, which led to the path outside.

"Who were you talking to Michal?" Max walked over and put his hand on her shoulder. "You're shaking."

"I—I'll be—" She looked blankly at the door. "I wasn't talking to anyone. Now how about that drink? Are you talking about evil still?" She took Max's hand and walked up to the bar.

She always had a gold rush of shinies from the room where the humans slept when the night light came out looking like a big hunk of cheese. She could easily wander about—quiet and quick—but wander she could. The big sharp-tooth growly beasts never knew when she was there. She could collect her favorites to put in her foot-cloth. The one that smelled like the man-human who would always come around for a visit. A single dangly jangly with a big red button on it. A shiny round thing with a few little sparklies. A tiny sharp dazzle with a human letter. If only she could get that paw bit—the thing that the human wore on her paw. (Of course she knew that the human was a she. She wasn't just a stupid beast. . . .) But she could never get that one. It was always moved around, sometimes without her moving it. Sometimes the man-human would move it. Sometimes it just seemed to find its way to some other place. She wasn't sure, but she knew that it was just too heavy for her to take to her little mousey home.

FOUR

Heterosexuality is not normal, it's just common.
DOROTHY PARKER

THE NEXT DAY. *At the RTSS*

"You know," Max began, "all of this talk about hetero sex in the Garden leaves some of us out."

"Right, Maxie," Michal replied. "We should discuss homosexuality and the Bible. What with all of these same-sex marriage debates, and the direction our country is moving, I'd be interested in hearing your views about it."

"You mean that God hates fags? You know, *your kind.*" Phil made air quotes with his fingers, then looked at them as if they were foreign things. "I hate it when they do that." He put his hands behind his back. "Well, God hates fags at least according to the Westboro Baptist Church and your Holy Book." Max and Michal stared at him incredulously. "Oh, right. God hates the *sin*, not the sinner."

"You know that neither one of us is going to go along with you here, Phil. So what's your take on it, Max? You're a *gay deacon*, after all," Michal said.

"I love this topic," Max said. "To your point, Phil, our Holy Book doesn't condemn homosexuality at all. Top scholars have shown those who believe the Bible condemns homosexuality are misled by faulty translations, poor interpretation, or just don't know the cultural context. As you know, the Bible has been used to justify slavery, anti-miscegenation laws, and the subjugation of women, and now, in an equally damning and rights-denying way, homosexuality."[22]

"Well, I personally think that your imaginary god-being cares *very much* about what people do in the privacy of their own bedrooms. How they have sex—as laid out in Leviticus 18—when they have sex, with whom they have sex. And particularly if they are having *gay* sex. If you're talking about the God of the Bible—you know, the only document from which we derive knowledge about the imaginary Über-Being"—Phil struck a bodybuilder pose, displaying his not-so-developed physique—"and if you're trying to suggest that the Bible doesn't condemn homosexuality, well, I've got an iceberg to sell you—in Africa." He laughed. "How can your God condemn homosexuality because it violates God-designed human functioning, since so *obviously* penises are not supposed to penetrate rectums—which is weird since God put the prostate there, you know, the male G-spot—but at the same time He condones and even encourages violence? Evidently God designed humans to be penetrated by swords but not flesh—or so said Hector Avalos."

"I agree with Phil that the Bible condemns homosexuality—actually, let's speak more accurately, it condemns male-male homoeroticism. The term 'homosexual' wasn't coined until the nineteenth century," Michal pointed out. "Anyway,

I agree with Phil at least on this. The Bible *does* condemn it, but not for the reasons that people might think. But I'd like to hear your argument, first, Max."

"I warn you, Max," Phil began, "that whatever you say, I'm going to challenge why you don't take the Bible literally here, but you do elsewhere."

"Oh, I'm taking it literally, my friend. People just don't understand the context."

Phil rolled his eyes and held up a finger in protest. "That was fast."

"Let me explain. Consider the most often-cited supposed condemnation of homosexuality in the Old Testament: Leviticus 18:22. 'You shall not lie with a man as with a woman. It is an abomination.' The prohibition of male-male sex occurs only in the Holiness Code of Leviticus, with its so-called 'purity laws.'" Max stopped himself from making air quotes mid-gesture.

Phil laughed. "They have a life of their own, don't they?"

Max smiled. "The condemnation doesn't occur anywhere else. The implication, then, is that the *only* reason for forbidding male-male sex is concern about uncleanness or ritual impurity. So the passage in Leviticus—*passages*, actually, because you find the condemnation again in Leviticus 20:13—so the *passages* in Leviticus are religious, not moral. Here, 'abomination' simply and only means 'unclean.'"

Michal shifted in her seat. "I have something to say about 'abomination,' but I'll let it pass for now."

"You said you would challenge," Max beseeched his friends. "You didn't say it would be every single word."

"I warned you, henpecker." Phil smiled at Michal and then waved Max on.

"Fine." Max took the tiny victory and continued: "Indeed, almost immediately after Leviticus 20:13 we find the passage 'you shall make a distinction between the clean animals, and the unclean, and between unclean bird and the clean. You shall not bring abomination on yourself by animal or bird.' So since we aren't ancient Israelite priests concerned with ritual purity in our offerings to God, we needn't worry about it."

"This makes some sense to me, Max," Michal agreed. "The Hebrew word for 'abomination' here is *toevah,* which often means 'impurity' or 'religious taboo.' If the authors wanted it to mean 'wrongdoing' or 'sin' they would have used the word '*zimah.*'"

Phil chuckled and stabbed an accusing finger at Max. "Don't mess with the Hebrew scholar and world traveller."

Michal laughed and then went on, "But you haven't got a prayer, Max, if you think that the Leviticus writings were only addressed to the priests regarding their behavior. I grant that Leviticus does have to do with matters associated with the priests, but not exclusively. Rather, it is addressed to Israelite males, and concerns their relationships with other people, with God, and with their land."

"In other words, it's addressed to the only people who mattered in most of the Bible," Phil said smugly.

"Sadly so, Phil." Michal said. "But hear me out. Remember, too, that the Leviticus writings do not come from a single source or tradition, and both the Holiness School and the Priestly Torah were mostly written between the early exilic period and the end of the exile. This is significant. Their asses had been thoroughly kicked by the Babylonians, so badly that they even had to resort to cannibalizing their children because they were starving to death. And so all sorts of superstitions about mixings, confusions, and boundary crossings appear. Such superstitions likely existed before, but now they were being invoked as reasons why Yahweh was punishing them. Think about what they were doing. They were mixing with foreign women. That is, they were mixing blood. And they were confusing created for creator. They were idolaters, big time. We see all sorts of prohibitions against mixings and confusions in both Leviticus and Deuteronomy."[23]

Michal continued speaking, lecture-style. "Consider Leviticus 18 where as you noted, Max, we find homoeroticism being called an abomination. We also find a prohibition against sleeping with a menstruating woman. Here we have mixing semen with blood. Both are defiling. We also see an apparently random prohibition against sacrificing one's child to Molech. But this is a paradigmatic example of idolatry—confusing created for creator. Bestiality is confusing species. I realize they didn't have that terminology then, but they definitely had some notion of natural kinds. Bestiality is crossing the boundaries between human and animal. Bestiality also means mixing semen in the receptive woman—human semen with animal semen. Incest is mixing potential sexual partners and one's kin. Adultery is confusing one's own sexual property with one's neighbor's property. Male homoeroticism is big-time mixing and confusion, and this is why I think that, here in Leviticus, it alone of all the prohibited sexual practices is singled out as an abomination. Homoeroticism mixes semen, and it mixes semen and excrement—excrement, by the way, is called defiling in Ezekiel. And homoeroticism also confuses gender. The submissive partner is acting like a woman, thus reducing his status in society, and the active partner is treating the submissive partner like a woman. Homoeroticism uniquely displays three kinds of mixings and confusions, and that's why it's called an abomination. Only penetrative homoerotic sex acts are prohibited. Non-penetrative sex acts do not blur the lines between male and female. The woman is supposed to be penetrated and the man is the penetrator. The Hebrew word for woman is *naqeba*, which means 'orifice bearer.'" She snorted. "As if there are no orifices in the male body."

While Michal 'lectured,' Max and Phil assumed their 'student' stance, sitting dutifully and respectfully, pretending to take notes.

"Is this all going to be on the test?" Phil asked in a nasal voice.

"What did you get for that bit after adultery?" Max whispered to Phil, sounding very much like an addled schoolboy.

"Knock it off, you guys." Michal shook her head.

"Well, you could have taken a breath in there. Though it's all good stuff." Phil grinned. "Besides, I am quite confident that I can locate all six of my orifices."

"Do you know something that I don't?" Michal asked.

"Do you want me to name them?" Phil held up his finger, pointing at himself. "Asshole. . . ."

"Of course you would go there first, Phil. But it's good as an orifice-descriptor *and* general overall self-description," Max joked.

"Well, I know one orifice that you overuse," Michal jabbed.

"And that would be my *kisser?*" Phil swooned. "Alas, it's been out of commission for some time." He puckered his lips.

"Enough! Let me get back to what I was saying," Michal said. "With the awesome designation 'orifice bearer,' the woman is to be the one to receive the male. . . ."

Max and Phil went back to taking imaginary notes. Michal rolled her eyes and continued. "So a man who was sexually penetrated by another man in anal intercourse was confusing societal norms of maleness and femaleness. . . ."

EIGHT YEARS EARLIER. *Santa Barbara*

Dozens of bars cluttered State Street in downtown Santa Barbara. It was easy to find a watering hole offering local brew, cheap grub, music, pool tables, darts, and big-screen TVs. But turning west onto one of the side streets, it was easy to miss a smaller pub, not nearly so raucous. Patrons of this establishment had to make their way past two bohemian shops and one selling various "smoking products" to reach their destination.

The sign above the heavy wooden door named the creature painted on the wall—a large, brightly colored wall mural of a cartoon slug, colors still fresh after years of repainting. Sitting in a fashion recalling the hookah-smoking caterpillar in *Alice in Wonderland*, the slug was a blue- and ochre-colored creature with two antennae protruding from its head, curling out toward the smoke shop next door, always reaching for that building but never quite getting there. One could almost make out its name, long forgotten. One of the middle letters was an 'e' and the last was 'y.' Was it Betty? Or maybe Henry? The answer was a mystery but 'The Slug' heralded the entrance to a well-known grad-student pub catering to students of nearby UC Santa Barbara since at least the '70s.

Michal entered, gliding through the (mostly) studious throng of students. Every kind of discussion could be had here, from philosophy to physics, politics to chemistry. The pub was a beehive of intellectual exploration, with liberal lubrication from a local brewery's Blue-eyed Frog or the newly arrived Bear Crap Stout. The stench of greasy hamburgers and fries offended Michal's newly vegetarian nose, but she loved to listen to the activity of the next generation of professors or activists. She intended to be one of the former, though the latter would not be completely unwelcome either. A fellow grad student brushed past her holding two pints of bright cornflower brew. She had seen him a few times in the library and they had spoken occasionally. His name was Brian and he was getting his Ph.D. in marine biology. Michal suspected that he would end up at the Scripps Institution of Oceanography doing some kind of research. He was brilliant and had worked hard to lift himself from a broken family in Los Angeles. He kept to himself, being on the quiet side, though he had at least once expressed some painfully shy interest in Michal.

He noticed her and turned. "Hey, Michal. How are you?" His Afro swayed before settling back into place.

"I'm doing all right, Brian. Busy—but who isn't? Who's the other beer for?" She motioned to the second pint he carried.

He gave her a nervous smile and then stared at the floor. "It's for Zandra. She's a grad student in linguistics."

Michal smiled and straightened her red and yellow zigzag-print skirt as Brian's eyes eventually met hers.

She winked. "I'll let you get back to her." She waved at Zandra and smiled.

Zandra smiled back.

Brian mumbled something like "See you in the library" as he quickly walked back to the table by the window.

Michal smiled at the thought of Brian finding someone. He seemed happy. He was a nice boy, but that was exactly the problem: he was just a boy. He had years of education and growing up to do and Michal had no interest in that kind of relationship. Teaching a boy how to become a man was the furthest thing from her mind.

She turned and spotted her professor, James, in a corner booth. He hadn't noticed her just yet as he pored over some aged-leather book. She watched him gingerly turn each of the delicate pages of what appeared to be a hundred-year-old copy of the *Book of Enoch*. He brushed his disheveled, shoulder-length, wavy brown hair away from his eyes in a motion that better suited a man much younger, yet nonetheless seemed natural for him.

James raised his hand to straighten his reading glasses and noticed her watching him. He gave her a familiar smile as he tipped down his glasses and motioned for her to join him. He took a sip of what must have been the stout as she made her way through the crowd.

She straightened her skirt again and sat at the table.

"Michal. . . . glad you could make it. Sit down. Can I get you a drink?"

"Sure. What are you having?" She plopped down her heavy satchel at the side of the two-person booth. Her arm welcomed the rest.

"The Bear Crap Stout." He chuckled at the name. "You would think that some of these micro-brewers would try for something a bit more cosmopolitan rather than resorting to sophomoric humor. Though I must admit it's rather good. Take a sip to see if you like it."

Michal reached for the glass, at first hesitantly, brushing his fingers as he offered it to her.

The foam tickled her nose as she took a long draw. She thought it might have been too much, but she was more than just a little nervous. The chocolate notes added a luscious quality, and something else—maybe molasses and a hint of orange—combined nicely with the malty beverage. She took two full swallows then handed it back.

"That's good. I'll take it." Michal felt increasingly tense. She imagined that it was because she was so attracted to him. That attraction was challenged momentarily as James looked at her with stifled laughter. He pointed discreetly at his own upper lip, motioned at her, and then extended a napkin toward her mouth. At first she didn't catch on to what he was noting, until she felt the remnants of that malty, *foamy* stout still on her lightly painted lips. Her cheeks reddened, but that blush turned from embarrassment to other feelings, as he gently dabbed her lips.

"Don't worry, it happened to me too." James smiled at her, showing another part of the napkin still holding the stain of his stout mustache.

He held up his hand to motion the server. In the quiet buzz of the place, she immediately recognized him and winked. James made the sign for "two" while pointing at his glass, smiling the amazingly charming smile that Michal so adored.

James seemed able to charm anyone. Even in class he carried his students along with his pleasing mannerisms and words. She loved that he was so socially capable, but more than anything she loved his brain.

Michal sat quietly while he described what he was reading. She heard the words and understood their meaning—1917 edition, Dead Sea Scrolls, theological significance—but to say that she listened to most of it would be less than accurate. She was drinking in his presence.

When the server arrived with the drinks, James lifted his glass.

"Listen to me going on. Today isn't about me and *my* brilliance." He winked at her and chuckled, "It's about yours. . . . Cheers. To your last class before you start tackling that dissertation."

"Cheers." She wished she had thought of a better response. Phrases flitted about her brain: bits of Latin, witty Victorian prose, even a few contemporary comeback lines that she had heard and appreciated. Ultimately they all fluttered away like the butterflies in her stomach.

"I must say, you saved the best class for last." He smiled again. Michal smiled back. His smiles were infectious.

"Of course, you would have had an easier time with your studies had you tackled it earlier."

"Always a scheduling conflict. . . ." How many years of college and that was the best she could come up with? She decided that she needed to get her head on straight. What would James see in a bumbling female? He had hundreds of those from which to choose, impropriety or not.

No, he appreciates intelligence.

They both took a long draw of the stout. The chocolate made way for the molasses on Michal's palate. As she had already sampled the stronger flavor, it had now been conditioned for something subtler. She closed her eyes and enjoyed the savor as she swallowed. When she opened her eyes, she giggled. James had his own fresh stout mustache. She handed him a napkin but couldn't bring herself to wipe away the foam, her hands failing halfway across the table. He smiled as he took her napkin and wiped his lips. She thought that he puckered them at the end, sending her a light kiss. She dismissed that as silly. *A bit too "romance-novel."*

"So what do you think of my textual criticism class? —Great stuff, right?"

"I love it. I'm really surprised that there are so few corruptions of the Hebrew text or, I guess I should say, that those corruptions that we do find don't significantly affect the sense." She was happy with her ability to keep up, as her confidence grew.

"Right. . . . The scribes were meticulous, and so we find few copy errors and none that compromise the integrity of the text." He ran his hand sensuously down the leather cover of his book as he spoke. "And certainly compared to the New Testament, as you just learned in class today." James smiled again and tilted the fresh glass of stout toward her. "I got a head start on you. . . . I've been reading *Enoch* while you were in Nomi's Prophecy class. Well, if you stay here with me long enough tonight, you'll catch up."

"I love *Enoch*," Michal exclaimed, then immediately thought better of it. *I love Enoch. I sound like an excited little girl.*

"We should read it together, then. It offers a great alternative narrative to the origin of evil. Would you be interested in doing that some time?"

Michal felt the flush coming, and fought hard not to show it. Her cheeks, she was certain, were betraying her thoughts right now. *Are you hitting on me?* She hoped so.

"I would love that. Yeah, I remember that part of *Enoch*—in the *Watchers*, right?"

Not a little girl, not a little girl. I am a woman and I should start acting like one. Her twenty-six years of age should have been ample evidence of that fact, but her behavior belied her maturity.

"Right. . . . So what did you think about today's discussion of the New Testament?" James redirected.

"I've got to say, I'm glad I'm not a Christian taking your class. There are so many interpolations, redactions and missing words, phrases, and verses in the New Testament. I know a lot of the interpolations are found in the medieval manuscripts, as you noted. But since the *King James* is based on these later manuscripts, I'd feel betrayed if I were a Christian taking your class, who trusted in the *King James*." Her poise continued to grow with each word. Every syllable made her feel more of an equal with this man. "And I was shocked to hear that the New Testament writers did not even read the original Hebrew texts but the more corrupted Greek Septuagint. You blew me away today, James."

Another smile. "Well, thank you, Michal. It's such a joy having you in class. My colleagues and I think so highly of you. You have more than established yourself as a mental force with which to be reckoned. You always offer refreshing alternative views and I'm not ashamed to say that you've frequently challenged my own thoughts on many subjects." He smiled as he took another long draw of his stout.

Michal watched his throat work as he swallowed. He wiped his lips and looked at her very seriously.

"I'd love it if we could study the texts together. I could teach you so much." James paused, which made Michal feel uncomfortable.

"Let's get out of here, Michal." He extended his hand, then drew it back deftly and grabbed his leather satchel, placing his copy of *Enoch* into its folds.

"OK. . . . Where are we going?" She tried to sound seductive, even a little sensual. She hoped it didn't come off as too forward.

"Follow me. . . ." The tone of his voice changed suddenly and made alluring promises.

She downed her beer and picked up her satchel.

As they got up to walk out of the pub, the two glasses sat forgotten on the table. One mostly empty, the other nearly full, their offerings had been cast aside for other sensations. The server came over and quickly bussed the secluded booth, making it available for some new tryst. She watched them, enjoying a moment of voyeurism, when James' hand momentarily rested on Michal's as they both pushed on the door. They exited the pub.

Back at the RTSS

Phil chuckled. "So basically, most of the prohibited sex acts that we find in Leviticus 18 are on the list of things that people do anyway. The bestiality thing is not so common, but I've seen some websites. . . . Sorry." He covered his mouth with his hand, "I'll shut up. Go on."

Michal shook her head and then smiled. "You know, bestiality is legal in Washington State."

"No shit?"

"No shit."

"*No shit*. . . ." Phil smirked.

"Can we get on with it already?" Max asked. "Michal was in the middle of—"

Phil looked at Michal and motioned toward Max who was smiling. "I'm sorry. I return you to your previous target. He's right over there."

Max sat attentively, a smile on his face. "Please proceed."

"OK. . . . Not convinced yet? As scholars have pointed out, we see even more prohibitions against mixings and confusions in, for example, Deuteronomy. Unclean foods often involve animals, birds, fish, and insects crossing boundaries. So animals that have 'hands,' that is, paws, instead of feet, birds that dive into water, fish that don't swim with fins, insects that fly, and so on are all deemed 'unclean.' There is also a prohibition against cross-dressing because it confuses gender. . . . Ancient Israelites were not supposed to mix seeds when they sowed, plow fields with two different kinds of animals, or mix different kinds of thread."

"Hmmm. There goes my polyester-wool blend suit. It doesn't wrinkle, but I suppose it *is* in bad taste." Phil laughed hard at his own joke. "Oh, and Maxie has to stop dressing up in those girly clothes on the weekend."

"Funny guy. . . ." Max shook his head. "Interesting argument, Michal, and a very long-winded one. I thought you wanted me to share *my* views. Or was that just a set-up to present yours?" he teased.

"Sorry, Max. You know how I get. Go on."

"You are my friends for a reason, so I know what I'm getting into. . . . Let's look at the New Testament now. Most homophobic Christians, or ill-informed ones, cite Paul's passage in Romans 1:26-27 to prove that God hates gay people or at least our sin. This is like saying that Lady Gaga likes meat because she wore a dress made of it. It's important to keep context in mind when you are looking at literal meanings. Here Paul suggests that homoeroticism is unnatural. While it is clear that Paul disapproves of this act, he is not making a moral condemnation. Paul could have used the Greek or Hebrew words that mean 'morally wrong,' but he didn't. He chose the same type of language that we find in Leviticus. So Paul, too, is disapproving of homoerotic acts, but only because they are religiously impure."

"So 'unnatural' means 'impure'?" Phil asked.

"'Unnatural' here means something like 'socially unacceptable,'" Max said.

"I believe my argument about mixings and confusions works better here, Max," Michal cut in. "Israelites were driven by all kinds of superstitions of this sort. In their minds, Yahweh punished them for this. I believe that Paul followed this tradition, being the good Pharisaic Jew that he was before his conversion. If you look at Romans 1:26 and 27, Paul had just been talking about people who confused the created for the creator. Then he launches into talking about how *these very same people* then confused gender by lying down with a man as with a woman. And consider the so-called lesbian reference we find here. It's not about lesbians at all. Paul is referring to women who engage in non-procreative sex. Their partners are confusing 'holes,' if you will, inserting their penises in places they don't belong.... Don't believe me? Read what Paul says: 'the women exchanged natural intercourse for unnatural.' Well, what is 'natural intercourse'? Procreative intercourse, obviously. We see Paul, or writers who later wrote in Paul's name, suggesting other confusions. Look where we see him referring to the apocryphal *Book of Enoch* in his letter to the Corinthians. He implicitly suggests that angels want to mix their flesh with female human flesh by having sex with good, church-going women. This is why the women are told to cover their heads—to hide their beauty from the lustful angels above, so as not to be so tempting. Of course, most people miss the Enoch reference entirely."

"This is beginning to sound like a really bad sci-fi movie," Phil joked.

"So what you're saying, Michal, is that the translation or rather the interpretation by man is flawed?"

Michal looked at Max, who wore the hint of a smile. "Yes, that is what I'm saying."

"Good, just wanted to clear that up." Max continued, "This makes sense, Michal. We also find Paul stating that men should not wear their hair unnaturally long and women should not wear their hair unnaturally short. This is gender confusion, too. Maybe Paul *was* following that tradition. But let's now consider the so-called condemnations of homoeroticism in First Corinthians and First Timothy. As you know, there are only a handful of homosexuality passages in the *entire Bible*. Compared to other sins, like social injustice and idolatry, this is small potatoes. I've always wondered, why all the uproar?"

"Good atheists can use this argument as well," Phil said. "I mean, it's a laundry list in 1 Corinthians 6:9. *Idolaters, adulterers, drunkards, slanderers....* Honestly, I'm not sure if *anyone* is spared. According to this, nobody will inherit the kingdom of heaven. Not that I believe in heaven anyway, but it's a bad sign when an atheist can use the Bible to disprove itself. After all, Paul is talking about believers, so it's already assumed these people are washed in the blood, or what-have you."

Michal looked at Phil. He shrugged. "You know, I research this stuff to better crush my enemy."

She smiled. "But Paul's lists of sins are just examples of contemporary moral decay. If Paul were around now, or at least in the 1960s, he'd denounce sex, drugs and rock-'n-roll."

"Anyway," Max began, trying to bring the conversation back to himself, "in Corinthians and Timothy we find the Greek words 'arsenokoita' and 'malakoi.' *Arsenokoita* has been widely translated as meaning 'homosexual' or 'sodomite,' or even 'homosexual pervert' or 'pedophile.' The literal translation is 'man-bed.' 'Arseno' means 'man' or 'men' and 'koita' means 'bed' or 'bedroom.' So: 'man-bed-room.' Some scholars have suggested that *arsenokoita* means the active partner in male-male sex, or the male who pays the *malakoi*, who is the 'soft' or 'effeminate' male in a sexual exchange. So the *malakoi* would be the passive partner. *Arsenokoita* and *malakoi* are paired together for a reason. I'm inclined to think that Paul is prohibiting prostitution—condemning male-male prostitution or exploitative sex. We see the same kind of thing in Timothy."

"First of all, Max," Michal countered, "we don't exactly know *what* is going on here since, as you pointed out, the language is so obscure. I actually think that Paul made up the word *'arsenokoita.'* But a very good case can be made that the *malakoi*, being the submissive partner in a male-male sexual encounter, confuses gender by assuming the role of a woman, and the *arsenokoita*, being the active partner, is also confusing gender. So the New Testament writers bought into the same superstitions about mixings and confusions that the Israelites accepted. And should we be so surprised? My personal opinion, given that this is all superstition anyway, is that God himself likely doesn't give a damn about homosexuality, but the Jews and early Christians sure thought He did."

"Many Christians still think He does," Max said.

Phil clapped his hands several times deliberately and emphatically. "Very nice arguments, you two. I'd say especially nice in that you utilized both the Old and New Testaments. And I certainly don't think we'll get any argument about the Israelites, or in fact any ancient humans, being wildly superstitious. You know, I've heard from some of my *homosexual apologist* friends"—Phil stifled a laugh— "that the Bible actually gives evidence in *support* of homosexual relationships. David and Jonathan, Ruth and Naomi. . . ."

"There's better evidence than that," Max said. "Probably the strongest argument in favor of homosexuality comes from Jesus himself, as scholars have pointed out. First of all, Jesus doesn't say anything about homosexuality anywhere, but even more importantly, he seems to accept it. He certainly never condemns it. We find this in the story of the centurion and his servant or slave in the Gospels of Matthew and Luke. The centurion who asks Jesus to heal his slave refers to his slave by the Greek word *pais*, which means 'my boy.' This word was commonly and affectionately used in the Greco-Roman world to refer to a slave used for male-male sex, and also meant a male lover. It was a term of endearment. By contrast, the centurion refers to his other servants as *doulos*, which was a generic word for slave or servant. Almost certainly, the servant whom Jesus heals at the request of the centurion is the centurion's male lover. It was common practice for Roman military leaders to take their male sex slaves with them on campaigns. Jesus obviously understood this. He wasn't an idiot, after all—unless you're willing to call God an idiot. Jesus did not condemn homoerotic relationships, nor was he in the least disturbed by them."

Michal added, "Jesus was a product of his time. He took so-called homosexuality for granted, just as He took slavery for granted."

"Hmmm. . . . Jesus took slavery for granted? So Jesus, being God, was *OK with slavery*? Slavery isn't *evil* in God's eyes?" Phil asked.

"Conversation for another day, my friend." Max smiled.

"Fair enough," Phil said. "You've both neglected to address the most often repeated argument, however. That God intended humans to be heterosexual. We've all heard this before: It's Adam and Eve, not Adam and Steve."

"You're actually going with *that*?" Max asked incredulously.

"Do I have to say again that I am only playing devil's advocate? Of course it's a crap argument, but someone has to represent it, since your literal approach is not exactly the common interpretation of the masses. Ironic, that. . . ." Phil chuckled. "But I get it. Being gay is who you are to the very core. You certainly didn't choose it the way Michal chooses vanilla over chocolate."

"Actually, I was bitten by a gay mosquito." Max laughed.

"Funny, Maxie." Phil laughed along. "Like I was saying, you didn't choose to be gay, like Michal chooses vanilla over chocolate."

"MMM—mmm, vanilla ice cream." Phil and Max both looked at Michal. She closed her eyes and thought about enjoying a bowl.

Phil took a deep breath. "Michal wonderfully likes vanilla and you wonderfully like men. You didn't choose *your* preference the way she chose hers. Let's consider the argument in your Bible: Adam and Eve, not Adam and Steve. Jesus did in fact—at least that's what the literalists say—speak about homosexuality, when he answered questions about sexuality by invoking Genesis and the creation narrative. Genesis 1:27 states that 'God created Adam in his image, in the image of God he created him, male and female he created them.' God created two different kinds of complementary humans with two different kinds of sexual parts that naturally fit together. Indeed, this was God's *very good plan*, supposedly. This union of male and female is so important that the Bible takes marriage between a man and woman to be a mirror of God's love for His people and Christ's love for His Church. We also find Jesus commanding heterosexual marriage in both Matthew and Mark: 'What God has joined together let no man pull apart.' According to your Bible, God clearly decrees 'Adam and Eve,' not 'Adam and Steve.'"[24]

"Invoking this passage introduces so many problems, as feminists have pointed out," Michal began. "Many feminists argue that the creation stories are not so much about human *sexuality* as they are about the male-centered, priestly writers of Leviticus, who want to put women in their place." She waggled a finger at Phil. "Remember, this is the religion in which men would pray 'Thank God I was not born a woman.' My Jewish grandfather told me this. He was mocking, of course, but the truth of it was there. The blessing goes like this: *Shelo Asani Isha*. 'Blessed are you Lord for not making me a woman.'"

"Biblically, God made two kinds of humans, male and female, and they are designed to populate the planet. 'Be fruitful and multiply,' right?" Phil said.

"Actually, this is yet another reason why male homoeroticism is supposedly wrong. It's 'wasting seed.' It's the failure of the mitzvah to 'be fruitful and multiply and fill the earth,' as you just pointed out. This was Onan's sin. Remember Onan, the second son of Judah, who was killed by Yahweh? He refused to 'raise up seed' for his dead brother. The eighteenth- and nineteenth-century term 'onanism,' which comes from the story of Onan, means 'masturbation,' but that's not what Onan was doing. He was practicing coitus interruptus with his widowed sister-in-law, not whacking off. . . ." She smirked. "But about that first creation story—" Michal paused to draw a breath. "The first creation story doesn't get at this misogyny so much as the second. In this first one, God does not establish a ranking or worth of genders. It just notes that humans are of two complementary kinds. But the second story. . . ."

"Oh, that second story gives us a wonderfully male-dominated world. Women are beneath men—man big and strong, and smarter and better in every way, except of course baby-making." Phil struck his famous bodybuilder pose, flexing his underdeveloped muscles.

"Well, Phil, you clearly have demonstrated your ability to read. It would be nice if you had also demonstrated your ability to understand." Max held up his hand and looked at Michal with imploring eyes. "The argument from nature is a tried and true attack. Tried and true for non-thinking persons, that is." He glanced at Phil. "And I thought you liked being a thinking person?"

"Please, go on. Remember, I'm playing devil's advocate. It requires a lot of thinking to try to put my brain into illogical mode."

"I've had this discussion with several people in my congregation. The argument from nature only works if your eyes are closed. The whole of Psalm 119 reminds us to keep our eyes open to God, His works, and His laws. The world provides evidence of the truth of God's word. Adam and Eve, not Adam and Steve? Well if that's the case, homosexuality wouldn't be reflected in nature, right? But it does occur, in cats, swans, dolphins, elephants, giraffes, sheep, and, of course, in bonobos. I could go on and on."

"I think you just did." Phil smiled.

"I actually knew a guy who returned his rescue dog to the shelter because he said that his dog was gay." Michal laughed.

Phil and Max both rolled their eyes. "We're trying to be serious here."

"Sorry," Michal said. "But Max, to your point about the world providing evidence of the truth of God's word in this case. You know, God quite clearly created things He wants no one to have any part of, at least if we go with what's in the Bible. God made shellfish and pigs, for example, made them edible—"

"And tasty. . . ." Phil smacked his lips.

Michal shook her head. "—Made them edible, but forbids us from eating them. Of course God changes His mind, as He so often does. Remember Peter's vision in Acts 10? He saw heaven open up and a large sheet containing all sorts of animals, including unclean animals, being let down to earth, and God tells Peter to get up, kill, and eat: 'Do not call anything impure that God has made clean.' In my mind, this was to make Christianity more attractive to the Gentiles. They didn't have to become Jewish first, didn't have to follow all of the rituals. . . . But even more damning than this is the fact that in the Bible homoeroticism is a *choice*. Remember 1 Corinthian 10:13? 'No temptation has overtaken you that is not common to man. God is faithful. He will not let you be tempted beyond what you can bear. But when you are tempted, He will also provide a way out, so that you can endure it'. . . . You know, the nineteenth-century human rights advocate, Karl Heinrich Ulrichs, argued that Paul could not understand homosexuals as anything other than *depraved* heterosexuals. There was no way he could understand homosexuality as being anything other than a choice. The science just wasn't available then."[25]

"All that might be true, Michal, but current studies show that, genetically, gays are predisposed toward homosexuality, just as there are genetic predispositions toward many other characteristics, including a fondness for vanilla ice cream. . . . Well, at least *you* have a preference for vanilla," Max said. Then he scowled at Phil.

"Don't look at me." Phil pointed at himself. "Devil's advocate, and in this case, weak argument."

"You do need to be careful, Max, if you are suggesting something like a gay gene," Michal said. "But I *would* agree, if you're suggesting that sexual preference is a combination of biology and environment."

"OK, so we all agree that the Bible is wrong about homosexuality," Max said.

"Again, you didn't listen to what Michal and I were saying," Phil began. "The Bible isn't wrong. People are wrong. Their interpretations and translations, like everything else, are off."

"I think it's more nuanced than this, right? We just don't have the ability to know exactly what these ancient Israelites and early Christians were thinking. About this topic, or pretty much anything else in the Bible. Were they motivated by superstition? Misogyny? Fear? Prejudice? We weren't there and in any case the words just don't translate well." Michal looked at Phil with a smile. "I can't get vanilla ice cream out of my head since you mentioned it. Do you have any hanging around?"

"Of course. You know I stock it when you're coming. By the way, to help boost Max's argument, do you remember when you started liking vanilla, or were you born with that preference?"

"Well, I used to love chocolate far more than vanilla."

"So you had a preference that you overcame?" Phil smiled.

"That's right. Until my brother and I had a chocolate ice-cream eating contest. After finishing off a gallon or so in about ten minutes. . . . You can understand why I never touched it again."

"How old were you, *five*?"

"Twenty-five. And drunk. At least I won the contest."

"This doesn't really help Max's argument, since it would suggest that nature does *not* override nurture."

"On the contrary, it supports my argument quite well. Keep in mind that my argument is not that nature is stronger than nurture, nor the other way around, but that they are both part of God's design. They simply *are*." Max picked a bit of errant lint off his shirt. "Since homosexuality exists in nature, and God exists, they must be part of His plan, from cats, to giraffes, to chimps, to humans."

"Does seem like you have made your point, Max. So putting my devil's advocate pitchfork aside, I'll retreat to my old grind, *science*. Although there is by no means a consensus, a convergence of scientific evidence suggests that homosexuality is at least in part natural. Many accept that genes, hormones, and brain structure all affect sexual preference. Of course, this isn't the whole story, since social influences also come into play. It's nature and nurture, neither of which hold sway over the other. So 'Adam and Eve' falls by the wayside. . . . No surprise to me."

"Adam and Eve. So we're back to socio-political influences, like I pointed out earlier. We've already established that the Bible is a book strongly influenced by the world views of both the ancient Israelites and the surrounding cultures. Israelite culture was definitely patriarchal to the extreme, and it's no surprise we see this reflected in the Bible." Michal flexed her muscles. "Man good. Woman bad." She giggled at Phil.

"I think her muscles are bigger than yours, Phil," Max said.

"Oh, thank you very much. . . . But the fact remains, Max, *we* can agree that homosexuality is not wrong, but the Bible still holds a very negative view of it. Remember what it says? Homosexuals must be put to death. Leviticus 20:13. You've pointed it out yourself."

"If you read it without taking into consideration context or interpretation—and taking things in context is the very definition of literal."

"Except for the bit where the words in the Bible *literally* say that homosexuality is detestable. And to interpret it otherwise makes it not literal, but figurative. Do we really need to call up all the memes?" Phil took out his cell phone.

"No, I think that once again we're all just at the 'agree to disagree' point," Max said.

"I hate that phrase," Phil said. "It's just giving up. The whole point of discussion is to come to some kind of agreement after considering varying viewpoints. If we're lucky, we might even be able to change someone's mind based on the facts, at least the facts as one might be able to argue them." He looked back and forth between Max and Michal, eagerly seeking understanding.

"What are you talking about, Phil? You know how we are. We almost never agree on anything." Michal looked at Phil curiously. "He's babbling more than usual, wouldn't you agree, Max?"

"I do understand that he's trying to find consensus, but babbling might be a bit—" Max paused, looking for the right word.

"Harsh?" Phil said. "Thanks, Max. I knew I could count on you."

"I was going to say a bit too generous. Your stuff at the end there was somewhat disjointed." Max chuckled. "But it does mimic the modern-day conservative Christian view quite nicely. So when did you become the foil? I thought that was my job?" Max tapped Phil on the shoulder as they turned toward the bar.

Seemingly out of nowhere, a voice spoke from the corner of the room. "Evolutionarily. . . ."

"Where did *you* come from?" Phil asked. He stared at the man in blue and green plaid pants and white loafers, looking very much like a Palm Springs golfer or a used car salesman, his black hairpiece sliding down his forehead. "When did you sneak in? You're not invited, and you're certainly not invited to our conversation."

Michal looked at Phil. "Be nice for a change. Let the guy speak. What's the harm, really? Plus, he might infuse our discussion with new energy. . . . What were you saying, sir? Please come join us."

"Thank you." The man approached them. "I've been listening to your argument from nature. I wanted to say that from an evolutionary standpoint, homosexuality as a trait is an outlier. This includes the animal kingdom as well. In terms of fitness and goodness in a species, homosexuality is, without a doubt, *a very bad trait to have.* And since the possession of traits is the only way that we can measure the goodness or badness of instantiations of a species, we must conclude that homosexuals are *very bad people.*[26] The Bible merely echoes the facts of evolutionary science. This makes sense, since God is Lord and Master of Scientific Truth. So of course the Bible would speak truth in this regard."

The man's words sent a shudder down Max's spine. He felt himself growing visibly angry, an emotion that he rarely felt, and only when he was defending his very existence as a gay man to others—more often than not, to Christian others.

"This guy is spewing hate. I've come across this kind of hate-filled bullshit on the Internet, sometimes from people who profess to be God-loving Christians," Michal said.

"Get out of here!" Phil yelled at the man. "We don't tolerate such hateful intolerance."

Max patted Phil on the shoulder. "Thank you, good Sir Knight, but I've got this one." He addressed the man, "You know, from an evolutionary perspective, most of us think that the only point of sexual behavior is reproduction. But it turns out that since sexual behavior is both intimate and pleasurable, it is found in many species, not just humans, to help form and maintain social bonds. Homosexuality helps humans form beneficial relationships with each other, and this enhances community survival. Researchers have connected homosexual behavior with the presence of higher levels of the social hormone progesterone. We can make sense of homosexuality from an evolutionary perspective."[27]

The man smiled contemptuously, turned, and walked out of the bar.

"Thanks for having my back, friends," Max said.

"We've always got your back, Maxie. Some people are just not worth the effort to try to change their minds. It's too exhausting. Besides, there was something about that guy. I didn't catch it at first. He just felt evil to me, you know?" Michal put her hand on Max's back. "Come on. Let's get out of here. I think we could all use some fresh air. The sun will be down before we know it."

You might wonder about Phil and Michal "having Max's back." He was a big guy—big enough to take care of himself. Plus, if you didn't know any better, he looked mean. Of course, friends look out for each other, but there was a particu-

lar reason Phil and Michal wanted Max to know that they understood—or at least tried to understand.

The papers had labeled it a racially motivated hate crime. Some called it a drug deal gone bad, given the amphetamines they found on him. But Max knew better. His friend, Jayden, was dead. And the case—yet another black youth dead by violence—had already gone characteristically cold.

It was their freshman year. Jayden had told Max about a Christian group on campus that was putting on a panel session, open to the public, on Thursday night, 7 p.m.

"The posters are plastered all over campus," Jayden began. "The speakers include a former atheist, a former Muslim, and a former homosexual." Jayden was particularly interested in this. His boyfriend back home was a Muslim. "I'm surprised they don't have a 'former nigger.'"

"I'm surprised administration lets them stay on campus," Max said. "I suppose they have the right to say what they will, but I'm pissed that they're putting lipstick on that pig and calling it Christianity."

"I want to go. Give them a piece of my mind. Will you join me?" Jayden asked.

Max was hesitant to say 'yes.' Some people just weren't worth the effort. What did his big brother always tell him? "There's no point arguing with emotionally disturbed people." But Max really liked Jayden and wanted to show his support. No way they'd mess with Jayden, if Max came along.

"OK, I'll go," Max finally said.

They showed up to a packed room, probably breaking fire code. The former Muslim spoke first:

"Only true followers of Christ go to heaven. Muslims do not follow Christ. Islam's Allah is not the God of the Bible, the real word, the *only* word of God. The Qur'an is not a book of God. It is a book of the devil." She continued on like this for some time.

A man from the audience stood up. "Muslims, Hindus, and people of all faith traditions can go to heaven, so long as they live in accordance with their faith in sincerity and devotion. God knows the heart. God is not a god of any particular religion. He is God to *all people.*"

Jayden stood up and clapped. A few others followed. Max pulled on Jayden's shirt bottom, urging him to sit down. He didn't want any trouble and this place did not feel safe. Jayden looked at Max and sat down.

After some back-and-forth, including the former Muslim's testimony about how she found Christ, the former homosexual stood up.

"I honestly believed I was gay," he began. "But I was blinded by a demonic spirit of homosexuality. Those who think they are gay come from emotionally and spiritually broken homes. Nobody is born gay. Don't believe the lie. I know many gays who were molested by father figures. I was one of them. This is the only love we knew. Love through perverted sex. The enemy of our soul, the devil, exploits this brokenness. But I sought out deliverance, and the demon was cast out of me. This was just a few months ago. I am already engaged to a good Christian girl."

The good Christian girl stood up and smiled. Several members of the audience cheered. "God bless you, brother" others chorused.

"That's bullshit and you know it!" Jayden shouted. Max looked at him sternly.

"Let's get out of here," Max said urgently. He grabbed Jayden's shoulder and led him out of the room.

"Sissy fags," a man said as they were leaving. Max ignored him and kept pushing Jayden toward the door. When they reached it, Jayden turned and shouted again. "Fuck you all! You all go to hell."

Max quickened their pace. They had a long walk across campus to the dorm.

It was dark. Max tried to calm Jayden down, but made sure that they were walking briskly.

Suddenly Max was hit on the back of the head with a beer bottle. He was knocked out cold, falling to the cement path. He woke up some time later, blood matted in his hair. Jayden was gone. In a panic, Max ran through the deserted campus, yelling for his friend. He finally found Jayden, chained face-down to a bicycle rack, his pants around his ankles and blood running out of his rectum. Several bloodied beer bottles lay next to him.

"My God! Help! Somebody help!" Max grabbed hold of his friend and cried.

The police never found out who did it. There were no witnesses, and the police found amphetamines on Jayden's body, so justice was neither blind nor swift. The police went dutifully through the motions. They interviewed everyone who attended the event. It didn't really matter. The forensic investigation was so shoddy that all the evidence was tainted. After a few months the police declared the case "cold."

Christian, Gay Rights, and ethnic groups of all stripes protested on campus and in the city streets. They protested the senseless violence and the slovenly police practices. More than once, the leaders of the campus group, Reclaiming Christ in Christianity, were told that they had neither the spirit nor the actions of God and Christ in mind. There was also speculation that had the victim been a white male, the police would have found a suspect and delivered swift justice. But the incident was swept under the carpet, like so many others. The victims were blamed for their bad behavior, and the criminals were secretly applauded for ridding the world of the wrong kind of people. The local media marched in jackbooted lockstep with common, decent folk.

Jayden's parents sued the university for five million dollars in damages, for allowing that group on campus and not providing adequate campus security. Jayden's father ended up hanging himself before the case ever went to trial. The university had good lawyers and the case was settled out of court for a significantly smaller sum.

Max would often visit Jayden's mother. He also visited Jayden's boyfriend, Abdul Ghafur, whose name, Max later learned, meant "Servant of the Forgiving."

SUMMER

Summer is shorter than any one—
Life is shorter than Summer—
Seventy years is spent as quick
As an only Dollar—

EMILY DICKINSON

§

FIVE

If it feels to us like free will, then let's treat it as free will and get on with our lives.
J.W. IRONMONGER, *THE COINCIDENCE AUTHORITY*

EIGHT YEARS EARLIER. *The Gulf of Mexico, fifty miles off the Texas coast*
"Careful with that box, airman!" Phil looked disapprovingly at the man in uniform loading his material onto the company evacuation helicopter. He was sure that even if the young man couldn't hear the tone in his voice, he would definitely see the disdain in his eyes. Phil could barely hear anything over the helicopter blades, but he could easily see the half-hearted "Sorry, sir" on the young man's lips.

You ought to be sorry. That half-million dollar equipment box is more than you'll make in a lifetime. He continued to load the helicopter while waving away the noxious smells and smoke wafting from the center of the rig. He looked over at the firefighting team. They seemed to have everything well under control—at least as far as he could tell from his mandatory training. Why did he have to leave anyway? He should be staying, if for no other reason than to see what it was like to fight a real fire. Phil had watched the fire-teams practice putting out fires a dozen times, but had participated in only one drill. Sure, this fire was a bit bigger than the practice runs, but they totally had this. This bucket list item dangled in front of him, impossible to reach.

One drill—but man, I'd like to be out there helping out. Phil watched the men move back and forth, almost elegantly, engaging in a dance that belied the effort it took them to handle that fire hose. He continued to tie down his many belongings. As he did, he noticed that the men seemed to be struggling a bit more than usual. No matter, they just needed to remember their training. The looks on their faces told a different story. This thing was starting to cause them some concern.

The fire had started about twenty minutes earlier on the oil rig *Crawfish*, positioned one hundred miles off the coast of Texas. Fed by a fuel line, it quickly grew beyond the scope of fire extinguishers. And so the fire-team was called in.

Ten minutes after that, they were pumping seawater to try to douse the flames. Five more minutes and Phil was being rushed to the helipad. At the time Phil thought it was overkill to evacuate him and his data, but he figured the company just wanted to protect its investment—both in him and his research. After the acoustic testing told them where to initially drill, Phil's own research told them which direction to go and how deep the pocket might be. It was currently pumping 120,000 barrels a day, but his research showed that they could improve that to 250,000 with a new location and going a bit deeper. He would be making the final recommendations next week at the officers' meeting. *Guess that's going to take a bit longer than expected.*

The airman tapped him on the shoulder, handing him the audio cable. Phil plugged it in. "We have to go now, sir!" There was no fear in the airman's voice, but Phil could sense some urgency.

"Why the rush? We're not in an emergency evacuation, are we?" Phil wondered what was going on behind the scenes.

"Top brass wants you back on dry land. Needs all that expensive research and their top geotechnical engineer to explain it all!" The airman winked.

Phil smirked, acknowledging the backhanded compliment. He operated the lever to cinch down his belongings in the chopper. He looked around at the cargo area. There was an empty seat next to where he was going to sit. He looked over at the three boxes of mineral sample testing materials. Realistically, if his research played out, the content of those boxes could be worth millions. He looked over at one of the men standing near the firefighting crew and beckoned to him.

The young man, twenty maybe, approached, fear in his eyes. Phil pointed at him and then over at the empty seat. The young man smiled and began to get onboard the helicopter. He was just about to sit down when he felt a box tapping him. Phil pantomimed the box in the seat. The young man's face fell as he placed the box in the seat, then the next, and finally the third. He strapped them in place, jostling them a bit to make sure that they didn't come loose. He stepped off the helicopter and began to walk back to his post. Phil tapped the airman on the shoulder as he keyed the mike to talk to him.

"This thing looks like it's getting bad. Is there another transport coming?"

"I heard they're prepping another bird just in case. The control room hasn't called the general evac yet." The airman pointed at the windows of the control room where people could be seen working, talking on the phone, coordinating the procedures. "Besides, this helo isn't big enough for more than four."

"OK." Phil sounded less confident to himself than he thought he should. He pulled his headphone aside and looked back at the young rig-worker.

"You're fine!" He yelled over the drone of the helicopter blades. "There's another bird coming. Besides, there're backups for the backups on this rig!" He pointed at the control room. "They've got this!"

The young man nodded, but the downturned eyes and sunken look were anything but confident. Phil looked at the fire. It was now burning out of control. He sat down in the helicopter. As they rose up and away from the platform he could see more men moving toward the blaze. He took one last look at the rig before he turned around and looked toward the horizon to the north—where he knew that the coast of Texas and a five-star hotel were waiting.

Unfortunately, the backups to the backups failed. Later, the investigation would center on a pump that was improperly maintained and sign-off sheets carelessly overlooked. In the end, the rig was not a total loss, and only three men died in the blaze. One was the young rig-worker with the frightened eyes. It had been his first offshore employment.

The company, RNAS Subsea Drilling, tried to shift responsibility for the disaster to the inspection company, which fired their regional inspector when it was found that he had been falsifying reports. Ultimately RNAS paid out half a billion dollars in fines and legal settlements. The inspection company folded, declaring bankruptcy instead of paying the fines, and the inspector was sentenced to five years' probation.

None of that stopped RNAS from repairing the damage and re-starting operations two years later, with promises to improve safety across the board and enhance secondary check-on inspections. Pumping 200,000 barrels a day, the restored rig earned the company $2 million in revenue even on a slow day. It took less than a year for RNAS to recoup their losses and replenish their legal fund.

And none of that mattered to Phil as he sat in his luxury hotel and watched the news. He looked over at the sample boxes, now empty with their contents shipped off to headquarters for further analysis. He poured himself a highball of bourbon and drained it in one swallow. He refilled it and stared at the empty boxes, mindlessly calculating how much the materials weighed and how much each ounce had been worth, then comparing that number to the $125,000 each dead man's family would receive: $757.58 per pound. He never worked in the private sector again.

MAY 26, 2014. *Dawn breaks at the RTSS*

Sunlight was just peaking over the mountains, as our three friends strolled through a field of what looked to Max like buffalo grass. Interspersed throughout were little yellow blossoms in full bloom. Phil reached out and ran his hand over the almost waist-high grass, describing lazy arcs in the vegetation as he walked.

"OK, Mr. Costner, enjoying your spiritual moment?" Max jibed as he sipped from his thermos of tea.

"As a matter of fact, I am. But I must correct you. It's not a *spiritual* moment. Remember, I'm the godless heathen who doesn't believe in spirit." Phil slurped his tea loudly, earning pointed stares from his companions.

"Would you two shut up? I'm trying to enjoy this beautiful open field. See how the petals turn from yellow to gold in just the right light? It seems to go on forever." Michal gestured toward the large expanse of grass and flowers.

"Feeling the freedom of this field are you?" Phil turned to Michal.

"Here it comes." Max looked skyward. "Forgive him, for he knows—well, not much of anything."

"You're going to find something unpleasant, even here? You really know how to fuck up a person's day," Michal chided.

"No, not unpleasant. Just true." Phil smiled.

"OK, I'll bite, *yes, I am feeling the freedom of this field,*" Michal droned like the ending of a knock-knock joke.

"Your eyes deceive you. Is it still freedom if there is a fence surrounding this place? Freedom, like the freedom of this field, is an illusion." Phil scuffed his bunny slippers on the tall grass, the ears bobbing to and fro as they caught on some of the leaves.

"We are free for all practical purposes if we do not know the fence is there." Max thrust his jaw defiantly forward as he put his hand up to shade his eyes while trying to see the "hidden" fence.

"You won't see it, Maxie." Phil waved around the surrounding area. "It's invisible, intangible, and you can't prove it. Just like your heavenly—"

"Don't start that," Michal interrupted as she looked in the direction that Max was surveying. "It *is* there, isn't it? Or is this just another elaborate demonstration of yours, Phil?"

"This isn't even my land. Belongs to some farmer, y'know. I don't know whose it is. But it's next to mine so I walk on it. Good thing we're not talking about morality, eh?" Phil smiled mischievously.

Max and Michal continued to look around—off into the trees, out toward the horizon—but no fence could be seen.

"But for *all practical purposes*, my dear Maxie, the fence *is* there and your freedom *is* an illusion. Doubly so because you can't even see the fence. But because I suggested it, you now think it *might* be there. And since you think it might be there, you're wondering whether maybe I'm right and that you aren't actually free. Freedom is like free will. It only exists if you don't question it."

"Now isn't that a bit of sunshine." Michal glowered at Phil. "But to your point. Isn't it the case that if one begins to question their freedom and free will, as you say, then one is *freely* questioning it? Kind of like Descartes' 'the demon can make me doubt the existence of everything, but he can't stop me from doubting.' And aren't you here conflating epistemology with metaphysics? That is, believing and *questioning,* as you put it, with existence? Something's existence does not depend on our confidence in it. That makes you more of a Berkeleian than I supposed. . . ."

Phil stared at her blankly.

"George Berkeley, if you recall." Michal nudged Phil. "But I trust that if you're going to throw out something like that, we have to define them both. —Are you going to play Godzilla now, swatting down those two nasty monsters Freedom and Free Will?"

"Nah, I don't believe that either of them exists anyway. Freedom is only achieved in increments, but never totality. Free will is a bit more confusing, but I don't think it exists either. There is just too much evidence against it." Phil shrugged.

Max looked at Phil. "God has given us free will so that we can learn to make the right choices. So sorry, Phil, but I believe in free will." He squeezed Phil's shoulder affectionately. "Free will is a gift from God, the ultimate gift, offered to us so that we can better know His love, and understand how complete it is. God loves us so much that He is willing to let us make mistakes. Consider this analogy: Suppose a father puts a piece of chocolate cake and a bowl of Brussels sprouts in front of his son, and he tells his son to choose which he will eat for dinner. . . ."

Michal interrupted him. "Clearly the boy's mother wasn't home." Max and Phil chuckled.

Max continued, "The father knows that his son will pick the chocolate cake, even though Brussels sprouts are better for him. Yet the father lets the boy choose the cake."

Phil piped in, "Even if it means throwing the kid into diabetic shock?"

Max shook his head disapprovingly.

"Ah, but does God actually let us make mistakes of our own volition? Or does He predetermine us to make mistakes so that He can, what, get a little endorphin kick from watching His creation get it right once in a while? And how is that even remotely free will?" Phil crossed his arms and stared at his two friends.

"So you are admitting that you don't understand the mind of God?" Max's smile was coming out in his words. "I'm sorry, Phil, you're smart—I dare say brilliant, even—but how can you even pretend to know the mind of God?"

"Tell you what, Max," Phil took a long draw of tea, "you explain how predestination and free will can be anything other than irreconcilable, and maybe *you* will know the mind of God. Remember Paul says in 2 Thessalonians 2:13 that God predestines some of us to heaven. And I will even quote from memory: 'But we ought always to give thanks to God for you, brothers beloved by the Lord, because God *chose you* from the beginning to be saved.' . . . But in the Good Book's typically contradictory way, it also says in Joshua 24:15 that we have free will. I will impress you even more with my memory"—Phil adjusted his imaginary bowtie—"'But if serving the LORD seems undesirable to you, then *choose for yourselves* this day whom you will serve' . . . blah, blah, blah. I often wonder why I waste brain-space memorizing snippets from your so-called Holy Book. Anyway, if all-powerful God makes us do something, and in fact designs us so that we must in fact do that very thing, but also makes us feel as if we actually had a hand in making that choice, then how can we do anything but that thing? Aristotle's 'sea battle' argument makes a similar point. Do you remember what it says?"

"Sort of. But go ahead, Phil," Max said.

"Aristotle begins by telling us that every proposition about the future must be either true or false. He presents the following proposition: 'Either there will be a sea battle tomorrow or there won't.' Both can't be true, right? If there is going to be a sea battle tomorrow, that has been true since the beginning of time. But then this makes it *necessarily* true. It could not have been otherwise. Aristotle concludes from this that nothing is possible except what actually happens."[28] Phil beamed confidently.

"Actually, Phil," Max responded, "Aristotle seems to reject this view, if you remember correctly. He *rejects* the move from truth to necessity. Just because something *is* true doesn't make it *necessarily* true. This is particularly the case in relation to propositions about future contingents, about what is neither necessary nor impossible. So while it *is* necessary for a sea battle to occur or not to occur tomorrow, it is not necessary for a sea battle to occur, nor is it necessary for a sea battle *not* to occur."

Phil smiled widely at Max and then turned toward Michal. "And you, Michal, you've been a bit quiet here in this discussion. Do *you* believe in free will anymore? There was a time when you did. . . ."

Michal had turned away and was looking for the fence again. "I'm sorry—did you say something to me?"

"I asked whether you still believe in free will."

Michal hadn't always been a determinist. Phil was, because the science just made sense. Michal never really attended to the science; she just felt as if most of her actions were freely chosen. Max was different. When he read the Bible, he saw that the decision to accept Christ was a choice—the most serious choice—that every person had to make. But even more than that, Jesus, the Son of Man, spoke of His freely giving His life for the sins of mankind. Didn't Jesus say that "no one takes this life from me, but I lay it down on my own accord. I have the authority to lay it down, and I have the authority to take it up again"? But it wasn't just the Word of God that convinced Max of the truth of free will. He experienced it in his own life. Being raised in the church, he later freely ran from God, only to run back to him. Of course, when he told the story to Michal, after she had become a Christian and a determinist, she suggested that God had done an awful lot of nudging, even some divine maneuvering, to bring Max back to the fold.

As I said, Michal wasn't always a determinist. But she became one through what she considered to be nothing other than a series of divine interventions. And, of course, she could find Biblical support for her determinism in, for example, Paul's words in Romans: "For whom he did foreknow, he also did predestinate. . . . Moreover whom he did predestinate, them he also called: and whom he called, them he also justified: and whom he justified, them he also glorified." She wasn't in the least surprised that the Bible was inconsistent in this, as in so many other "facts."

Michal knew that God had chosen her, had known that ever since her first angelic visit at the age of twelve—at least, that's what she would say looking back as a Christian at the events of her life. Michal's father was as atheist as can go, while Michal's mother was a Catholic-turned-reincarnation-Native-American-mystic. She dabbled in everything, trying to cover all her afterlife bases. It was as if she'd gone all-in on Pascal's wager. Of course, there was her Aunt Vi, but she never talked to Michal much about angels, except during her telling of the Christmas story. Michal certainly hadn't expected that an angel would sit on her bed, but it was as real as can be. But then she forgot about it, and focused on her acting and singing career (ages ten to thirteen), and then neighborhood veterinarian to the injured and stray (thirteen to fourteen), before her focus turned to boys and books.

After her "procedure" and her devastating break-up with Phil, Michal got to know Maria, a middle-aged waitress at the Denny's near Michal's apartment, where she always ordered banana-walnut pancakes every Saturday morning after her jog.

Maria noticed that Michal was uncharacteristically smashing her pancakes with her fork and then pushing them to the sides of the plate, her eyes welling up in tears. A few minutes later, Maria walked up to Michal's booth and freshened her coffee, something which she had been doing for countless Saturdays.

"Are you all right? Usually you finish those cakes before I blink my eyes." Maria gave a warm smile. "May I sit down?"

Michal set down her fork, picked up her napkin to wipe a few tears, and looked at the mess she created on her plate. "Sure, why not? Though I'm not much company."

Maria sat down, explaining that she had asked the manager if she could take her fifteen-minute break early, because God told her that Michal was hurting deeply inside and needed His forgiveness.

"Why don't you come to church with me tomorrow?"

"I haven't been to church since I was a girl. I wouldn't know what to do."

"You just do as the Lord leads. Why don't you meet me here about 9:45 tomorrow morning? The church is right around the corner. You can come over for homemade pie after. My daughter Rosaria and I have been baking the past few days. Just please don't say anything to Rosaria about being pregnant. The baby's daddy ran out on her."

Michal felt sick inside. "I just don't think I have time to go with you tomorrow, Maria."

"Please come tomorrow. It'll lift your soul."

Michal showed up the next morning to her own surprise. She wanted the company. They walked the five minutes to church, which was so packed it was standing room only.

The pastor went to the front of the congregation after the opening hymn—*I Need Thee Ev'ry Hour*—and looked directly at Michal.

"The Spirit of our Lord is going to come upon you, young lady. Close your eyes and lift your hands up to the Lord."

Michal realized she couldn't leave. She played along. She closed her eyes and didn't know what to do or what to expect. She began to pray, which she hadn't done since her Aunt Vi taught her the Lord's Prayer.

The pastor yelled out, "Don't pray!"

How did he know that I was praying?

Suddenly she felt dozens of hands on her shoulders, her head, her back. And then people starting speaking in tongues.

"The Spirit of the Lord moves!" the pastor shouted.

Michal felt a stirring through her whole body, as if the Spirit *was* moving through her. It felt invigorating, even thrilling. She was getting into what was happening to her. She felt every sensation: the laying-on of hands, the alien, sometimes guttural sounds, the Spirit awakening her soul. And then it happened. . . .

"Uuma ma' ten' rashwe, ta tuluva a' lle."

She heard herself speaking in tongues, as if she were a conduit for the Spirit's voice.

"Praise God! Praise God!" she heard all around her. She opened her eyes and Maria was smiling widely. Maria gave her a hug. Michal was utterly blown away. What curious thing had just happened to her?

That was weird. . . . Exciting, but weird. . . . Scary, but weird. Completely unexplainable and. . . . WEIRD.

After the service, Maria invited Michal to her home, introducing her to seventeen-year-old Rosaria, who served them each a slice of cherry pie.

"Did you know that Mama baked a pie last night and the filling bubbled out of it *in the image of Jesus.*"

"Oh, really?" Michal said, allowing herself to get drawn into this absurd conversation.

Rosaria walked up to the refrigerator and took down a photo stuck to the door with a magnet that read *Jesus is the Answer.*

"See? Mama took a Polaroid."

Michal grabbed the photo. The red-cherry filling had indeed bubbled out of the top of the pie crust looking like Jesus in Rembrandt's *Head of Christ.*

"Isn't that amazing?" Rosaria exclaimed.

"Quite," Michal said. She didn't quite know what to make of it.

"The Good Lord must love my pies." Maria laughed. "It's just such a blessing, don't you think, Michal?"

"Sure, I guess."

"Do you have any questions about what happened in service?"

"You mean speaking in tongues? My Aunt Vi claimed she could do it. That is, before she switched to Greek Orthodox. Now she says that it's the tongue of the Devil."

"Where two or three are gathered in my name, there am I among them," Maria began. "The devil wouldn't show where our Lord is."

"I suppose not." Michal was so completely confused that she didn't know what to think. "So how do I do it again?" She did enjoy the experience. It felt like a carnival ride.

"Well, it usually happens to me when I'm washing my hair," Maria explained.

Arriving home at her apartment, Michal quickly took off her clothes and rushed into the shower like an addict needing another fix.

"Come, Holy Spirit. Come, Holy Spirit. Come, Holy Spirit," she kept chanting with soapy hair, her hands lifted up to the Lord.

Nothing happened.

That night while lying in bed she repeated, "Come, Holy Spirit. . . ." She even moved her mouth trying to force the words. Nothing happened. After a few minutes of trying, she laughed at herself.

What a sucker.

The next time that God intervened was in graduate school. Gretchen was a blonde beauty, an over-the-top Christian but with a very sensual nature, as so many of her male peers liked to point out. She quickly befriended Michal and worked hard at proselytizing her. But she also had an intense curiosity about all things pornographic. This altogether unexpected side first showed itself when she invited Michal to her apartment.

"What does cum taste like?"

"What?" Michal was taken aback by the directness of the question coming from a twenty-three-year-old Christian woman.

"What does it taste like? Have you tasted it? Do you swallow? How do you do it?"

Michal laughed. "A good Christian woman like you—?"

"The *Song of Solomon* is our God-given sex manual, you know? But I don't see any directions about giving head. The third verse of Chapter Two says I'm supposed to do it. I just need the mechanics."

Michal tried to contain her laughter.

Suddenly Gretchen looked startled as she stared at her bookshelf. "Did you see that?"

"What?" Michal was thinking that Gretchen had seen a big spider or something.

"That demon. He was grabbing for my *Lolita*."

"Are you OK, Gretchen? I didn't see anything," Michal said.

"*That demon.*" Gretchen gestured at the bookshelf again. "You know, my pastor says I have a spiritual gift. Seeing demons. . . . There's an exorcism at our church tonight. Seven o'clock. Wanna come?"

"Gretchen, that's just not my thing. . . ." Michal was trying desperately not to alienate her best friend. At the same time she didn't want to end up swept away by another charismatic leader. Looking back at the time with Maria, she likened the speaking-in-tongues episode to a rock concert where everyone was carried away by chemically created emotions. Only the chemicals manifested at the revival were internal and self-created. She looked everywhere, except at Gretchen.

"Come on—do it for me," Gretchen cooed in Michal's ear. Her breath sent a fiery hot streak through Michal that had nothing to do with Christian churches.

"Well, just because you're so pretty. . . ." They had many such teases.

Michal and Gretchen walked up to the church, which was a converted former grocery store. Gretchen pulled Michal aside just before they entered through the doors.

"I have to warn you, our church is small, and we've just recently had to move to this new location after our last lease expired and we were forced out by a landlord who is not a believer."

Michal nodded, "OK, that's fine."

Gretchen held up her hand, "And our pastor was called by God at a very early age. He's still quite young, but he's a powerful tool for God."

"Gotcha, he's a *powerful tool.*" Michal looked at Gretchen who completely missed the joke. She was far too nervous. Michal tapped her on the shoulder, "Hey, it's OK, I understand. I won't be disappointed."

Gretchen gave a seraphic smile and nodded.

Michal couldn't remember a time when she had lied better. Looking at the outside she wasn't sure how she was going to pull off the lie. She took Gretchen's arm in hers and they entered the church.

Overhead, the many ceiling fans never quite seemed to get into sync, the result a chaotic clatter of noise. The many people seated in folding chairs didn't seem to mind. They fanned themselves with their programs and immediately Michal had to stifle a laugh.

"This looks like a scene from *The Devil's Advocate*," she whispered in Gretchen's ear, finishing with a playful *puff.* Gretchen giggled.

Almost as one the congregation turned their sweaty, well-dressed forms to shush the newcomers. It was obvious that they were waiting for something other than Michal and Gretchen's arrival.

They were awaiting the *Event.*

A woman stood up and approached them. She had a full round face, and when she spoke her jowls—yes, jowls—wiggled. To say that she filled out her blue-, orange-, and purple-flowered Mumu would have been generous—to the Mumu, that is, which sagged under the heavy load. Instead of clicking, her pumps clunked as she approached. At the last possible moment she turned her scowl into a smile, making sure the two girls knew that they had done something wrong, but trying to be welcoming, as the Bible would have her do.

"Hello, Gretchen, I haven't seen your friend before. Why don't you sit right over here by me? I'll make sure you know what to do and don't get yourself embarrassed." With that, she put her sweaty arms and overstuffed lace gloves on the girls' backs and led them to their very own ultra-luxurious metal folding chairs. Michal's wobbled if she didn't hold very still, and after a few clacks back and forth, their new friend, the flowered warden, cast disapproving stares at her.

A hush fell over the crowd as five people walked from what was once the meat department to a small podium. A long white freezer still stood there. No one had bothered to remove it. Michal thought the podium might be left over from a warehouse, as remnants of a sticker posing the question *"Do you know what to do in the event of a fire?"* still clung to it.

Michal coughed because the alternative—stifling a laugh—would have elicited another baleful stare. The pastor couldn't have been more than twenty-five years old. He had long orange-red hair that fell in straight hanks around his face. He glowered through piercing blue eyes from beneath his prominent brow. His Kelly-green suit was something straight off a Goodwill rack. He swam in an XXL, the only size tall enough to hold his height. Michal couldn't help but think of some kind of upside-down carrot: green on the bottom and orange on the top.

The elders more than made up for his youth. Every one of them was definitely an AARP member. They stood flanking their spiritual leader. A full minute ticked by. The elders stood stock-still, sweat dripping off their dark, equally cheap suits. Finally it was time to start, as the boy in green raised his hands up and out, apparently channeling Christ on the cross, while continuing to stare at the floor.

"LET US PRAY!" The voice that issued forth from this young man was disconcertingly louder, older, and deeper than it seemed he should possess. Universal choruses of *Amens* and *Hallelujahs* momentarily drowned out the incessant noise of the fans.

After a prayer that involved thanking God for not erasing them from existence or giving them all a horrible disease—and other such groveling that went on for a full ten minutes—Pastor Upside-Down-Carrot finally lowered his hands. The elders moved in one fluid motion, delivering him from the feigned cross on which he had hung himself. Thrusting his chest and face heavenward he stared up into the spinning fan blades above and called out:

"Who amongst you is afflicted with a demon? Who amongst you wishes to be freed from the millstone that keeps you from our Lord? Who amongst you needs the strength that GOD ALMIGHTY, through me HIS SERVANT, can deliver to you, to be rescued from your demon?"

The appropriately respectful amount of time passed before several people walked to the altar. The pastor looked at them all, assessing them as though he were inspecting a car, checking to see if they had the proper exterior, a few but not too many dents and dings. And then he seemed to inspect their interior, his eyes penetrating through them, looking at afflictions to which only he was privy. He perused the penitent, then began to survey the congregation. When he passed down Michal's row, the warden averted her eyes in a most melodramatic way. But he didn't even pause there. He moved on to Michal and stopped abruptly. He stared directly into her soul. She felt an eerie reminiscence of the time she'd gone to church with Maria. She turned away from his devastatingly penetrating gaze.

Gretchen, who had been staring at the black-and-white-checkered tiled floor, poked Michal in the arm. "Go on up there."

Michal knew that she was making her own choices, but before she could decide whether to go up or not, she found herself kneeling at the altar with the rest of the contrite. She thought that she should get up before it was too late. *Just get up and go sit back down, Michal.* It would be a mistake, another charade to avoid. *No, really, I'm good with a little bit of demonic possession. Don't mind me.* She knelt there mimicking the others, debating whether to leave. While her internal dialogue spun on, she watched as the pastor approached each of the gathered.

He walked with the confidence of a much older man, striding toward each, placing his hand upon their skull, uttering something in tongues. And then moving with all of the grace and force of an ocean, he sent his energy to the person in the form of a neck-snapping slam to the forehead, whereupon the penitent collapsed to the floor, shrieking.

Time to go back to your seat, Michal! She had just about decided to leave when she looked up at a greasy, dinner-plate-sized hand descending on her head with a clap. She winced.

He uttered some unintelligible gibberish and shoved her forehead. But something strange happened.

Years before, Michal had watched a demonstration at an outdoor fair. Next to a pretzel stand, a little old Asian man performed impossible-to-believe martial-arts demonstrations. He spoke in broken English of his *qi*—the life force of the universe, that elemental force one can harness to defeat one's enemies, to be both an unstoppable force *and* an immovable object. Using the power and force of his *qi* and a five-inch punch, he chucked men around the pavement. Letting the *qi* flow around him, he moved with a well nigh inconceivable grace, evading multiple attackers. And harnessing and controlling his *qi,* he was able to prevent five men from the audience, each of them at least twice his weight, from moving his little body, no matter how hard they tried pushing him from his seated position. A collective " *What the fuck?*" could be heard all around.

Michal was reminded of this as the pastor turned to push, swiveling at the waist. She saw the little old Asian man of years past in this Kelly-green-wearing youth. She winced in anticipation of the oncoming "energy" that would likely leave her with an unwelcome case of whiplash.

But when she opened her eyes, she was still kneeling there, and the pastor had moved on to the next person. She had felt nothing. No force, no impact, no sensation of being sent hurtling away like a tiny little sock monkey. *Nothing.* She looked around at the rest of the congregation, who all seemed to be suffering from some kind of shared epileptic seizure.

That was the moment when the pastor-boy stopped and slowly, ominously, turned back to Michal. He raised a massive bony finger and pointed to the empty seat next to Gretchen. Gretchen looked at Michal, then at her pastor, then at the floor. Most of the congregation stopped chanting and stared at the pastor, standing there beaming his energy at an empty seat. All eyes turned to the empty seat, then to Gretchen, then up to the meat department where Michal was still kneeling. Even the disobedient ceiling fans were suddenly silent. Then the pastor's voice boomed out directly at Michal.

"Leave this altar! You have rejected the Spirit! You do not have the WILL to give up ALL!"

His words echoed off the black construction paper blocking out the windows and boomed back across the room. Silence. Michal looked at the pastor, then at the congregation, then back at the pastor, whose hair now obscured his face entirely like some kind of mad Rasputin. —Then back at Gretchen staring at the floor following their friend the warden's lead. Finally Michal stood up. She half-expected the pastor to grab her hand, spin around, and throw her halfway across the room, professional-wrestling style, in a painful display of ferocity and strength.

She flinched when she had to duck to avoid touching his outstretched hand, then turned and walked purposefully back to her seat. The whole congregation shouted *Amen,* save for Michal, Gretchen, and Pastor Eternal Condemnation.

Michal grabbed Gretchen's arm. "Let's get out of here."

Gretchen didn't know what to do. Emotions ranging from disappointment to shame to fear raged within her. She allowed Michal to drag her from the defunct grocery-store-become-church.

Outside in the parking lot, Michal leaned against Gretchen's car. She waved wildly at the swirls of the Van Gogh sky, at the beaming streetlight, at a beat-up red Cadillac passing by. Finally, she turned to Gretchen. "Don't you see how completely taken in you are by all this utter *bullshit?*"

"What do you mean, Michal? Demons are real. I've seen them myself. I've seen people in my own congregation delivered from them." Gretchen's eyes implored Michal to take it back—to make it all better.

A phrase popped into Michal's head only moments before it plowed into Gretchen like a bulldozer. "Someone whom I love dearly once used these words:

unicorn juice. All of this is unicorn juice, Gretchen! Come on! Can't you see what you're doing? You're trading real life for a fantasy. You're living in Fantasyland. How 'bout we chase a rabbit down a hole next? Maybe have a spot of tea with the Mad Hatter? Couldn't be any crazier than tonight. . . ."

Gretchen started to cry. "Michal, you can't mean it. You just don't believe enough. You don't have enough faith. Why didn't you—?"

"Don't cry, Gretchen." Michal wiped tears from Gretchen's cheek. "I don't mean to hurt you. I care about you. If God is real, I don't need faith. If God is real, that charlatan and his theatre of puppets could have ejected me out of that wannabe church like a shot. That's why I'm trying to rescue you from all this nonsense."

Gretchen stared at Michal, then glanced back at the blacked-out windows of her family church. The place where she had learned right from wrong and a healthy fear of God. Then she looked back at Michal. "You didn't move. Why—?"

"Because it's all smoke and mirrors, Gretchen. It's all *unicorn juice.* That thing, whatever it is, back in there? It's only as real as you make it." She took Gretchen's face in her hands and held her close, their noses just a butterfly's wing apart. "It's all spiritual garbage."

Equal measures of hope and doubt expressed themselves on Gretchen's face. "Really? How can you know? What if—"

Michal saw Gretchen's familiar argument for fire insurance coming and decided to cut it off. "Gretchen, no one can know whether God's real. Nobody's offered any incontrovertible evidence for God in over two thousand years. And not surprisingly, with better technology and more ubiquitous recording devices, there's even less evidence for God today. I'm talking about God, the Creator of the Universe—no evidence."

Gretchen was starting to regain some control. Michal wiped away the few remaining tears. "There is no God, there are no demons, and best of all, *You are free to give head*, since there's no God telling you that you have to wait to start acting out those naughty, delicious scenes in *Song of Solomon.* "

A naughty, delicious smile crept over Gretchen's face. "Really? Can we? I think we should. . . ." Her eyes promised other naughty, delicious things.

"Yes, Gretchen. Let's get out of here and start living *our* lives on *our* terms."

Until her conversion some years later, Michal looked on these acts as ones of pure self-determination. She had chosen to act. She had chosen to feel something or not to feel something. She had chosen to speak in tongues. It was obvious to her. Didn't she know a few extra languages? Wasn't it just self-hypnosis? She had chosen not to be moved by the charlatan boy-pastor. It was choice, and her own will, that ruled her life, not external forces, not some God.

However, after Michal's spiritual battle with a demon, after she had become a Christian, she looked back on the encounters with Maria and Gretchen as nothing short of divine intervention. They were moments leading up to the Ultimate Intervention, which, despite her devotion, she couldn't help but see as some kind of epic wrestling match. A classic matchup between Goliath-God in one corner, clocking in at infinite weight, wearing golden, heavenly trunks and a purple face mask, and in the other corner, tiny little David-Michal clad only in doubt and despair. Only this time Goliath would win. In the cosmic scheme of things, it was over in a blink, in a twinkling if you will, with God delivering a divine body slam so forcefully upon her that she could not help but believe.

Determinism comes in many guises. For those who love science, it shows itself in mathematics, and chaos theory, and the mysteries of neuronal preemptive action. For Michal, it came as two seemingly charlatan pastors and a final battle royale. She too bent to the will and plan of God.

"Michal?" Phil was still trying to get her attention, which had drifted back to the field. She turned to look at Phil and smiled.

"I asked whether you still believe in free will."

"Well, there are a few really good arguments for it. We certainly *act* as if we are free, as if our choices are our own. And there's that very persuasive argument that without free will there is no responsibility, which all but throws out the possibility of morality. —Oh, and God wants us to love Him. He doesn't want automatons, and love seems impossible without free will. . . ." Michal paused to consider what she would offer next. "You know, Hegel said that freedom can only be realized in community. Or, I should say, that freedom is most realized in participating in the practices, shared understandings, and institutions of a community. He makes a distinction between subjective and objective freedom. An agent is subjectively free when she reflects on, and is able to find some satisfaction in, her actions and relationships. She's objectively free when her determinations are prescribed by reason, whether she engages in reflection or not."[29]

"Hegel is damned near impenetrable," Phil said. "I'm impressed."

"Thank you, darling. —And I agree." She smiled. "You know, Hegel was trying to defend a Kantian understanding of freedom, but he wanted to ground it in community, rather than in the individual. He took Kant to be way too abstract and formal—but don't we all?" She winked. "If you remember, Kant ties freedom to morality. A will that is free is one that gives itself its own law, which means that autonomy of the will and free will are the same. A will is free only when it follows the moral law, the Categorical Imperative. As Kant says, we can understand ourselves either in terms of the laws of reason or the laws of nature. Insofar as we understand ourselves in terms of the laws of reason, we understand that we possess free will. Reason would not be reason, Kant says, if it were subject to the laws of nature, to forces outside of our selves. Freedom only truly exists in the noumenal world."[30]

Michal took a breath and continued. "If I *were* to believe in free will, it would be something along the lines of Hegel, or maybe Simone de Beauvoir, who argues that our freedom is conditioned by our society, by our position in society. She was specifically talking about women, but it applies to any marginalized member of society who has less freedom than those privileged white guys." She shook her finger at Phil. "Not everyone is as radically free as Sartre suggests.[31] Ayer also presents a really interesting idea that relates to Beauvoir's.[32] A compatibilist notion of free will. He distinguishes between being constrained to act and being caused to act. Just because my actions may be causally determined, it doesn't necessarily follow that I am not free. I am constrained when I am compelled by another person to do what he wants. Being constrained doesn't necessarily mean that I am completely deprived of the power of choice, though. I don't have to be hypnotized. I don't even have to have a gun to my head. I might be *implicitly* coerced. If I'm constrained, then I'm not free. And if I'm not free in this sense, then I'm not morally responsible. Well, at least that's what Ayer says. On this view, free will is not an all-or-nothing affair—like we either have it or we don't. It comes in degrees and depends on our relationships with other people. . . . Anyway, having said all that, I really don't believe in free will, except maybe in Ayer's sense of not being constrained. If we look at the Bible, as you pointed out, it seems to suggest in many places that we don't have free will at all. *I* certainly didn't freely choose God. He imposed Himself on me and against my will, as I was pretty viciously atheistic, as you both know. Paul, when he was Saul, had a similar experience. And if we look at certain key figures in the Bible like the Pharaoh or Judas Iscariot, or even Adam whose disobedience was necessary for God's 'Jesus plan'—well, they don't seem to be acting freely, either."

"Ah yes, Pharaoh's hardened heart. . . ." Phil mused.

"And as Susan Wolf argues, an agent's actions must at the very least be determined by her interests. Wolf offers a great example, which goes something like this: Suppose you think that your next-door neighbor is a perfectly nice guy. He feeds your dogs and waters your plants when you're on vacation. He checks in on you when you're sick. One day you wake up, knock on your neighbor's door, and when he answers it, you punch him in the nose. As Wolf explains, we wouldn't consider this to be an action at all, but more like some kind of involuntary spasm. If we did consider it to be an action, we would consider it bizarre in the extreme. We would think ourselves to be utterly crazy to have performed it. So our actions cannot be completely undetermined," Michal concluded. "They must at least be determined by our interests."[33]

"Well, Michal, I think—" Phil tried to interrupt.

"But Michal—" Max tried to say.

Michal ignored them and continued in her long-winded way: "And science seems to support determinism. Look at evolutionary social biology or genetics. There's a reason, Phil, why you're more of a slut than I am—evolutionarily, you are trying to spread your genes around. . . ."

Max laughed out loud. Phil just shook his head.

"Your culture, your environment, your upbringing, all determine your beliefs and desires, which in turn determine your choices," Michal said.

Out of the blue something very odd occurred. The world suddenly seemed to drop away—for Michal, at least. And then it came back with a thud. Michal was gripped with terror. She wanted to run away, but she didn't have anywhere to go. She paled, wiped her forehead, and grabbed Phil's familiar arm.

He looked at her with concern. "Are you OK? You zoned out for a few." He held her arm and could feel a slight trembling.

Max extended his thermos. "Here, have a sip of tea. It *is* getting kind of warm out here. I've also got some edamame in this little baggie. Why don't you have some?"

"I'm fine. I must just be tired. . . . What were we talking about?"

"Free will—" Phil began. "If you're OK to continue, Michal." She nodded, giving Phil the go-ahead. He paused and looked into Michal's eyes. Something danced behind the windows of her soul. Phil wondered what it was and then laughed at the reference. "I don't even believe in the soul," he mumbled.

"What's that?" Now it was Michal's turn to wonder.

"Nothing—just a silly childish notion that I am doomed to keep in my mind but fully able to deny. —A lot like the notion of free will. It's something we *want* to believe in, but which has become harder and harder to defend." Phil thought for a moment. "Think about this. Remember the sea battle? You two are currently in your own version." Phil smiled, casting a quick glance at Michal and patting her arm.

She looked at him, wondering whether he was being reassuring or condescending. With Phil it was always so hard to tell.

"Are you referring to the idea that we are doing what we were bound to do, by God or the stars, and so we were inescapably drawn to the right-here-and-now regardless of our decisions?" Max looked at Phil skeptically. "If so, I don't buy it."

"Yep, exactly. And the support for this is that you two are currently in Japan, out in the middle of a field. Though—" Phil paused.

"That's fundamentally the same argument some Christians use to prove that God exists," Max said. "We have such a wonderful world and God made it this way and my proof for this is that it *is* this way—and therefore God exists. Kinda like Leibniz's best of all possible worlds, which Voltaire so hilariously satirized.[34] You debunk this argument as circular and yet you are now willing to employ it to oppose free will? If so, then you must accept the equivalent argument for God's existence. So not only are you arguing in a circle, as you accuse me of doing, but you are also now displaying your most hated characteristic. You're being hypo critical. Back to you, my friend." Max smiled at Phil.

"True enough." Phil affected a British accent, "I shan't attempt to eat my cake and have it too, shan't I?"

"Don't you mean have your cake and eat it?" Max asked, a bit perplexed.

"Nope, this one I'm sure of. Anyone can have their cake and then eat it, but it's impossible to eat your cake and then have it, at least in the same form. If you insist, I can share some of my favorite scatological humor that shows how I can have my cake *after* I've eaten it. . . ." Phil smirked. "It's very easy to make statements like '*free will exists*.' But when you start to actually think deeply about it, the notion gets a bit muddled."

"Well, it's a pleasant surprise that you're admitting you were wrong, Phil. That you went all circular-argument on us." Michal mockingly punched his shoulder. "Maybe you should drink more of your tea. You must be suffering from sunstroke or heat exhaustion."

"I'll do my best to make sure it doesn't happen again." Phil smiled. "OK, so that's a terrible argument. But still— Think about it. You are in Japan, and we are in a field. Correct?" Phil gestured at the yellow-dotted grasses.

"I'm afraid to say 'yes,' but. . . ." Michal looked at Max. They both nodded.

"So that being said, three weeks ago, when I purchased the tickets, had you freely chosen to come here?"

"Nope," said Max. "I could never have imagined that I would be travelling here again so soon. How am I to say with any honesty that I chose to be here? — But I can see where you are going."

"Neither did I. —Though I must say that hearing you admit that you're wrong is worth the trip." Michal smiled broadly.

Phil stuck out his tongue. "Thanks for reminding me. So on to something about which I actually am right, then. Neither of you chose to be here, yet the wheels were set in motion to get you here. You did accept the invitation, though even that was strongly influenced by the past, *our past*, the relationship we share, and the really great first-class tickets I got you."

"As I said, I see where you are going. You're saying that we didn't *freely choose* to be here, at least not in any absolute sense." Max poked Phil's shoulder. "But we may have chosen the intermediate steps. Accepting your argument, Phil, nobody chooses anything. Since I did not choose to be born, I have not chosen anything after that. Tell me that you have something more to bring to the table."

"The problem, Max, is that it's all but impossible to distinguish between those actions caused by prior influences and those which were, as you say, freely chosen. You do admit that some of our actions are determined by prior influences? Like you being a Christian, for example," Michal said.

Max shrugged. "I admit that due to my previous bad life choices, I chose to live a wretched existence, and that led me to be extremely receptive to somebody—in my case *God*—rescuing me from my hellish misery. But I still can't accept that I did not actively choose this path, these decisions. God gave me this free will, and I use it both as an affirmation of His love and in thanksgiving for that same love."

"So you won't be swayed by logic on this one, eh, Maxie?" Phil jibed.

"Logic tells me that there are things that I don't understand, and even though I have very little control over God's plan, I am given the ability to make choices within that plan. It's much like approaching the end of a hallway and being confronted with two doors. One is open, the other is not. You can choose the closed door if you wish; you can stubbornly pound on it; but it will never open unless God wills it. God opens some doors for us and closes others."

"Like the Reverend Mother said to Maria in the *Sound of Music*: 'When God closes a door, somewhere he opens a window,'" Michal said.

"I'm sure that phrase makes the devil himself gloat unconscionably." Phil laughed. "If there were such thing as a devil—well, Jonathan Sarkos, maybe."

Max shook his head. "We all have to leave this world. Some of us will join Him in the afterlife. This is God's plan." Max produced a small Bible and held it up. "How you spend that afterlife depends entirely on whether you choose to follow the advice God so lovingly gave us in His Book. Perhaps I am willing to admit that our long-term choices are limited, but our immediate and short-term choices belong to us alone."

Phil rubbed his temples. "I truly don't know where to begin with the many problems you just introduced. . . . Let's just go with the idea that you believe that our short-term decisions belong to us alone. Is that how you would put it?"

"Yes. I believe that God gave us the freedom to make these decisions in the here and now," Max responded, "and before you say that there is no proof that God gave it to us, your objection is noted."

Phil pretended to write something in a book. "Entered by the bailiff. —So you say we have free will with regard to our short-term choices. But what if I told you that even that was questionable?"

"Obviously I would disagree," Max said.

"Well, how about the choice not to be eaten? What if I told you that there is a parasite that—"

"Oh yes, the *toxoplasma gondii*. I've heard of that. It's a parasite that infects rodents, making them attracted to cats and cat urine," Michal interrupted. "And since the rodents are attracted to the cat urine, they can more easily be caught. They even approach the cats, which makes them easier to be eaten by them. In this way, the parasite can end up in the stomach of the cat where it can procreate. Cats are considered to be the definitive hosts, since they are the only place where the parasite can breed."

Phil and Max stared at Michal.

"What, just because I believe in the Spirit doesn't mean I'm not allowed to read?"

"Fair enough. I just didn't expect you to know that right off the top of your head. But then again I guess I'm not entirely surprised that you did." Phil chuckled.

"So are you saying that because rats don't have free will, then humans don't have free will? Again, I think you're slipping, my friend." Max poked at Phil.

"Ah, but that's where the fun begins. Ol' *t. gondii* can live in humans too. And further, its existence in humans has been loosely linked to schizophrenia, suicide, and self-destructive behaviors. One in four people in America are said to have this parasite active in their bodies, and specifically in their brains. When you engage in self-destructive or even highly risky behavior, it may be because you're infected. The true cause of your actions, then, could be less your own choices and more the doings of this fiendish little parasite," Phil said.

"Well, that's a pretty specific example and there are a lot of suppositions there. . . ." Max felt like Lucy had just pulled the football away.

"I've read that even religious fervor is determined. Explains why some folks have a hard time getting all intoxicated about God. And I recently read that scientists can accurately predict a person's political leanings, whether conservative or liberal, based on their reactions to non-political images such as a woman holding a dead mouse. Conservatives tend to be naturally more fearful and intolerant, the scientists say, so they will freak out or be disgusted by the image. But liberals like me feel sorry for the poor little mouse. Being conservative or liberal is an inborn trait. I can no more change from liberal to conservative than I can change the color of my skin." Michal smiled. "OK, John Howard Griffin notwithstanding. —

And obviously being liberal or conservative strongly influences what we believe and do."

"Not only that, Maxie," Phil said, "but there is evidence that even at the neuronal level free will is questionable. Research by Peter Tse shows that although the neurons receive stimuli to act, they are *already* acting—primed and firing if you will—before the stimuli are received.[35] So what is actually controlling the neurons? Is our free will pushing the buttons, so to speak, or is something else? I would argue that even if the evidence isn't conclusive, free will is called into question."

"It seems, Phil, that once again you have actually argued against yourself in trying to prove your point. You are saying that there is something outside of our understanding. Consider your example from neuroscience in particular. —Think about it." Max tapped his head and gave an exaggeratedly puzzled look. "Even the best scientists cannot understand all of the details of the world. You call it lack of free will, but I call it God's infinite and unknowable will. You are unwilling to allow that there could be a God who controls elements of this world that are beyond our understanding. You are just *choosing* to have a different god. The atheistic Nietzsche, if you recall, claimed that those who reject God elevate Science and worship *it.*"

"He's got a point, Phil," Michal said and smiled.

"Max, you are my dear friend, but there are times when I think you are hopeless." Phil shook his head. "You're not going to accept my argument that on both the macro and micro levels there are situations in which we don't have free will, even though you've agreed with all of my statements? Have you been getting drunk on *unicorn juice?*"

Fourteen-year-old Phil sat on his bed alternately reading Kant's Critique of Pure Reason *and this month's* Hustler. *He could hear his parents talking with a client in the next room. They were being their usual "chilled-out" selves. It didn't hurt that this client was into 'ludes and pot. Most of his parents' clients were into the more conventional drugs—including coke and meth—but their range of competencies in chemistry afforded them the skills to manufacture several different styles. Phil went back to* a priori *centerfolds until his door opened and his mom came in.*

It's important to note that although Phil had a Hustler *subscription, he hadn't purchased it himself, since he was under eighteen. His parents ordered it for him when he'd started showing interest in the female form about a year before. Feeling that most experiences in life held some value, they encouraged their son to experience almost everything, much like Rousseau's education of Émile. But they understood that one had to be judicious about such experiences.*

Phil's parents—both engineers with Dow Chemical—sold drugs on the side. They seldom worried whether their customers were responsible people who would use those drugs properly. Usually cash talked and platitudes walked. They were in the habit of throwing talk-of-the-neighborhood Playboy Bunny parties. On party night, they'd have a five-foot-tall pink-painted wooden rabbit decked out in Christmas lights proudly displayed on their rooftop—thanks to Phil's mother's artistic talent. They'd play games like Pin-the-Pasties-on-the-Bunny and Centerfold Roulette, while passing around drops of acid. Phil would often put on his dark sunglasses and walk through the guests on his way to the kitchen for a tall glass of chocolate milk, earning big smiles and high-fives along the way. He felt like Tom Cruise in Risky Business.

Phillip and Charlotte Foster met in their Advanced Organic Chemistry class in their senior year of college. They were excellent students and they both planned to work for a major company after they graduated.

They were in the same mandatory 8 a.m. study session. Typically they would arrive about ten minutes early, before anybody else. For the first few weeks of the semester they sat silently while Phillip nervously stared at the table, never quite getting up the guts to talk to Charlotte. That is, until one morning when he woke up late and decided to grab a coffee on the way to the session. He ran into Charlotte already in line at the Daily Grind. Phillip smiled at the opportunity to finally talk with her, but he still couldn't quite find the nerve. Luckily, Charlotte spotted him, breaking the ice.

"Hi," Charlotte said.

"Hi," Phillip replied, barely meeting her eyes.

"You're in my Organic study session, right? —The one that starts *right now?*" She glanced at her watch and smiled.

"Oh, you're in that session?" Phillip said, pretending he had never noticed her before.

"Why don't you join me in line." She gestured at Phillip to cut in front of her. "So you like coffee?"

"I love coffee." Phillip smiled, taking his place in line. "Especially their Hawaiian Kona Reserve."

"I do, too," Charlotte said. "So what else do we have in common, besides coffee and chemistry?"

After ordering their drinks they decided to skip the study session altogether. They found a table and sat down.

"It's not like me to be late for the session," Charlotte began, "but the—"

Phillip finished her sentence: "—football game."

"Right! The football game. . . . I really don't care much about football, but a friend dragged me out."

"Me too."

They talked merrily about coffee and 2001: A Space Odyssey. And their favorite: zombie movies. Then Charlotte introduced a subject about which she was very passionate: the growing disparity between classes in America.

Phillip never got comfortable with this topic, though he'd heard it raised often enough. He knew about class disparity firsthand. He was the son of an extraordinarily wealthy man, one who was even famous in some circles. But he always tried to hide that fact. He didn't want to be different from the other kids. He felt different enough already.

That was why he insisted on paying for his college education. He wasn't going to be some trust-fund kid who would never make anything of himself. He'd succeed on his own.

The summer after graduation, Phillip and Charlotte would hold a simple June wedding in the countryside. Charlotte would wear a cream-and-cocoa lace country-truffles dress and a flowered head wreath. Phillip would be in khaki shorts and Birkenstocks. Phillip's parents missed the wedding because they were traveling to the Greek Isles. The newlywed Fosters would get hired at Dow, but their love for all things thrilling and dangerous quickly led them to launch their "side job," which was the source of most of their sizeable income. Phillip III would be the beneficiary of both his parents' and his grandfather's wealth.

When his mom opened the door, Phil didn't put his Hustler between the folds of his Kant book. He just kept reading, jumping between the two as his mood drew him. His mom, who wore her Dark Side of the Moon t-shirt and leather and suede biker's jacket, sporting buttons from all the major concerts, just looked at him and giggled.

"Got any questions, kiddo?" She pointed at his reading material.

Phil looked up, set his *Hustler* down beside him, and raised his Kant. "I know that *a priori* statements can be understood to be true by pure reason alone, independent of experience. We don't need empirical evidence to know that they are true. *A priori* statements are necessarily true. Some even call them 'God-given' truths. . . ." He paused to collect his thoughts. "But can *God* be known *a priori*? Can our knowledge of God be *God-given*?" Phil laughed at his ability to play with language. "No need to answer, Mom. I've been reading both Anselm and Descartes. Their arguments suck. 'God, being the most perfect being, must exist. If God did not exist, then God would not be God, since He lacked that perfection. He would be less perfect than a being who shared all of His characteristics, but also existed.'"[36]

"Well done, Phillip." She looked at him through her round, rosy-pink John Lennon glasses.

"But you haven't heard my whole argument, Mom. The problem with Anselm and Descartes is that their arguments rest on a definition. Definitions tell you what properties something must have to fit the definition, but nothing about whether that thing exists. Their arguments lead us to believe in the existence of *perfect unicorns!*"

"How's that?" His mother played along, enjoying her son's sense of intellectual curiosity.

"Think of it like this. A unicorn is a magical, horse-type creature with a spiraling horn on its head that can only be ridden by virgins, right? Well since it's better to exist than not exist, the perfect unicorn *must exist!* I don't know about you, Mom, but I haven't seen one lately. . . . Then again, I haven't seen God either."

"Perhaps you'll see Him tomorrow." His mother chuckled.

"Yeah, while I'm in our backyard feeding my pet unicorn." Phil laughed. He put down his weathered *Critique of Pure Reason* and held up his *Hustler*, seamlessly changing topics. "Have you and dad ever had a threesome?" Phil loved to try to embarrass his parents, though he rarely succeeded.

She laughed again, sounding a bit like bamboo wind chimes. "Not this week, sweetheart. . . . It's time for you to get some sleep. You have AP math first thing tomorrow morning."

"OK, Mom." Phil placed his reading material on his bed stand, turned out the lights, and entered the land of Nod.

"Nah, Phil," Max began. "I gave up on unicorn juice at rehab. So let me answer you. The many things that God has given us are beyond our understanding. First Corinthians 13:12 states that 'for now we see through a glass, darkly, but then face-to-face. Now I know in part, but then shall I know even as also I am known.' But Paul also tells us in Romans that 'we know that in all things God works for the good of those who love Him, who have been called according to His purpose.' I believe that I have free will because God has given it to me."

"Why did God choose to give it to *you,* Max, when He skipped over so many others? Think about it: the senile—people with significantly diminished cognitive capacities—addicts—psychotics. . . . Shall I go on? Certainly *they* don't have free will in any meaningful sense of the word. If as you say God gave us free will, then He *selectively* gave us free will. Why didn't God give *everyone* free will? God certainly didn't make free will *freely available,*" Phil crowed.

Michal beamed at this, but Max didn't have an answer. Instead, he switched gears: "OK, so here's something you might not want to contemplate, Phil. . . . Think about the good things that God has given us through free will. Even better, think about your world *without* free will. Then nobody is actually responsible for their actions at all, are they? Michal already raised this argument... Do you remember Ivan Karamazov in Dostoevsky's novel? 'If God does not exist, then everything is permitted.' The result would be a world of rampant selfishness and anarchy."

Max crossed his arms, displaying the comportment of an Oxford don. "I'm not sure you really want to live in such a renegade world. And aren't you very utilitarian, Phil, in always invoking the practicality of decisions? How is your regurgitated cake tasting now?"

Phil looked at the ground. He was sure that if he looked hard enough he could find the layer of roots of the grasses underneath, or more fancifully, the roots of his friend's logic. "Look, Max, I'm simply saying that just because we don't like the consequences of the truth, it doesn't make it any less true."

"Kind of like God. Just because we can't prove that He exists doesn't mean that He doesn't. And just because we can't prove that God gave us free will doesn't mean that He didn't. And your hypothesis would give us a dreadful world in which to live, so why would we want to have that kind of understanding guide our decisions? God gives us the practicality that you so crave."

"Gaah! You're hopeless." Phil spun on his heel and stared at the ground again.

"But I'm not necessarily wrong." Max laughed.

Michal saw that Phil was still staring at the ground, looking a bit disheartened. "I can help you out, Phil," she began in a cheery voice. "It only *seems* that Max is right. After all, how can we hold people morally responsible if they have no choice in how they behave? Remember what Richard Taylor says? 'Ultimate responsibility for anything that exists, and hence for any person and his deeds, can thus rest only with the first cause of all things, if there is such a cause, or nowhere at all, if there is not.'[37] If all events are determined by the sum total of previous events, then morality seems to lose its *raison d'être*. However, both Daniel Dennett and Strawson argue that determinism does *not* rule out morality and personal responsibility. Indeed in claiming that it does, one makes two faulty assumptions.[38]

"First," Michal went on, "one assumes that were we to concede that our universe is deterministic, we would have to abandon what Strawson calls our 'moral reactive attitudes.' One also assumes that morality does not possess a free-floating rationale independent of the truth of determinism. But in fact, both morality and holding people morally responsible are rational and socially advantageous.[39] This is your utilitarian argument, Phil. And so we needn't be so freaked out at the thought of a deterministic world." She smiled. "Look, Max, whether or not we're actually free, morality still exists. I can still pick my favorite moral theory and follow it like a recipe if I want. I can still will that my maxim should become a universal law, I can still aim at the mean between two extremes, I can still do that action that leads to the greatest good for the greatest number of people—nothing changes.[40]

"But even more so, Max, you are blurring the distinction between determinism and fatalism, suggesting that a determinist holds that even the edamame that you just popped into your mouth, and indeed all of our behaviors, every last tiny little one, is determined. But while this is one version of determinism, it is certainly not the most widely accepted. What Phil and I are suggesting is that human behavior is the result of a complex of genetic, environmental and cultural influences, as well as responses to and interpretations of prior events. Given this initial set of conditions, only one so-called choice or behavior will result."

"Well played, Michal." Phil became enlivened again. "Max, what *you* are suggesting is that our decision-making is like so-called 'forking paths,' that a person's future choices branch out to a garden of forking paths, as some philosophers have argued, following Jorge Borges' short story. And a person acts of his own free will in selecting among these paths. He could have chosen any one of those paths. And at each decision, a new garden of forking paths presents itself. What I'm arguing is that given the preceding conditions, all the things that Michal just mentioned, one could *not* choose otherwise. You could never have been a Botswanan shepherd, for example."

Phil paused. "Now you're going to prove me wrong and move to Gaborone. . . . But you get what I'm saying. Imagine the initial set of conditions as being like my foot, getting ready to kick a soccer ball—I wish I had one for effect—anyway, we cannot imagine the soccer ball going anywhere but in the direction I kick it."

"Good one," Michal said. "And remember the words of Schopenhauer: 'Man can do what he wills but he cannot will what he wills.'"

Max shook his head impatiently. "Obviously we are at a standstill. Shall we move on?"

"OK, Max, I'll change directions," Phil said. "And have I got a doozy for you."

"I'm on pins and needles." Max popped another edamame in his mouth, washing it down with a slurp of tea.

"So do we lose our free will when we get to heaven? If not, then very quickly heaven won't be so heavenly because people would choose to go against God, just as one-third of His angels did. Or would you say that people *wouldn't* be free to choose to go against God once we get to heaven? —Well, once *you two* get there, since I'm obviously not going. . . ." Phil smirked.

"Ah, easy answer, my friend. God has created us all gods-in-the-making. When we get to heaven we will be *like God*. As Paul says in 1 Corinthians 'Just as we have borne the image of the man of dust, we will also bear the image of the man of heaven,'" Max said.

"This is a bit blasphemous in my mind," Michal said. "But then again, this does seem to be the mystery that Paul talks about. God is creating gods-in-the-making as part of a heavenly family in which Jesus is God's firstborn Son. But you do know that this wasn't *Jesus'* teaching.[41] Anyway. . . ."

"And," Phil piped in, "if one, being god-like, cannot choose to go against God, then there is something that God, or gods, cannot do. Then your God is not omnipotent."

"Well, *I* don't have a problem with that," Michal said.

"Sure, and the next thing that you are going to say, Phil, is that God cannot create a rock that is too heavy for Him to lift. . . ." Max stopped talking when he suddenly heard movement in the grass. His lizard brain jumped to scenes in books and movies where evil, menacing, or just downright deadly things emerged from the tall grasses. Years of living on the street rushed back to him and he shifted to defend his territory, his only weapons being his size and the thermos of tea clutched firmly in his hand. He spotted a short, wrinkly, hunched-over man wearing a *sugegasa* and dirt-stained, green- and gray-striped gardening pants. The old man walked toward them through the grass, parting the leaves with an ornamented walking stick.

The man's stentorian tenor had been softened by age, making him sound like crackling paper. He called out weakly, "You young people are always having the most interesting conversations. Most interesting indeed. It makes me happy to think that you are not talking about Hatsune Miku."

As he walked toward the group, Michal leaned over and whispered to Phil. "Where did he come from? And how could he have possibly heard us?"

The man's face could just be seen beneath the *sugegasa*, the shade of his hat affording him some relief from the morning sun. Max stepped forward and offered him some tea.

"Perhaps he's the farmer who owns this land," Phil whispered back to Michal. "I've never seen him before. He must have snuck up on us when we were absorbed in conversation. It happens from time to time here."

"There's no way. . . . My eyes haven't left these sundrenched poppies. I've been so mesmerized by the way they change colors."

The old man took the tea and gave a short bow. After taking a drink, he turned to Max. "Young man, you are so kind to offer an old man your tea. It is very refreshing in this lovely morning sun." He returned the thermos to Max, leaning wobbly against his walking stick. "That is much better, thank you. What manner of things occupies the minds of you young people today?"

"The mysterious nature of free will and determinism," Phil shot off casually. He secretly hoped he would intimidate the man to leave.

"I'm not sure that I can keep up with your young minds on such things, but maybe I can give you some insight from my many years."

"By all means. Please join us," Michal said and smiled.

She noted the scrollwork on the old man's walking stick. It hinted at a pattern that she couldn't quite make out.

"Interesting scrollwork, isn't it?" said the old man.

Michal looked at the man curiously.

"How can you say that heaven is not so heavenly, young man?" the old man asked Phil. "I always thought the afterlife was a chance to try again. I expect that I will return as a small bug and my soul will become another small pebble in my family's garden. . . ." He slowly crouched down and picked up a small beetle. The shell reflected the sun in a magnificent metallic red and black. "To have a different perspective." He smiled warmly.

"I imagine that my friend here will come back as a bug right before a frigid winter in Chicago," Michal said, smirking at Phil.

"Thank you very much," Phil grimaced. Max laughed.

"But you Americans believe that you all go to heaven, don't you? —I am not important enough for that. Heaven is reserved for the important people, like you Mr. Phil." The old man smiled again.

"Have we met?" Phil asked.

"You are the owner of this very unfortunate *ryokan* are you not?" His voice held no malice, just a matter-of-fact tone, as if he was telling someone that it was two o'clock.

"Oh yes, of course. That's how you know me," Phil said. "Hey, what do you mean *unfortunate?*"

"I mean no disrespect, Mr. Phil, but your *ryokan* is not only unfavorable to many Japanese, but very, ehm, empty," he replied with the same flat tone.

"I like my privacy," Phil said. Max and Michal laughed at their friend's predicament.

"And thank you very much for your support." Phil frowned.

"I am sorry, Mr. Phil, it is most dishonorable for me to insult you when you and your friends have extended your hospitality. You were speaking about heaven not being so heavenly?" He lifted up his palm in a welcoming gesture. "Can you forgive me by explaining your complex philosophy?"

Max and Michal continued to laugh, but then made a small attempt to stifle it. A very small attempt.

"*Et tu, Brute and Brut—a?* Blast." Phil shrugged. "We were saying that if people have free will in the Christian heaven, it won't likely be any better than earth."

"I never agreed with that," Max said. "That assumes that negative consequences must always accompany free will. That may well be the case here on earth, but it will be different in heaven. First of all, we will see God and so we will necessarily want to do His will. Think of it this way. If an unquestioned expert on, say, origami, told you how to fold a crane, then wouldn't you listen to his advice?" Max folded his arms, obviously happy with himself.

"Well, *if* I wanted to learn origami, I might be inclined to do so because of *her* expertise." Michal smiled at Max and Phil. "Of course, an expert on origami would be a woman."

"I might be able to go along with that, but I promise you won't like my follow-up, Max," Phil said.

"Really, O Business-Acumen-Deficient One? Fine, I'll continue despite your warning. So if this *woman* were to offer you advice, you would take it. She is an origami expert. How much more so would you follow the Creator's advice on how to live life in heaven? Not only did He create everything, He's had the most experience with the affairs of heaven. . . ." Max stopped, realizing what followed from what he just said. He looked at Phil and began to open his mouth, but Phil had already started to jump in:

"He created *everything,* including the fall of Lucifer and all sin? Yep, I would really take the advice of that yokel. Not only did He give His angels free will, but that free will, given to them *BY GOD ALMIGHTY*—Phil raised his voice while pointing skyward—"led them to rebel against Him, something which gave rise to our never-ending misery, including painful childbirth, long hours in waiting rooms, root canals. . . ." Phil winked at Max. "I believe I've got you."

"I think he's right, Max." Michal patted her friend's back.

"OK, but that's just it. You see, free will and God's plan—" Max stammered, searching for a response.

The old man rested his hand on Max's arm. "May I have some more of that tea, young man?"

Max poured the tea and handed it to him. "Here you are, sir."

"Thank you." He handed Max his walking stick and held the tea with both hands, treating the thermos cup like a sacrificial goblet or golden bowl. He raised it to his lips. "The problem with you young people is that you are always looking for the answer, when you should understand the value of asking the question." He sipped the tea.

Suddenly a gust of wind blew through the grass, playing a soothing tone and then rising to a small crescendo before dying down. Our three friends looked at the old man curiously, and then looked at each other. Not surprisingly, Phil broke the silence first.

"Who are you? Yoda?" Phil smiled in spite of himself. He felt a calm that he had not enjoyed for months.

"Just an old man with many years of experience. . . . I try to bring what little I can to others, much like the fruit in my orchard."

Phil thought about several bowls of fruit that had mysteriously appeared on his doorstep over the past few years. "I guess that means that you don't mind me walking in your field, then?"

"Not at all. I imagine you need all the peace you can find, given the lack of customers you have." He smiled from under the shade of his *sugegasa.*

Phil smiled. "So what's the point of asking the question? We were talking about how heaven was buggered up by God giving His angels free will and how it will be exponentially buggered by giving humans, who notoriously misuse their free will, access to heaven."

"Not to be disrespectful," said the little old man, "but we should be discussing the journey, not the destination. You are so wrapped up in finding your destination that you are missing the lovely field around you." He retrieved his walking stick from Max and gestured with it at the field. "You worry that heaven, as you seem to understand it, might become less heavenly, because of the unpredictability of those beings who will be there, whether humans, angels, or *kami*. . . . But heaven *could be* a time of great exploration, and the very act of exploring would be a tremendous good. Never mind that there might be negative consequences that outweigh the good of having that freedom. Humans will finally know that they have it. Maybe they had that freedom all along, but they will finally *know* it." He returned to leaning on his walking stick, suddenly looking even older and more enfeebled. "And that knowledge would be more important than any negative consequences, whether they are real or like the passing wind."

"Um—yeah, so that's very Zen of you," Phil said.

"Thank you," said the little old man.

"I think we need to head back. Would you like to return with us? Free drink on the house, since I'm not selling it anyway," Phil said.

"No, thank you. I must return to my orchard and see to the fruit." He turned to Max, thanked him again for the tea, and then wandered off into the field.

Our three friends watched him leave, the soft breeze playing through the grasses.

Max turned to Michal and Phil. "That was interesting."

Phil nodded. "Boy, you've got that right." Then he looked at Michal, as if he just had a brilliant idea. Suddenly a funny smile took over his face.

"I don't suppose you want to walk into the village, and get another one of your silly snow globes." Phil gestured toward the tree-lined dirt road. Max laughed.

"Don't make fun. I'm sitting on a fortune with them. You do know that I own one of the original 1878 Paris Universal Expo globes. This was the same exposition that displayed Alexander Graham Bell's telephone. Grandma gave the globe to me before she died. It's a little snow cabin made with a heavy lead glass dome and a gold-painted ceramic base. Kinda like the one in the opening of *Citizen Kane*. —Nah, I'm good this trip."

"OK, let's head back then."

Our three friends walked back to the *ryokan*.

Michal got her first snow globe when she was eleven years old. Her little brother, Jack, walked uninvited into her bedroom. He saw Michal sitting on her *He-Man* bedspread, facing the window with headphones on. She was singing Madonna's *Vogue* and using her Barbie as a microphone. Barbie wasn't good for much else.

She stood up, gyrating her hips to the music. Jack started to laugh so hard that Michal turned to look. "Get out of my room!" She took off her headphones. "I'm telling Mama. Get out."

"You sing really good." Nine-year-old Jack said. "Your dancing is good too.... Here, I have something for you." He presented a little box that he was holding behind his back.

"What's this for?" Michal smiled, but she was puzzled. *Why's he being so nice? Did he lose Sebastian again?*

Sebastian was Michal's pet hamster. The one that Daddy would end up releasing to her death a year later. Michal had named her Sebastian after the crab in *The Little Mermaid.*

"But she's a girl hamster," Jack had objected. "You can't name a girl hamster 'Sebastian.' That just wouldn't be right. Why don't you name her Ariel?"

"Because I like 'Sebastian.' I can name her anything I please."

Jack would often take Sebastian out of her cage and give her rides in his wagon. Sometimes she'd try to jump out.

He extended the little box to Michal, "It's because I love you." Michal opened it and saw a little snow globe of Sebastian and Ariel. Her eyes grew big with excitement.

While Michal was inspecting it, Jack tried to explain why Ariel was in there, too. He seemed to be apologizing. "I know you don't like Ariel, but she's the main character. They don't sell snow globes with just Sebastian."

Michal smiled. "I love it. Thank you, Jack." She hopped off the bed and gave him a big hug.

Looking back, Michal thought that this was the sweetest thing her little brother could ever do. She found out that he had paid for it with the money he made in his neighborhood business: "Jack's Famous Lawn Mows of the Stars."

Daddy would end up breaking it in a fit of rage when Michal was talking too long on the telephone.

The reason Michal loved snow globes so much now was not only for the many memories each one offered, but because they symbolized her relationship with God. Every night, before she drifted off to sleep, she would imagine that she was in God's snow globe, protected from all the dangers of the world. In God's snow globe, snow gently fell to the ground, but she was never cold, and little angels would fly all about.

SIX

Do those people who hold up the Bible as an inspiration to moral rectitude
have the slightest notion of what is actually written in it?
RICHARD DAWKINS

SOMETIME IN THE THE SUMMER OF MAX'S SIXTEENTH YEAR

It was not quite six o'clock in the morning but Max could already hear the sounds of grasshoppers and cicadas singing a hallelujah chorus. Before long the temperature would be unbearable. One hundred and five in the shade, the weatherman reported the night before. Max glanced at the thermometer, its cracked face forlornly reporting a still-temperate eighty degrees. A deep voice gruff from years of cigarette smoking startled him: "Thought you were going to sleep the day away again." Max looked across the garden, noting that the sun was already bright in the sky. "Are you going to stand there all morning, boy, or are you going to get to work? The okra won't pick itself."

Max took a diagonal path to the edge of the garden. Northern wheatears flew overhead and landed on a nearby peach tree, the leaves rustling a counterpoint to the little tambourine-shaking sounds of the cicadas. Sweat beaded on his upper lip. Avoiding the rough edge of the garden glove, he wiped his mouth with the sleeve of his denim shirt, all the while lamenting the handkerchief still sitting on his bedside table.

Three rows of bright green plants stood defiantly heavy with yield, their tops brushing the waistband of his worn jeans. Max contemplated the bright yellow flowers peeking from underneath the leaves that suspiciously resembled poison oak.

Such a cheery looking plant.

Carefully, Max positioned the small knife against the stem of the plant, just above the cap of the pod. It went easily through. "If it won't cut, it's too old, and Mother won't cook it," his father's voice echoed in his head, as he cut pod after pod and tossed them into the bright orange bucket. They landed with a thud.

An hour passed as Max made his way down the first row, spines from the okra branches and leaves catching repeatedly on his shirt. The back of his shirt was already soaked through with sweat and he could feel his short-cropped hair plastered to his head underneath the cowboy hat he wore. Occasionally a few sweat drops hit the dirt as he bent to cut one of the lower pods. He should have cleaned the garage instead.

"Maxwell! Time to get ready for mass." His mother, dressed in her Sunday finest, including her trademark white kid gloves, waved at him from the garage door opening. His father scowled before striding alongside the house to intercept her, as she began walking toward the garden and Max.

"What do you think you're doing? He's not finished yet." Furrowed lines appeared between bushy white eyebrows as the eyes of a pilot bore through the unassuming woman dressed in lavender. Her eyes, brown and piercing, narrowed as her hands went to hips rounded from birthing six children. Her salt-and-pepper hair blew slightly in the breeze, mirroring the flutter of the sleeves on her dress. Her right eyebrow rose slightly before she spoke.

"What I'm doing is calling my son to get ready for church." Her body stood in direct challenge to the man dressed in khakis and a polo shirt, towering more than a foot over her. Her voice was calm with authority.

Max's father bent down to look her in the eyes. "And what is that envelope in your hand? More wasted money for that church of yours?" His jaw jutted forward, stubbornness evident on his tanned features.

She smiled. "What is that box in your hand? Did you buy that with wasted money for cigarettes?" The couple stared at each another, daring the other to break the standstill, until Max finally approached and dropped the bucket at their feet.

"You two have already agreed to disagree and you're just baiting each other. Give it a rest." He put his hand on his father's shoulder and kissed his mother's cheek before going into the house through the back door of the garage.

"Old coot." His mother shot to his father, as Max was walking away.

"Stubborn woman," his father volleyed back before picking up the bucket and returning to the garden. Max smiled on his way to the shower.

LATER IN THE DAY, AFTER THEIR MORNING WALK. *Back at the RTSS*

Phil tipped back in his chair, balancing unsteadily before rocking forward, catching himself on his toes, and repeating the cycle. The chair creaked every time he pushed back. An opened bottle of Three Ships single malt whiskey and a glass sat on the floor next to him.

"Seriously, Michal, in what sense are you a Christian if you're such a heretic? I've only heard heretical views from you." He caught himself with his toes as the chair came back down, then he pushed himself back again.

Michal watched his chair-based antics and just shook her head. "First of all, every Christian is a heretic of some sort, if you scratch deeply enough below the surface. But to your question, Phil. I am a Christian because I hold all of the essentials of the faith. That Jesus is both God and man. That Jesus died on the cross, was buried, and resurrected. That there is only one true God, and He exists in three persons. And that there is only one way to God and that is through Jesus. I know it's tough to understand how all of that can be balanced, but you're doing your own balancing act right now." Michal pointed at the chair on which Phil was teetering precariously. "Not everyone thinks that's an easy thing either."

"Touché, miss, but I thought you were a universalist? Doesn't that mean that you believe that there are many different paths to God? Doesn't that preclude your one-way-to-God ditty and require universal reconciliation? We will all be reconciled to God, without exception. Even the devil himself. Apocatastasis. No eternal punishment."

Michal frowned. "I am a universalist, but not in the sense you describe. Not all roads lead to the top of the mountain as the—what should I call them?—'mainstream' universalists proclaim. My universalism requires Jesus. Jesus is the only way to salvation. But whether one believes in Him or not, we still have the fact of Jesus on the cross. If even one soul were lost, then that would not be a complete victory for my Savior. And so all souls are reconciled to Him. God became a human in the person of Jesus, and we are all reconciled to God through that loving act. Jesus' love will transform and redeem everyone. In any case, universalism is not so heretical. Origen taught it in the third century and it was accepted until the sixth."

Phil smiled, "Just because it has some history behind it doesn't make it any less heretical. Heresy, at least as the dictionary defines it, is a belief or opinion contrary to the official position of a particular religion. So if I say, as Origen did, that hell does not literally mean the fires of hell, but the 'fire of conscience and the stings of remorse which torture the mind,' this may sound reasonable, but since that is contrary to the idea of hell that was accepted by the third-century church and by many people today, well, it's heretical." Phil rocked back in his chair again. "Of course, you could just say that was Jerome speaking and not Origen, but that's—"

"You do love to hear yourself talk, don't you?" Max said. "I would have thought that time would have given you more humility." He smiled, then looked seriously toward Michal. "Universalism is certainly a very attractive heresy, Michal. Probably the most attractive heresy, especially if you're in love with God's love, as you and I are. If God is love, and I mean total and complete love, it would seem that universal salvation is necessary. But to believe this is just blind optimism.[42] Assuming, of course, you want to stay within the bounds of scripture. And what you are saying is completely contrary to scripture, particularly Romans 5:18, where Paul flat out states that 'just as one act against God condemned all men, one act of righteousness brings life for all men.' Universalism is contrary to that idea."

"You weren't listening, Max. My universalism requires Jesus and so it *is* consistent with Romans 5:18," Michal said.

"Well, that makes you a heretical universalist, too," Phil said with a laugh.

"One of the greatest dangers of universalism is that it interferes with evangelism. What's the point of evangelizing, of spreading the Good News, if we're all going to heaven anyway? Michal, we've been friends for a very long time, and I have no more problem with you and your progressive Christianity than I do with Phil and his blatant atheism. But if you are going to call yourself a Christian, you need to find that Christian heart. You can't be confusing people and leading them astray by promoting universalism. You will be answering for a lot of souls." Max's tone resonated with well-rehearsed pastoral concern.

"Well, we can't have *that*. It would be a pity if all of those unprovable objects were sent to that unprovable place of eternal damnation." Phil held up his feet as he rocked forward and then struck the floor with a loud thump. His head fell forward. He slowly raised it and spoke ominously. "Be prepared to be cast into utter darkness."

Michal clapped her hands. "Aren't you the dramatic one? But I am a universalist because a loving God, an all-good, loving God, would not condemn people who commit finite sins, no matter how monstrous, to eternal torment in hell. So, yes, I am in love with God's love. And He would never do that. Not my God. Either everyone goes to heaven or no one does. Of course, I'd still love God even if there were no such thing as heaven, for He has given me a big slice of heaven here on earth. He transformed my hate-filled life into one of peace and joy. I wonder how many Christians would still follow Jesus if they knew there wasn't an afterlife? They'd probably wonder 'what's the point?' Like Ivan Karamazov: if God does not exist we can do whatever we want. —Well, I still would follow Him. He's still my Savior. Jesus saved me from a wretched existence. But in any case, I choose to believe that we all go to heaven. —Of course, this means that there must be some sort of a cleansing process before we are fully reconciled to God."

"Don't you remember, Michal? Sheep go to heaven. Goats go to hell." Phil laughed. "You may believe in universal salvation but that makes you no less heretical." He pretended to open a book, licking his finger with the turn of each imaginary page. "Remember the bit about not leaning on your own understanding? You should follow the example of our friend here and just accept what's in that book of yours. This whole cleansing thing that you're suggesting—it sounds like an idea grounded in logic, not something from the Bible. What is it? Some version of purgatory?"

"Kind of, yes. Think of heaven like a grand ball. I'm speaking metaphorically, of course. Everyone is dressed in tuxedos and gowns, dancing all around the floor, and you show up filthy, clothed only in tattered rags. Wouldn't you want to clean up before entering the ball? Even if the host welcomes you as you are?[43] —I would."

Max shook his head. "Michal, your view runs counter to the Bible. Jesus taught us that those who reject Him will spend eternity in hell. We find this repeated throughout the gospels, in Matthew, Luke, and in John."

Phil held up his hands and wiggled his fingers while making a whooshing fire sound. "The great Bertrand Russell says that makes Jesus cruel. Not even a humane person could believe in everlasting punishment. No humane person could have such a vindictive nature. You certainly don't find Socrates holding this view. Compared to Socrates, Jesus was morally defective. Jesus was cruel."[44]

"Jesus was *just*, Phil," Max said. Phil opened his mouth to protest, but before he could say a word, Max turned back to Michal. "If Mr. Mummenschanz is done with his act, let me continue. Universalism focuses exclusively on God's love and mercy while altogether ignoring an equally important part of His character: His justice and wrath. In order for God to be a good God, He must also be a just God—righting wrongs and all that. Universalists trivialize sin, essentially cancel-ing out the need for Christ's redeeming sacrifice.[45] That in itself would make you a heretic." Max turned to Phil. "Wouldn't you agree?"

Phil opened his mouth and moved his lips but no sound came out. He pounded on an invisible wall and proceeded to feel around for its edges.

Max smiled. "That's right, mimes are silent. Any chance you'll keep it that way?" He winked at Phil.

"No—as if you had to ask. . . "

Michal laughed. "I am *not* minimizing sin. Not in the least. You say that Jesus said these things. But how do you know that He did? You've already agreed with me that not everything in the Bible is true, so how do you know Jesus really made these statements? That's especially true when it comes to the Gospel of John, which some scholars argue is a reaction against the Gospel of Thomas and the Gnostic Thomasine sect. There's a slew of textual support for this."

"Ah, the classic the-Bible-isn't-necessarily-the-complete-Word-of-God argu-ment. I was wondering when you would try that, Michal. I expect that from Phil, but I'm not sure why you would take that tack. You do realize that God is capable of ensuring the Bible we have today is the Bible that He wants us to have. There's a reason we read the Gospel of John and not the Gospel of Thomas," Max said. "God's hand is clearly visible in the canonization of the Bible. We should approach it through both tradition and reason."

Phil huffed. "That's your argument? You know very well, Max, no one can prove what you're claiming. I realize you're now a pastor, and therefore you'd rather accept things on faith than lean on your own understanding, but presum-ably you do still remember what a circular argument is. You've called me out on it. . . . "

"Deacon, not pastor, and neither can you prove that what I say is not true," Max shot back.

"The canon was created by an elite group of literate males who privileged cer-tain narratives, calling them inspired and authoritative, because they supported a particular patriarchal world view in which women were subordinate to men," Michal said, all feminist-afire. "And that settles that!"

"Unfalsifiable," Max said.

TWO WEEKS EARLIER

Max stood next to his mentor, Father Manganiello, and waited. Calm had tran-scended his earlier apprehension. The peace of the Holy Spirit filled his heart. He looked out over the small congregation. Family and friends who had supported him since his early teens smiled and nodded their support—everyone except Gideon Morrison, who wore a scowl darker than a Texas twister cloud.

Blood pumped in Max's ears and sweat beaded on his upper lip. Jeffrey Taylor, Max's sponsor, stood up, straightened his navy-blue suit and yellow fleur-de-lis tie, and walked down the blood-red carpet to Father Manganiello's side on the first step of the dais. He towered over the priest by more than half-a-foot. Absently running his fingers through his blond hair, Jeffrey smiled at Max before looking forward again.

Sunlight poured through three stained glass windows, painting the bishop with the dappled blues, reds, and golds of St. Joseph's resplendent robe. Father Manganiello and Jeffrey approached the bishop.

"Bishop Ackerman, bishop in the Church of God, on behalf of the clergy and the people of the Diocese of Texas, we present to you Maxwell Cardin to be ordained a deacon in Christ's holy catholic church."

A smile spread across Bishop Ackerman's wizened features. He looked at Father Manganiello and Jeffrey. "Has he been selected in accordance with the canons of this Church? And do you believe his manner of life to be suitable to the exercise of this ministry?"

"We certify to you that he has satisfied the requirements of the canons and we believe him to be qualified for this order." They both stepped back and motioned Max to step forward as the bishop addressed him.

"Will you be loyal to the doctrine, discipline, and worship of Christ, as this Church has received them? And will you, in accordance with the canons of this Church, obey your bishop and other ministers who may have authority over you and your work?"

Max turned and looked into the crowd, trying not to settle his gaze on Gideon. "I am willing and ready to do so. And I solemnly declare that I do believe the Holy Scriptures of the Old and New Testaments to be the Word of God and to contain all things necessary to salvation, and I solemnly engage to conform to the doctrine, discipline, and worship of the Episcopal Church." He reached for the quill pen that the bishop offered and signed his name to the declaration.

Bishop Ackerman watched Max's eyes as they passed over the congregation. He remembered his own signing of the Deacon Declaration so many years ago. He smiled. Max was a good candidate in spite—and because—of his personal tribulations. God's mercy and will and all of the joy of the Holy Spirit were truly alive in this young man. But the bishop's brow furrowed when he noticed Max suddenly looking down.

Ah, Mr. Morrison—the only parishioner against young Cardin's path.

The parish had given their support, so a lone parishioner's misgivings should be of little consequence. He motioned for the congregation to stand. "Dear friends in Christ, you know the importance of this ministry and the weight of your responsibility in presenting Maxwell Cardin for ordination to the sacred order of deacons. Therefore, if any of you know any impediment or crime because of which we should not proceed, come forward now, and make it known."

Gideon Morrison moved into the aisle. "I know why he shouldn't go on. He's a faggot, plain and simple." A collective gasp rippled through the congregation as all heads turned in disbelief toward Gideon.

"How can you speak like that in the House of God, Gideon Morrison? You ought to be ashamed of yourself." A woman dressed in a pale peach suit glared at the interruption. Several others looked on in disapproval while others looked at Max with pained eyes.

"*Me* ashamed? He's got loose morals and unholy desires. Says so right here in his di-a-ry." Gideon drew out the last word, slurring it into an insult.

Max started forward, alarm flushing his pale cheeks. "How did you—?" His words were cut off as Bishop Ackerman's hand rose, urging him to stop.

Gideon made a grand gesture of licking his thumb as he turned to a book-marked page: "'It was cold at the beach. The gray sky held clouds as dark as my inner turmoil.'" Gideon snorted. "'A young college student, barefoot, the hairs of his legs light against his dark tan, walked hand-in-hand with another man out toward the heaving gulf water splashing over the jetty. How I envy them. . . .' Shall I go on, Bishop?"

Bishop Ackerman walked down the aisle, his slippers silent on the red carpet. "May I see that please?" He reached for the leatherbound book in Gideon's hands. Gideon handed it to the bishop, a satisfied smirk creeping across his features. The book felt worn, smooth with use. The bishop opened it to the page that Gideon had read and noted the date: four years ago.

"My apologies to the congregation for this interruption. Were any of you not aware that postulant Cardin was a homosexual?"

No one raised a hand. They were all shaking their heads 'no.'

"Well, Gideon, it appears as though the parish has already discussed this. What was the outcome, Father Manganiello?"

"The ordinand has always been forthright in his struggles and he remains celibate as per his agreement with the parish, while he is on the road to the priesthood. It was the recommendation of this parish that all ordinands, regardless of disposition, follow this path to demonstrate the seriousness of their commitment."

Bishop Ackerman nodded to the rector. "Then I see no other reason for an objection. Please sit down, Mr. Morrison, or depart this ceremony in peace. Oh, and you might want to brush up on your Bible study, beginning with Exodus 20:1-20. And be sure to revisit Matthew 22 verse 37. . . ."

Gideon got up and left through the back doors of the small chapel. After his exit, the bishop returned to the dais and addressed the congregation.

"St. Joseph's Church, is it your will that Maxwell be ordained a deacon?"

The congregation responded, "It is."

The bishop continued, "Will you uphold him in this ministry?"

Firmly, the parish responded in unison, "We will uphold Maxwell on his path."

"In peace, let us pray to the Lord." Max finally exhaled. He hadn't realized that he'd been holding his breath this whole time.

The bishop began to recite the litanies. His voice was soothing and sure, and filled with the Holy Spirit. "From all blindness of heart; from pride, vainglory, and hypocrisy; from envy, hatred, and malice; and from all want of charity. . . ." Ackerman raised his arms as he looked heavenward, then bowed his head once more as the congregation responded in recitative, "Good Lord, deliver us."

As the bishop followed with the traditional litanies, including the Kyrie Eleison, a bright beam of light from the stained glass window of St. Joseph touched his white robe just over his heart. Max felt the calm return. As he waited for each call and answer, Max bowed his head. His voice rang out every response to the bishop's words until the bishop finished with the call to "illumine all bishops, priests, and deacons . . . with true knowledge and understanding of God's word. . . ." Max was still grappling with what that truly meant—especially in the wake of Gideon's accusations.

Back at the RTSS

"Unfalsifiable? You're going with that? Circular backed up by unfalsifiable?" Phil waved his arms wildly. "Well, I have an invisible force field, created by undetectable, unicorn-riding leprechauns that protects me from nonsensical arguments. They have shot you with invisible rays that are influencing you to agree with me, even now. You just can't prove that they don't exist." He took a sip of his whiskey.

"I can prove they don't exist because I don't plan on agreeing with you on this subject anytime ever," Max poked at Phil.

"Hang on, guys. . . . Max, you invoke God's justice and wrath. We find evidence of these qualities throughout the Bible. Take Ezekiel 16. God is so pissed at Israel's apostasy and idolatry that He tells her He will gather together all of her lovers to gang-rape her. —If God really said this, I'm not interested in following Him."

Max stared at Michal, eyes wide, mouth gaping. "What translation are you using? The Michal International Version? Sure, Ezekiel does have God comparing Jerusalem to a prostitute, although not really, since Jerusalem isn't paid by her lovers but, as we might say today, gives it away for free. But gang rape? Not unless you think 'thrusting thee with their swords' is meant as a euphemism, not literally. But then you might want to interpret being 'stoned' as getting baked with your bros. . . . Not gang rape at all, Michal. More like bringing Jerusalem's various lovers back to stone and hack her to pieces."

Phil laughed. "You two are arguing over whose translation of the Bible is correct and which bits. Go ahead and argue which flavor of unicorn juice tastes better. No matter who's right, whether we're talking about crushing with stones and hacking to pieces or stripping naked and gang raping, why would anyone want to worship such a sadistic God? Whichever version you go with, He's a real sicko."

Michal frowned, her eyelids low and heavy. "God's not sadistic. Humans are. In any case, this is just human interpretation of the political and natural events. Israel had a history of being seriously ass-whooped, by the Egyptians, Assyrians, Babylonians, Greeks, Seleucids, to name just some of the big players. And of course the people in Jesus' day were subject to persecution by the Romans. No wonder the gospel writers have Jesus talking about eternal punishment in hell. That was the shiny light at the end of a dark tunnel of persecution. All their enemies would suffer an eternity of punishment for their actions."

Max stood up from his chair. "I know that eternal hell is a tough pill to swallow, but I also know from personal experience that hell and the metaphorical flames of suffering exist in *this* life. In the afterlife it's worse. It's eternal. There is no hope of redemption from the silence and darkness of death. In Christ we have eternal life. Rejection of God is separation from Him for all eternity."

Now it was Michal's turn to sit back, her face beaming. "You do know, Max, that the ancient Israelites had no conception of hell. None. Even the concept of an afterlife was introduced very late, during the Hellenistic period, likely drawing on Greek mythology or religion. They're basically the same thing. Gehenna— actually Gehinnom, or the Valley of Hinnon—was the site of a garbage dump outside ancient Jerusalem, and trash was always burning there. It eventually came to mean the place where the wicked go after death. That's also where the prophet Jeremiah condemned the apostates who burned their children in sacrifice to Baal. And it's almost certainly where we get all the hell-fire imagery. But it is *not* like our understanding of everlasting hell. It's a place where the soul goes to get purified, kind of like purgatory, or a waiting room for heaven. Nobody is there for eternity. The spiritual purification is limited to twelve months. Hades or Sheol was the abode of the dead. Both the righteous and the wicked end up there. The Christian conceptions of hell and an afterlife derive from Gehenna and Hades or Sheol. Jesus invokes the word 'Gehenna' as a metaphor for punishment of the wicked."[46]

"I agree that the Christian conceptions of hell and the afterlife draw on Gehenna and Hades or Sheol," Max said. "And I, too, can't agree with many Christian traditions that take hell to be a literal place of eternal flames. I'm not really sure whether Jesus believed in it or not. We definitely see Him invoking the fiery torment image in the Gospel of Matthew. In Matthew 25:41, for example, He says that those who are cursed are destined for the eternal fire prepared for the devil and his angels. Or what about Matthew 13:42 and 50, where they will be thrown into the blazing furnace and there will be weeping and gnashing of teeth? —I agree with you, Michal. I don't think that Jesus meant for us to take it literally, as something other than metaphor.... But I do believe that Jesus meant for us to take it very seriously. Hell is far more horrible than what Jesus' fiery image suggests. . . ."

"Even more horrible than lapping up scalding water like thirsty camels, as the Qur'an puts it?" Phil asked with a laugh.

Max shook his head. "Look, guys. I've been—um—OK, so I'm having a hard time getting this out." He laughed. "I've been playing around with an idea of hell, if you don't mind me sharing it.[47] Remember *The Brothers Karamazov*? Michal and I have mentioned it before. Zosima's older brother Markel was an atheist." Max jabbed Phil's arm. "Anyway, he becomes dangerously ill—consumption—and, facing death, he suddenly changes. Looking at the garden through his window, he even asks the singing birds to forgive him, because he had overlooked the beauty and the glory of God all around him as expressed through nature. As he comforts his grieving mother, Markel says something like 'We are all in paradise, but we do not want to know it, and if we did want to know it, tomorrow there would be paradise the world over. . . .' Heaven and hell are the same place but different orientations. You hate the Beach Boys, right? But I love them. Imagine that we are sitting side by side at a never-ending Beach Boys concert. What is heaven to me is hell to you. Heaven and hell are nothing but states of mind."

Phil chuckled. "I can go along with you here, Maxie. For me, floating in the clouds in our white gowns before the Almighty, strumming harps and singing hallelujahs, would be nauseatingly boring, while the two of you might enjoy it. . . . Or maybe the other guys got it right and I'll end up with a collection of houris, not harps." Phil grinned widely. "Think about it. In all these fairy tales of the afterlife, the one thing that we take with us is our personalities. Our desires come from our personalities. So while I might not have the same desires any longer, since I'll be transformed or cleaned up or whatever, those desires come from somewhere. In your mythos that somewhere is the soul."

Max shook his head, then gazed upward at his god. "Pearls before swine—?" He looked at his two friends. "If I may?"

Michal laughed. "Sure. But first I want to say something more about this heaven and hell stuff, whether we get there, and how it might connect to a meaningful life."

"Go on—although this seems like a bit of a derail," Phil said. "That is, if you don't mind the lady cutting in?" He smiled at Max.

"By all means, she has my permission to derail."

"Maybe just a bit, but a worthwhile one. . . . I can imagine that when we die, when we approach the so-called 'Pearly Gate' with St. Peter jangling the keys in front of our noses, instead of asking us 'What do you believe?' or 'Do you believe in God?' he asks us whether our lives were meaningful. God gave us this life, for crying out loud. Did we do something with it? Did we accomplish anything? Or did we waste it? Why would God give us everlasting life if we squandered this one? We'd just fritter away our afterlife, too. . . . You know, Susan Wolf wrote a lot about meaningless and meaningful lives.[48] We can all think of a paradigmatic example of a wasted life: the couch potato who spends day after day, or night after night, drinking beer and eating cardboard pizza while watching other peoples' lives on reality shows. This guy lets life go by in utter passivity. John Stuart Mill was on to something when he made a distinction between the higher and lower pleasures.[49] But Wolf discusses other types of wasted lives, too. Think about the idle rich, who flit about life trying to avoid utter boredom, engaging in one amusement after the other. I tried this kind of life once. Remember that guy I lived with in Malibu?"

"Was this before or after you dated the professional boxer and minor-league baseball player?" Phil said with a laugh.

Max joined in. "Hey, what ever happened to that stunt double with the irritable bowel?"

Michal rolled her eyes. "As I was saying. . . . I quit teaching for a year. Every day I'd go surfing, shopping, out for a fancy lunch, maybe a pedicure after an hour with my personal trainer. Then I'd party with my girlfriends at night. After a year I was ready to pull my hair out. I had to get back into academia and start using my brain again. . . ." She did not say: *I was caught in the pantry with the Brazilian cook.* She looked at Phil very seriously. "You know, Phil, you're in danger of slipping into this kind of life. All of your adventure travels, and now holed up in this—this place."

"Michal, you've got no idea what you're talking about. But I won't defend my life to you. You're not worth my trouble," Phil huffed and then looked away.

"Let's all calm down. . . . Michal, you have a point with all of this?" Max said, trying yet again to bring peace between his two friends.

"Sure I do." She looked at Phil. "I'm sorry—that was way out of line. You're not like that. I don't know why I said that. Anyway, that kind of life, which has no resemblance to your own, is also meaningless, pointless, empty. But there's another type. What about the corporate executive who works twelve hours a day, maybe six or seven days a week, always on the road, missing his wedding anniversary or his children's birthdays, suffering tremendous stress, maybe even poor health, for the sole purpose of accumulating more and more wealth? As Wolf puts it, this is just like David Wiggins' example of the pig farmer who buys more land to grow more corn to feed more pigs to buy more land to grow more corn to feed more pigs.[50] Another example of a meaningless, utterly useless life."

"And, of course, the mythical figure of Sisyphus represents total meaninglessness," Max said.

"Remember, Camus says at the end of his essay that we must imagine Sisyphus happy," Phil said. "In any event, in all of those examples you gave, Michal, their lives might not be meaningless from their perspectives. Maybe the lazy guy on the couch, or the rich girl who spends her daddy's or her husband's money on fancy new shoes or purses, or the executive who wants to make a shit-ton of money, maybe their lives are worthwhile to them," Phil said. "Who decides what makes life meaningful anyway? The same people who say what makes art valuable?"

"Your relativism won't fly here, Phil. Wolf makes a great point. For those people who are living truly meaningless lives, we can imagine them having some kind of epiphany, where one day they wake up—either literally or figuratively—and recognize that their lives up to that point have been meaningless. As Wolf says, such an experience would be nearly unintelligible if we took the definition of a meaningful life to be purely subjective, as you're trying to do."

"Meaningful lives *are* subjective, Michal. Think about those who lived during the time of Homer's stories—Odysseus, for example. Were their lives meaningful? Odysseus wasn't happy unless he killed at least one person per day," Phil said.

"Happiness is not necessarily connected to meaningfulness, Phil," Michal said. "Remember all of Nietzsche's 'heroes'—the higher men—suffered tremendously, but their suffering made possible our greatest cultural achievements."

"I think Camus got it right when he spoke about the absurdity of life, of our futile search for meaning in the face of an unintelligible world, completely devoid of God and any God-given eternal truths and meanings," Phil said, frowning.

"So what does make life meaningful, Michal?" Max interjected. "I can think of a few people in history who led really meaningful lives, like Mother Teresa or Gandhi. But what was it about their lives that made them meaningful? Do you or Susan Wolf offer any criteria? Or are we to rely on our intuition here? —It seems that we must include 'helping others' as necessary to a meaningful life. Or 'being moral'?"

"I can think of plenty of so-called 'meaningful' lives that were not particularly 'moral,' that were not judged to be moral," Phil replied. "Think about Gauguin, for example. Didn't he quit his job and abandon his family to poverty to pursue his artistic career, which included living a primitive life in a jungle hut in Tahiti? Some of his greatest paintings depict Tahitian life. Many would consider his life to be worthwhile despite the fact he left his family behind and denied his children a father. Indeed, at least Michal would say that our world would be poorer had he not done that."

"Phil's right, Max. A meaningful life might not be especially moral. Gauguin did lead a meaningful life. And Wolf does provide criteria for meaningfulness. A meaningful life is one that actively and, according to her, at least somewhat successfully engages in projects of positive value. I might amend that slightly by saying 'actively engages in creative pursuits that serve as a testament to a life well-lived.'"

"This seems more than a bit elitist, Michal. Not everyone is as creative as a Gauguin, or all those other 'higher men' that Nietzsche would give an appreciative nod to. Are you saying that you have to be a higher man—or woman—to lead a meaningful life? What about the person who is not particularly creative—never wrote a novel, even a boring one—yet engages in charity work, maybe digging wells in a Third World village. . . . Doesn't take much creativity to dig a well. Would you say that this person's life lacks meaning?" Max said.

"Michal, unless we want to revisit our whole discussion about relativism, whether it's with respect to art or morality or in this case what constitutes a meaningful life, we aren't going to get anywhere. . . . And your view leads to the paradoxical result that Nietzsche's higher men, who reject Christianity, and even mock it, end up in the Christian heaven. —So where were we before we got so magnificently sidetracked? Although I will say, Michal, that it was a worthwhile and meaningful sidetrack." Phil smirked.

"I'll just let what I said settle into your big brains for a bit. Go ahead, Max, you wanted to say something?"

"Yes—so back to our discussion before you ran us off track." Max smiled. "We were talking about heaven, hell and purgatory. What I wanted to say was that as far as purgatory goes, Michal, it cannot be a place. We're not in Dante's *Divine Comedy*. There is no Mount Purgatory. If there were, Phil would be on the seventh terrace of lust with all of his houris."

Phil gave a thumbs-up, then said, "Michal puts purgatory somewhere below Filene's Basement and slightly above Sears." He laughed.

Max just shook his head. "Let's consider Paul's words in First Corinthians. At the moment when we come face-to-face with God, all of our works will be tested by fire, if you will. If, as Paul puts it, our works are laid on a foundation of gold or silver or costly stone, they will survive the fire. But if our works are laid on a foundation of wood or hay or straw, they will be burnt up, although we ourselves will be saved. So I guess Paul's words might fit your theory of universal salvation, Michal, although I still hesitate to accept it, especially since all the hell-talk comes from Jesus' very own lips. It seems that Paul, not Jesus, flirted with universalism."

"Right," Michal began. "At the moment of death we are still imperfect and we still need to be purified and perfected. C.S. Lewis observed that our souls demand purgatory. Indeed, my idea of the ball comes almost directly from Lewis, and from Peter Kreeft, who talks about him. Lewis said, 'Would it not break the heart, if God said to us: It is true that your breath smells and your rags drip with mud and slime, but even so, enter into this joy? Wouldn't we reply: I'd rather be cleansed first?' Sin is purged, as you suggest Max, in this cleansing fire."

"So long as you agree that this happens all at once, not over the course of some indefinable time spent prettifying ourselves for God."

"Right, I agree with you here. I was only speaking metaphorically."

"Unicorn juice," Phil huffed. "And Phil did sayeth unto the believers, Again I sayeth unto thee, you talketh of Unicorn Juice. You two can argue what flavor of heaven and hell or purgatory exists, what form the afterlife will take. It's all speculation and as you continue to show, speculation based on interpretations about which very few agree. I think that if we're to believe in a heaven or hell or afterlife, why not choose one that makes sense? —That actually rewards our actions on this planet? Think about it. Valhalla is a reward for being a good warrior and for dying in battle. This afterlife makes sense. It rewards a lifetime of heroic activity. Nirvana is freedom from the cycle of birth and death, ostensibly for 'getting it right.' Thank you, Indigo Girls.

"Most Christians believe, and I want to emphasize the word *believe*," Phil continued, "that the afterlife depends on one particular action that you must carry out during this life. 'That whosoever believeth in him. . . .' Well, that's pretty cut-and-dried. We can argue about which parts of the Bible are more accurate, but I would think most believers would rattle off John 3:16 as their sword-and-shield against the perils of hell. This is precisely why I am so opposed to this heaven-or-hell concept. Just one single little action gets you your one-way ticket to heaven. And if you don't do it, it doesn't matter whether you've lived a good life or a bad one. You're still going to hell."

"Not so fast, Phil," Michal began. "Many Christians invoke passages in the Bible which emphasize the importance of one's actions on earth and not just belief. It's not like swallowing a little heaven-pill. Think about what Jesus says in Matthew: 'When I was hungry, you fed me, when I was thirsty, you gave me drink.' His disciples asked him, 'Lord, when did we feed you?' and Jesus responded, 'When you did this for the least of these, you did it for me.' We who do not help those in need are cast into the eternal fire. If you believe that—and remember what Jesus' brother James says: 'Even the demons believe, and they shudder'—belief alone doesn't cut it. —But you were saying, Phil?"

"Michal, while you're correct about those passages, most Protestants still claim that John 3:16 is the formula for heaven. Many Christians believe that a person who lives any kind of life can have a deathbed conversion. I'll grant that it requires real belief. That is, you can't 'trick' God. But the fact the deathbed conversion supposedly works shows that there *is* a Christian one-way ticket. . . . Do I have to quote Ephesians 2:8? 'It is by grace that you are saved.' Not actions. Not works. Grace.

"You two take an educated, elevated view of the Christian afterlife. But let's look at some other afterlife myths, particularly Nirvana. It's not something where you make one decision and you're good. In the case of Buddhism and Hinduism, it's a lifetime dedication to nothingness."

"You mean emptiness, don't you, Phil?" Michal said. "Emptiness is not nothingness. That would be a very nihilistic view. Remember what the Buddhist master Nagarjuna said: 'Emptiness wrongly grasped is like picking up a poisonous snake from the wrong end.' Define emptiness as nothingness and you get bitten. Nagarjuna's point is that things do not exist the way we think that they do. We grasp at things, thinking that we can possess their essence with our tiny little egos, thinking that they are somehow fixed and permanent. Emptiness is seeing through this illusion, putting to death our ego-selves and opening ourselves up to the ungraspable, fleeting, and incomprehensible reality."[51]

Max and Phil stared first at each other and then at Michal. Phil finally asked, "When did you become a student of Buddhism?"

Michal chuckled. "That's pretty much my entire knowledge of Buddhism displayed right there. And I'm not even sure I've got it right."

"Not that I want to go off on a wrong tangent, but I'd agree with that last statement of yours," said Phil. "Nirvana is the release from the endless cycle of birth and rebirth. To be released to what? That would be the snuffing-out of this candle of existence. To me, that's nothingness, since we're still talking about some kind of afterlife from which nobody has ever come back." Phil waved his hands. "It's exactly the problem as before, though—we are talking about interpretations, and ultimately relying on the words of some person taken to be an authority. So now that Michal has given us her version of Buddhism 101, let's get back to the Christian afterlife.

"Think about Christian scholarship, from the Church Fathers and all the rest. It's like a mulligan stew of doctrines, with ingredients that don't go well together, spices that do battle in your mouth. My point is that there is no universal agreement in the Christian faith." Phil took a drink. "Besides, getting agreement from Christian scholars is like trying to get comic-book geeks to agree on who's stronger—Superman or the Hulk—or sports aficionados to agree on who was the greatest boxer of all time. . . ."

"Well, I for one like Wonder Woman and Muhammad Ali, and not just for what he's done in the ring. But why don't you pour me another drink, Phil, and let's put this discussion to bed." Michal extended her glass to him.

"Good idea. It's beginning to feel like we're stuck in the '71 Ali-Frazier fight at Madison Square Garden," Phil said.

"So long as I'm Smokin' Joe," Max smirked.

SEVEN

So long as you write what you wish to write, that is all that matters; and whether it matters for ages or only for hours, nobody can say.

VIRGINIA WOOLF

THE NEXT DAY. *At the RTSS*

Michal sat at the little desk in her room, writing in a notebook. She looked up at Kwan Yin and imagined her smiling. Just then, Phil and Max barged through the door.

"Don't you guys know how to knock?" Michal asked.

They ignored her. "Whatcha writing?" Max said.

"A story I've been working on—a novel. Now, if only I could work in a strong female character. —Someone that the toy companies could turn into an action figure. That's where the real money comes in."

"Writing a novel, eh? And in a room of your own. . . ." Phil laughed at the reference.

"Virginia Woolf," Michal began. "She said that no woman can produce a creative work without *privacy.* Privacy is necessary for creativity. Evidently this concept is totally alien to the two of you."

"A novel. Cool." Max smiled.

"You know," Phil began, "we should help you write it. We'd make great material for a novel, we three. And with Max's and my name on it—you know, *guys' names*—well it would surely get published."

"You forget, Phil, she kind of has a guy's name already," Max said. He smiled at Michal and then added, "You'd make a great action figure."

"Of course, she needs to master jumping off rooftops first." Phil laughed.

"Stop being so ridiculous. But you two are making a good point, at least a good historical point, about which Woolf was writing," Michal said.

"Do tell," Phil said. "Wait, I probably need a drink for this."

"There's an opened bottle of Red Zin right here." Michal lifted up the bottle from the desk. "I snuck it in from your bar. We can share my glass."

Phil poured himself a drink. Max and Phil sat down on her futon. Michal closed her notebook and turned her chair to face them.

"In *A Room of One's Own,* Woolf invents a fictionalized character, Judith Shakespeare, William's sister. Judith was her brother's equal. As Woolf writes, 'She was as adventurous, as imaginative, as agog to see the world as he was.' Unfortunately, she was living in Elizabethan England. Not the best time for women. For centuries before, and even after, women had little or no access to education."

"Am I going to grow a nice set of tits listening to all of this?" Phil asked. "I'm suffocating in estrogen here." He and Max laughed.

"Seriously. Can't we have an intellectual discussion about women—obstacles to women's success, women and literature, even women in philosophy—without you making fun?" Michal asked.

Phil made a very serious face. "Go on. We're listening."

"Good. So back to Judith. Well, let's start with William first, by way of contrast," Michal said.

"Phil and I love Bill the Bard," Max said. He leaned against the wall. "Any chance you snuck some food in here too? I'm famished."

"My stash is in the corner right there," Michal said. "Have at."

"I'm going to have to charge you by the item. You know, to restock my kitchen," Phil said and laughed.

Michal rolled her eyes. "As I was saying. William Shakespeare. Obviously Shakespeare was extraordinarily gifted. But unlike his sister, his genius was nurtured. He was sent to school, where he likely learned Latin, read the likes of Virgil, Ovid, and Horace. He even sought his fortune in London. He had a taste for the theater, became a successful actor and, well, we all know what an amazing playwright and poet he was."

"What's your favorite play?" Phil asked Max.

"Derailing," Michal said.

"I like the comedies best. But you know that. I'm also a fan of the tragedies. I don't much like the histories, though *Henry V* was pretty good. I'd say *Tempest, Much Ado About Nothing.* Maybe *Twelfth Night.*"

"Derailing," Michal said again.

"Sorry, go on," Max said with a mouthful of Kaki-peanuts.

"Pass me the wine," Michal said. Phil extended the glass.

"Not the glass. The bottle." She took a swig and continued. "Now as you can see, William got a good education, opportunities left and right, all because he was a male. Judith, on the other hand, though she was just as gifted, was doomed by her gender. So much so that she ends up killing herself."

"Didn't Virginia Woolf do that, too? Kill herself, I mean?" Max asked.

"She did. And I kinda understand why. Actually Judith Shakespeare was Woolf's demon," Michal said. "May I continue?"

Phil looked down his robe. "Sure. It doesn't look like I have to change bra sizes quite yet and this is kinda interesting. So please continue, darling."

Michal and Max laughed. Michal took another swig and then handed the bottle back to Phil, whose glass was empty.

"OK, back to Judith Shakespeare. Unlike her brother, she had to stay at home. She didn't get a formal education. She had no chance of learning Latin, of reading Virgil, Ovid, and Horace. Maybe she'd pick up a book now and again, probably her brother William's. She might scribble a few ideas down on a page, when she had a bit of free time. But her mother would invariably interrupt her. Tell her to mend the stockings, mop the floor, or mind the stew on the stove. She was gifted like her brother, but it was extinguished. Patriarchal society prevented her from even achieving anything like her brother's acclaim. Everything was stacked against her, just because of her gender. It would have been impossible, completely and totally impossible, for any woman to have written Shakespeare, *in the age of Shakespeare*. From the very start, Judith was doomed to inconsequentiality."

"There were some great women writers. You know, the Brontë sisters, Jane Austen, George Eliot, George Sand, Katherine Mansfield," Max said.

"I forgot you took that Women's Lit course," Phil said.

"Oh, and I forgot one of your favorites, Michal—Sylvia Plath. Though I don't get why you like her. She's so dark," Max said.

"Michal has a dark side," Phil said.

"I *had* a dark side," Michal said. "Anyway, in the *Second Sex,* Simone de Beauvoir writes that there are no women geniuses because women don't do anything. What can they write about, if they don't experience anything? But the women you mention, Max, were much later than our imagined Judith Shakespeare. Mostly nineteenth century. Not Plath, of course."

"You know, you've got a point with all this, Michal. Whenever we open a history book and read about a witch being burned at the stake, or a woman possessed by devils or whatnot, we are likely on the trail of some lost novelist or poet. Women who didn't obey the rules and stay in their place. Makes sense," Phil said.

"You're right, Phil," Michal said. "Woolf says as much. —And suppressed philosophers, too."

"I was wondering when we'd get to that."

"Mary Ellen Waithe has documented at least sixteen women philosophers in the classical world, seventeen women philosophers from 500 to 1600, and over thirty from 1600 to 1900.[52] Some of them are well-known, like Mary Wollstonecraft, Sor Juana, or Harriet Taylor Mill. But most have been utterly disregarded by the male-dominated discipline of philosophy, as if they didn't exist or weren't important," Michal said. "And it's still pretty bad. If *I* were in charge of the canon, I'd also include Hannah Arendt and Beauvoir. I'm sure I could come up with others."

"I'd agree that historically, at least, philosophy has been a male enterprise," Phil said.

"And a misogynistic one. Much of the philosophical canon is deeply misogynistic. Many feminist philosophers have noted this. Genevieve Lloyd and Susan Bordo, for example, have pointed out that 'reason' and 'objectivity' are gendered notions. Male notions. At least in the history of philosophy," Michal said.[53]

"So now reason has a penis?" Phil asked. "What, women can't engage in reason?"

"No, that's not what I am saying, nor what they're saying. Philosophical norms like reason and objectivity are valued as male traits, in contrast with emotionality, which is likened to irrationality and associated with the feminine," Michal said. "Max, toss me the peanuts. I also want another swig of wine, Phil." They obliged.

She continued, "Canonical philosophers have had plenty to say about women's character and nature."

"Like Aristotle," Phil said. "Aristotle called the female a deformed male and he claimed to have proven it: women have fewer teeth. I love what Russell says about it. Aristotle could have just asked Mrs. Aristotle to open her mouth so he could count. But instead, he was blinded by what he thought he already knew and so he never bothered to check."

"Remember Socrates' wisdom? Socrates realized that unlike all the other folks in Athens who claimed to know what they did not know—evidently Aristotle would have been one of them—he *knew* that he knew nothing. . . . Well, actually he knew a hell of a lot," Max added.

"Historically, canonical philosophy has been explicitly misogynistic. Not just Aristotle, of course. Mary Wollstonecraft was responding to Rousseau's sexism."

"Didn't Wollstonecraft's daughter write *Frankenstein*? Mary Shelley, right?" Max said.

"Right, Max. Have you guys ever read the education of Sophie in Rousseau's *Émile*? Sophie was educated to be pleasing to men. Wollstonecraft called women 'spaniels' and 'toys,' but not because of any innate deficiency of the female mind. It was because men denied them a formal education," Michal said. "I can multiply examples of misogynistic philosophy. Much of Kant's writings are overtly sexist. The question is whether the sexism is intrinsic or extrinsic to his philosophy. Well, there are many female Kantian scholars, so I'd say that's been settled."

"But Michal, give credit to at least *some* male philosophers. . . . You know John Stuart Mill was a feminist of sorts. Didn't he write *The Subjection of Women*, arguing in favor of equality between the sexes?"

"Sure, Max, though some scholars think that his wife Harriet Taylor Mill actually wrote it. But it would never have been taken seriously were her name on it. Mill at least credits his wife with co-authoring the essay. Some of the arguments are very similar to ones she makes in her own essay *The Enfranchisement of Women*."

"I've gotta say, Michal, this discussion turned out to be more fun than I expected. Now let's go back to the bar and get something more to drink, since this bottle is empty and poor Maxie needs some tea. Then we'll talk more about that novel of yours." Phil smiled.

EIGHT

There is an old illusion. It is called good and evil.
FRIEDRICH NIETZSCHE

LATER THAT AFTERNOON. *At the RTSS*

Michal strolled past the many stone *tōrōs* and bright red and pink azaleas, which lined the wooden path leading to the teahouse. She finally sat down on a bench to read *Uncle Tom's Cabin*. As her eyes passed over the words, she heard the calls of nearby peacocks. She glanced up and noted a brilliant blue and purple peacock with his harem of peahens pecking at what looked to be a big pile of rice sitting atop an ornamented plate.

"Blue Onion china." Michal shook her head. "Why doesn't this surprise me?"

Just then Michal heard Phil's voice from close by. "I would think that after all this time few things would surprise you."

"Few things, yes," she called out, not turning to look for him. "Do you actually feed your peacocks cooked rice on Blue Onion china?" She spoke as if accusing Phil of some grave sin.

Phil appeared from behind a large, twisted old pine tree. He smiled widely. "Ah yes—they won't eat it any other way. Very sophisticated, don't you think?" He walked toward her on the wooden path. "Hey, I've got a piece of cheese in my pocket. The albino one loves it." Phil reached into his pocket and pulled out a piece of cheese, handing it to Michal with a flourish. "Here, I'll call him for you." Suddenly Phil made a loud screech, which sounded like a woman screaming. The white peacock soon appeared through the shrubs.

"I can't believe it," Michal began incredulously. "You know, I haven't seen a white peacock since the one who crossed our path in Rome. Do you remember?"

"How could I forget?"

"Did you know that peacocks symbolize immortality and white peacocks are often found in mosaics and paintings representing Jesus Christ?" Michal extended her hand, taking the cheese from Phil.

"Just put out your hand and he'll come right up to you," he whispered as the peacock cautiously walked forward.

"Where did you get him?" Michal whispered back.

"I know the right people." Phil shrugged. "What good is being eccentric if you can't have obscure animals wandering around?" He smiled. "Though I was thinking about getting a big cat. —You know, to complete the evil genius look."

Michal stifled a laugh as the peacock drew closer. Holding the cheese in her open palm, she bent over and reached out toward the bird. The peacock looked at her, then closed the distance between them, its tail-feathers trailing behind like some great wedding train. He pecked at the cheese as Phil looked on. Suddenly, the bird looked up and around, reverberations on the wooden path a harbinger of further company. The peacock snatched the cheese and dashed for the bushes.

Max approached, slurping his tea from a thermos.

"Can't you be a little quieter?" Phil jabbed. "This is supposed to be a tranquil place."

"You just missed—" Michal began with a whisper, then, realizing that she was still being quiet for no reason, she stood up and grinned. "You just missed the white peacock. He grabbed a piece of cheese right out of my hand and ran away through there." She pointed at the silver-blue juniper bush.

"Did you guys know that white peacocks represent our Savior?" Max asked.

Michal nodded. "I was just telling Phil that."

Just then, an old man in grass-stained, camel-colored coveralls walked by carrying a pair of pruning shears in one hand and a chisel in the other. Phil smiled at him and nodded. The old man smiled and nodded back.

"Who's that?" Max asked.

"My gardener," Phil said.

"Your gardener? I didn't know you had a gardener. What's his name?"

"I don't know. He doesn't speak English and he can't understand my Japanese."

"Fancy that."

"He just showed up one day with some gardening tools, so I showed him around the place."

"Well," Michal said, "your gardens are immaculate—except for that one bush where he seems to have slipped with his shears."

"I put a lot of work into it. Takes a lot of time, but I enjoy it."

"You mean your gardener doesn't do it?" Max asked.

"Oh no. He's a terrible gardener. But I need him so that my establishment— you know, my establishment that never seems to have any decent customers—can have a certain level of *respectability*. He was afraid I would fire him—I could tell by the look on his face—so he tried to make himself 'differently useful' and started chiseling stone for me. . . . You know all of my wonderful stone benches around the place? The dragon, the tiger. . . ."

"Yes—I love them," Michal said.

"Well, he didn't do those. . . . He's a horrible stonemason, too. But I just can't bring myself to fire the guy, and I need him for my image. I keep all of his 'attempts' at stone carvings in the shed. I tell him that I haven't yet found the perfect place for them. Of course, he doesn't understand me, but he smiles just the same and keeps . . . *carving*. I can show you, if you'd like. They're perfectly dreadful. —Maybe I can teach him how to do some light carpentry."

Max looked down at Michal's book. "Harriet Beecher Stowe. I haven't read that since college."

"I love it. I'm almost done. I just started a really difficult chapter though—a discussion between Cassy and Tom. Sambo and Quimbo have just beaten the shit out of Tom. Let me read what it says. . . ."

Michal opened the book and proceeded to read:

"'"There's no use calling on the Lord. He never hears," said the woman stead-ily.'" Before continuing, Michal clarified, "Cassy is speaking to Tom. . . . *"'"There isn't any God, I believe. Or if there is, he's taken sides against us. All goes against us, heaven and earth. Everything is pushing us into hell. Why shouldn't we go?'"'"*

Michal put the book on the bench and looked up at her friends, waiting for a response.

"Obviously she's having a crisis of faith and has lost patience with God. She's no Job," Max said. "I can understand that kind of attitude, though. I've had it my-self. It is a difficult thing to come face to face with *Ha-Satan* and come out of it choosing to believe in God's grace and mercy. It never seems like it's going to happen when you are in that kind of desperate situation. But that's what free will is all about, isn't it? Being faced with evil and choosing to walk the path of right-eousness and faith in God's purpose for you."

 Phil held out a hand full of rice as a peacock came over and began to eat. "*Uncle Tom's Cabin* is apropos to our discussion, since the slaves were in an un-tenable situation, like the Israelites. Slavery, subjugation to a more powerful group that imposed its will, and loss of their own traditions and culture were part of everyday life. So Job and Tom alike are tested, told to reject their beliefs. Like good people they stick to their principles. The ironic part is that Tom's reward is death, whereas we give honor and praise"—Phil looked directly at Michal—"and a whole new family and household to Job. . . . Maybe the God of the Old Testament isn't quite such a bastard after all." Phil sneered at Max, while brushing the pea-cock gently aside.

"Are you saying that the evil that Legree inflicted on Tom and the evil done to Job are equivalent?" Max sat down on a large rock across from the bench, his hand absently feeling the rough texture and coldness of the stone. "I get that they both could be seen as obstacles to the believer's faith in God. I might think that Uncle Tom had a better time of it, since his death presumably brought him into the presence of God, while Job had to wait around and remember all the evil he'd endured."

"Let me have you think on that, while I go get myself a drink in the teahouse," Phil said. "Besides it looks like it's going to rain." Our three friends walked along the path toward the teahouse adjacent to the main building.

"Do you think that your God sits in the clouds, contemplating all of the evil that He has done?" Phil asked, pointing accusingly skyward as they stood in front of the teahouse. "Or perhaps He doesn't consider it to be evil. . . . Or perhaps even more evil awaits us in the afterlife."

They walked through the teahouse door. Phil reached behind the bar for some sake cups and a bottle of Junmai.

"That's interesting," Max said.

"Yes, it is," Michal said. "Usually he just ignores our talk about the afterlife. What's gotten into him, I wonder?"

Max brushed off a bit of stray moss from his pants and took the barstool next to Phil. *What could Phil be thinking?*

"Phil, God does not think about the evil He has done, since He is not the one committing the evil. He merely created it, or more accurately, created the possibilities for evil to exist. . . . Once again, though," Max said, "it looks like I need to remind you that there is no evil in the afterlife, since the afterlife is full communion with God."

Phil stared off into space. "You don't see that as obvious, I suppose."

"What exactly is obvious, Phil?" Max rested his chin in his hands and eyed the edamame pods sitting in a blue ceramic bowl on the counter.

"Two things. First, that your God is complicit in the creation of evil, since He created all the circumstances necessary for evil, and B—" Phil winked. "Don'tcha hate when people mix their numbering systems? —And B, not only is evil possible in order for God's little free-will experiment to be of any use whatsoever, but evil must necessarily take place. Otherwise it is simply an unrealized alternative."

"Humans are flawed creatures, Phil, through-and-through, and though I hate to invoke this, I have to believe that this aspect of things is part of God's good plan." Max pointed his finger at Phil. "Don't say it. . . ."

"Without getting into specifics, let's just say that if the purpose of God's free-will experiment is to show people that there are right and wrong choices and those choices have consequences, then at least some poor slob is going to have to make a wrong choice to act as an example." Phil uncorked the sake bottle and poured it into two cups, extending one to Michal. "Otherwise, we might as well remove the possibility of choice. Everyone will do the right thing, knowing that the alternative is evil, and we shouldn't do *that* because it's, well, evil. . . . But then we have no free will after all, do we? In order for free will to have any meaning whatsoever, the subjects in the experiment *must* see the consequences. Thus God would have to accept that there would be some, if not a great deal of, evil." Phil downed the sake in one swallow. "Therefore God created not just the possibility of evil, but its *necessity.*"

Michal heard the door open and turned to look. A single patron walked up to the bar and hopped up on a stool. He was a one-armed man wearing a dusty green work shirt. Likely from a local farm, he smelled of sewer water or rotting fish. Michal wrinkled her nose then turned away to look directly at Phil and Max. Phil noted the patron and poured him a cup of sake. "This what you want?" He smiled and turned back to his friends.

"As you often do, Phil, you make a good point. However, how can you know the will of God? How can you know what He considers to be evil? Only God knows."

"You're exactly right, Max. We keep trying to put God into a knowable scope, but by definition God is unknowable. Here we are talking about God doing evil or whatnot when 'good' and 'evil' are man-made constructs. God isn't bound by our finite definitions," Phil said.

"And our attempt to bind finite definitions to God limits Him to the realm of the finite, which is impossible, since God is infinite," Max said. "The Neoplatonists, like Plotinus, argue that God exceeds *all categories* of finite thought. And remember what the medieval Jewish philosopher Moses Maimonides, or Rambam, said in his *Guide for the Perplexed:* while we can know by argument *that* God is, this does not entitle us to say anything about *what* God is. We can only know what God *isn't*. We can only describe God through negative attributes."

"Wait, wait, wait. . . ." Michal said.

"What?" Max asked.

"First of all, the politically correct term is *human-made* constructs." She smirked. "But Max, how can you believe in an Omni God and yet claim that He created evil? I know what you are going to say: God created evil insofar as He created humans with free will. Evil enters into the world as punishment, because of Adam and Eve's disobedience, and then evil continues, because of either evil use or misuse of our God-given free will. Of course this doesn't explain so-called 'natural' evils like floods, tornados, earthquakes, and the like, which aren't even evils in my book."

"Let's get right to the point: God is *the Omni God* and therefore created everything," Phil insisted, "including all pain and misery." He thumbed at his chest, pantomiming a knife. "Of course, that has problems too, but you get the point. —Michal, are you ignoring what Max and I just said about trying to put God into a knowable scope?"

"Well, if we're actually going to follow *those* rules, our conversations would be quite short and not nearly as much fun."

"You've got us there," Phil said.

"To your point about evil and free will," Max began. "That's not exactly right, Michal. Remember Iranaeus? God is the origin of everything. God is everything. God is omniscient, omnipotent, and omnipresent. But God is not omni-benevolent. Not only is that thought illogical, there are just too many examples in the Bible that contradict that statement. —Well, at least according to many Christians, who would cite Isaiah 45:7, '*I form the light, and create darkness. I make peace, and create evil. I the Lord do all these things.*' Or how about Deuteronomy 30:15, Lamentations 3:38, Ecclesiastes 7:14, and several more? It is very clear that God created everything, including evil. Iranaeus said that God created *children.* Adam and Eve were children. God wanted humans to take a long time to develop into godly, moral beings. And so He made the world a very difficult—and I dare say *evil*—place so that His children could learn moral lessons and become more god-like. —I guess the word 'calamity' or 'adversity' fits these contexts better than 'evil,'" Max corrected himself. He swirled the dregs of his green tea in the thermos cup and emptied it in one swallow.

Michal looked at Max incredulously. "So God is not omnibenevolent? Max, this is a terrifying God. Indeed, the most terrifying of gods. He's certainly not one worthy of worship. And this makes you a heretic, too, Max. Throughout history, philosophers and theologians, in discussing the problem of evil, have invoked God's three Omni characteristics: How can an all-knowing, all-powerful, and all-loving God permit evil? If God is all-knowing, He knows about the evil. If He is all-powerful, He can stop it, and if He is all-loving, He *wants* to stop it. So God can't be all three and evil still exist. Of course, I agree with you that if we take the words of the Bible to accurately describe God's character and actions, then He is implicated in evil—too much evil for me to love and accept Him, *if* He's truly like that. He would be bipolar and sadistic to the extreme. I can give you numerous examples, which I am sure you already know. There are plenty in the Old Testament, of course, and we've discussed a few of them already, including how God ruthlessly punishes the Israelites for apostasy and idolatry, and how He commands the Israelites to slaughter every living thing in sight when they conquer a people, including innocent women, children, and even animals. Doesn't this go against the sixth of the Ten Commandments? As nineteenth-century Argentinian philosopher Alejandro Korn said, the author of this commandment must have been a very *word-minded person*. What the sixth commandment should have said—but it would have taken up too much room on the tablet—is: 'You should not kill, unless you are a warrior, a judge, or a priest. You should not kill, except for members of another tribe. You should not kill, except for those who profess a different god. You should not kill, except in defense of your life, your honor, or your property. . . . ,'"[54]

"And to make a similar point, how is Deuteronomy 20:17 any different from Hitler's Final Solution?" Phil asked.

"It wasn't only *Hitler's* Final Solution, Phil. It required the best efforts of millions of Germans of every stripe: from businessmen to doctors to factory workers—butchers, bakers, and candlestick makers," Michal said. "Both are a weighing of evils. But let's first look at Deuteronomy. You can't just abstract 20:17 without looking at what's around it. God has given the Israelites their promised land. He tells them to completely destroy every living, breathing thing, because otherwise the conquered people will teach them to follow the evil ways of their gods and the Israelites will sin against the one true God. Both are evils, but it's evidently more evil to engage in apostasy and idolatry than to annihilate a people. —But I don't believe for a second that God really said this. This is the ancient Israelites' way of trying to understand their history. And in fact, they didn't slaughter everyone. They intermarried, they committed idolatry, and their asses were thoroughly kicked by the Babylonians. Now about the Final Solution: This, too, was a weighing of evils, at least in Hitler's warped mind. Before the war, Hitler blamed international Jewish financiers for the world's economic troubles and claimed they would plunge the nations into another war. Hitler said that the only way to stop this imminent disaster was to annihilate the Jewish people. I suppose that the same kind of sick logic was used when we decided to drop the bomb on Hiroshima. Or the way Stalin treated his own people: *'U nas mnogo lyudey'*—'We have many people, who cares?' Anyway, back to Biblical examples of God's sadism." She smiled. "I know that was a bit longwinded. —Let's look at what the gospels say about Jesus, in case you think that God is only evil in the Old Testament. Remember the pigs and the fig? Jesus casts demons into pigs that run off a cliff and die. What did those poor pigs do to deserve that—?"

"Wait a minute, Michal. I think you may have just run the facts around the barn," Max chided. "Hitler hated and persecuted the Jews, financiers and otherwise, long before the Second World War. After all, *Mein Kampf* was published as early as 1925. But it wasn't until the second half of 1941—after Germany invaded the Soviet Union—that Hitler's number-two, Hermann Göring, ordered a 'complete solution of the Jewish problem.' The Nazis didn't implement the Final Solution to try to *prevent* a war. In fact, the outbreak of war allowed them to widen their persecution of the Jews far beyond Germany itself, and to set about eliminating *all* the Jews in Europe—and especially the millions of Jews in Eastern Europe who until then were largely beyond their grasp."

"*You* wait a minute, Max. What I've given you are the *facts,* exactly as my Jewish grandfather told me when I was a little girl," Michal huffed.

"Whoa, Michal!" Phil interrupted. "Appealing to authority does not make something true. If that were the case, Hitler might have been able to claim the high road because of his support from Nietzsche—well, Nietzsche's Nazi sister."

"Phil, I know what I know. You have to accept—"

"Michal, I don't have to accept anything, except the truth. I would love to be able to trust the firsthand account of your neighbor's brother's hair-stylist's dog-groomer's venerable grandfather. But we've agreed that we're searching for *truth.*"

Michal opened her mouth to protest, but before she could Phil cut her off. "Besides, I wanted to take your side."

Michal gave him a quizzical look.

"What Max said about the *real* history still doesn't change the point. The point is that Hitler had his motivations, which he thought justified his horrible actions. Just as Truman had his motivations, and Mengele had his motivations, and if I may be so bold"—Phil reached for the sake bottle—"just as your all-mighty God has *His* motivations to justify *His* evils."

Max laughed. "Hey, what do you know, we've gone off on a tangent again. Can we get back to Jesus? He had just cast out a legion of demons from a demoniac. They had to go *somewhere*. And unfortunately for the pigs—"

"Lame," countered Michal. "Jesus casts out demons all over the place in the gospels and this is the only time He casts them into other living beings. Jesus is God. He doesn't have to do that. He could have cast them into oblivion like all the others. But there's a better explanation for the pig story. Jesus likely didn't do this at all. Remember, Jesus encounters a demoniac. And when the demoniac sees Jesus, he addresses Him: 'What have you to do with me, Son of the Most High God?' When Jesus asks him his name, the guy says, 'My name is Legion, for we are many.' Now you guys know this: a legion was a division of about five thousand troops of the Roman military who would conquer and then occupy a country. Jesus casts the legion into pigs—unclean animals—that charge into the sea and are destroyed. The author of Mark is invoking an incredible militaristic image here. Doesn't this remind you of something? —Moses and the destruction of Pharaoh's army in the Exodus deliverance.[55] Of course, Exodus 15—the so-called 'Song of the Sea,' which celebrates Yahweh's drowning of the Egyptian chariots in the Red Sea—recounts a mythical event, a fable that the Israelites likely told about how they were no longer under the all-powerful Egypt's oppressive thumb. You know, many Jews believed that the messianic figure would deliver Jews from Roman oppression, just as Moses had with the Egyptians, or Cyrus of Persia with the Babylonians. It's no wonder so many of Jesus' followers deserted Him at the end. He disappointed their messianic hopes. . . . But let's turn to that poor fig tree. It wasn't the season for fruit, but Jesus is hungry, throws a temper tantrum, and curses and kills an innocent tree."

Max chimed in again: "C'mon, Michal, as you know, Jesus was using this as a teachable moment: those who do not produce good fruit will not inherit the Kingdom of God."

Phil couldn't help adding his two bits. "I think Michal is making a good case that Jesus, at least as depicted in the gospels—and by the way, *that's all we've got to go on*—is a pretty cruel guy. And don't forget all His talk about hell-fire and torture. We've mentioned this before. I love that parable in Matthew where Jesus talks about the king who demands ten thousand talents from one of his subjects. One talent was more than fifteen years' wages for an average laborer! The subject begs the king to forgive him his debt and the king, feeling sorry for the guy, does. But then the guy goes to his buddy who owes him only one hundred denarii. That's not much at all, compared to what he owed the king. A denarius was only a day's wages. His buddy can't pay him back, so the guy throws him in prison. The king hears about this and takes the guy whom he had forgiven the ten thousand talents and *tortures* him. The really fucked-up part of this story is when Jesus says that 'this is what my heavenly Father will do to you, if you do not forgive your brother.'"

"Yeah, that's pretty extreme," Michal said. "So all of us who have ever harbored a grudge, for example, will be *tortured* by our *Loving Father*. Nope, I can't accept that Jesus said this. But I want to add one more thing about Max's version of the Omni God. . . . Max, you say that God is Omni everything, except omni-benevolent, and claim that this is supported by scripture?"

"Right."

"Well, I argue that scripture suggests that God is *not Omni anything*. Let's start with God's omnipotence. You say that God is omnipotent and He created everything."

"I did say that."

"Look at Genesis 1. The first creation story. God does not create everything. He does not create out of nothing. He creates out of *found stuff*: watery chaos. Who created the watery chaos? Did God create it earlier, then got bored, came back to it, and decided to create something more spectacular from it?"

"Oh, I am loving this," Phil relished.

"And regarding omniscience, just consider what God says right before He destroys the earth with a flood. —Another evil act, by the way, since God drowns many innocents, including animals. Don't tell me that absolutely everybody was evil except for Noah and Mrs. Noah. Genesis says that the Lord was sorry that He made humankind. He says that He will obliterate all the people and all the animals—except for Noah and his family and the pairs of animals in the ark—since He was sorry that He had made them. This suggests that when God created humans, He did not know that they would disappoint Him so much."

"God does not foresee, He sees all at once in His Unbounded Now," Max explained. "So He must have seen that tremendous goodness would result in the end."

"But then why did He say He was sorry?" Michal asked.

"This all goes to show that we can't trust what's in the Bible," Phil said.

"You know the Gnostics had a different understanding of all this. Our world began by a mistake. The creator of our world wanted to make it perfect, but he failed. Some would say *'she failed'*—it was the goddess Wisdom, or Sophia, who was tasked with creating the world." Michal said. "There's also the pretty persuasive argument that the universe cannot be perfect, because otherwise it would be coextensive with God. So it must have defects, and we call those defects 'evil.'"

"But then why so many defects? Why so many dents and dings?" Phil asked.

"Can we get back to my main point already?" Max began. "About God creating evil? I have a good argument for it."

Michal and Phil nodded. "Go on."

"Thank you. *FINALLY.* . . ." he said in mock-exasperation. "Why did God create evil? That is the important thing. I look at it this way. Without evil, free will is meaningless. It's an illusion. There is nothing for us to choose between, nothing for us to strive for or against. It follows then, that evil, like free will, was God's greatest gift to us before the gift of His Son. I do not believe that evil exists only in the hearts of men. Evil is all around us, in stimuli that we must respond to, righteously or not. *That* is the gift—the choice to do so. Besides, God created evil before the fall of Adam and Eve. In Genesis, wasn't the Tree created before humans were? Third day versus sixth day."

"First of all, Max," Michal began, "God did not create the Tree of Knowledge before man, if that is indeed what you are referring to. You need to look at the second creation story, not the first, since the second creation story is the one that discusses Adam and Eve. The second creation story says that *on the day* that God created the heavens and the earth, and before any plant had sprung from the earth, God formed man from the dust of the ground. And *then* He planted a garden in Eden, and there He planted the Trees of Life and of Good and Evil. *Then* He put the man in the garden. But you can still argue that evil existed before the fall of Adam and Eve, since God placed the serpent in the garden and it was the serpent who tempted them to sin."

"I have no problem agreeing with you on this point, Michal," Phil began. "There are two contradictory creation stories in the Bible from two different sources, the so-called 'E' or Elohim source, and the 'J' or Yahweh source. So your argument has been weakened, Max, and both of your arguments for the Biblical god are weaker as well, because, yet again, we have found inherent contradictions. You are either forced to accept both stories, or accept that the contradictions are further evidence that the Bible is not of, from, inspired, or even remotely *about* God."

"How does that follow, Phil?" Max asked. "The Bible was written by fallible men, that's true. It's also true that many cultural and political influences are part of it and color the content. But the true message of scripture is clear and we must take these passages and filter them through logic, reason, and our own understanding. We can argue all day about conflicting minutiae within any text."

"Couldn't God have created humans who have free will but who always choose the good?" Michal asked.

"The gentleman from Japan would like to request that he be able to field the question for the gentleman from Texas." Phil gestured in a deep bow toward Max, flourishing his hand in Max's direction.

Max smiled and nodded. "So yielded to the gentleman from Japan."

"We spoke about this before, but essentially that would be no choice at all. If you grant that we are destined to have free will, then we must have a choice and that choice must be an actual choice, a real honest-to-God choice." Phil chuckled. "I'll borrow some words from A.J. Ayer here. I would say that we likely agree that things that are empirically verifiable 'hold more degree of confirmation' than things that are not. Any kind of God-talk, either for or against His existence, *since unverifiable*, is literally nonsense. —At least in Ayer's mind."[56]

"You do know that Ayer claimed to have had a near-death experience. He claimed to have seen God. He even said that he'd have to rethink his whole philosophy because of it," Michal said.

"I don't buy it," Phil said.

"I won't take you to task for invoking Ayer, since others have already done that work for me. But I will agree that events that we experience hold more weight than those we consider or imagine." Michal gave a little smile. "At least for me. But even still, what about this: Your argument suggests that good cannot exist without evil. That evil is a necessary counterpart to good. But doesn't this limit God's omnipotence? For there is something that God cannot do. He cannot create good without evil. But let's suppose you are right. That God had to create evil, so that humans could choose good. To learn lessons, as Max would say. But then why so *much* evil? There are so many horrible, horrible human evils. And what about so-called natural evils? Like I said, Max's free will defense doesn't work here. —But I can't even go with you this far, for we can exercise our free will all day long without ever having to choose between good and evil. I can choose between two goods or between something good and something morally neutral, and so on. Surely you are not saying that evil is necessary in order to *recognize* good? What is the real added value in recognizing good? Perhaps we need evil to always be threatening the good—you know, to make life more interesting. Or so said Alan Watts. —Well, that's fucked-up."

"The only way to eliminate all of these horrible evils that you speak of, Michal, or even significantly reduce evil, is for God to restrict free will. But that effectively turns us into mindless sycophants. And although it solves the problem of evil, it destroys the primary reason for God creating humans in the first place. That is, so that we can *choose* to love him." Max caught himself beginning to raise his hand, palm up. "Some Christians have suggested that God *has* restricted evil by limiting the human lifespan to one hundred and twenty years, so that evil people can't live very long, and that God can't do any better than this, since evil begins in our hearts and minds."

Phil poured himself some more sake, rolling the cup between his hands, watching as the liquid swirled. "I can see your point about choosing, though I still don't agree that's His only goal. However, I think we'll all agree that limiting our lifespan so that we can screw up only so long is bordering on some new brand of cruelty. At least *that* Omni He got right: Omni-cruel." Phil sipped at the sake. "Or as I like to put it, God's a dick."

Michal frowned at Phil, and then turned to Max. "I just can't agree with you, Max, that God is responsible for evil. Although you know in the Qur'an God did create evil spirits, the jinn, before He created men, from the fire of scorching wind. Jinn have free will. The jinn Iblīs refused to bow down to Adam, as God demanded that he do. Because of his disobedience, God expels Iblīs from Paradise, and he is called 'Shaytān' or 'Satan.' Sound like a familiar story?" She winked. "Anyway, I could go all Manichaean on you and argue that there exist two equally Omni but opposing forces: one omnipotent and omnibenevolent, God, and the other omnipotent but omnimalevolent, like Descartes' evil demon. But I'm not inclined to believe that. I could go Augustinian on you, and say that evil does not really exist as a positive quality, but is only a privation or corruption of goodness, the absence of goodness. But I know that evil is real. I have experienced it. I believe in both demons and angels. . . . I just can't explain it."

"So you admit that you can't explain evil?" Phil smirked. "Have you ever read James Morrow's novel *Blameless in Abaddon?* Morrow invokes Manichaeanism to help us understand the morality of God."

"I read that novel," Max said. "A small-town justice of the peace, Martin Candle, decides to have God tried by the World Court at The Hague for crimes against humanity."

"Right, Maxie. After a series of personal tragedies—including painful metastatic prostate cancer and the death of his wife in a freak automobile accident involving a runaway Irish setter and some ravenous termites"—Phil took a deep exaggerated breath and then continued—"Candle, very much like Job, decides that humanity needs to call God into account. He calls attention to many of the lesser-known horrors of human history in his indictment."

"So have *you* ever felt the desire to suck on the ears of a hippopotamus?" Max asked. Phil laughed out loud.

"What?" Michal's face was confused.

"Isn't that what St. Augustine asks Candle?" Max asked.

"It is," Phil said with a laugh. "Concupiscence—it does us all in."

"Some of us more than others." Michal laughed. "Sounds like I should get my hands on this book."

"It's offensive, Michal. Blasphemous to the extreme," Max said. "Perverse." He shook his head.

"When *I* do offensive, I like to wrap it up in a pretty silk bow," Phil said with a smirk.

"You don't always succeed," Michal said. "Anyway, I'd like to get that book."

"Especially for Morrow's use of Manichaeanism, as I said. That's the big bombshell at the end of the novel. Since God is omnipotent and infinite, there can't be another infinite being opposing Him. If there were, then God would be less than omnipotent. It makes more sense to understand that God is *both* infinitely good and infinitely evil. He must be, in order to encompass everything," Phil said. "God has a dark side. A radically evil side. As Jesus—now the Devil—

says to Candle, 'I am what I am. I am Christ and Antichrist, God and Satan, Heaven and Hiroshima, Arcadia and Auschwitz.'"

"And remember what Jesus says in Revelation 22:13: 'I am the Alpha and the Omega,'" Max said. "God must have *all* the opposing qualities."

"So when we praise God, we are praising His benevolent aspects, but when we denounce a disaster, say, or a devastating illness, we are rejecting God's vindictive nature. Arcadia and Auschwitz. . . ." Michal said with a shudder. "Hmmm. . . . I'm not sure about this. This isn't really a God I'd like to believe in."

"It's the only God I *could* believe in, Michal," Phil said. "If there is a God, the only logical explanation is that He is both infinitely good and infinitely evil."

"Hang on a second," Michal began. "Maybe it's not so logical after all, Phil." She paused and then smiled. "I need to channel my old lover, the math prof—" She closed her eyes.

"Is he dead?" Max asked.

"No. He's not dead, he's in Denver." Michal grinned. "Bear with me as I work this out. —The argument that since God is infinite He must encompass everything is weak. An infinite being doesn't have to be infinitely everything. We can understand this with sets. There are infinitely many integers. There are infinitely many coordinates of points on a line, and still infinitely many of them are *not integers*. . . . Or consider this: if God encompasses everything, that means He has infinitely many attributes, but then God does *not* encompass everything, because He does not have the attribute *of not having attributes*. . . . Or what about this: if God encompasses everything, then He is His own attribute. He encompasses Himself, who is encompassing Himself, who is encompassing Himself, *ad infinitum*. . . . I guess that might not be a problem. He *has* to encompass Himself, because if God does not encompass Himself then He does not encompass everything. Anyway. . . ."

"That was a bit of mental masturbation," Phil laughed. "Do you need to clean up after that? —But seriously, Michal, God doesn't follow our logic. Or, rather, He isn't confined by our logic. God has His own logic. He gets to make up any rules He pleases. He gets to make shit up as He goes."

"If God encompasses everything, then we can capture Him by enumerating an infinite set of attributes that He possesses. So God is pink and He is not pink. He likes to hike and He doesn't like to hike. He loves chocolate-covered ants and He hates them. But this makes no sense," Michal said.

"This is all so ridiculous, it just goes to show that God does not exist," Phil said.

"I'm not sure I'm wrapping my head around all of this," Max said, a bit befuddled.

"Sorry, Max," Michal said laughing. "Back to my original point. I know that evil is real. And I just can't bring myself to believe that God is responsible for it."

"I have also experienced evil, Michal. I know that it is real. I don't deny that in the least. I just disagree with you about its origins," Max said, then added: "Thanks for getting us off of that logic ride. It was giving me extreme vertigo."

"And I believe in the tooth fairy and the Easter bunny," Phil said.

"Nice, Phil." Max's words, dripping with sarcasm, only inspired a smile from his friend. Max lifted the thermos to the light and stared at the empty cylinder. He walked behind the bar to look for a tea kettle. He finally found one in a box on a shelf. He pulled it out, filled it with water and plugged it in, then returned to his stool.

"How about the Flying Spaghetti Monster?" Phil asked. "Remember Bobby Henderson's 2005 open letter to protest the Kansas State Board of Education's decision to teach intelligent design? Well, I am a Pastafarian. Actually, a *Rastafarian Pastafarian.* I've been a member of the Church of the Flying Spaghetti Monster since 2006. I can even quote from Henderson's Gospel *and* sing Bob Marley's *Three Little Birds* at the same time." Phil opened an imaginary book and began turning pages while singing, in perfect pitch, "Don't worry about a thing. . . ."

"Phil, you make fun because you have never directly experienced angels and demons. Well, you think I have a mind, don't you? And a pretty sharp one, if I say so myself," Michal said. "Yet you have never seen my mind, nor heard it, nor touched it, nor smelled it. Indeed, you have never perceived my mind at all—or anyone else's mind, for that matter. And so by your own logic I have no mind. Indeed, no minds exist outside of your own."

"I have an answer to that, Michal. Actually, I have to give credit to Augustine here. He argued against this solipsistic thinking. He said that I can observe bodies external to mine that behave just as I behave, and so by analogy, I am justified in believing that these bodies have a similar mental life to my own.[57] —Now I want to be very clear here. I am not saying that this is absolutely verifiable, but it is a belief backed up by at least some good observations and good logic." Phil gave a wry smile. "But to your point about minds, I don't believe that any *minds* exist, but I do believe in the observable brain, which acts very much like our concept of a mind. If you ask me though, I think most of the planet is bereft of minds. People are just drones who react to stimuli in the most simple manner. That's our planet: mindless drones asleep at the wheel. Or zombies," Phil said, looking despondent.

Michal shook her head. "But to your point, Max, if Phil will allow us to be serious again. If I'm going to accept anything like free will, and I'm not saying I do, then I would side with the process theologians. They argue that God is not omnipotent in this sense: He cannot be coercive. He cannot force His will on us. This would be against His all-good nature. But He can divinely nudge us. Woo us. However, since He does not play a coercive role, He does not stop us when we do evil, even though it pains Him very much when we do."

"How does that square with Psalm 139:5, *'you hem me in, behind and before'*? Or do process theologians deny that this part of the Bible is accurate and/or inspired? It would seem that if we're to go with what the Bible says, God is quite coercive." Phil crossed his arms. "But just like the many other myths you hold dear, you're welcome to believe in whatever you wish." Phil walked behind the bar and poured himself a glass of Buillet, watching as the ice cubes clicked together, then took a long drink. "I need to switch to something a bit more appropriate for this discussion. . . ."

"First of all, Phil, you misunderstand that psalm—at least the way it speaks to me. What do you think it means to be hemmed in by God? I don't know whether your mother ever taught you how to sew, but a hem is sewn into fabric to keep it from unraveling. God has hemmed me in so that I don't completely fall apart," Michal explained. "In any case, as I've already said, I don't really believe that the Bible is accurate or divinely inspired. . . . Well, perhaps divinely inspired insofar as *some* men who loved God very much were inspired, by their love, to write some of the words that they did. But in terms of being accurate—I believe that much of what is written in the Bible is politically or superstitiously motivated, or written out of plain ignorance, and so on. At best, we have a historical glimpse at the figure of Jesus, which, of course, helps to show us God's character, as well as glimpses at Paul, Jesus' brother James, and perhaps Peter."

"How can you even say this, Michal? Since you've already rejected many things that Jesus said and did, in what sense can you discern the historical Jesus from the made-up Jesus, as you suggest?" Max then looked at Phil, noting his upturned lips and the humorous light in his eyes.

"I'm going to win this argument," Phil said. "Imagine this scenario. You have a teenage daughter who wants to go to a dance. You know that if she goes alone, she will be raped by a group of boys. Wouldn't you prevent her from going? Tie her up in her bedroom, if that's what it takes? You, being a loving parent, certainly wouldn't let her go, would you? Nor would you simply say, 'Honey, do not go to the dance, because some mean boys will hurt you.' She's a teenager, for crying out loud. She wouldn't listen. No nudging on your part could convince her to stay home. . . . But suppose you did let her go because her angelic pleas were so irresistible that you just couldn't say 'no.' Wouldn't you secretly follow her to the dance and as soon as the boys began to rape her wouldn't you jump in and rescue your daughter? You would certainly find no comfort were you to stay home instead and enjoy that third glass of wine, even if you knew the boys would be hit by a Mack truck on their way home as punishment for their sins, and you had One Direction concert tickets waiting for your daughter to make up for what had happened."

Michal and Max looked at each other and then at Phil, seemingly at a loss for words.

"You two have nothing to say? Was it that easy? Come on—I want to hear your responses. Here, Michal, a drink will help. Perhaps Dionysus will inspire you. . . . Max, this is my teahouse, but I don't have anything non-alcoholic to offer you. Not surprisingly, *my* teahouse is remarkably sparse in tea." Phil smiled at Max and took a slug of whiskey.

Max went behind the bar to pour hot water into his thermos cup. "Thanks, Phil, but I can get my own tea." He pulled a teabag from his shirt pocket and placed it in the water. Darjeeling this time—he needed something stronger for this discussion.

"Phil, I can see where you are going with this one, but really, I thought you knew your Biblical references better. God was put in almost this exact situation. Let's combine John 3:16 with Romans 5:9: God so loved the world that He gave His only Son and while we were still sinners Christ died for us. . . . God knew the horrific things that were going to happen to His only Son, but He also knew that Christ needed to decide of His own free will to walk down that pathway. God even sent the Adversary to tempt Him. But Christ chose to be stalwart in the face of temptation, chose to give His life, chose to do God's will. In John 10:17 and 18, Christ says of His own life that 'No one takes it from me, but I lay it down of my own accord. I have power to lay it down, and I have power to take it up again.'" Max turned away from Phil. "Michal, I must ask you, would you agree that Christ's sacrifice on the cross demonstrated God's love for us? God's most poignant example of a loving sacrifice? That, by His example, we can understand the depths of God's love for us and the extent to which we may be called to walk that path of righteousness?"

"God's greatest act of love was becoming a human in the person of Jesus, and teaching us how to love Him and each other by showing us, really *demonstrating* to us through His actions, such tremendous love. Jesus' *life* is more important than His death." Michal looked around the teahouse gathering her thoughts, watching them dance in the smoke wafting from the fireplace.

"Hang on, Michal—not so fast. Animals know how to love. Animals know how to love without knowing a whit about God—or Jesus, for that matter. Don't tell me that Buster and Barney don't love you. A dog's unconditional love is the paradigmatic example of love. If only we all loved each other in the way our dogs love us. I dare say that the world would be a far less evil place," Phil said.

"Yes, but—" It was clear that Michal was scrambling. Phil was right, of course. She decided to change the subject: "I know you'll scream 'heretic' here, but I just don't think that Jesus' sacrifice was necessary, Max. We are reconciled to God through His entering into this world. —I've got a really cute idea. So cute that I'm hoping to get it published somewhere. Here it is: All this sacrifice talk is not God-imposed, but created by humans and, I dare say, greedy Israelite priests who wanted to fatten their coffers and keep people in their places. I can say this, of course, since I've stated that the Bible is not the word of God but of men. Mostly powerful, greedy men. Yes, Jesus died on the cross and He was resurrected in order to conquer death, the greatest of evils, I guess. But we needn't interpret His crucifixion as sacrifice. Ancient Israelites thought that they could reconcile themselves to God by offering an unblemished female goat or sheep, or if they were too poor, two turtle doves or pigeons. I suppose God looked down and was saddened by all of this sacrifice and He wanted to put an end to it. So He died on the cross: *No more need to sacrifice, guys. Try to top the sacrifice of God.... You can't!*'

Max stared at Michal. "And you're a Christian how—?" He let his question hang there before continuing. "No matter, you're in good company. Many Christians don't believe in the whole word of God, in the Bible, but follow many of its tenets. So let's stick to the idea that the Bible is a set of guidelines or a road map to living a virtuous life. Not exactly a GPS but a general description." He paused and looked at Michal.

"We don't need that GPS to show us how to live," Phil said. "Haven't we already got a little angel sitting on one shoulder, whispering into our ear?" He laughed.

"Ah, but we've got a little devil sitting on our other shoulder, and he's shouting 'Concupiscence,'" Michal said and laughed.

"In any case, that little angel, that little devil, it's just our own minds talking to us," Phil said. "More trustworthy than your so-called Holy Book, especially since if you read it carefully enough it seems to justify *anything.*"

"For the sake of argument, Max," Michal began, ignoring Phil, "though what you're saying about the Bible being a good road map to living a good life is pretty sketchy, we'll go with it. But only for the sake of argument. —God definitely does speak to us using the words of the so-called divinely inspired but politically motivated, privileged, misogynistic writers.... You know, Beauvoir recognized the function of patriarchal religion as a legitimizer of male power. In her *Second Sex* she says that 'Man enjoys the great advantage of having a god endorse the code he writes, and since man exercises a sovereign authority over woman, it is *especially fortunate* that this authority has been vested in him by the Supreme Being.'" Michal glared dubiously at Max as if he were trying to pull the red queen from her ear to get a payout.

"Now that's the old skeptic I knew before. I'm glad to see she's still hiding in there behind that layer of faith," Phil smirked.

"That's enough out of you, unbeliever."

"Waiting for my houris to deflower," Phil said with a leering grin.

"If I may continue?" Max half-laughed at his two friends.

"Before you do—" Michal piped in. She gave Phil a serious look. "I know you like to poke fun and that you're an equal opportunity asshole but I'm tired of people, and especially so-called Christians, who demonize the Qur'an without even knowing what's in it."

"Michal, I'm equal opportunity in my scorn for religions of all stripes, but now are you going to say that I'm ignorant as well?" Phil looked genuinely hurt. "That would make me no better than those I target. Of course I'm aware of how loving, kind, and tolerant the Qur'an is. Muslims, Jews, Christians, Sabians—another monotheistic religious community—will all have their reward with God. After all, they worship the *same* God. God is the ally of all of those who believe and do good. Whoever rejects false gods and believes in the one true God, as revealed by His messengers, some of whom He favored above others—including Jesus, by the way—will be brought out of the depths of darkness and into the light. Now if that isn't love, kindness, and religious tolerance, what is? But so many religions on this planet feature a big, rainbow-swirl lollipop or a re-do waiting in the afterlife. Christians and Muslims have heaven or Paradise, pagans enjoy an ale in the Summerlands before coming back, and Buddhists hit Nirvana or get back on the bike. Hell, even Vikings have their feast in the halls of Vallhalla."

Max choked out a laugh while Michal—oblivious to Phil being of the same mind—began to wag her finger at him. "As my colleague, Justin, likes to say—you know, the *lamp guy?*—there seems to be an inverse correlation between extreme, shrill denunciations of *x*, and actual knowledge of *x*.... Do you even know how loving and accepting the Qur'an is, especially toward the so-called People of the Book—Jews and Christians? —Certainly compared to the xenophobic Hebrew

Bible. Of course, it also blames many of them for killing prophets and leading others astray. But that's true, isn't it? Yet God tells Muslims to overlook this and pardon them. It even says that Jesus was created like Adam. God said 'Be' and He Was. Muslims accept that Jesus was born of the Virgin Mary, a messenger of God to the children of Israel, who healed the blind and the leper, who brought the dead back to life, whom God took up and raised to Himself. Of course, God warns the People of the Book not to overstep the bounds of truth. I bet you didn't know all that. . . . So I'd stop with all that bullshit about the houris."

"Michal, are you OK?" Max asked softly.

Michal stared at the ceiling as if in thought, then looked back at Max and Phil, a bit teary-eyed. When she finally calmed down, she said, "I'm fine. It's—just a hot button topic of mine. Certainly you both understand that." She recovered some of her playfulness with a little smile.

"Michal, you can't deny that houris are in the Qur'an as a reward to the faithful." Phil made an arrogant face.

Max rubbed his temples, then covered his eyes with his hands. "Just give it a rest, Phil." He put down his hands and smiled, eyes bright. "Anyway, let's get back to our discussion. Would you both agree that, according to the Bible, the gift of free will is also a demonstration of God's love for man? And that Christ, made flesh, exercised this free will and chose to do God's will?"

"If I am forced to accept your set-up, then yes, according to the Bible that follows," Michal said. "But I don't agree with your premises. However, for the sake of argument, Max, I'll continue to go along with you"—Michal looked at Max suspiciously—"for now."

Max removed the tea bag and set it on a napkin. He took a sip of the spicy-flowery tea and looked directly at Michal. "How can we exercise our Father's gift of free will, if He did not also create evil to give us a true choice? Either free will is an illusion, or God created both—and created both with a purpose. In order to be worthy in God's eyes, must we not also choose the path of righteousness as Christ did? Not only choose it, but Job-like, when faced with the opportunity to curse God for that suffering, perhaps caused by our own choices, we must resist the temptation to curse God and rejoice instead." Max turned to Phil. "You gave the perfect analogy earlier, Phil. It proves my point exactly. Thank you." Max smiled, noting the prominent twitch of Phil's lips. He continued:

"Therefore God creates evil as an ultimate act of love. Without evil there is no ability to choose, there is no free will. To have a choice means we have the ability to choose between or among alternatives. We must have real choices whether to come to God or not, to hold no god above Him, to love our neighbors as ourselves, to believe that Christ died for our sins and that God loves us, even though we are faced with trials and tribulations. And though we doubt, God is always there as our bona-fide free-will choice. We are called by God to choose either death or everlasting salvation. Though we are all called by God, each of us can choose to let the phone go on ringing and never answer." Max walked behind the bar again to refill his cup with hot water. He plopped in a bag of green tea, which he found in a box on the shelf. "Michal, do you think Phil won this argument?"

Phil grumbled and began to say the words, "Unicor—"

"None of your unicorn juice," Max said. "I realize that it's difficult to accept some of the truths in the Bible. But if you accept as I do that the Bible is more than just a bunch of words, but a book that is divinely inspired insofar as the truth manages to shine through, despite the best efforts of man. . . ." He tilted his head at Michal, "Yes, Michal, *exclusively men*—then you have to accept that this is not just logical, but Biblically supported." Max sipped his tea with a loud slurping noise. "Look, Phil, I found something non-alcoholic in your teahouse."

"Phil, it's about time I stop you with all of this unicorn talk. It's getting really tiresome," Michal said. "You can't compare God's existence to the existence of unicorns or—let's make this interesting—*invisible pink unicorns*, as some of these atheist sites suggest. But you know what, Phil? We can scientifically determine that invisible pink unicorns simply do not exist. . . . See, I'm invoking your Science God here. The only chemical basis for living organisms on our planet is carbon-based, which would mean that they would always be visible, right? Of course the unicorns could be hiding really well. . . . Oh, but perhaps they are made out of antimatter, you might say. Well, then, anytime they interacted with ordinary matter, they would instantly, and I might add *spectacularly*, be destroyed.[58] I suppose you can say that they could be made out of some funky as yet undiscovered material straight out of the *X Files,* but—"

Phil glared scornfully at Max and Michal. "Michal, that argument is *so deeply stupid* I don't know what to say. So you're going to try to invoke science, when you believe in a being that is neither provable, observable, nor even consistent with the laws of science as we understand them?" Phil gritted his teeth and stared at the floor. "Unicorns *DON'T* exist, nor have they ever, nor has magic, nor have miracles, nor have gods, nor the afterlife! —Look, I've got a story to tell you. Actually, Anthony Flew was the first to tell it, I think. Or it was a retelling of a tale by John Wisdom. In any case, it goes like this: Two explorers came upon a clearing in the jungle with many flowers and weeds. One of the explorers said 'Some gardener must be tending this.' The other explorer wasn't convinced. So they pitched a tent and set watch. They never saw the gardener. So the first explorer said, 'Maybe it's an *invisible* gardener.' So they set up a barbed wire fence and electrified it, and had bloodhounds patrol it. No shrieks were heard to suggest a shock, no movement of the wire to suggest an invisible climber. No bloodhounds gave a howl. Yet the first explorer was still not convinced. 'There *is* a gardener,' he insisted, 'invisible, intangible, impervious to electric shock, who has no scent, makes no sound, who comes secretly to look after the garden, *which he so dearly loves*.' The second explorer just shakes his head. How can an invisible, intangible, eternally elusive gardener differ from *no gardener at all?*"[59]

Phil seemed to grow calmer. He spoke in a voice so soft that it was almost lost in the echo of his earlier tirade. "I don't think you understand how important this conversation is to me—how germane it is. . . ." He continued to stare at the floor.

Max and Michal looked at Phil, and then exchanged glances heavy with questions.

"What was that about, Phil?" Michal's words were suddenly soft.

Suddenly a string of Japanese words—drunken slurs, or what Michal and Max assumed were drunken slurs—erupted from the farmer at the bar, who our three friends had all but forgotten. The farmer's eyes wandered around while he gesticulated. He fired words like bullets at Phil, Michal and Max, then finally stopped and stared at them. Phil laughed and responded in Japanese, another string of words that neither Michal nor Max understood.

The farmer slapped his head with his one hand and laughed. "Of course you don't understand what I say. You Americans. . . . In my day we had to learn both Japanese *and* English. But that was because we were forced to." He glared at the foreigners and then continued:

"But that is not important. What *is* important is that you are talking about big ideas. Perhaps too big. *I no naka no kawazu taikai wo shirazu.* 'A frog in a well does not know the great sea.' You were talking about your American God creating evil. That's not a problem in Shinto." He looked at his sake cup. Seeing it empty, he attempted to refill it with the bottle of sake that was no longer there. He looked at Phil accusingly.

Phil shrugged and then moved behind the bar to fetch more sake for this local stranger. He returned with a ceramic carafe filled with cold sake. "On the house." Phil gave him a wholly fake smile.

"Thank you," the stranger said to Phil, accepting the sake. "As I said, it's not a problem in Shinto. But I am curious about this Isaiah verse that you spoke of before."

"You mean Isaiah 45:7?" Max asked. "*I form the light and create darkness—?*"

The stranger nodded.

"The important part of the verse," Max said, "is that Isaiah is challenging King Cyrus, telling him that he must put his faith in Isaiah's God rather than his own, since Isaiah's God made everything, including both good and evil. Well, 'calamity,' actually, if we take the Hebrew word 'ra' in context." He became momentarily lost in thought, chewing over the word.

The three looked at Max, until Phil waved at him. "You've thrown out the statement. The floor is yours."

"Did you know that God calls Cyrus His messiah? Cyrus was God's chosen messiah to deliver Israel from the Babylonians." Max was speaking out loud, but it was obvious that he was working something out internally. "It's interesting that he was the only named messiah in the Bible, except for Jesus, of course." Max shook his head, trying to gather his thoughts, and continued, "There's a problem here and I believe that we have fallen into some kind of fallacy of ambiguity. I think that we are all seeing evil through our own lens. That's not surprising. The Hebrews did as well. The hallmark of a good conversation is being able to speak on a subject about which you can also offer a countering view, by seeing it through someone else's lens." Max put up his fists and took a mock swing at Phil. "Hopefully without killing each other in the process. —We are talking about evil yet we haven't defined the term. We are all just going on about what we *claim to know,* like the phrase 'Everyone knows that only good things are desirable.' But there are a number of good things that are not desirable. . . ."

"You're not making sense, Max. Are you meaning to say that there are no bad things that are desirable?" Michal began. "Because that's what follows from what you just said. If so, that's just false. I think what you mean to say is that, among those good things, are desirable things. Take the phrase 'Only dogs go to heaven.' This means that if you go to heaven, you are a dog. It doesn't mean that all dogs go to heaven. There are some dogs who don't go to heaven. But if you're *not* a dog, you just forget about going to heaven. So given what you said, 'Everyone knows that only good things are desirable,' the interesting thing that follows from this is *not*, as you say, that there are some good things that are not desirable, but the far more controversial claim that if you're *not* a good thing—that is, if you're a *bad* thing—then you're *not* desirable. And like I said, that is blatantly, absolutely, positively FALSE. People desire bad things all the time. The three of us are perfect examples of this."

Phil laughed out loud. "That word 'only' can be a real bugger, right, Maxie?"

Max sipped his tea. "Fine, Michal, but to the point that *I am* trying to make, if you don't mind? —Tea is good when it's hot and so hot tea is desirable, right? But maybe we shouldn't be so hasty. Tea that is too hot is not desirable, nor is it desirable if we want a cool drink of iced tea on a hot day. That said, my hot tea"— he set the cup down, and rested his hands on either side of it—"is not always a good thing. So, first, we need to agree on terms. Are we talking about evil as opposed to good? If so, then the Isaiah passage doesn't seem to work, because the opposite of 'peace' is 'calamity,' not 'evil.' Isaiah was speaking in opposites: light and dark, peace and calamity. Unfortunately, the Hebrew language is more sparse than English, as Michal can tell you, and so we must look at the context to get the true intent and meaning of the Hebrew word. Since Isaiah is speaking in the language of opposites, clearly the better word here would be 'calamity,' not 'evil.' Regardless, though, God does create calamity, doesn't He?" Max waited only a pastor's moment for the rhetorical question, and then continued before anyone could answer:

"Sudden disaster, distress, or ruin? Tribulation, misfortune, and affliction? Just look at the Bible, and you find God doing this everywhere. This is God's doing, not man's. The Flood. The raining down of sulfur and fire on Sodom and Gomorrah. The Isaiah passage is likely not referring to evil, especially not evil at the hands of man, but *God-created calamity.*" Max stood up. "According to design arguments, even calamity passes the test, as it is extremely complex in its effect, and yet simple in its formation. A clear sign of a Designer. . . ."

Max stopped. Phil was smirking, Michal was smiling, and the stranger was just staring at him. Then he noticed that he was posing during his brief sermon, rather in the fashion of *The Motherland Calls.* His right hand was raised, his left hand extended in a calling gesture. Sheepishly, he lowered his hands and then laughed. "Maybe that was a bit more preachy than I expected, but you get the idea." He winked. "We need to define our terms." Max sat back down on the barstool.

"Preach it, brother! The power of logic compels me!" Phil cried out, his arms waving.

"Right, Maxie." Michal turned on her barstool to look at her friend. "The ancient Israelites also used the word 'toevah' to express evil or wickedness—abomination, actually—though other times toevah means 'ritual taboo.' Abominations are so detestable that they make God sick to the point of vomiting. Take Job 20:15. Zophar describes God vomiting out the wicked who mistreat the poor. In other passages, the *land* vomits people out. We see this in Leviticus, for example. In my mind, 'ra' should rarely be translated as 'evil.' 'Calamity' or 'adversity,' yes. But rarely 'evil.' Evil should be reserved for the most abominable things that make God sick. True atrocities. *We* consider every little pain, discomfort, or misfortune to be evil, but this is only from our Western eyes. Israelites were far more philosophical."

"Abominable, huh?" Phil smiled. "Then God must have vomited all over the Abominable Snow Monster in the *Rudolph the Red-Nosed Reindeer* television special." He laughed.

"I love that Christmas special," Max said. "I've always felt like one of the Misfit Toys."

"Cute." Michal giggled. "Well, the Snow Monster did make some trouble for Rudolph and his elf-dentist friend. . . . But stop being so serious and let's get back to our silly discussion. —So I mentioned understanding evil through both ancient Israelite and our own modern Western eyes. . . ."

"There's that ethnocentrism rearing its ugly head. OK, I can agree that we need to look at this from the proper historical and cultural perspective. But if we restrict evil to that which is an abomination to God, where does that leave us?" Max watched the old gentleman enjoy his sake.

Phil opened his mouth to speak, then noticed the stranger studying our three friends as they argued. *He seems like an anthropologist or sociologist, rather than a farmer. It's as if he's observing us, like some kind of researcher. I wonder if he's enjoying himself?* Phil walked around the bar to get another bottle of sake for the stranger. He noticed the stranger was chewing the nails on his only hand. He offered him some more to drink. The stranger looked up at Phil, then at the nearly full sake bottle, picked up his cup and took a small sip. He smiled. *"Arigatō gozaimasu. Kanpai."*

Michal and Max glanced at Phil, a puzzled look on their faces. Then Max offered, "My hovercraft is full of eels."

Phil laughed hard. "I think you mean to say, '*Watashi no hobākurafuto wa unagi de ippai desu.'*"

"I don't get the joke," Michal said.

"Python. —Anyway, our friend here is expressing his gratitude."

Michal shrugged. "At least *some* men know how to express gratitude." She turned to Max to finish her thought:

"—God vomits them out of His mouth. God doesn't just throw up over any little thing. He reserves this for the worst of the worst. So we really shouldn't include smaller adversities or misfortunes in this discussion, at least so far as the ancient Israelites were concerned," Michal said.

"True, but there are quite a few things that are abominable or abhorrent to God, foremost among them idolatry and social injustice, but also other behaviors."

Michal, you mentioned all those superstitions about mixings and confusions," Max said. "There are many ways to define evil. So what can we do to keep the definition short and sweet, and relevant to today?" He turned to Phil. "How would you define evil?"

"Well, I'm certainly not going to include some archaic notion of mixings or confusions. I like my polyester blends and my White Russians." Phil shrugged and poured himself a drink. "I think we should stick with those things we can all agree are actually evil. And, yes, that can include killer tornadoes and other freaks of nature."

"You're a freak of nature," Michal said with a laugh.

"Cute." Phil rolled his eyes. "Honestly, with friends like these, who needs politicians?" He laughed. "As I was saying, biblically God can make whatever He wants and that includes—on multiple occasions—actions, people, and events that are by almost everyone's standards evil. Well, in my book He can go ahead, because I don't believe in Him and I don't believe in evil. It's all make-believe and I can make-believe anything." Phil looked around the room. Max and Michal stared at him as though a large tree was growing out of his head exactly where it shouldn't. The one-armed stranger also gazed at him, his eyes bright and aware, while he absently picked a bit of wax out of his ear.

The strange man set down his sake cup atop the bar and hopped off his stool. He only stood about as high as a ten-year-old boy. Michal hadn't noticed that before. He approached Phil and took hold of his hand.

"You say that you do not believe in God or evil? I must say that your words are music to many ears. I suppose that you do not believe in the Devil then, either. Well, this wouldn't be a surprise, since he is so laughably depicted in your cartoons, donning those red tights, and sporting horns and a pointy tail. Oh, and let's not forget that pitchfork. This is better anyway, since people then blame the Almighty rather than place the blame where it squarely belongs. . . ." The stranger paused and then spoke in a very serious tone. "But you must trust me now in what I am about to say for I am bound to speak Truth." He dropped Phil's hand.

"Go on," Phil began, "you have piqued my interest."

"Mine too," Michal said. Max smiled and nodded for the man to continue.

"Your views, sir, remind me of Shinto belief. There is no absolute standard of good and evil. Things just are as they are. Even the so-called evil, blood-sucking *Kappa* has *some* redeeming qualities." The stranger walked back, hopped up on his stool and grabbed his sake cup. After downing his drink, he adjusted himself and continued. "Despite the Shinto view, evil is very, very real. . . . But of course, so is goodness and pleasure. Your God offers you so many pleasures. Just consider the many delights of the heart, and the senses, and the intellect."

"May I pour you more sake?" Phil offered.

"*Domo arigatou.*" The stranger looked intently at Phil. "Consider sun-kissed mornings in a field of golden flowers—or your tea, sir—" The stranger smiled warmly at Max. "Or this sake, or your wonderful koi pond at which I spend so many lazy afternoons."

"Or friendship, or love," Michal said and smiled.

The strange man continued, "But you *ignore* all of these pleasures. Or you take them for granted. And you dwell on the miseries and pains. Every wrongdoing, every bump in the road, you call 'evil.' It's like you're given a glazed donut and complain about the hole. This utterly delights the Angels of Darkness, for then you take your focus off the Creator and your fellow man, and dwell on your own misery or the misery of the world.... But evil, *real evil*, is so vile, so heinous, so cruel, and so inhumane, that you simply *cannot imagine* a human doing it. And indeed no human *could do it,* were it not for the Agents of the Inferno."

"I'd say that so-called 'inhuman' acts are *human-all-too-human,*" Phil said.

Max leaned over to Phil and whispered, "Angels of Darkness? Agents of the Inferno? I thought he was Shinto. —Archaic superstition. Bad science fiction. Or drunken nonsense."

The stranger smiled at Max. "I may be drunk, young man, but I do not speak nonsense."

Michal hung on the man's every word. "Please continue." She smiled broadly.

"Thank you, beauty, I will.... When such evil occurs, it seems that we"—the stranger paused—"I meant to say 'the demons' and 'the Father Below'—when such evil happens, it seems that *they* have the advantage. The world *seems* to be in the palm of their hands. But as much as so many have tried to rewrite the script...."

"So it's like re-watching a really distressing movie and so desperately hoping that this time the ending will be different," Michal added, a bit too excited.

"Right. The script has already been written," the stranger reiterated. "Trust me. All they can hope to do is make man miserable *on this earth.*"

Michal's eyes were fixed on him.

The man turned and addressed Phil: "You say that there is no God, but at your death, you must choose either the Father Above or the Father Below. You cannot *not* choose. At the hour of your death...."

"Do you mean to include even the unbelievers and doubters?" Michal asked.

"Yes, even the unbelievers and doubters," the stranger continued. "I truly hate saying this, but I told you that I am bound by Truth. At the hour of your death, you will see *Them* and then you will know that *you have always known them,* and you realize what part each of them has played at the many hours in your life when you—when you *supposed yourself to be alone,* and then you will say, 'So it was *you,* all along.' And you will not only see them, but you will see *Him* in his *Glaring Luminosity....* The other side will be there, too, but they will only be looking on, having been crowded out of the room. Of course, they do manage to win a *few stubborn souls.* The Honorable SCREWTAPE was right...."

Max nudged Phil. "He's taking C.S. Lewis to be a historian. Or a biographer...."

"Shhh, Max. This guy is so intriguing," Michal whispered.

The stranger smiled at Michal. "I am happy my words are so inviting to you, beauty."

Phil looked at Michal and smiled widely, tapping her on the arm. "Beauty." He smirked.

The stranger then addressed Phil: "So what do *you* think of my words? You have been remarkably quiet. My words should have rattled you. You should be unsettled to the bone. . . . Or perhaps you are comforted. I'm never quite sure how people like you will react."

Phil held up a single finger at the stranger as he tapped quietly on his cell phone. He had already pulled up a stock quote on RNAS. His investments had been steadily gaining in value and there was no sign anything was amiss. He checked a few other sites as well, noting no unusual trading activity or rousing of the economic beast. He began to wonder who this man was. He was certainly not a local. Who had the resources to pass themselves off as a philosophical and theological expert on such short notice? He looked up at the stranger, who was chewing at his nails again.

Phil looked at the man mistrustfully, out of the corner of his eye. "You're good," he said quietly.

"Hrrm?" The man's eyes flitted about—seemingly bright and insightful but then suddenly vacant, dim and shallow. *Nope. Not a hint of intelligence there.*

"Nothing. Just remarking on your knowledge of theology. C.S. Lewis is well-known for his fantasy books, but few people, at least few average folk"—he gestured at the man's attire—"would quote him. But then again, Japan is known for its advanced educational system. It's sad that Americans can't quite catch up in that category."

"You are being elusive, friend, but it won't work. The village has many rumors about you as a recluse, a connoisseur of philosophy and theology, and a complete narcissist. I just did my homework since you seem to be lonely. Alas, your friends showed up, so perhaps my visit was unnecessary." He waved at Michal and Max. "But we are here now, so let's make the best of it. Whether we were destined to be here or not, we should take advantage of all opportunities to learn about the world and each other. Let's be frogs who hop out of the well." He sipped his sake and looked at Phil. "I believe you have a response."

"I do," Phil said. "For the sake of discussion, let's say that I don't want to reject your argument out of hand, even though it is based on the premise that there is an afterlife, which is, of course, completely untenable." Phil sipped at his whiskey and looked at his friends. "They have been working on me for some years now and have yet to sway me. But let's just say that I'm a bit more receptive to the idea right now. So let's proceed on those grounds."

"Yes, let's." The man spoke as if addressing an ignorant child.

"Assuming there is an afterlife, let's also give a nod to our previous discussion about determinism and say that it's not relevant to this discussion. You seem to be saying that we dwell on the negative to the exclusion of appreciating the positive. Is that correct?" Phil eyed the stranger, his hand resting on his chin like Rodin's famous statue, watching for any sign of deeper understanding—anything.

The stranger nodded, still looking vacant.

He's pretending to be a halfwit, but I know better. Phil looked at the man, who smiled stupidly. "So who defines negative and positive?" Phil asked.

"You think you have me, do you, by invoking a relativistic argument?" The stranger leaned toward Phil and clenched his fist.

"Not at all. I hope that's not your only weapon in this match, though if it is, I would have to say 'yes.' Is a mother giving birth a positive event? Of course it is, most would say, particularly anyone steeped in any kind of major religion. Children are a blessing from God, right? But what if that child's birth brings about a greater burden on the family? Because the child is severely disabled, say, or the extra mouth to feed impoverishes the family. As we previously discussed, it's all context." Phil tilted his whiskey glass at the stranger. "And before you respond, I want you to understand that I'm OK with context, with relativism. I'm OK with the Stoics and their opinion that good and evil are states of mind—how we react to what life deals us."

"I would say that you *seem* to believe that you have a firm grasp on your version of reality. But what if your version of reality"—the stranger gestured around the room, then tapped his own head—"is just as relative?"

"Now I *know* you're an evil demon trying to argue against me with skepticism. Of course, I can't imagine *real* evil demons. If I could they would somehow not be—real." Phil smirked. "We've already been down this road. . . . If it is all relative to the observer, then that just *is* the only reality and we must act in that. If it is not relative, but the observer is deluded, then still, that is *his* reality and he must act in that. Unless you can offer me some evidence that I'm sitting inside a vat of gelatin, being used for my electricity. . . ."

"I'm sorry, but I don't understand your American pop-culture reference." The stranger scratched the back of his head.

"Of course you don't, except that it's not just an American reference. No matter, let's continue, shall we?" Phil shot back his best schoolmarm look.

The stranger wrinkled his nose and tried to smile.

"Phil, don't you think you're being a little rude?" Michal was trying to soften her own feelings. Why Phil was behaving in such a manner to a stranger was threatening her sense of propriety.

"If only it were as easy as pulling back the curtain and exposing the Wizard." Phil downed his whiskey. "We keep dancing around this whole evil, sin and abomination thing. I think we all agree that there is some matter of perspective there, but just how much perspective? Instead of 'evil' let's just call it 'cruelty,' since cruelty implies intent. We can set 'apathy' aside for now, though I would argue that apathy is the ultimate in cruelty."

"You know, Claudia Card argues that evil doesn't require intent. Evildoers can be negligent, for example. What makes an act evil is culpable wrongdoing and foreseeable, intolerable harm,"[60] Michal said. "So I won't agree with you about intent. . . . But go on, Phil, the floor is yours."

Max sat back and smiled. "Look out, Phil is on a tear. Go ahead, my friend."

"Please proceed," the stranger said.

"So if we avoid my last overarching statement, which I intend to back up, by the way, let's talk only about cruelty. Cruelty, like evil, is entirely relative."

Michal groaned. "I don't like this argument. . . ."

"Would you argue that cruel actions tend to be those that are done in the actor's self-interest?"

"Wait. . . . I believe that before the debate begins, we should define this word 'cruelty.' Are you referring to the word meaning 'callous indifference to, or pleasure in, causing pain and suffering,' as defined in"—Max raised his Oxford pocket dictionary—"this dictionary?"

"How many books do you carry around with you?" Phil playfully chided.

Max shrugged. "As many as I need for conversations with you."

The strange man turned slowly toward Max, a half-grin splitting his leathered features. "I would agree with that definition. What about you, Phil-san?"

"I can agree with that." Phil stared at Max and then glanced over at the stranger. "Shall I continue?"

"Of course."

"So would you agree that cruel actions tend to be viewed as those that are done in the actor's self-interest?"

"Certainly they do not go against the actor's desires." The stranger's hand, gnarled by too much time laboring in the sun, brought the sake cup to his lips. "I do not think that I can agree that they are always deliberately done in the actor's self-interest." The corners of his lips turned upward slightly as his eyes sparkled in challenge.

"Can we at least agree that actions are, in general, seen as being done in one's self-interest, according to one's desires? At least temporarily?" Phil glanced at Max, who was frowning. "Yes, I know sometimes desires are not ultimately good for you, but at the time would you say that you *believed* that they were in your self-interest? No matter how reprehensible they might have seemed afterward?"

"I can desire to slowly drink myself to death because I find my life unbearably miserable, even if I might be wrong about that judgment. How is this in my self-interest, especially if all living beings act self-interestedly toward their own survival, or even their own flourishing? Even my houseplants seem to do this. Stubbornly refuse to die when I love them to death with over-watering and fertilizer," Michal said. She looked at Phil who was waiting patiently.

"Please, go on," Phil said. Michal wasn't entirely sure whether he was being sincere or sarcastic.

"I'm reminded of Socrates in the *Meno*. Nobody knowingly does what is bad for them because that brings misery. And nobody would knowingly bring misery upon themselves. It is in their self-interest to avoid misery. If someone acts in ways that bring about their own misery, then they are not acting out of self-interest. Well, people do this all of the time. Knowingly doing what is bad for them. So obviously people are not always acting self-interestedly."

"Your comment suggests that self-interest is always directed towards a person's benefit. Further, it suggests a level of control and more importantly foreknowledge. But this is not what I am saying. We self-interestedly desire to do things that do bring on misery. This is more due to weakness of will and lack of foreknowledge than actual intent. Finally, we heap misery not only upon ourselves, but upon others. So I don't agree with Socrates," Phil said. "Let us all relish that people aren't as easily swayed and logically out-maneuvered as Meno. Otherwise, we wouldn't need any other philosophy, because Socrates would have gotten it all right." He frowned.

Max looked from Phil to the stranger, and wondered where all of this was going. "Fine, Phil, for the sake of discussion, I think we can agree that those who are performing cruel actions are doing so because they choose to, intend to, and therefore self-interestedly want or desire to do so."

"I can't agree with you," Michal said. "I can compulsively act cruelly, even cruelly to the extreme, because I am compelled to do so, such as when I act out of an addiction or a sickness. Or I can be coerced to do so from the outside. Take the pedophile who hates what he is doing. It sickens and disgusts him. He goes out on an errand, to the grocery store, say, and doesn't intend to do it. But then he sees a kid in the parking lot and finds himself suddenly immersed in his sickness and acts. He doesn't choose to do so.... Unless you consider compulsions to be choices, and I don't. He certainly doesn't intend to do so, nor does he—by my example—want or desire to do so."

"Ah, but the problem with your example is intent. Specifically, cruelty has to do with intent, not with actions taken as a result of being driven by something that has control over our choices, such as an addiction. Remember, cruelty is defined as callous indifference or pleasure in causing pain and suffering. When I was causing pain to others as a result of my addiction, I did not feel pleasure at the suffering and pain of others. On the contrary, I was devastatingly aware of the pain I was causing, but I couldn't stop. The drugs made me indifferent. This is not cruelty." Max folded his arms.

"Well, I am not inclined to agree with your dictionary definition of cruelty, Max. I know that it's Oxford, but still. I would say that callous indifference or pleasure in causing pain and suffering is certainly *sufficient* for cruelty, but not necessary. I'd widen the definition a bit. Cruelty can happen accidentally, without intent. What you are suggesting, Max, is that the pedophile, because he acted as a result of a sickness that was out of his control, did not act cruelly because he did not desire to act in this way. I would say that if you ask *damn near anybody* they would say that, despite the pedophile's intent not to harm the child, he engaged in a very cruel act. I'd even hazard to say that *you* acted cruelly, Max, while in the throes of your addiction." Michal ran her fingers through her hair.

"So you are proposing that any action that causes some degree of pain and/or suffering could or should be considered cruel, regardless of intent? And what about the victim's understanding of the situation?" Max's eyes goggled. "I'm not sure you realize the ramifications of that statement." He shook his head.

"Come on, Max. You weren't listening to what I was saying. Either that or you are trying to make a straw man out of what I said. Of course it's not true that any action that causes some degree of pain or suffering is cruel. That would be ridiculous to the extreme. I never suggested that. I said that we must *widen* the definition of cruelty, to allow us to say that some actions are cruel even if there wasn't intent. We don't want to just throw the word 'cruel' around willy-nilly. Like 'abomination,' it should be reserved for extremely wicked acts, but I don't think that intent is always necessary. Consider the Holocaust. Much of what happened during the Holocaust was not the result of intentionally cruel acts, but of bystanders acting indifferently. Ignoring suffering, being indifferent or oblivious to it, can be just as cruel as intentionally inflicting it, even though there is no intent to act cruelly."

"*Damn near anybody?* Since you have already introduced the straw man, I will call you out on your appeal to popularity," Max said. "If I can come up with people who disagree with your assertion, do I win? I know several sociopaths who would disagree. . . ."

Michal squinted her eyes and bit her lip. It was clear to her two friends that she was getting pissed.

"Some of the Holocaust *might* have been unintentional, Michal, which means, implicitly anyway, that some or even much of it was quite intentional. Which brings me back to my original point and why I went with 'intent' and used the words '*tend to*.' I fully accepted that there would be counter-examples. I'm with you. I don't agree with Max. I gave an example of intent as something upon which we could hopefully all agree." Phil laughed. "Guess that didn't work so well. . . . So I ask, can cruelty and evil be unintentional?"

"I already gave my answer," Michal grumbled. "But to drive my point home: Can giving a young girl a teddy bear at a Christmas party be evil? Doesn't seem so, does it? But what if, unbeknownst to the giver, the teddy bear was taken from a Jewish girl who had just arrived at Auschwitz, the bear being left behind with her clothing at the entrance to the 'showers'? Holocaust survivor Charlotte Delbo writes about this.[61] Since the giver didn't know where the teddy bear came from, obviously it's not intentional, but I'd argue that the act is evil."

"You seem to be suggesting that things can be tainted with evil. What kind of weird metaphysical hocus-pocus are you going to offer to try to defend *that* view?" Phil said impatiently.

Michal stared at him blank-faced.

"It looks like we're all still sitting in the well, trying frantically to hop out," the stranger said. "I expect that one of you will come up with a better argument, likely in dramatic fashion."

"Back to your original question, Phil. At best I can say that *some* acts of cruelty are motivated by self-interest," Michal said.

"Some acts of cruelty are relative to the beholder, to the target of the cruelty. I'll offer a pretty simple example. A child might think his mother is cruel for taking away his favorite toy after he punched his little brother." Phil reached for his whiskey and started to take a drink, but then suddenly stopped. "Well, I would go so far as to say that cruelty is entirely a social construction, derived from hundreds if not thousands of years of human interactions, expressing a particular society's preferences." Phil took a sip of whiskey and awaited the expected retorts.

"You're referring to the dehumanization of some groups of people based upon the socio-political or cultural viewpoint of the aggressor, such as the views of the Hutus about the Tutsis. Think about all of the shed blood between these two groups—the Burundian and Rwandan Genocides and the two Congo wars. Such viewpoints often result in the systematic cruelty towards any group or individual considered to be subhuman by the other group, right?" Max went to the electric kettle and filled it up with water.

"Yep, that kind of cruelty," Phil said. "If we pause and consider all of the bloodshed throughout history—well, I might be inclined to agree with Ferdinand's words: 'Hell is empty and all the devils are here.'"

Michal stamped her foot. "Sorry, Phil, but I don't buy it. You're talking about making cruelty relative, relative to someone or something, and I. Just. Don't. Buy. It." She punctuated each word with her index finger, jabbing the air in Phil's direction. "When every week we hear about something horrible happening, some despicable act, just like in the news the other day. Somebody decided it would be a fun time to pour bleach—down a puppy's throat." Her words caught in her own throat. "I don't think that person did that for self-interest. I think that person is just plain cruel. And that is something that anybody"—she looked around at the others—"ANYBODY should be able to see. I don't care who you are."

"You are referring to things we might call 'absolute' cruelty, such as the puppy incident or the Holocaust?" Max watched Michal's features carefully.

"Yes, exactly. Absolute cruelty. Things that, regardless of your culture, should be considered cruel by any reasonable, feeling person." Michal shook her head, sparks almost flying from her eyes.

The stranger studied this exchange between Max and Michal with interest. Phil watched the stranger, suspicion evident in his drawn brow.

"So what then can we define as this so-called *absolute* cruelty Michal?" Phil all but spat the words at her. "Is it cruel to take the life of another living being? Is it cruel to end the life of a cute fuzzy little puppy by pouring bleach down its throat? Is it cruel to club a baby seal for its fur, or breed wittle fuzzy wuzzy minks for their soft luxurious fur, but perfectly OK to breed cattle and kill them for meat and use their skin for a fancy jacket?"

Michal glared at Phil. She began to speak, but her words failed her. Phil looked at her waiting expectantly. She waved her hand at him.

"Shall I take that as a 'no'? A go-ahead? Either way you get the point. *The world can't always be kittens and cotton candy,* Michal."

"Think about this scenario," Phil continued. "A beautiful summer day, green grass, freshly mown, bare feet, and the undeniable urge to take a stroll. So you walk out and trod across the lawn, the grass feeling like plush carpet under your toes. What a lovely sensation, little tickles and itches as you enjoy the luxurious Western decadence of a well-manicured lawn. Utterly cruel, right? At any point did you consider this to be cruel? I would hazard to say that you did not. However, you just killed at least a few small bugs, and if you didn't, you at least disturbed their ecosystem." Phil gestured with his glass. "These bugs mean no more to you than we would mean to a capricious and vastly more powerful god. This is the very heart of apathy. Who cares about some little bugs? They're already working to make a hundred more in just that little area."

Phil gazed out the window. He got up and walked toward the door and motioned them to follow. "Come on. Let me show you something." He opened the door in exaggerated fashion and walked out into his garden. It was raining. The crunch of the compressed granite surface played out a staccato rhythm as he marched out to the riot of color.

Max grabbed an umbrella from the stand and motioned Michal to follow. "Like I said before, he's on a tear. It's always amusing, to say the least." He walked to the opened door to see Phil standing in the rain. "Amusing. . . ."

Purple and white orchids, pink lilies and orange birds of paradise were in full bloom, dripping from the rain. Phil walked along the path toward the bench sitting next to the koi pond. The pond had a little moving water sculpture that ticked as it dumped out its newly full bucket of water.

Tick.

The bucket righted itself as Phil kicked off his bunny slippers, which made a squish-plop noise. He walked around on the nearby moss. The rain fell steadily on him, drenching his tattered robe and running down his hair and face. He turned to look at his friends, dry beneath their umbrella. Michal and Max stared at Phil, someone most people would consider to be well beyond peculiar because of this and many other actions. But to them, this was just another outlandish demonstration. Phil's displays frequently ended by painting him in a less-than-flattering light but—at least to Max—they were usually amusing.

The bucket filled again and emptied. *Tick.*

They watched as Phil walked barefoot on the moss, arms outstretched like an entertainer taking in the applause. Or perhaps he was drinking in the water through his now utterly drenched robe, through some kind of strange osmosis. His rain-soaked clothes fit like a second skin.

Max stifled laughter, fully aware that it would shortly be replaced by an unsettling jolt at whatever was about to occur. He braced himself as Phil began to speak.

"If we're talking about ants, one particular queen can lay fifteen hundred eggs a day for seven years. That's about 550,000 ants per year. So really it's no big loss. Why don't you care about the poor beleaguered ants you just killed? Because we don't care about these little insignificant critters. Sure, they perform a function in the world. But who really cares?"

The bucket filled and emptied. *Tick.*

Phil bent over and pulled away the moss to reveal a thriving community of ants. They scurried toward the dark and relative safety of the undisturbed moss. Some began to burrow into the ground. He put out his hand and let a few crawl onto it. Their scent glands no longer sensing a path, the ants desperately searched for some kind of sanctuary. Phil reached out with his other hand and picked up the carcass of a dead ant. He made an overly dramatic show of holding it up toward the heavens. He began to sob uncontrollably, his whole body seemingly wracked with pain. He yelled out skyward, his voice quaking:

"NOOOOOO!"

Even though her daddy made a habit of it, Michal could never stand shouting, turmoil, cries of rage and other such eruptions. And so Phil's antics threw her into a terrible fright.

Hell, his outburst even scared a grey-headed woodpecker right out of a nearby maple tree. The bird, completely disoriented, smashed into the window and dropped dizzily onto the ground.

At that exact moment thunder cracked across the open courtyard, so powerfully that our friends could feel it in their chests. They saw the water in the pond disturbed by the impact of the sound.

"WHYYYY? YOU HEARTLESS BASTARD! WHAT WERE YOU THINKING? OH MY GOD! I CAN'T BELIEVE YOU COULD DO SUCH A CRUEL AND INHUMANE THING! THIS CREATURE HAD A LIFE! A COLONY TO SUPPORT! IT WAS A LIVING THING! HOW? How? How? How?" His voice quieted. His tears mixed with the droplets of rainwater.

Then Phil looked at his other hand, on which two little ants continued to crawl. He plucked one up, absently dropping the first dead insect onto the ground as he did. He held the little living ant—held it forward to show his friends that it was still alive. Then without taking his eyes off of his friends, he crushed the insect between his thumb and forefinger, grinding it into a tiny black paste. He licked off his fingers with wet, over-exaggerated sucking sounds.

Tick.

He looked at the remaining insect as it continued to scurry up his arm. Delicately, reverently, he knelt down and placed his arm on the moss. Hesitantly, the tiny ant moved toward the ground. It stopped, its feelers frantically twitching and probing. Then it crawled down to the moss, quickly crawled to the apparent safety of its cover underneath, and disappeared from sight.

Phil put the moss back in place, tapping it down lightly with his toes. He turned to his friends. Michal's face was buried in Max's chest.

"Cruel or kind? These words are used to categorize and help us relate to our world. They are, however, ethnocentric to the extreme. And yes, I realize that this borders on an *argumentum ad absurdum* but I believe that in this case it is nonetheless justifiable. I can see you're unconvinced. . . . If you like, I can do the exact same exercise with some mice, or some puppies, or maybe even some local beef." He rubbed his hands together, a look of madness spreading over his face. Grinchlike, the crinkles of his smile reached toward his ears. He began to assume the very semblance of insanity.

Michal and Max stared blankly at Phil. The stranger now stood by their side.

"These creatures are nothing more than a tool with which I can explain my point of view." Phil ground his hands together, as if making more invisible paste, ecstasy flashing across his features. "It is in my self-interest to do so. And at least with insects, there should be no reason for you to have me arrested and thrown in the clink for cruelty." He knelt and took some water from the pond and drank it. When he rose again, his face was as affable and friendly as a parson on a Sunday morning. "Though you might have me put away for being totally bat-shit crazy. But hey, that's nothing new, right?" Phil plopped down on the bench with a wet squish as the rain continued to fall.

Tick.

"*Now* who's the evil demon, Phil-san?" The stranger asked softly. As he was speaking, the rain stopped and the sky turned from a dark black to a brilliant blue. A soft rainbow arched over them. Phil and Max looked up at the sky.

The stranger smiled and then looked at Michal, resting his hand on her lower back. She was still visibly shaken and in tears. "Let me rein you back in," offered the stranger. "Mr. Phil, it's time you stop your theatrics and listen once more to Truth. Let's sit over there on those dry benches." The stranger motioned to the two curved stone benches, which faced each other under a giant Kobushi magnolia.

Phil rose from his bench, which was hand-carved in the shape of an ancient-looking dragon. The water dripped off of his robe. He gave a courtly bow. "Please, after you." His eyes never left the stranger, who returned a short bow before walking over to the benches.

The stranger sat next to Michal on one bench. Phil and Max faced them on the other. The stranger looked at Phil and spoke, "You present two arguments. One is that evil, or *cruelty*, as you say, is nothing but self-interest gone amuck. The other is that morality is entirely relative."

"You've got it," Phil said.

"You're such an ass," Michal said to Phil through tears.

"Let me engage you here," began the stranger." Let's discuss your self-interest argument first."

"I relish the opportunity," Phil answered with a wide grin, seemingly oblivious to Michal's state. He was beginning to calm down. "Kant embraced this sort of argument, too. He claimed that evil occurs when we subordinate the requirement of duty to those of self-interest.[62] Anyway, please go on."

"Your argument is that evil or cruelty, as you have so graphically demonstrated it, is self-interest gone amuck. This suggests that we are hard-wired to be self-interested. And so evil or cruelty must be our self-interest going dangerously awry, rather like buggy programming. Do I have this right?"

"Evolutionary theory seems to have established that we are hard-wired in this way," Phil responded. "Just consider the ruthlessness of natural selection."

"But evolutionary theorists are now realizing that humans could not have survived without cooperation, charity, and reciprocity," the stranger countered. "Early human life was a collective effort, not an entirely self-interested one, and this has shaped the evolution of our brains."

"But it can all still be explained by self-interest. It's in my interest to cooperate," Phil continued. "Remember *Atlas Shrugged*? Human nature is naturally selfish."

"Most people grow out of the Ayn Rand phase, Phil," Michal said under her breath. She crossed her arms and looked down at the ground. "Claudia Card rejects Kant's argument from self-interest. As she rightly notes, we can do evil for evil's sake."

"Ah, but humans also act altruistically, Phil," the stranger began. "I can offer you some examples. Recently, anthropologists discovered a pygmy tribe in the Congo. The tribe hunted collectively, stretching a large net, sometimes three hundred feet across, to catch prey. Once the net was in place, the women and children would shout to frighten the animals into the net. One pygmy decided to live according to your Randian ideal. He snuck away from the tribe and hung his own net in front of the other. He was caught. Not surprisingly, the tribe banished him for life.[63] This was essentially a death sentence for this self-interested little man. . . . Or consider that a selfish soldier is considered to be a *coward*, not a hero. I can offer even more examples and more anthropological and sociological cases. Or have you heard enough?"

"And think about this, Phil," Max said. "In times of tragedy, people engage in selfless heroism, not selfish panics. And consider when you rescued me. Was that selfishness on your part, or were you doing it out of selfless love for a good friend?"

"He's got you there, Phil," Michal said. She was brightening up.

"The position I'm advocating," Phil began, "is psychological egoism. Humans are always motivated by self-interest, even in so-called acts of altruism. Even when people choose to help others, they do so for personal benefit. 'It feels good to help.' 'I want recognition or praise, or a future favor.' 'You'll help me someday, if I help you now.'" He puffed out his cheeks and thrust out his lower jaw, looking more like a bulldog than his intended Brando. Slowly, deliberately, he walked over to Michal, and put his soaked, tattered-robed arm around her shoulders, "Some day, and that day may never come, I'll call upon you to do a service for me."

The stranger and Max stared at Phil. Max held his hand in front of his mouth to hide his expression. Michal looked up into Phil's eyes and smiled. Phil winked at her, taking her hand, and spinning her away toward Max with all of the sudden grace of a ballroom queen. "Besides, I really like what Nietzsche says. Witnessing the suffering of another threatens my own happiness, because it reveals my own vulnerability to misfortune. And so I help in order to alleviate those feelings that threaten my own happiness."[64]

"Nonsense," Max said. "People act altruistically even when the altruistic action is far outweighed by the reward of acting selfishly. —Especially those who act in Christ's love. And don't tell me they're only acting in Christ's love because they expect a heavenly reward. The Holy Spirit, which dwells within, moves them to act in this way."

Phil rolled his eyes.

"And remember Hume's example. Consider a mother who risks her own health by attending to her sick child. Weakened by grief at her child's sudden death, she dies herself.[65] How is this selfish?" Michal asked.

"Come on, Michal. You can do better than that," Phil said. "It's easy to answer Hume here. She wanted to be perceived as a good mother. Or she wanted to gain respect or recognition, or she wanted a reward in the afterlife, or even she was motivated—subconsciously, perhaps—by the more earthly reward of passing on her genes."

"What about a soldier who falls on a grenade in order to save his comrade-in-arms? There is no time to think through any positive future reward or recognition," Max said.

"All right, guys," Phil said. "What about Richard Dawkins? Organisms may seem to be altruistic, but genes are selfish. Genes want to reproduce themselves, and they control the organisms, even if the organisms don't know it. So the conviction that we love our children more than ourselves is natural. It's hard-wired. It's just our genes manipulating us to get their way."[66]

"You can't prove this, Phil," Max said.

"But neither can you disprove psychological egoism," Phil retorted.

The stranger shook his head. "To say that you cannot disprove egoism is not a virtue of your theory. It is a fatal drawback. A theory that claims to tell us something about the world, as psychological egoism does, must be falsifiable. Not false, of course, but falsifiable. —Capable of being tested and possibly proven false. Psychological egoism fails here. Much as you'd like it to be, it is not empirically demonstrable. But even more to your point: Psychological egoism rests on the confused notion that considering one's *own* welfare—what you have been calling 'acting from self-interest'—is incompatible with taking into account the welfare of others. This is simply false."[67] The stranger picked at his ear again.

Michal clapped her hands and smiled. The stranger tapped her on the shoulder in appreciation. "Thank you, beauty." He turned to Phil again. "I'd like to address your second argument now, Phil-san. You suggest that morality is relative. Good and evil are in the eyes of the beholder, so you say?"

"You actually think that you are going to have the last word on psychological egoism? Self-interest is *primal.* What about the Stanford Prison Experiment? People will often act in ways that advance their own self-interest at the expense of others. Or what about our wonderful American physicians who sell their souls to pharmaceutical companies and equipment suppliers for the sake of paid dinners, fancy vacations and other goodies, to the degradation of their profession? I could go on and on," Phil said.

They all looked at him in frustration.

"Oh, very well," he conceded. "Let's talk about moral relativism. That was one point of my ingenious demonstration."

"You know, Phil, moral relativism might be trendy but it is very simpleminded," Michal said with a crooked grin.

"If I may have this one?" the stranger asked politely, before continuing. "Let's first consider the opposite: moral realism or objectivism. One powerful argument in favor of moral realism involves pointing out certain seemingly objective moral truths. Cruelty for its own sake is wrong. Or boiling babies for fun is wrong. With a bit of thought we can produce a very long list and secure considerable agreement. . . ." The stranger paused to collect his thoughts. "If you are a moral relativist, if you think morality is merely a matter of perspective—as you do, Phil—you must reject those claims. But this position is completely indefensible or, at the very least, extremely disagreeable, both personally and philosophically."

Phil's telltale smirk returned as he replied, "I agree with your last statement that it may be disagreeable, but it is no less true. In my mind, we'd be better off replacing propositions of morality with propositions of utility. We call an act 'beneficial' and we sanction that act if it helps more people than it harms. Otherwise we should condemn it. So-called moral truths are merely useful constructs— inventions. No less inventions than neo-Gothic architecture or baroque music. You know, Richard Rorty argues that even though moral judgments cannot be justified, we have no choice but to act on our own view of the good and to try to persuade others to accept that view. Following Dewey's pragmatism, he says that we should promote moral views that make this world a better place, as best we know how. That's all we can do."[68] His eyes moved from the stranger, to Michal, to Max. "Has anyone even shown the slightest bit of concern for the bugs we walked on to reach these benches? —No. Max spoke about the Hutus and the Tutsis earlier. Cruelty is relative in that case, and I can advance other examples. Take the early nineteenth-century yellow fever outbreak among French soldiers sent by Napoleon to keep the peace in Saint-Domingue. More than half the soldiers died. Cruel, right? Well, cruel on God's part. But then again, it helped free the slaves and found the Republic of Haiti. *But then again*, it produced Dessalines, who slaughtered countless numbers of people. . . . And just look at the extent of disagreement about so many moral issues. You overstate the points of agreement. There are no objective moral truths."

"That's a *non sequitur* as any baby logic book will tell you," Michal said. "Consider a different argument and one which we have been exhaustively pondering. It goes like this: There is extensive disagreement about the existence and nature of God. Therefore it follows that there is no truth of the matter about God's existence and nature—but there *is* truth of the matter. There either *is* a God as Max and I firmly maintain, or there is not. And if there is a God, then that God is either a Judeo-Christian God, or a Muslim God, which is of course the same god. Or perhaps God satisfies some conception we have yet to imagine. Remember the rabbit-duck image popularized by Wittgenstein? Some see it as a rabbit. Others see the exact same drawing as a duck. Just like God—we might see Him differently, understand Him differently, but *God is God*. Some of us worship the duck-god and others of us worship the rabbit-god. We even go to war over it. Remember that *New Yorker* cartoon of the two armies going to battle, each proudly flying the same rabbit-duck flag? The caption reads, 'There will be no peace until they renounce their Rabbit God and accept our Duck God.'"

"Our Duck, who art in our pond, Donald be thy name. . . . Give us this day our daily—um, what do ducks eat? —ah yes, *cracked corn*, and forgive us our waddles as we forgive those who waddle against us. . . ."[69] Phil laughed heartily. "You guys worship your Christian God, but it seems that Walt Disney got it right—it would certainly explain God's short temper."

Michal and Max laughed along. "Back to my point," Michal continued. "I understand that the point of Wittgenstein's rabbit-duck was not to show any underlying objectivity, any real truth of the matter. In fact, it shows the exact opposite, but I think you still get what I'm saying. In any case, there is still the fact of the matter of God's existence even if we do not know what it is, though I personally believe in the truth of the Christian God." She smiled at Phil. "You are confusing metaphysics with epistemology. You've done this before, Phil, and I've called you out on it. You're doing it again. Believing something does not make it true. And not believing does not make it false. This is true of morality, too. Disagreement, even extensive disagreement, as you yourself point out, does not entail that there is no truth. We just haven't grasped that truth yet." Michal gave a smug smile.

"You think you've got me, do you?" Phil said to Michal through gritted teeth. "Well, from what you just said, it also follows that considerable *agreement* about so-called 'moral truths,' as our friend here so kindly noted"—Phil motioned to the stranger—"does not entail that there *is* truth." He huffed.

"Fine, Phil, so I'll drive my point home even further. Philippa Foot said that it is impossible that there should be two moral codes the mirror images of each other, such that what we consider to be fundamentally right in one community would be considered completely wrong in the other. There is a great deal that all people have in common, something deep and fundamental in human nature that grounds our morality: affection, cooperation, a desire for help in times of trouble, a desire to work, love of freedom and truth. . . ."[70] Our moral sense is an innate part of our shared human nature," Michal said. "It's *not* all relative. And this by the way, my friend, is *science.*"

"You feel satisfied? Remember when Nietzsche says in *The Gay Science* and *Thus Spoke Zarathustra* that 'God is dead'? He is suggesting in part that any belief in some kind of transcendent or objective justification for our moral claims, whether God or even the Platonic forms, no longer holds water. Although Nietzsche certainly ranks moralities according to whether they express strength or weakness, health or sickness, freedom or slavery—that is, according to whether they should be considered a master or slave morality—he never suggests that these criteria of rank are derived from anything like some objectively privileged vantage point from which they can be compared. In any case, I've got other tricks in my bag. Let's consider my ant demonstration again. We are all ants in God's little ant farm. Sometimes he drops little sugar bits for us to viciously fight over. Sometimes he pours water on us and floods us out. Sometimes he adds ant lions. . . . Have you ever heard of these demon-type insects, the doodlebugs? They are ants' deadliest natural enemies. They seize the ants by their fierce jaws and suck out all their blood. Sometimes God adds ant lions just to make things interesting. . . . Yes, God is cruel. I'm just waiting for him to pick up his heavenly magnifying glass and give us a good fry." Phil said.

"Phil, what's gotten into you?" Michal asked weakly. "Please don't do this again. . . . Please—I'll leave. I swear."

Max wasn't amused either.

"Ok, then, I'll tame my argument a bit for your sake. Your God is a relativist. At least according to your Holy Book. Genocide is wrong when people do it to God's chosen, the Jews. Well, except when they're being punished. But genocide is perfectly acceptable—indeed, God even demands it—when it's the ancient Israelites committing the genocide. When the Israelites conquer a people, God tells them to kill every living thing. Man, woman, child, even the animals, as you've pointed out, Michal. And they are viciously punished when they *don't* do it."

"Like I've said, Phil, this is the ancient Israelites' interpretation of events around them—their claim that it's God's will to act as they do. God's not a relativist. As Creator of all, He would deeply mourn the annihilation of *any* people, whether they were God's chosen or not. He would mourn the death of the Canaanites, or the Ammonites, or the Moabites—any of Israel's enemies. And the Palestinians today, I dare say. The vicious slaughter of a people is *never* God's will," Michal said. "I love to invoke a passage that shows *me*, anyway, that much of the Bible cannot truly reflect God's will. And if it can't *here,* why should we expect that it can *anywhere*? It's just so ridiculous. It's found in Numbers 5. If a man suspects that his wife has committed adultery but has no proof, he takes his wife to a priest who is acting on behalf of God. The man first presents a jealousy offering. Some kind of bread. Then the priest mixes up some poison called 'bitter water.' He dishevels the woman's hair—I guess so that she looks like the slut that she supposedly is—and forces her to drink it. If she is innocent the poison will not harm her. But if she is guilty, the bitter water will cause her uterus to drop and she will be in severe pain, and if she's pregnant with another man's baby, well, God is carrying out an abortion—let us never say that the God of the Bible is not a divine abortionist! The priest acting on God's behalf is forcing her to drink poison! Whether the woman is innocent or guilty, she'll likely get sick from drinking the poison and it's just a matter of luck if she *doesn't* get sick. Of course, this validates the man's suspicion that his wife was cheating, whether she was or not. This is pretty fitting for a patriarchal society, where women are under men's thumbs. Clearly God's not doing any of this fucked-up stuff. This is the action of humans and I dare say *cruel* humans. *Men*, to be more specific—not God."

Phil smiled at Michal, who was now sitting alone on the bench. "Hmmm, I wonder when our new friend snuck away?" he asked.

"He was likely turned off by our discussion. It was definitely more heated than usual," Max said.

"Well, let's get back to it," Phil began. "I want to revisit my claim that evil or cruelty is relative. You like Zhuangzi, Michal. I've heard you cite him on more than one occasion. Consider his story of the Peng and the dove."[71] Phil looked at his friends waiting for some encouragement to continue.

"Go on." Michal smiled.

"OK, so I've steeped myself in the culture of my currently chosen land," Phil said.

Max gave him a puzzled look.

"Right, he was Chinese, not Japanese. . . . You get the picture."

Michal and Max laughed.

"Zhuangzi tells one of my favorite stories about the butterfly. Remind me how Peng goes," Michal said.

"So remember, Peng is actually the transformed fish, K'un. Peng is so large that its size cannot even be estimated. When it flies, it soars ninety thousand li into the sky. Which for those of you who don't know ancient *Chinese* math. . . ." Phil looked at Max and smiled. "That's about thirty-six thousand feet, or roughly cruising altitude for them thar more modern commercial airliners. Now, when we consider Peng and the little dove, their difference, of course, lies in more than just size. While the dove is just an ordinary bird, the Peng is a numinous creature. It provokes a derisive reaction from the dove, since it challenges the dove's worldview. The Peng's worldview seems absurd to the little dove, since it is incomprehensible to it. But the smallness of the dove's view is also incomprehensible to the Peng. When the Peng flies up to ninety thousand li, both the sky and the earth appear blue, since at that height the detail is indistinguishable. Each creature sees the world according to its own unique perspective. In the case of these two creatures, not only do we have a tremendous difference in size and perspective, but we have different biology altogether—if a mythical creature can be said to have a biology.

"Different creatures see things differently," Phil continued. "Cats see the world differently than we do. They don't really see colors like we do. So when we say 'red'—if they could comprehend the word—they wouldn't really understand it, any more than we would understand *that thing in the dark that you can't see* when they'd say that. But whose perspective is right? The answer is that perhaps *neither* perspective is right—or both are." Phil mused at the thought. "Another paradox, as if we don't have enough of those in this life. —And can *we* compare perspectives and make some kind of objective decision that determines which perspective is the true one? No, not at all. We are just introducing another perspective. Reality is a matter of perspective and evil, being an inherent part of that reality, is also a matter of perspective."

"Reality is not a matter of perspective, Phil, unless we're talking about God's perspective. And God's perspective makes reality objective," Max said.

"Huh?"

"I can kinda get why you might say this, Phil," Michal said, as she glanced at the dogwood tree just in front of the big window of the teahouse. She watched it stir in the light wind. "I have a friend who had a squirrel's nest in a big tree in his backyard. The squirrel had babies. He tells me they were so cute." Michal pointed at the tree, imagining the little squirrels jumping around like little pudgy, clumsy, furry children. Then her expression darkened. "One night he woke up to screams. He looked out his window and a big raccoon was pulling the babies out of the nest and eating them. I just cringe when I think about witnessing that scene. . . . From the squirrels' perspective, this seems like a horrendous evil. But the raccoon was just looking for a midnight snack. Perhaps human life is a bit like this. Sometimes we have the perspective of the squirrel and other times the raccoon."

Michal thought about some large, raccoon-like creature looking down at humanity through glassy black eyes, regarding people as nothing more than little morsels with which to play and then eat. The thought reminded her of other, more powerful beings, or, more specifically, *one* more powerful being. She quickly added: "Not that God does that."

Phil chuckled. "Of course He wouldn't because He's omnibenevolent. —Oh wait, Max, you don't believe that."

Michal looked at Phil with curiosity and a measure of pity. "Phil, you may make an interesting and fairly defensible argument with some good analogies. But I just can't accept that kind of a world. —That kind of a God. It's horrifying. What is it like to think that you live in such a place?"

"Honest." Phil walked over to his neglected bunny slippers, squeezed out the water and put them on. "So then God must have created evil or God Himself is evil. This of course is completely contradictory. The very definition of God includes His omnibenevolence, so God can't be evil—unless of course we go with Morrow's hypothesis."

Max raised a hand in protest.

"Objection noted," Phil said. "But then if God can't be evil, how is it that evil can so overpower the will of God? If God is perfectly good, as they like to say in

Sunday school, then shouldn't He promote and protect the good? And if so, shouldn't He be able to squash all evil? If you say that the exercise of our free will causes all this evil rather than God, then I ask you: Why does He allow *all this evil?* So that we can learn lessons to become more God-like? What of all the people who fail? Are they just part of some crazy eugenics program designed to create a better human being or maybe a better human soul? How can you square a God who is trying to create the best human soul with all the evil He allows to exist just to achieve His goal? Are you willing to accept that God is some kind of mega-powerful Josef Mengele?"

"You wear your cynicism like a tattoo," Michal said.

"Well, let's hope it's less permanent than that tiger tattoo you've got on your shoulder blade," Max smiled.

"Where is God? Where is God *now?* What would you two like to hear? That God willed Himself onto life support to help us realize how much we need Him? Or because He thought we'd do a better job at it without Him around?" Phil frowned.

The Home of Kami

Metal eyes stared down at the cold desk. A single placard sat with its lettering facing outward. Those metal eyes would never see the name printed on the other side of the placard, since it had never been turned around and the eyes could not move from their place on the wall. Only those who came into the stark white-and-glass office could read the placard. If those eyes could read, they might wonder if the placard said M. Bellowes, or maybe T. Sudempkin, or possibly G. Gekko. But of course they couldn't read. The eyes were attached to a bust of a stringy black goat mounted on the wall.

A keyboard imbedded in the LED desk offered letters, numbers, symbols, all begging to be touched so that its job could be complete. It promised to provide many enticing images, documents, feelings, sensations. All one needed to do was touch it. *Touch me,* it quietly, incredibly seemed to cry out. Misshapen hands obliged and tapped seemingly random numbers and letters for the span of thirty seconds. The keys made no noise save for the sound of gnarled fingers striking the clear surface. The only evidence that anything was happening was a slight bluish-green hue emanating from the glass desk. Not-so-metallic eyes turned and looked up at the bust looming over the desk, eternally keeping watch over all that transpired there.

All at once, images and videos began to bubble up from some virtual well deep within the uncharted lands of the monitor-desk's storage centers. In this one, a woman sat staring at a watch. In that one, a man watched as a younger man waved at a departing helicopter. In another, a woman cradled an ashen-faced man. Another screen showed the audio waveform of a distressed male's voice. On another, a meadow of green and gold welcomed three friends and the rising sun. Multiple images bubbled up from the desk, crowding it, until every space was occupied by some image of this man, that woman, and another man—all the same, all familiar. A single gnarled finger tapped in the center, instantly freezing all of the images in place.

"4wq#09&8xcdz@720! Come in here." The voice was other-worldly.

A glowing being of the faintest green entered through the wall and hovered in front of the desk.

The voice, as gnarled as the finger, spoke again. "Take a form. The Research Department says it is urgent. You are going to Japan." The second 'a' of 'Japan' seemed to go on for eons.

The glowing-green-being metamorphosed into a suit-and-tie with a vaguely anthropoid form. It shifted from male to female before finally settling on its choice. The voice from the desk spoke again. The same knobbly hand tapped at one of the images. Its voice careened about the room, finally striking the being in the suit-and-tie. Its words spanned multiple languages but the meaning was clear: *"This one."*

The gnarled finger repeatedly rapped at a single moving image, the rest sucked back down into the well from whence they came. The single image hovered in the middle of the desk just above the keys, which glowed redly.

The body in the suit-and-tie looked at the image, nodded, turned and left. It could be seen walking away, down the corridors of glass. It turned at the last hallway and descended the stairs, briefly stopping on the last step before jumping off into the void. The only evidence of its passing was a small eddy of space-time where it had stood. The eyes that accompanied the gnarled hands turned and looked at the bust. "A most excellent choice, don't you think?"

The bust nodded its approval. Or at least it might have nodded if it could move, if it weren't incapable of moving for all eternity. It had but one job: to loom over this desk, forever staring at all the goings-on. It had an itch on its left hoof—the one that didn't actually exist—that it could never scratch. It had attempted to move. After many failed attempts, it had tried to will the itch away. But it never could. It thought of the many different jobs that others held here. It tried to imagine itself happy for this small punishment, but it could not bring itself to do so.

"Maybe in another billion millennia you will learn," puffed the being at the desk, offering false promises. The eyes attempted to cry, but the mind behind them couldn't get past the itch.

I must say that of our three friends, Michal knows evil intimately in the most INTIMATE sense of the word. Of course, Phil knows the evil of the oil-rig accident and Max knows the evil of Jayden's death. Without doubt they both could cite numerous examples. But Michal knows evil INCARNATE. —Let me explain how it all began.

One night, a few summers ago, Michal was in her study reading the Euthyphro, preparing to teach her freshman students the next day. She took notes as she merrily chewed over the argument. She was relishing the thought of confounding them with the dilemma presented in the dialogue: Does God command the morally good because it is morally good, or is it morally good because God commands it? If God commands the morally good because it is morally good, then there are moral standards outside of God to which God appeals. But that means that God is bound by laws—moral laws outside of Himself—rather than being the creator of these laws.

Michal looked up from her notes when she heard a crackling sound in the hallway. It could have been her Yorkie, Buster, running from one room to another. Looking up from her desk, she didn't see anything in the hallway. She called out to Buster but he didn't answer. Since there seemed to be nothing to investigate, she continued:

But if it is morally good because God commands it, then that means that there are no moral laws outside of God's will and God could have willed otherwise. Instead of giving us the Ten Commandments, He could have given us the Ten Anti-Commandments: You shall have other gods besides me, do not honor your mother and father, go ahead, commit adultery and steal your neighbor's stuff.

The noise returned. Buster was now lying in the vintage red-velvet armchair in the corner of her study. She stood up from her writing and looked down the hallway to the living area. Since it was dark, it was difficult to make out anything near the burning candle on the end table. She called out to her boyfriend.

"Sam?" —No answer. She thought she saw movement and dismissed it as Barney, her three-legged rescue Chihuahua. "Mommy's writing. You better not be peeing on Mommy's rug in there." She couldn't make out anything except for the flickering candle. She shrugged and went back to her writing.

This should present a particular challenge to those of you in class who are believers. Now, I'm not calling you out nor criticizing your beliefs, but I do expect you to be critical enough to question yourself. This may undermine your faith altogether but then you'll be freed from the debilitating illusion of Christianity.

She beamed at the thought of her student believers finally questioning their faith. She was pretty sure that her administration would get an earful from the Campus Crusaders who had set up shop in the student commons. She entertained the thought of those students marching into the dean's office, complaining about her proselytizing atheism and attacking their faith. Though she would love to think of Dean Mbanefo telling those idiots that their religion had no grounds, she was also pretty sure that—

Somewhere in her mind the words "candle" and "end table" finally registered. *She didn't have a candle on the end table.* It suddenly seemed as if the apartment was getting warmer. Then she heard the crackling noise again from the living area. She wanted to get some tea anyway, so she got up to check out the sound. It was likely Barney—or so she thought.

As she left her study, Barney walked up to her for a pet. She looked past him down the hallway and glimpsed a monstrous sight. A giant creature as tall as the ceiling was squatting on the floor, warming itself by the flames—yet nothing was burning. The flames that had seemed to come from a flickering candle moments before now looked more like a small campfire. The creature defied description, but it most resembled a bull-like figure with knotty, brownish-green skin.

Michal approached it curiously. She wasn't afraid. She was excited. She felt as if her whole worldview was about to change. Something drew her forward to what should have certainly sent her—or anyone—running away screaming.

Indeed, the closer Michal moved toward the creature, the more inviting it seemed to be. It beckoned her with a knowing glance, but when she had almost reached it, she was suddenly pushed away into the sliding glass door, as if by some mighty, invisible force. The creature and the fire instantly disappeared.

The next morning she was having coffee with her boyfriend, Sam.

"This sounds crazy, but last night, I think I was visited by a demon."

"I don't much believe in demons, Michal—nor God for that matter. And neither do you."

There now. There are no monsters under your bed. Calm down. Here's a cookie.

Sam looked up from the *Times* crossword he was solving. "It was probably a bad dream. If you really want to know about the devil, read *Master and Margarita*. . . . So what's a five letter word for 'ridiculous'?"

"But I was wide awake. I was reading Plato in my study. —'Inane,' 'funny,' 'silly'. . ." Then Michal realized he was making fun of her.

"You must have fallen asleep in your chair. That happens to me all the time," Sam said.

Sam finally convinced Michal that she had been dreaming. But two nights later something curious happened again. This time she felt a loving, heavenly presence, and she even heard Jesus speaking to her. Michal then realized—or she thought she realized—that the previous night she had indeed had a spiritual battle with a demon who was trying to take her soul, before God snatched it away.

She became a Christian that night, to everyone's total surprise—most of all her own. But evil would not leave her alone. . . .

A few nights later, before she drifted off to sleep, Michal saw another creature sitting next to her bed, making some indiscernible noises as if speaking an alien language. A glowing light illuminated the creature. It too defied description, but it most resembled a little green sea monster, though of course Michal had never seen a sea monster. This time she thought to invoke the name of her new Savior: "In the name of Jesus and by the power of His blood, LEAVE!" The creature instantly disappeared.

Over the next several months, Michal experienced many such visitations. She could not understand why. Why would demons bother her now that she belonged to God? She was afraid to tell anybody—anybody except for Sam, whom she thought she could trust with anything—for fear that they would think she needed to be committed.

For a time, Michal even thought that demons were trying to kill her. There was the ski-trip incident two Christmases ago. Driving back from Bear Valley, Michal suddenly felt something seize the wheel. Her Jeep plowed into a snow-packed embankment and flipped. But everything seemed like it was occurring in slow motion, and the Jeep ever so gently landed back on its wheels as if nothing had happened. She looked in her rearview mirror and noticed an angel-like figure standing in the road. She told Sam that evening when she stopped by his place on the way home.

"Michal, seriously. This has got to stop. The first time it was kind of cute, but now you just sound—*unstable*. Did you have imaginary friends when you were a kid?"

It was apparent that Sam was getting impatient. Michal tried not to tell him when it happened again but he was with her the morning her watch went missing. They both looked high and low for it, to no avail. But Michal felt a mischievous—even evil—spiritual presence. At this point she was pretty good at discerning them and, most importantly, at getting rid of them. —At least temporarily. She said her all-too-well-rehearsed Jesus-incantation and when she came back from the laundry room, the watch was suddenly there on the floor in such an obvious spot that she and Sam could never have overlooked it.

"I told you, Sam, demons won't leave me alone." She presented the watch to him, explaining where she had found it.

"Michal, would you like *me* to phone the psychiatrist or will you?"

Michal laughed, but Sam wasn't laughing.

"I mean it." He gulped his last drops of coffee, silently gathered his belongings and walked to the door. As he was leaving he said, "Call me if the old Michal ever comes back."

She never saw Sam again, and now she couldn't. He had died last summer, choking on a piping-hot, straight-from-the-campfire toasted marshmallow. As luck would have it, the bears got to him before the park rangers did, and so the coroner's report read "death by mauling," which is a far more manly way to go than dying from a little ball of whipped sugar lodged in one's throat.

As I said, she never saw Sam again, and except for her pastor—who seemed to respond in the same suspicious way—and a few brief mentions to Max, she learned to never tell another soul.

And now the demons would not leave her alone—or so Michal thought. It was as if they were on a mission to drive her mad. Even in Phil's *ryokan*, it seemed. The night before, in the middle of the night, Michal awoke to an incessant *tap, tap, tap*. The annoying noises went on for several minutes. She glanced out the window, but not surprisingly nothing was there. She crawled back under the comforter and covered her ears with her pillow, but then the noise grew even louder:

TAP, TAP, TAP. TAP, TAP, TAP.

Once again, Michal thought to say the magical words *In the name of Jesus.* . . . And POOF—the sound instantly stopped.

Demons and angels had become regular features in Michal's life. They were as much a fabric of this world—*just as real*—as people, poppies and snow globes.

NINE

Nothing weighs on us so heavily as a secret.
JEAN DE LA FONTAINE

LATER THAT EVENING. *At the RTSS*

Several hours had passed. Michal and Max were growing increasingly impatient with their friend's drinking and dramatics. Phil stood in front of them, arms crossed, every indication he had no intention of changing his behavior.

"What? Is that *too much truth for you?*" He walked up to the bar. "Oh right, we're all looking for truth, aren't we? But at every turn, throughout history, all the major ground-shaking philosophers have whored themselves out for *some belief!*" Phil spat out the words like they were obscenities. "Descartes? Our great skeptic? Tell me he didn't just want to avoid getting sent to his room. And now my own friends? They cling to *their* beliefs as well. And why? Because it feels good! Because it makes life comfortable! You need something to think about to keep you from thinking! Well, if you need that, how about this? Go ahead and start thinking about what happens to atheists when they die. Think about *that* long and hard, and tell me that your belief is a good one. . . ." He uncharacteristically grabbed a bottle of Bacardi 151, cinnamon schnapps, and Tabasco, mixed up a diabolical concoction and poured it into a little shot glass.

"Drink of the devil," he said.

He shot back the alcohol, looked at the empty glass, then savagely threw it across the room, laughing as it shattered against a wooden pillar, tiny bits of glass flying everywhere. He smiled smugly as he began to calculate the spray pattern in his head while he reached for the Bacardi again.

Max grabbed Phil's arm and began to pull it away from the bottle. Phil half-heartedly fought his motion.

"I think you've had enough, Phil."

"You think you're my *savior* now?" Phil snarled.

All that could be heard in the bar was the gentle hiss of the gas-fed fireplace. A light breeze played against the rice-paper shutters—the yellow ones with the white painted cranes. Michal could almost hear the water sculpture ticking in the pond next to the carcass of one ant and the still animate body of the other—scurrying about and oblivious to all these larger questions.

Michal spoke just above a whisper, "Phil, you've never really been interested in the afterlife, other than to mock it." She took a gulp of air as she tried to work past feelings welling up within her. "Why are you asking about this now?"

Phil smiled wickedly. "Why do *you* want to know? You've got your afterlife all buttoned up with your completely fabricated, comfy belief system." He saw a blur from his right before stars exploded in his eyes. The world went black for what seemed like an eternity. Or maybe it was only for an instant—he couldn't tell. When he came to, his breath blew back at him from the floor, smelling of vinegar. He opened his eyes to the blur of the bamboo hardwood. He flipped over onto his back. He could hear something through his ringing ears.

". . . Know . . . the . . . 'ell has got . . . you but . . . too far even for you! You can stop acting like a bastard now. Apologize to Michal!" The rings morphed into Max's yells. The words *bar fight* wandered around his brain. *Perfect ending to this little argument.* He took a swing at Max's groin only to be met by stabbing pain from Max's knee incapacitating his arm.

"You always were a shit fighter, Phil. Now's not the time to learn." Max took a step back. "You went off to cushy desk jobs and executive salaries. I went out to minister to the homeless. You know what it takes to handle yourself on the street, especially as a gay man?" Max stared him down until Phil finally looked away. He tried not to look sheepish. This proved all but impossible, given the screaming pain in his face and arm. He winced.

"That's right. You know nothing about that type of life. Which is why you're gonna apologize to Michal or I'm gonna make you eat your bar," Max said matter-of-factly.

Michal thought that if she had blinked she would have missed the whole exchange. She tried to speak with authority, but her voice came out as a whisper, "I can take care of myself, Max." She walked over and looked down at Phil. He had managed to turn on his side. The red blooming on his face would end up a nasty bruise. She couldn't help but think that he deserved it.

"Phil, you're scaring me. What is the point of all your questions? You've always asked questions with a certain calculation, with forethought. Manipulation, even. —You began asking me about lemons, so you could get me to agree to a particular restaurant when we were in Italy." She smiled, pleasant remembrances dancing around the hurt.

"I remember—and we did end up at that restaurant, as I recall." Phil smiled through the pain.

"You don't even get to pretend to gloat, ya jackass," Max said with a twisted look on his face. "'Pologize or get another ass whoopin'." Max thought about the many times he had ass-whooped homophobic jerks outside bars. "There's still time to show off my Kung Fu Grip. . . ."

Phil opened his mouth, then closed it as Max loomed over him. For a moment he thought about kicking Max's legs out from under him like some kind of action hero, but then he remembered how he had ended up on the floor in the first place.

He sat up on one elbow and immediately regretted it. The change in position caused a pounding in his head. He looked at Michal, shamefaced.

"Well, excuse me all to hell." Phil chuffed a laugh, which caused his face to explode in pain again. He returned to a much more neutral expression. "I'm sorry, Michal. I was out of line."

Max extended his hand to help Phil up to his feet. "It ain't the end of the world to be wrong, y'know." He winked at Phil while examining his face. "Now you can check something else off your bucket list."

"You remember that?"

"Of course," Max said. "You missed out on fighting an oil-rig fire as I recall, but did you ever fulfill that '*being with two women from different continents at once*' bit?" Max's eyes sparkled bright with suspended laughter.

Michal touched Phil's shoulder. "That aside, you playboy, why are you asking all these questions about the afterlife?"

"Can't I just engage in a riveting discussion with my good friends?"

"I don't think that's it. And we're your good friends because we're smart enough to know when you're stringing together a line of bullshit." Michal's eyes wavered between sadness and laughter.

"You and Max know what will happen to you after you die. You, Michal, will get your white-picket fence and heavenly-designer-dog breed, which will be superior to your neighbor's designer-dog breed, and you will get together at heavenly block parties and tell your neighbor that she looks good in purple 'cause that's the only other color you can wear in heaven, while secretly you wish she'd gain twenty pounds. . . ."[72] He frowned. "Well, I've never known what will happen to me. People often call atheists 'arrogant elitists,' as if we act superior to those who believe because we think our views are infallibly right." Instinctively, Phil reached for his glass, only to be met by Max putting his hand down on the bar to block him. Deprived of his favorite nervous tic, Phil continued: "But atheists are not arrogant, because we don't presume to have any idea about the afterlife. Ultimately, we say that this life is it. We don't conjure up visions of heavenly hosts or some great opportunity to talk to Socrates, or Descartes, or Hume, or Nagel—oh wait, he's still alive." Phil smiled weakly. "Death is nothing. The end. That takes more bravery and *honesty* than believing in some pleasant eternity where God will wipe away every tear. We *want* to believe that at the end of our lives we don't turn into worm food, because if that's all there is, it seems like our lives had no point, like they were a terrible waste. But the reality is, that's precisely what happens. At best we'll leave some testament behind to a life well-lived."

Michal's eyes welled with tears. Phil hadn't been so poetic in a long time.

—A very long time.

She put her hand on Phil's shoulder and gave a pained smile. She was certain she knew what he was trying to say, but she didn't want to accept it. She held his gaze and asked anyway.

"Phil, are you saying what we think you're saying?" Michal whispered.

Phil gave her a cockeyed smile, "I think you know what I'm saying." His gaze drifted to Max. "I'm dying."

AUTUMN

Know'st thou not at the fall of the leaf
How the heart feels a languid grief
Laid on it for a covering,
And how sleep seems a goodly thing
In Autumn at the fall of the leaf?

DANTE GABRIEL ROSSETTI

§

TEN

No one here gets out alive.
JIM MORRISON

The White House, Act 1, Scene 1.
(NOT TO BE CONFUSED WITH THE RESIDENCE AT 1600 PENNYSYLVANIA AVENUE)

SCENE. Exterior of a house. It is white. The walls are white, the door is white, even all the windows are white. There is light all around. This heightens the sheer whiteness of the house, eliminating even a hint of shade or texture. Footsteps can be heard coming from stage left. They keep the same tempo, maintain the same volume, grow no louder even as a man appears out of a fog of—even more white. He is wearing a dark-green jacket and has charcoal-black hair pulled back with just the right amount of gel to keep everything perfectly in place without looking greasy. He is unabashedly attractive with a striking physique—what some might even call "beefcake" or "eye candy," considering how he fills out his jacket. His looks are exotic, perhaps Middle Eastern. He walks toward the house and stops fifteen feet away. He looks at the walls and at the second-story gables, squinting and holding up his hand to block the incandescent blaze of the house. He can barely withstand the implacably bright light. Finally, he pulls out dark glasses from his khaki pants and puts them on. They are wrap-around-your-face glasses, the kind that Arnie wore in *Terminator.* He gets a stern look on his face and turns to the audience. "I'm ba-a-ack ." He smiles, then approaches the house. Cautiously, he knocks on the door. The sound is hollow and echoes all around the stage. The man pushes lightly on the door and the entire house moves from the effort. He walks to the left of the house and sees that it is nothing more than a facade, a bit of stage prop. He laughs quietly to himself, then immediately stops and looks around. Apparently satisfied that his laughter has gone unnoticed, he walks around the facade into a living-room set. An overstuffed chair in (you guessed it) white sits before a crackling yellowish-red fire in a free-standing glass fireplace, the only bit of color to be seen. Smiling, the man approaches the chair. He pulls out a cigar and bites off the end. He looks around again and makes a motion to spit it out. Before he can, something offstage startles him. He looks stage right and his eyes go wide.

(Speaking through a bit-off cigar) "Of course you're here. You would wait until I'm about to—yes—well, I was thinking of that—don't you have an ashtray?"

Moments tick by, as the man in the green jacket listens intently to a sound that the audience cannot hear. He continues a dialogue with the inaudible presence.

"OK, but I think I'll just—no? All right." The man screws up his face and swallows the cigar tip. "Do you mind if I light it now? OK, thank you . . . Sir." He addresses the air with an equal measure of fear and respect. Plopping the cigar between his lips, he produces a flame from his fingertips and lights the cigar. Two long puffs and four short ones and the cherry is burning well.

"May I sit?" (Man gestures at the seat)

"Thank you. —You've extended an open invitation. I'm here. C'mon, you've kept worse company: gluttons, drunkards. . . ."

"What? Where have I been? All around, doing my usual work for— Right, it's a secret. Mum's the word."

"You know. . . . I've been here and there. East and west—mostly east, recently. . . . But you know that."

"Of course you know what I'm going to ask. Is there any point in—ah, you want me to say the words? —Fine."

"Sorry. It's just that—you know what's been going on. I've heard that you even know about that incident. I didn't think anybody knew about that. . . ."

The man in green, now sitting in the chair, now enjoying his cigar, takes multiple puffs and looks particularly contented with himself. "Yes, that. . . . Fine work if I do say so." He goes to tap some of his cigar cherry on the floor and stops mid-motion. He looks at the cherry and then seems to strain to hear something.

"Oh, come on! —No ashtray and not on the floor? Really, is that necessary?" He spends a moment looking defiantly at the cigar, craning his neck to hear. "And not in the fireplace either? Look, I appreciate the homey touches, but I would like to put them to some good use."

The cherry is starting to get dangerously close to falling off. The man looks at the cherry, looks at the chair, looks at the fireplace, looks quickly but carefully around the "room" and finally exhales in exasperation, whereupon he stands up and taps out the cherry on his pants. He wiggles around, uncomfortably moving the cherry away from anything vital. He grits his teeth as he seems not to have succeeded, squinches his eyes for ten seconds, and then settles back into the seat.

"There, I won't sully your precious fake house. . . . This reminds me of all those other houses of yours. Great on the outside, but filled with fakes." He smiles at his own jest, then immediately frowns. "I was just having some fun at your— No, Sir. It won't happen again." He stares at the floor sheepishly, twists his foot and seems to lose track of time.

"What? Oh, right, I'm here for a reason. That is, of course, if you don't mind, if you have the time . . . y'know, if it's OK and you're not too busy. . . . Well, of course, you *do* have the time, what was I thinking? —Um—what *was* I here for?" Seconds pass. "You have that effect on a being, you know that? Um. . . .

"Oh, yeah, *beings.* I'm a *being,* right? And in fact you have said—and I don't mean this in a bad way to remind you of something you obviously know—but you have promised that I—I mean *anyone*—can ask for anything. I just need to ask.

"Didn't you say that I just have to ask? —I just have to ask, right? Well, I'm here asking. Yep, that's me, just sitting here in this incredibly wonderful, comfy chair asking. Going to ask—going to ask right now—yep—asking. . . ." He grits his teeth and winces preemptively.

"I know—I know that you're not part of our crowd. I know they gave you a bad rap. I get it. You can do pretty much anything. I know about all that Bad Ass stuff you've done. You must know that you've got *quite* a reputation."

He quickly gets up from the chair, suddenly aware of what he has just said.

"A GOOD reputation. Yes, very good, at least relative to you know. . . ." He points up. "You know. . . ." He points up again. "You know?" Then he smiles the same sheepish smile. "Of course you know. What was I thinking?" He sits down. His smile turns to confusion as he tries to regain his train of thought. Then suddenly he stands up.

"I know you can do it. I won't overstep my bounds—*I swear.*"

Cupping his ears, as if a great thunderous sound has just erupted, he yells inaudibly. His every muscle strains to get his words out over the sound, but he can't. He tries again, but can offer nothing but the silence of an open mouth trying to defy the deafening boom. Finally the man's voice returns as a great anguished cry.

"Wow. . . . OK, you're right. . . . Sorry to have presumed. It won't happen again. In that case, *I won't swear.* You just have my honest 'yes.' My 'yes' as a servant and a tempter. Great work if you can get it. . . ." He looks offstage. "No, I mean it. Great work, really great, wonderful, *honorable work.* I'm lucky—*blessed even*—to have the job."

He gets up from the chair and looks around for somewhere to get rid of his cigar. He turns one way, then the other, looking very much like a child lost in the mall or a dog chasing its own tail. Finally, exasperated, he starts to eat the remainder of the cigar.

(Through full mouth) "Just give me three days. Three days is all I ask."

(He continues to take bites of his cigar)

(Exit stage left)

How Phil Got the RTSS

You might be curious about how Phil acquired the Rashomon ryokan and how he ended up with so much money in the first place. It's a fascinating story, worth a few minutes to tell. His grandfather was none other than the enormously wealthy Phillip Foster, inventor of the TV dinner. He got the idea from the prepackaged airline meals that he consumed on his many trips between New York and

California. He pitched the idea to a big food products company in the early fifties. They loved it and soon these frozen meals were found on every American family's kitchen table. The company later challenged Foster's claim that he was the inventor, but in the end, Phillip Foster was a multi-millionaire. He soon bought a competing company himself, started marketing the dinners in oven-ready aluminum trays, and became wealthier than ever.

Phil often visited his grandfather, especially at Christmas time, when brightly colored decorations adorned the mansion filled with priceless artwork, intermingled with various artifacts from his grandfather's world travels. Phil was especially mesmerized by the eight-foot tall, nine-hundred-pound grizzly that welcomed guests in the atrium. At Christmas it wore a red velvet Santa hat. Phil's grandmother had died when he was just a young boy. She had fallen off their 90-foot luxury yacht, The Gloria—it had been named after her—in the Mediterranean, just off Porto Cervo in Sardinia, Italy. Earlier that evening, his grandparents had dined at the Billionaire Nightclub. Phil's grandmother had had too much to drink, even before they returned to the yacht. She was standing at the stern, drinking her fifth pomegranate martini. She twirled around in her full length, red-beaded evening gown, begging Foster to take her photograph. As she struck a movie-star pose, she stepped back too far and fell overboard. Her body washed up on shore three days later. Foster mothballed The Gloria until his grandson started college, at which point Phil brought her to the Santa Barbara harbor.

A few years ago, Phil had been on one of his many adventures when he got word that his grandfather had died. He had been hiking in the Nubra Valley of the Indian Himalayas and had just negotiated buying a few Buddhist relics from the monks at Diskit Gompa. Only Phil could pull that off. He cut his trip short to make the funeral and the reading of the will. Much to Phil's surprise, his grandfather left him a Cezanne worth over $35 million. It hung in Phil's apartment for several months, right next to his Patrick Nagel signed by the artist himself. Otherwise the walls were bare. It made for great conversations at parties, but Phil started to worry that word might get out that the painting was sitting in his apartment, ripe for the taking. He decided to donate it to the Metropolitan Museum of Art—that is, right after he got back from his trip to Japan.

He found a high-end broker-and-storage firm, and had them keep it. Five hundred a month seemed a bit steep to him, but it turned out to be quite a deal. So he stored his Cezanne and his Nagel and took off for Japan. Phil took no small joy at watching the proprietor's face drop when he brought out his framed canvases and the Nagel seemed the more valuable piece.

Phil had never been to Japan, but had wanted to go ever since his Boston trip with Michal. He flew into the oppressive heat and humidity of Kansai International Airport, carrying just his travelling backpack, then he took the express train to the city. He visited the many Buddhist temples, Shinto shrines, palaces, and gardens, and marveled at the architecture. He stayed in hostels, love hotels, and coffins. He met a beautiful Japanese college student, Yuma, who was eager to practice her English with him in exchange for her giving him a tour of Kyoto. It

was a good deal for both parties, with some great side benefits when it turned
into a very intimate tour of Japan—or at least of one of its citizens.

On one of their excursions, Yuma took him to a stone pillar on Kujo Street.
She explained that this was what remained of the Rashomon—one of the two city
gates built during the Heian Period. She told him of its history and how this had
been the setting for Kurosawa's 1950 film. Walking back to Phil's hotel room,
they passed a real-estate office with photos taped to the window. There he spotted a ryokan within a few miles of the lake region of Otsu, for sale for only $153
million. . . . —Wait, that's in yen—so about 1.5 million in US dollars. The ryokan
was in an amazing location, within walking distance of a small village, near a field
of yellow-gold poppies and nestled in the Hira Mountains, complete with a natural hot spring. It would need a hell of a lot of work. Phil thought about the oil rig,
his life, and fleeting opportunities, and almost instantly decided that he would
sell—not donate—his Cezanne and buy the ryokan. What good was a painting of
a bunch of apples when he could have new, exciting experiences? Besides, the
museum had enough Cezannes anyway. . . .

Back in New York, he set about finding a buyer for his painting, something
which was actually harder than finding a buyer for his apartment. But two weeks
later, he was down to his travel backpack, one piece of art (he would never get rid
of his Nagel) and two boxes of personal items. He donated his furniture, most of
his clothes, and nearly everything else, to the local Goodwill.

After returning to Japan, he found that Yuma had gone back to school, so his
very broken Japanese had to sustain him through the sale. Thankfully, large sums
of cash speak clearly the world over. He bought the ryokan, renaming it The
Rashomon Tea and Sake Shop. The walls were nearly falling down, the spring
was overgrown with weeds and the road was atrocious. He spent the next two
years fixing it up, hiring contractors and doing some of the work himself. Ultimately he'd fix everything. Except the roads—he still liked his privacy.

Room with a View

Two men stood talking in a cold white room. Last year's magazines sat neglected
in a wall-holder. A glass jar of cotton swabs sat next to another piece of medical
equipment, which more resembled a celestial screwdriver than a conventional
device. One man was slowly putting on his shirt, while the other, wearing a long
white coat over his khakis and Stratford, adjusted his red-yellow-and-blue Jerry
Garcia silk tie. The first man looked at the tie while he dressed. The many colors
were supposed to be whimsical, inviting, to put him at ease. Right now they just
looked comical, like a clown's clothing. The first man opened his mouth to speak.
The words that followed were the typical questioning protest for which the man
in white had adopted a standard answer given with a friendly smile. Of course, he
could get a second opinion, but he was confident in his analysis of the results.

Eons and light years away, something watched the exchange. It smiled at the
proceedings. It was always amusing when these creatures were faced with their
own demise. It laughed, unrestrained. What foolish little ignorant beings these
are.

It switched its gaze to another of the trio. She was talking with a priest on the phone. They were making arrangements to talk in a few months. Too bad that his schedule was so full of other more important matters of God. . . .

Another shift, and a different man was talking to a group of people in a basement room of a church. They were drinking bad coffee and store-bought lemon pound-cake. The coffee had been brewed yesterday. It had boiled down to a well-nigh undrinkable murky black liquid that everyone gritted their teeth to swallow, smiles plastered on their faces in self-defense.

Many questions were being asked of the man. Questions about morality, sexual preference, pedophilia, adoptions. Another laugh as it watched the proceedings. *What fools. They think that any of this is absolute. They think they know, and yet the truth is far grander than any of that.*

The man in the basement room seemed able to answer the questions. The woman hung up the phone and gazed out the window. The first man put on his shirt, took a piece of paper and left the room. The observer watched it all.

"Yes, that one will do quite nicely," it said.

It laughed at the thought of time and space. *It's already happened—and yet it won't be happening soon enough.*

It laughed again.

THE NEXT MORNING. *At the RTSS*

A scruffy mouse with a crazy bulging eye that could never fix on any one thing emerged from the tall grass on the side of the road. He stopped and sat on his hind legs, sniffing the air. Satisfied, he squatted down and made a dash for the mound with the bright colors and the water, avoiding a line of marching ants. As he paused for a quick drink, he thought about his cousin in California, where all of the movie stars lived and everyone carried guns and rode horses. She had a much easier life. Once she showed him all of the glitz-and-glam that she had collected from a human who wasn't a movie star, but who looked and played the part. If only he could manage to sneak into a human's suitcase to pay his cousin another visit. He'd stay a lot longer this time to lounge by the pool.

After wiping off his whiskers, he bounded across the compressed granite road toward the building where the man lived. He came to a big orange-flowered bush and stopped. He wandered around for a few minutes, looking for a snack. He found a very unappetizing grub carcass, not at all to his liking—not even if he were to add a honeysuckle condiment.

He scurried up to the big door and squeezed through a small crack between the boards, wriggling his way inside as he had done at least a dozen times before. He began to search for a morsel to tide him over.

Phil sat at the bar watching the invisible customers, imagining their conversations. He relished the hush. He felt the gentle breeze outside through the opened shutters and heard the creak of the floorboards as he shifted in his seat. He could even hear the tiny scamper of a field mouse running across the floor. He hopped off the seat to get a broom. It was a quiet bar, but it was *his* bar, and it was going to be clear of *pests*. He said the words out loud as he grabbed the broom.

I am not a pest. I am a respectable field mouse and I have a name. My name is Randall. You wouldn't think me a pest if you got to know me.

Phil saw the mouse stop by a chair leg. Holding the broom tighter, he wondered whether the mouse actually was a pest. He thought about his own behavior, especially of late. Maybe he and this little mouse had more in common than he thought. He wouldn't shoo *himself* out of a room. Or maybe he would. Even *he* got on his nerves some times.

He stared at the mouse. The mouse stared back. Finally, he slowly reached behind the bar and grabbed a pack of rice crackers. He opened the little cellophane packet. Randall—whose name Phil still didn't know, as he had never thought to ask—twitched his nose and whiskers in anticipation. Phil tossed the little cracker to the mouse. Randall cautiously made his way to the cracker and grabbed it between his paws. He looked at the man who showed no sign of approaching, and so he sat back on his haunches and began to eat.

When Randall finished, he tried desperately to get the man's attention to give him another rice cracker. He especially liked it wrapped in *nori*. But how could he possibly communicate *that*? This was going to be a bigger challenge than he had first thought, for the man spoke American human (of which he knew just a little to get by) and he spoke mouse and *Japanese* mouse to boot (which had its own special dialect)—and he'd heard the man try to speak Japanese. So Randall decided to jump up and down and do a little twist, hoping *that* would get the man's attention.

"Is that the only customer you can attract these days?" Michal said, as she walked into the room. Randall studied her. She looked exactly like the photo he'd seen when he visited his cousin. He noticed a shiny thing hanging from her neck. Yep, this was the same woman. Now he just needed to find out where she was hiding her suitcase.

Michal stamped her foot. Randall scampered away into the darkness. He'd heard about this woman's dramatic performances from his cousin and he wasn't certain what to expect. Little did he know, Phil engaged in his own dramatic performances, too.

"Well, *that* was unnecessary," Phil said. He looked at Michal. "I was thinking about identity and I was about to debate my only customer." Phil motioned to a few small crumbs sitting on the floor. "And now he's gone. . . . See, this is why I don't have any customers."

"Because you engage them in existential debates and scare them away?" Michal asked. "Well, I believe it." She smiled.

"Only the weak-minded ones," Phil jabbed.

"Three, two, one. . . . Asshole," Max chimed in as he walked into the bar. "Look at the performance on this machine. It'll go from zero to asshole in three seconds. You can't get that kind of performance out of just any bar-owner." He grinned.

"I'm a well-oiled machine," Phil said. "Interesting—now I'm a machine."

"What are you on about now?" Michal asked with a smile. She was still trying to figure out Phil's mood. She wondered whether he was ready to talk about his imminent death.

"Apparently I'm a machine, and Max is a gay man—unless something changed recently that I don't know about. And you, well you're a. . . ."

"Not so fast, Phil. But I welcome a discussion about personal identity, especially since your mouse-friend seems to have run away," Michal said.

"You mean since my mouse-friend was *scared* away," Phil said.

"I'm sure you're breaking all sorts of Japanese health codes by having him around. I mean look at *that*." Michal motioned to a few droppings on the floor.

"Oh, *that*," Phil began, "*That* would be a token of his appreciation. I wonder if he'd like *nori* with that rice cracker next time. I love it like that and I get the feeling that this little guy is not so different from me."

"I wonder what it would take for a little mouse to be a person?" Max wondered. "Or a Martian, or a computer?"

"Well, all it would take for a little mouse to be a Martian would be to ship it off to Mars." Phil laughed. "To become a computer, well, that would take some complicated brain transfer, switching out mouse brain-matter for silicon, copper, and whatnot."

"OK, so my question came out badly." Max mock-frowned. "I mean: what would it take for a little mouse, a Martian, or a computer *to become a person*? Can there be non-human persons?"

"Great question, Max," Michal said. "It really gets to the question: Just what *are* we? Are we material bodies, or thinking things, or some combination of immaterial souls and material bodies? Which of our properties are essential and which are only accidental or contingent?"

"This goes back to my comment about whether Max could ever be a Botswanan shepherd. Or was it a goat herder?" Phil smiled.

"I know what phenomenologists like Merleau-Ponty would say about that," Michal began. "Max would be a different person altogether. The self is embodied and situated in a world of other embodied selves. The self is constituted in, with, and through the body in a deeply relational world. . . . You know, the East African poet, Okot p'Bitek, also understood that we are constituted in relation to others. He says we are 'son,' 'mother,' 'daughter,' 'father,' uncle,' husband,' grandfather,' 'wife,' 'clansman' 'chief,' 'medicine man.' The central question 'who am I?' cannot be answered in any meaningful way, unless we understand all of these relationships. As p'Bitek explains it, even a hermit peoples his cave, his forest, or his mountaintop with gods, spirits, devils and angels, and enters into communion with them as well as with nature—with birds, flowers, animals, trees and rocks.[73] Sartre said that our being is not just for-itself, but for-others. I wonder why, then, Sartre said that we are radically free? How can we be radically free, when we find ourselves interacting in a world of differing relations of power? Simone De Beauvoir got that. She said that our freedom is limited by our situation. Of course, in the *Second Sex,* she was speaking about women—as I've said before—but this applies to every marginalized person in society. Anyway, our Botswanan Max would not be our same, lovable, Texan Max. He would not survive a brain transfer." Michal smiled and gave Max's big arm a squeeze.

"I love talking about brain transfer experiments. They're so much fun," Max said. "Remember Locke's prince-and-cobbler example?[74] The prince's memories and consciousness go into the cobbler's body and vice versa. It would suck to be the prince after that. He could try everything to get back into the castle, but people would just think he's crazy."

"Like Descartes' madman, who thinks he's a king when he's only a pauper," Michal said.

"But in this case the pauper really *is* the king—well, a prince anyway," Max said.

"You know, these brain transfer cases really make one think about moral responsibility," Phil said. "Imagine that a surgeon puts my brain into Max's body, and given Max's burly size, I open a big can of whoop ass on some disagreeable folks. So, now I'm Max. . . ."

"Locke would say that you're Phil *the person,* Max *the body,* and an *entirely new man,*" Michal said.

"The point is: Who is responsible? Presumably I am, but then it's Max's body that gets punished. Of course, since it's *Max's* body and not my own, I really don't give a shit," Phil said and grinned.

"Thanks a lot," Max said.

"And where did Max's brain go? Into *your* body?" Michal asked.

"Nah, I've always wanted to be a zombie," Phil said.

"Maybe my brain went into your little mouse friend. Then I'd say that little mouse is now a person," Max said. "And a very sweet one, if you don't mind me saying so." He smiled.

"The problem with these transplant experiments," Michal began, "is that they regard the body as an exchangeable container or receptacle for our character or memories. Rae Langton and Susan James make this point.[75] Body swapping does not preserve psychological continuity. Swapping between a man and a woman, or a prince and a cobbler, or a black man and white man, or gay and straight, would almost certainly change psychological traits. Suppose a female supermodel's brain was transplanted into a greasy, obese male car mechanic's body. As Langton says, when we imagine the memories and character traits of a person being transplanted from one body to another, we imagine that person feeling much the same as before, committed to similar projects, to their own future as before, maintaining many of the same relationships as before. If the new body is sufficiently different, all that is up for grabs. They might even lose emotional investment in the new life they find themselves in."

"Well, if *your* brain were transferred into a supermodel's body, you'd be *you* only better," Phil said with a laugh, then immediately regretted it.

Max chuckled.

"No, that wouldn't be me, you ass. The problem with these transplant experiments is that they assume that there can be continuity of memory without continuity of body. But this is at odds with the phenomenology of memory. Some memories, such as trauma memories, are experienced at least in part by the body. So those memories would fail to survive the transplant. . . . And I'm perfectly happy with my body. —You've certainly never complained about it before," Michal said with a frown.

"Your body has always been *luscious,* darling." Phil smiled. "It was just my attempt at a lame joke. . . . Now, what we're trying to answer is a version of the persistence question. Under what possible circumstances is a person who exists at one time identical to someone who exists at another time? There are a couple of obvious approaches: the psychological approach and the somatic approach. The psychological approach is Locke's, of course. He invokes a memory criterion. If Person 2 at time $t=2$ can remember an experience of Person 1 at time $t=1$, then Person 2 is identical to Person 1."

"There's an obvious problem with this view," Max said. "I wouldn't be identical to my fetus, having no memories of when I was a fetus, nor even of my very early childhood. And God forbid I'm ever in a permanent vegetative state or suffer extreme dementia—I wouldn't be identical with that person either. The memory criterion just doesn't work."

"It also fails transitivity," Phil pointed out. "If A is identical to B, and B is identical to C, then A is identical to C. But suppose that an awkward, shy teen has a miserable time in high school. In his thirties, he becomes a successful, charismatic CEO of some awesome company and he remembers those painful teen years. As a very old man, he remembers his successful career as a CEO, but he doesn't remember his teen years. In this case, the awkward teen is identical to the CEO and the CEO is identical to the old man but the awkward teen is not identical to the very old man."[76]

"And, of course, since I can't remember anything in a dreamless sleep, I am not the same person as the person sleeping," Michal said.

"OK, so this view is pretty screwed up," Phil said. "You do realize, then, that you two will not be the same people in your glorified, resurrected bodies. Especially you, Michal, who insists on this phenomenological understanding of the embodied self. I wonder if you can find your way out of this one."

"Maybe Max and I can invoke a metaphysics of temporal parts," Michal suggested. "We are a sum of person-stages or parts, temporally contiguous with each other and not with anything else. For every period of time that I exist, there is a temporal part of me that exists only then. Temporal parts have different properties, just as different spatial parts have different properties. Ted Sider talks about this.[77] We are four-dimensional objects with temporal parts. So the same 'person' can have a fetus-part, an awkward teen-part, a successful CEO-part, a demented old man-part, a worm food-part, and a resurrected body-part."

"There's a fancy word for this: 'perdurantism,'" Phil said. "But there seems to be a problem with this, too. Perdurantism can't explain real change. The whole four-dimensional object does not change, it only has different parts."

"At least it explains how I can be the same person at the resurrection," Max said.

"And of course you need to secure *that.*" Phil winked. "So, we have arrived at probably the best approach: the somatic approach," he said. "Person 1 and Person 2 are identical, if they are the same organism."

"Instead of 'Person 1' and 'Person 2,' let's refer to them as 'Tweedledum' and 'Tweedledee.'" Michal smiled.

Phil smirked. "So let's get to the *Tweedledoozy:* the somatic approach. . . ."

"But then how can you make sense of brain transplants, Phil? It seems that if your brain went into a different body, then you'd be in two different places," Max said. "Most of you would be in one place as an empty-headed vegetable—well, that's weird."

"Isn't he already an empty-headed vegetable?" Michal socked Phil in the arm and grinned. "Sorry, I couldn't resist."

"Funny. . . ." Phil said. "I am a *thinking animal*. Notice that this does not imply that all human animals are people. Fetuses and empty-headed vegetables would not be people. . . ."

"There could potentially be serious problems with this view, if our moral scope is limited to people," Max said.

"I don't think too many folks limit their moral scope to people anymore. We aren't living in the nineteenth century, you know," Michal said.

"So then where do you draw the line? Sentient animals? Cute animals? All animals? All plants? Well, except for weeds. But weeds are just *ugly plants*. . . ."

"We are derailing here, boys," Michal said.

"Max started it," Phil said and stuck out his tongue. "So to rein it back in: Being a person is only a temporary property of being a human animal. The other cool thing about this view is that it doesn't imply that all people are carbon-based organisms. Angels, aliens from outer space, conscious robots, could all be people."

"You know, John Searle's Chinese room example challenges what he calls the 'strong AI view,' showing that even the smartest computers do not have a mind, do not understand, do not have consciousness,"[78] Michal said. "Remember the example?"

Phil and Max looked at each other, turned to Michal and responded, "Shi."

Michal grimaced. "Fine, then you guys explain it."

Phil winked at Michal, "No, I'd like to hear *you* explain it."

"OK. —Suppose I'm locked in a room and know that I'm going to be asked questions in Chinese. I don't understand Chinese, either spoken or written. I have a set of rules written in English that allow me to respond in written Chinese to questions also written in Chinese. The people asking me the questions who understand Chinese believe that I also understand the language. But, of course, I don't. —Searle says that computers do the same thing. They appear to be genuinely communicating, but they don't really understand the conversation."

Phil nodded his head approvingly and said, "Duìbùqǐ. Wǒ bù míngbái."

Michal looked at him for a moment, then said, "You do know I understand a bit of Chinese. I think you just said 'I'm sorry. I don't understand.'"

"Merely emphasizing your point. Sounded like I knew what I was saying, right?"

"Any time Phil can say *I don't understand* in any language, we should take it," Max cut in.

"There's certainly a possible world of conscious robots," Phil said. "And that was my point."

"So after all this, I'm really not sure *what* we are, but I can say this—I'm hungry. Phil, go fetch me a sandwich," Max said and smiled.

ELEVEN
"Rasho-Ramen"

Man just wants to forget the bad stuff, and believe in the made-up good stuff.
It's easier that way.
COMMONER, *RASHOMON*

MID-AFTERNOON THE NEXT DAY. *At the RTSS*

Michal touched the pendant that hung from her neck. It just didn't mean the same anymore. She stabbed her spoon back into the pint of vanilla ice cream. Real vanilla beans, cream, egg yolks, sugar. Not guar gum, not cellulose gum, not mono- nor di-glyceride, not polysorbate 80 (*what is that?*) nor artificial vanilla flavoring. She remembered one of Phil's more sophomoric—and drunk— moments, years ago, when he told her: "Don't ever eat vanilla ice cream with that artificial vanilla flavoring. Do you know what's in it? Castoreum. The juice from a beaver's anal glands. I am not making this shit up, Michal. Fake vanilla ice cream is nothing other than frozen beaver-butt juice."

Michal laughed as she brought the spoon to her mouth. She imagined the assembly line at a Ben and Jerry's—beavers on the conveyors, butts raised in the air, with women in hairnets and latex gloves squeezing the juice from their glands into big pickle jars. *Nope. Ben and Jerry's is the real deal.*

Despite Phil's recent antics, Michal could not quite bring herself to call him an asshole. Not now. Not now that he's dying. . . .

Hold it. Sure she could. He had been an asshole—an asshole for bringing them here like this. Besides, maybe he's wrong. Maybe the doctors are wrong. . . .

Nah, Phil likely insisted on ordering extra tests. He'd done his own research. *He was dying.* But then again—

Michal was definitely working through the first two stages of grief.

Max walked into the kitchen. Michal handed him a spoon and offered him the carton. He looked at her neck and smiled.

"I see Phil finally broke down and gave that to you."

"Yeah, but it doesn't mean anything. What was *he* going do with it? Wear it himself, when he's six feet under? —Sorry. Not funny." Michal frowned. "Do you think it's really true?"

"You mean what Phil told us the other night? That he's dying?"

"What else?"

"I think so. You know Phil. He likely ordered extra tests. I'm sure he did his own research, too. . . ." Max paused. "Yep, I'm sure it's true." Another pause.

"Truth—" He let the word linger. "Truth is a funny thing. You know, in the Gospel of John, Pontius Pilate asks Jesus 'What is truth?' which is pretty doggone ironic *since Truth was staring him right in the face!* Jesus doesn't answer Pilate. But of course you know that. . . ."

"Pilate didn't want to stick around for an answer." Michal tried to smile. "Or maybe Pilate meant that truth is really hard to grasp. It's always dangling just out of our reach—like this 'truth' about Phil dying. . . ."

Just then, Phil walked through the door. "Oh, I'm dying all right. I don't think science is wrong here. You could send me to fortunetellers, necromancers, sorcerers, *quacks,* and they'd all tell me the same thing: I'm dying. —So how are you guys today? I wanted to give you a little free time this morning."

"Of course you'd believe the so-called 'truths' of science. You know what standpoint theorists, like Sandra Harding, say about science, Phil? Scientists *think* that they are being objective—dispassionate, detached, disinterested, impartial, value-free—but this is only one perspective, one *privileged* perspective. There is no such thing as objectivity in the sense that science describes. What scientists choose to study, what they choose to take interest in while ignoring other puzzles and problems—how is this in any way objective? Science is a powerful institution that *appears* to be in the business of creating or discovering beneficial knowledge for everyone, but really it only advances and protects the interests of the dominant group, *their* group.[79] You know, science is a very *manly* institution, and more specifically, white, economically privileged, heterosexual males, although it is getting a tiny bit better. Virginia Woolf was right: 'Science is not sexless. She is a man, a father, and *infected* too. . . .'"

"But Michal, remember what Max Weber says in his lecture 'Science as a Vocation'? While science gives us the methods and means of justifying a position, science cannot tell us how to live or what to value. Value comes from our personal beliefs, like our religious beliefs," Max said, mouth full of ice cream. "So science *is* objective."

"You're missing my point, Max. No science is free from suppositions. Weber even admits as much. And suppositions always contain underlying value judgments. Science is never value-free. And science constructs truth and passes it off as a 'given.' Science is in the business of *myth-making.*" Michal took another stab at the ice cream.

"Are you *serious,* Michal?" Phil gave her an incredulous stare as he walked to the cupboard. "*Religion,* not science, is in the business of myth-making. . . ."

"Of course I'm serious, Phil. Science *never* gets us truth. As Harding says, further counterevidence can always—" Michal stopped and stared at Phil. "You're baiting me, aren't you?"

Phil smiled. "Please go on."

Undeterred, she continued: "Counterevidence can always be collected and conceptual shifts can cast old claims into new frameworks. As Harding says, scientific claims are not true *but only provisionally least false.* And the standards for what counts as *least false* are changing all of the time.[80] Scientific 'truths' are no truer than the so-called truths of the Bible."

"Michal, you just opened a big can of worms. Watch out. You might need another pint of ice cream," Max said. He looked over at Phil, who was opening a package of ramen noodles and dumping them into a saucepan.

"What you just said, Michal, is *wronger than wrong*," Phil began as he added some water to the pan. "Have you ever read Isaac Asimov's essay 'The Relativity of Wrong'? Science progresses from more to less false. It's just not true that all explanations of the world are *equally* wrong. Believing that the earth is a sphere is less wrong than believing that the earth is flat, since it's a closer fit to objective reality. But it's still wrong since the earth is actually an oblate spheroid. . . . Well, in fact, it's ever-so-slightly pear-shaped, as the first satellites discovered." Phil smiled wistfully. "Just like some women. I guess the whole Mother Earth thing has some merit after all." Max and Michal rolled their eyes. "Anyway, to equate the wrongness of the theory that the earth is flat with the wrongness of the theory that the earth is a sphere is wronger than wrong, since obviously one of the errors is more wrong than the other."

"Ramen noodles, Phil? Honestly, I thought that was beneath you." Max laughed.

"Yes, friend, ramen noodles. The Japanese love them. They consider instant ramen their best invention. When ramen noodles first hit the supermarket shelves, they were considered a luxury item. They were expensive." Phil inspected the empty package. "Is 'Oriental' even a flavor?" He shook his head and read the package again. "'Oriental'—now isn't that just a nice bit of ethnocentrism for you. And I dare say even more than a bit racist. Americans tend to lump everyone from East and South Asia into the same category and exoticize them."

"You're right, of course, but that's a discussion for another time," Max said. "Let's keep to this one."

"When I was a girl, I used to eat chunks of uncooked ramen noodles sprinkled with salt," Michal said.

"Have you ever tried it with paprika?" Phil asked. "Or how about drizzled with balsamic? I mean you should be more experimental with your cooking. . . . I know: topped with *sauce mornay.* —Actually, that might be pretty good."

"If you ate only ramen for every meal, you'd spend less than two hundred bucks a year on groceries," Max pointed out. "That even includes throwing in a fancy"—Max looked over at Michal—"a fancy *Tofurkey* for Thanksgiving." He laughed.

"Only a guy who lived on Skid Row would say something like that." Phil smiled, then looked away. "Sorry, Max."

"How many days in a row can someone eat only ramen noodles before they die?" Michal asked and then frowned when she realized the unintentional pun.

Phil laughed. "I don't know, Michal. Maybe we should conduct a scientific experiment. Of course, that would never get us *truth.*"

Max laughed. "Phil's got you there."

"Speaking of which, I think your feminism has been robbing you of your rationality, Michal," Phil said. "Yep, I'm baiting you again. I love the way your face gets all flushed."

Michal ignored the comment. "There you go again with your *faith* in scientific rationality, *enshrined* in all of the textbooks we've read since grade school."

"Michal, I am going to set you straight. Are you rejecting *reason* now? Do you now only appeal to intuition or *emotion*?" Phil asked.

"*You* appeal to *authority*. Scientific authority. You worship science as if it were your god. Nietzsche warns of this danger. As he says, there are no facts, only *interpretations*. Science is but one of many interpretations."

"There are *facts*, Michal. God's facts. Facts of the Bible. But I'll let Phil at you first," Max said.

Phil sat down at the table with his bowl of ramen noodles. "Science offers us many criteria for truth. And yes, Michal, *real truths*. At least truths so far as one is able to say that anything is true forever." He looked at Max. "Except God-boy over here who says *his* truths are eternal. . . . True beliefs portray the world as it really is. False beliefs portray the world other than it is. Take the claim that we are in Japan. The proposition 'We are in Japan' is true only if we are *actually in Japan*. This is the correspondence theory of truth. Its early advocates included G.E. Moore and Russell. Actually, it can be traced back to the ancient Greeks and Aquinas. Correspondence is one criterion for truth.[81] But science offers us many more. How about the principle of non-contradiction? The propositions 'This knife is straight' and 'This knife is not straight' cannot both be true at the same time, as simple observation will show."

"Not so fast, Phil. It's not that simple. This simple observable truth seems to change when the knife enters the water," Michal said.

"But it's still straight, Michal, even though it *appears* otherwise. The statement 'This knife is straight' is *still true*. . . ." He shook his head. "Anyway, let's move on. Consistency. A true proposition *fits the facts*. It is *in principle* falsifiable but not falsified. It does not contradict the facts. And how about coherence? A true proposition coheres with everything else we consider true. It confirms or at least fails to contradict the rest of our established knowledge. Or perhaps better: Truth is a property of a whole set of propositions and can only be ascribed to individual propositions insofar as they cohere with the whole. Spinoza, Leibniz, Hegel, and Bradley have proposed this kind of theory. And, of course, truths are useful. They give us mastery over our environment."

"There are a ton of problems with the coherence theory of truth, Phil," Michal began, "What if one lived in a ridiculous world where people believed that everything is colored pink. The drunk guy who claimed he saw a pink elephant would be considered credible. A true proposition is true if—what? It coheres with the beliefs of the majority? Or with the majority of the intellectuals in a given society? Or with those in power? Well, it's certainly *true*"—Michal laughed—"that those in power make a lot of shit up and pass it off as truth. Like those climate change deniers.... I can imagine that a powerful enough group could convince members of a given society that the whole world is colored pink. Of course, as they say, this would be sacrosanct—a *Sunday school* truth, if you will. Everyone would continue to see things differently colored but *really, truly, deep down,* people would know that everything is pink...."

"Kinda like the little wafers and wine you guys eat and drink on a Sunday." Phil grinned.

"Yep. Kinda like that," Michal said. "If you mean that we see and taste the wafer and wine but we know that it's *really* the body and blood of our Savior.... You know, the coherence theory of truth really only works with an omniscient mind, who has a 'God's eye view' of all the so-called facts."

"OK, so maybe coherence doesn't really work if it stands on its own. But as one criterion for truth amongst many, I think it's still helpful."

"I want to go back to that 'truth is useful' bit you mentioned earlier," Michal said. "Usefulness is an awful criterion. The problem is that it may be useful for some people to believe some proposition p but useful for other people to disbelieve it. Freud makes this point when he says that it may be useful for some people to believe in God to avoid despair, but for others it is useful *not* to believe in God."[82]

"Like my friend Crager," Phil observed. "'I won't go running to comfort and ignorance. I'd rather have pain and truth....'"

"Huh?" Max asked. "Who was that?"

"My friend Crager—"

"You know," Michal cut in, "both Foucault and William James talk about how truth is related to power and perspective.[83] We have a proclivity to forget how truths have been established. For James and Foucault, truths are made, not given. José Medina does a great job discussing their views.[84] Following James and Foucault, he says that truths are made in and through our practices, experiences and valuations, but we are prone to forget their origins. For instance, truths are 'made' by people in positions of power, but we forget that. —Like a lot of those so-called truths in the Bible."

"I'm not sure that you've got James exactly right, or that Medina does either," Phil said. "I've got nothing to say about Foucault. I can't speak to that, but only to James' pragmatic theory of truth. I thought that the pragmatic theories of Pierce, James, and Dewey held that truth is verified and confirmed through practice and experience. It takes a long time, then, to 'settle' truth. It's not that truth is just 'made up.'"

"Truth is a matter of perspective," Michal said. "Even Max believes this."

"What?" Max exclaimed. "No, I don't! Truth is objective. There are real facts. Real *honest-to-God* facts. *God's* facts and the facts of His word, the Bible. We don't always understand those facts or how they are filtered through *man's* facts, which leaves us with distortions and with different, sometimes contradictory, perspectives. *That's* the only *way*, Michal, that I believe that truth is a matter of perspective. People's subjective perspectives of God's *objective* facts."

"Max, you believe in transcendental, theological perspectivalism. I know that's a mouthful," Michal said. "For you there is one transcendental, or ideal, epistemic perspective, and a proposition is true only if it agrees with this—with God's—perspective. This transcendental truth is out of human reach. This is how you can explain people's different, often contradictory understandings and perspectives. But truth, *real truth*, is only what is accepted as true from this ideal perspective. For you, Max, truth is a matter of perspective—God's perspective, that is."

"OK, if that's what you mean, then I accept *that* kind of perspectivalism. I certainly don't believe your ridiculously relativistic, wishy-washy, progressive notion of truth as a matter of individual or group perspective," Max said.

"It's even worse than that," Phil argued. "Michal doesn't even take truth seriously. She seems to hold some kind of minimalist or deflationary theory of truth, which 'deflates' the supposed importance of the words 'true' and 'truth.' She takes the words 'is true' to be merely some sort of expressive convenience. It's certainly not a property that requires deep analysis.[85] Isn't that right, Michal? . . . Which is why you refuse to accept the truth that I'm dying."

"Hey, you know Kurosawa's movie *Rashomon* is all about truth. Did you know that, Phil?" Max interjected, trying to change the subject.

Phil rolled his eyes. "Where are you at right now, Maxie? What did I name this place? You're always trying to tell me things I already know."

"Oh, of course." Max shook his head. "Y'know, in *Rashomon* we have four different, contradictory, but equally plausible accounts of the murder of the samurai and the rape of his wife. But in the movie, even the dead guy lies. That is, if you're to believe that he's actually speaking through the medium. And in the end, it seems that the woodcutter's version of the story turns out to be *actually true*. So is each of the characters really seeing things differently? Are they really embracing different truths? Or are their stories motivated by self-interest while each of them knows the *real truth*?"

"Hmmm. Let's not get into all that right now," Phil said. "But I must admit that, except for that bit about Pilate and Jesus when I walked in—and Max, who can't help himself—you two managed to carry on a sustained philosophical discussion without bringing in that God fellow. I am impressed. Do you think it will last?"

"No chance in hell." Max smirked.

TWELVE

*I am a doubter, a questioner, a skeptic. When it can be proved to me that
there is immortality, that there is resurrection beyond the gates of death,
then will I believe. Until then, no.*
LUTHER BURBANK

LATE AT NIGHT. *At the RTSS*

Phil looked solemnly at his two friends. "I'm reminded of *Shanghai Express*. I bet
I've seen that old movie a couple dozen times. Why don't they make actresses like
Marlene Dietrich anymore?" He refilled the glass of the single bar patron who
was sitting at a table. The patron was wearing a faded pea-green tee with a screen
print of the female ninja Yukio from *X-Men*. He was slumped on the table, snor-
ing lightly. Phil clinked the glass with the bottle he held. The man barely stirred.

As Phil returned the bottle to the bar, Max said, "I've seen that movie more
times with you than I care to remember. There are some great lines in it. And
some of them are relevant to our recent discussions. Remember the exchange
between Reverend Carmichael and Shanghai Lily? The Reverend suggests that
Shanghai Lily get on her knees and pray. And she replies, 'If God is still on speaking terms with me.'"

Phil answered in his best Father Carmichael, "God remains on speaking terms
with *everybody.*" Stone-faced he looked at Max. "Are you trying to tell me something?"

"It's time for you to get on speaking terms with God."

Phil rolled his eyes and looked at his wrist, checking the watch that wasn't
there for the time. "Yeah, Max, I will—*later.* I'm not done sinning yet." He
laughed at his reference.

Max shook his head. "I know—why would you speak to an invisible unicorn?
But God can provide an enormous amount of comfort for you during this time.
Our words can only help so much. God's grace is another story. You just have to
let Him in."

"How long have we known each other?" Phil asked Max quietly.

"What, about fifteen years? Ever since college." He looked at Phil with the
hint of a smile. "Most of it good, except maybe the bit where you had me
interned. Oh, and that bonfire incident. What was her name? Stephanie?"

"Yes, well. . . ." Phil looked at the ceiling, a slight smile on his face as memories passed through his mind. "The bonfire incident—*Staci,* by the way." Then he
snapped back to the present. "But that's just it. . . . You'll say that *God* was there,
but that's your belief, whole cloth. The important thing to me is that *you* were
there. A real person, not my imaginary pet unicorn."

Phil looked at Max, shook his head and continued, "No, no—I want to share what Marlene Dietrich, the *luscious* Marlene Dietrich, said about death: 'When you're dead, you're dead. That's it.' And all you leave behind is food for weevils, which will be quite nasty if you're not quite dead."

Max gritted his teeth at Phil's horrible British accent, "You're using Python again, aren't you?"

Phil smacked the top of his head and replied, "NEE!"

"Why put your faith in the words of a movie star?" Michal asked, a hint of strain in her voice.

"I'm not putting my *faith* in a movie star." Phil's lips pursed, as he all but spat out the word. "I'm putting my faith *in you two,* the two people with whom I can engage with all of my senses—and anyway, I like what Marlene says."

Max raised his eyebrow to acknowledge Phil's revelation.

"Well, I like the words of Socrates much better," Michal said flatly. "For all we know, death could be the greatest blessing. It's either like a dreamless sleep, which is basically the best sleep in the world—except, of course, when I have flying dreams. Those can't be topped. Or it's hanging out and talking philosophy for all eternity.[86] That's pretty sweet to me, too." Michal chuckled, amused by her own tangent. "I really don't buy what Socrates is saying, but he *is* an awesome philosopher. You know where I stand. But you offer only *one* of many possibilities of what we become after death, Phil. Why should we suppose that you are right? You can't appeal to science here because no one has authority on this one."

"Michal, I accept what you say. You're right. Both philosophers and non-philosophers stand on pretty much an equal footing with respect to their understanding of death. There are no real experts. 'No one here gets out alive'—remember *The Doors?* Even those who study the process of death only know what happens to the body up until death. After that, once someone is dead, only the leftover gases and delightful decaying innards do anything that we can observe. We're all pretty much equals in thinking about death, and we all begin and end thinking about it from a position of ignorance.[87] Of course, we could just agree with Montaigne that death is a mystery and the purpose of philosophy is to learn how to die." He grimaced.

"But we have the truth of Jesus' life, death and Resurrection," Max argued. "*He suffered, and was buried, and on the third day, He rose again, in accordance with the scriptures....* Phil, I believe in the forgiveness of sins and the life everlasting with all my heart."

"When it comes to the Resurrection, Tillich said that dead men don't walk. Can't get any clearer than that," Phil said smugly.

Michal shook her head in frustration. "Max is right, Phil. But I won't proselytize you. Not right now, anyway.... You think we are nothing after death—worm food or weevil food, as you say. Completely gone. But as I said, there are *many* different possibilities, and since you just acknowledged that no one is really an authority here, you should be open to more of them."

"Well, it's possible that we are all reborn as purple-polka dotted kangaroos in some kangaroo heaven. —Of course, reason tells us this is pretty nutty, but no nuttier than hanging out in heaven with the angels, singing our hallelujahs, playing harps, polishing halos and mending broken angels' wings. And all that sounds pretty boring, if it *is* true. You know it's not. If it were, I'd rather have every atom in my body explode at the speed of light."

"Heaven is *not* like that, Phil," Max snapped. "As Peter Kreeft says, we may fear heaven because we fear boredom. We think that if there is an afterlife, either we will live eternally in boredom with God, or in agony separated from God. Life on earth seems far more interesting than heaven because we think there will be nothing to do there—or boring stuff, as you say, like playing harps, polishing halos and mending angels' wings."[88]

"But that's just heaven and we can revisit that in a moment," Michal said. "Remember, Phil doesn't believe in heaven." She waggled her finger at Max, looking every bit the schoolmarm. "So we should show Phil all of the possibilities that he has neglected. —Phil, you say death is the end of us?"

"I do. I'm a materialist," Phil explained. "It's a long-standing theory. *Theory*, by the way, is the operative word here. The father of modern materialism is Hobbes,[89] who followed in the footsteps of Democritus and Epicurus and other ancient Greeks. Hobbes argued that belief in incorporeal bodies and other such nonsense is one of the gross errors made by philosophers. You know, even in Jesus' day the Sadducees were materialists. They denied the soul's immortality and, indeed, the afterlife. *They were sad, you see, because they didn't believe in anything other than material reality*," he said, mimicking Michal's schoolmarmish tone. He snorted. "Without question, the Jews were pretty much all over the place here...."

"Reductive or eliminative, Phil?" Michal chided. "Come on, which are you? You must be an educated materialist, are you not? Do you believe that all mental states will eventually be explained away by scientific accounts of physiological processes, or are you even more radical, like the Churchlands?"[90]

Max interrupted, "The New Testament clearly asserts, in many passages, the existence of a soul and, after the body's death, of everlasting life through Christ." Max crossed his arms, willing Phil to change his mind.

"And Dickens asserts the existence of the Ghost of Christmas Past. Both equally fictitious." Phil's jaw jutted out slightly in challenge, his eyes sparkling.

"Really, Phil? You're comparing the inspired word of God to *A Christmas Carol,* a work of fiction?" Max asked incredulously.

"Fine. There might be some truth in Dickens.... But science does have something to say here. And while it might not be *definitive,* it seems the most likely. Certainly the most rational. You two have made the same mistake that most people make about atheists. You think that we *won't* believe in God, not that we *don't* believe in God. Atheism happens to be the current, most acceptable theory that has the most backing. By contrast, consider substance dualism. Descartes claimed that our intangible mental states proved the existence of a distinct mind or soul, utterly separate from the body. Being fond of fantastical explanations, Descartes located the point of interaction between mind and body in the pineal gland, since it seemed to have no other function. —Unless, of course, you've watched *From Beyond*. But while these intangible mental states *appear* utterly distinct from brain states, they are mere epiphenomena of those brain states, as Huxley has since pointed out.[91] In Descartes' time, it was hard to see how mind and brain could interact in any way other than by some strange hocus-pocus.

"I don't quite agree that our mental states have no influence whatsoever over physical states. Currently there isn't enough evidence to put this to rest. But it's what we have for now. Like atheism. Currently we don't have anything better to suggest as an alternative." Phil leaned against the barstool, arms crossed, face beaming.

"You know," Michal said, "John Hawthorne has argued that Cartesian dualism, which you have so satisfyingly mocked, meets the criteria of completeness, uniqueness, comprehensiveness, and exclusivity, and he warns that we should not so frivolously dismiss 'its pale caricature.'"[92]

"And Phil, merely finding relations, however close, between mental states and brain states does not move us any farther away from dualism. Sorry, my friend," Max said. "Humans are soul and body. But they are separated at death. The body may become 'worm food,' as you say, but the soul continues after the body returns to dust."

"Obviously I disagree with you, Maxie. I will allow there is the possibility you could be right in the same way that I will allow that suddenly we might no longer be affected by gravity. But I'm not going to start jumping off buildings any time soon, though Michal seems to have made a bad habit of that when she was a little girl." He smirked. "But let's move to evolution. You're smart people. You obviously believe in evolution. Don't scare me and tell me that there is a *creationist* in my midst." Phil exaggeratedly sneezed and wrinkled his nose.

"Evolution is the method by which God created us," Michal said.

"Wouldn't it have been simpler, less messy, less wasteful, less cruel, if God had just waved his magic wand and *Presto!*—humans existed? I guess your God didn't use a magic wand but"—Phil paused, searching for the right word—"*Play-Doh*—seems like it's good for something other than eating after all." He laughed. "Well, actually God molded us from dust, not Play-Doh. But it's the same idea."

Michal and Max looked at Phil disbelievingly.

"We know how creation is described in the Bible. We just don't usually refer to it with such tacky irreverence. But then, you don't care much about such things, do you?" Max said.

Phil shrugged. "I give it all the respect it deserves. Slightly above fan-fiction and roughly equal to *Star Trek* novels."

Max rolled his eyes. "Do go on, but you're a heretic and you need to be stoned immediately. . . . Michal, go get some rocks."

Phil continued, undaunted. "Check *your* Bible. It's not *my* Bible," he said, finger pointing to his chest. "Back to evolution. Evolution is an extremely gradual, extremely random process. So when did souls come about? Did the *Australopithecines* have souls? Or how about *Homo Erectus*? Weren't *they* in need of salvation?"[93]

"I don't know when in the evolutionary process God gave humans souls. But somewhere along the line He did," Michal said flatly.

"Remember, you rejected being spray-painted with the 'vaginal paint' of original sin," Phil argued. "You can't reject the vaginal-paint theory, or even a sperm-taint theory, but still hold that God, somewhere along the evolutionary line, inserted souls into humans. It's the same bad argument. This is just—" He stopped short. The many cruel things he could say swirled in his head. Finally he finished lamely: "It's just a bad argument and I think you recognize that."

"Fine. You've made your case for materialism or annihilation. Death ends us completely," Michal said in a tired voice.

"Except in the memories of our loved ones. . . . We remain alive, so to speak, until they forget about us. Then I suppose you could say that we are *really* dead. This view has been around a long time. Our man Epicurus held this view, and Lucretius, and Roy Batty."

"Let's consider other possibilities," Michal suggested. "Let's look at the viability of each of these. Shall we? Max mentioned Peter Kreeft and he can help us here."[94]

"I've got all the time in the world. . . . Well, at least a few months. Besides, that's why I invited you here earlier than usual. —In case you hadn't figured that out." Phil glanced behind the bar, noting his favorite anesthetic had dwindled to three bottles. He didn't notice Michal smile.

"Good. —Another possibility is that we survive death but only as ghosts. So we become mere shadows of our former selves," Michal said, fully aware that this was what Phil wanted—what he *needed*—right now. She said a silent prayer for wisdom and continued. "This is the mythological view of the shades of Hades. Remember, the Greeks would give libations to prevent the deceased, the *shades*, from haunting those who did not give them a proper burial. In the underworld, the far side of the river Acheron—that was the name of the river, wasn't it?—or was it the Styx?"

"Acheron, unless you are talking about one of the rivers *after* the dead enter Hades." Max looked at Michal. "Sorry—please continue."

"Anyway, the river was guarded by Cerberus, the three-headed dog defeated by Heracles. The Romans called him 'Hercules,' of course. Beyond Cerberus, the shades of the departed enter the Land of the Dead to be judged. Many ancient tribes and cultures embraced this view. Not just the Greeks, even the early Jews. And in fact there is plenty of evidence that ghosts exist. . . ."

"You getting all spooky on us now?" Max joked. "Are you going to tell us some haunted house story?"

"Not at all. As you guys know, without our action or invitation the dead often do appear to the living. I'm not just talking séances, which are creepily demonic. Enormous evidence of ghosts exists in all cultures. Consider, for example, that C.S. Lewis's dead wives appeared to *him.* Of course, they didn't scare the shit out of him, as we imagine ghosts doing. They offered him messages of hope and love, and the promise of heaven. Three kinds of ghosts seem to exist, as Kreeft sees it. First we have the ones who try to make the living miserable or afraid, who appear to be working on some unfinished earthly business and who feel little or no joy. Socrates describes them in the *Phaedo* as still being tied to their bodies. They prefer to try to resolve their earthly business, or hold onto their bodily pleasures or material possessions, rather than experience the joys of heaven. Then there are the malicious, deceptive, or evil ones. Of course they hardly ever appear that way, since they are deceptive. They're probably from Hell. Partners with demons, y'know? Or even demons themselves. And then there are those happy spirits of dead loved ones who appear without invitation and by God's will, like Lewis's wives."

Phil pointed his finger at Michal. "What are you drinking over there? I think I need to cut you off. —So let me get this straight. You're saying that because a great writer who believed in the *afterlife* claimed to have seen ghosts, and a guy who believed in the *four humors* and talked about the *existence of the soul* believed in ghosts, that *I* should believe in ghosts?"

"I don't care how crazy you think I am. There's plenty of evidence throughout all history and all cultures that they exist. In any case, I don't think we end up as ghosts. At least not permanently."

"Well, that's a relief. We only *temporarily* end up as something that fanciful writers describe. Good thing all those other fictional beings don't exist, like giant white whales hunted by revenge-hungry captains, monads, or even uni—"

Michal and Max cut Phil off. "Don't even say it!"

Phil paused. "Virgin-loving vampires that imprison their victims in abandoned castles?"

Both Michal and Max gave him an emphatic thumbs-down. "Epic fail. Save not successful."

"OK, you got me. I was going to say 'unicorns. . . .'"

"I've got another possibility," Max offered. "I don't believe it, but since we are talking about all the possibilities of what happens to us after death. . . ."

"Go on," Phil said. "It can't be much worse than ghosts."

"Reincarnation. This idea has been very popular in many times and places. We come back as a different body."

"Socrates even entertained this idea in the *Phaedo*. We come back as the animal that best represents the way we behaved on this earth. You'd come back as a *jackass*, Phil," Michal joked.

"Funny," Phil said.

"This is often a temporary destination," Max explained.

"I can play along here. In the *Rig Veda* and other liturgical books of India we find many references to the coming and going of *manas*—mind or soul. Indian philosophy, whether Brahman or Buddhist, with its various systems of metempsychosis, stress the distinction between soul and body, making the bodily life a mere transitory episode in the existence of the soul. They all teach the doctrine of limited immortality, ending either with the periodic world-destruction, in the case of Brahmanism, or with the attainment of Nirvana, in the case of Buddhism."[95]

Max and Michal looked at Phil and then shrugged.

"What? You know I read voraciously and death's been on my mind lately—go figure."

"So let's consider another possibility," Michal began. "Immortality of the soul. The disembodied soul survives as pure spirit, having been liberated by the death of the body. This belief comes from Greek philosophy—Platonism—but many people confuse it with Christianity. Christianity teaches the resurrection of the whole person, including the body, not just immortality of the soul."

"And, of course, the Bible speaks of resurrected bodies," Max agreed.

"All right, I've got another," Phil replied. "This exercise is really stretching my knowledge of Eastern thought. —The only thing that survives death is the cosmic consciousness, the One, Atman, the Buddha-mind, the perfect, eternal, transindividual spirit of Hinduism or Buddhism." Phil gestured around the bar. "See, I've got Hindu and Buddhist symbols aplenty, all around the bar." He mused. "But Japanese tend to be Shinto. Maybe *that's* why people don't come here. . . ."

"They don't come here because the proprietor is a drunk and an ass," Max said. "And most shamefully, your road isn't well-kept. *Very bad people* don't keep up their roads." Max wagged his finger at Phil. "Bad form, old man. Bad form."

Michal dutifully ignored Max' playful barbs at Phil. "So," she said, "there are *plenty* of possibilities besides complete annihilation. Christianity teaches that we will have a new resurrected body in a new heaven and earth. Real bodies. Solid bodies. At first we won't be recognizable in our new bodies. At least not by sight, but only by what we say or do. Mary Magdalene and the Emmaus disciples, for example, did not recognize Jesus in his resurrected body until he did and said stuff—well, if we take those accounts to be true."

"Right. He revealed scripture to his disciples and broke bread," Max said.

"This reminds me of Caravaggio's famous painting of the very transgender-looking Jesus. Remember? *The Supper at Emmaus.* Boy Jesus looks a bit girly there in his resurrected body. . . . But I'm still going with complete annihilation. Really, guys, it's the only view that makes scientific and logical sense," Phil concluded.

"Remember all the Caravaggios we saw in Rome? Too bad we never made it to London together to see that painting in the National Gallery," Michal smiled.

"You once said you loved me. Do you still?"

Rome was one of the two most exciting experiences of their relationship. The first was a trip to Boston. Michal had just finished a course in art theory and was going on and on about Claude Monet.

"Wanna go to the Louvre?" Phil asked with a big smile.

"I've got a lot going on this summer. Remember, two weddings? My brother Jack and my cousin Julia. I'm a bridesmaid in Jack's wedding. He's getting married so young. . . . Did you know I have to wear pink satin with a giant bow and puffy sleeves? Who would ever choose *puffy pink satin* for a bridesmaid dress? I'll look like cotton candy. —I can't really get away."

"Everybody will be paying attention to the bride. Besides, you'd look great in a burlap sack. . . . Hey, how about a quick trip to Boston, then? The Fine Arts Museum has quite a collection of Monet. One of the largest, I hear, outside of Paris."

The happy couple visited the Boston Fine Arts Museum and after spending several hours there, decided to walk to the liquor store on their way back to the Boston Park Plaza Hotel. They were strolling arm-in-arm, absorbed in conversation about what they had seen. Phil was prattling on about Hokusai. He had never paid much attention to Japanese art or culture before, but now he loved it. Michal had begun talking about the effects of light and the juxtaposition of colors in Monet's works and how they must go back tomorrow, when Phil opened the dark glass door of the liquor store right in the middle of an armed robbery. The young men, likely still teenagers, were nervously clutching pistols of some kind. Phil tried to back out the doorway when one of the kids yelled:

"You're not going anywhere."

Phil held Michal tightly as they stood in front of a long shelf of whiskey bottles. Michal was shaking in terror but Phil's blood was pumping with adrenaline. This was exciting! The kid who spoke to them took the money from the register and the two fled the scene, pushing Phil and Michal right into the shelf. They fell over, glass shattering everywhere. They were drenched in whiskey, their bodies pierced with shards of glass. The ambulance came and a police officer rode in the back, taking their statements. At the hospital they got stitched and bandaged up, and ended up going back to the museum the next day. Our obstreperously happy couple couldn't help but smile when tourists gawked at their beaten bodies as if they had just returned from some savage rugby match.

The second most exciting experience was their trip to Rome. When Phil had asked Michal to go to Italy with him, and whether she'd ever been there before, she'd lied, telling him her daddy had taken her to the Italian Alps as a high school graduation present, but that she'd love to go again. She cooked up a story about staying at Cortina d'Ampezzo. She remembered For Your Eyes Only *and Roger Moore being chased on skis, so she could describe the mountains and the architecture perfectly.*

You might be surprised to learn that they broke up only a few weeks after that trip. It happened like this. First, it's important to note that Michal was a virgin when she met Phil, but, passing herself off as a worldly feminist, she told him that she was experienced. She got away with it because she had already broken her hymen in a Moped accident a few years earlier. She was leaving her boyfriend's house on her scooter, waving goodbye, not paying any attention, when she ran into the back end of a green Volvo. She broke a rib and her hymen when she straddled the handle bar.

Michal swore when she started having sex with Phil that she would never get pregnant before she was finished with her education. She was already thinking about grad school. She wasn't going to be end up like her Aunt Vi, who got pregnant at the end of tenth grade and moved to Charlotte, North Carolina to live with her older cousin Mabel and her husband George. Vi kept the pregnancy a secret. She gave birth to a girl and gave her up for adoption. The family finally found out many years later when the girl, now a woman, located her mother through the adoption agency.

About a week after Phil and Michal got back from Rome, Phil phoned her. He had finally printed all of the photos from the vacation. Would she like to come over and look at them? He would take her to a fancy restaurant, her choice.

"I'm not feeling up to it." Michal seemed despondent.

"What's up? Come on, these photos are great. Besides, I haven't seen you all week."

Michal didn't know how she should say it. She could dance around the topic or just blurt it out. She decided on the latter.

"I'm pregnant." The two words sickened her when she heard herself say them out loud.

"Did you say *pregnant*? Michal, you're on birth control, right? How could—? No, I'm not that stupid. I know how this happened. Michal, I—"

Now as you may have figured out, Michal was a pretty smart girl, but not this time.

"I forgot to renew my prescription before the trip. I didn't think it was possible that I could get pregnant so quickly.... I'm sorry, Phil." Her voice was cracking.

Phil's mind was racing. Plans of graduate school at MIT, maybe Stanford, started to seem more difficult. But only difficult. "Michal, I don't know what to do. Hell, you're the strong feminist here. I want to ask you what *you* want to do but then that challenges *my power* and *my part* in this, so that's irresponsible. I want to make sure you know you have options and I'm behind you one-hundred-percent, but I also want to let you know that I'm not taking your power away from you. . . ." He felt dizzy, as he talked in long strings that would make a bumbling teenager sound eloquent.

"Phil, let's talk about this another day," Michal said, and hung up.

Phil was mid-sentence when the phone went dead, "Michal, I—"

He didn't know what to do. He asked Max to come over.

"I can't right now. I've got my li'l sis Jessica here with me," Max said.

Max was having his own crisis. Jessica had shown up on his doorstep the night before. She got the money for a bus ticket by selling her daddy's two cases of Salems (which he hid in the closet next to his box of pornos) to the neighbor boys up the street. She also pitched in thirty-five dollars that she'd been saving in allowance money.

"How did you get here?" Max shook his head incredulously.

Fifteen-year-old Jessica responded, "I ran away from home."

"Why on earth? Get in here." Max and his sister sat together on the chestnut-brown tweed couch (the one that Phil said he'd replace for free since it offended his aesthetic sense) while Jessica explained.

"It's on account of Daddy's not my daddy." She broke into tears.

"What do you mean, Daddy's not your daddy?"

"It's because our blood don't match. I learned this in school. Daddy's a positive and I'm a negative."

"*Blood doesn't match....* That's not how it works, Jessica. Daddy's your daddy as sure as I'm sittin' here. You've got his pretty eyes." Max touched her cheek. "I'm gonna call mom and tell her. She's gotta be worried sick."

It turns out that Jessica's mother was not particularly worried. Her daughter often ran away. "It's because you call her 'Jez'bel,'" Max's memaw would say to the rest of the family, shaking her head. "She's 'bout the wickedest woman in the Bible. What'd you expect? Poor girl didn't have a chance."

Jessica looked at Max and insisted, "I'm not going back to my *fake* daddy...."

Max would end up putting her back on the bus the next day. In the meantime, he explained all of this to Phil, who was listening impatiently on the other end of the phone.

"Can't you just give her a video game to play with and get over here? I'm having a crisis."

Max set Jessica up with the Sega and went over to see Phil, who explained the situation.

"You know, the Bible is ambiguous on this subject. Both pro-lifers and pro choicers can find arguments in it to support their views."

"I don't give a damn about your Bible right now, Max. Come on, what should I do? My brain isn't working to find a good solution."

"Well, you know the right thing to do—the decent thing to do. You love her, right?"

"Of course I do." Phil thought on the words—*of course I do*. This realization was one of the wonderful moments in Phil's life.

"Then the answer's simple." Max held Phil's hand, the hand that wasn't holding a drink....

It turns out that Phil did do the decent thing. After Max had left, he called Michal.

"Let's get married," Phil said, trying to sound excited. Actually, it wasn't that hard. In the half-hour or so that he'd had time to think about this kind of future with Michal, he had managed to convince himself that it would be *good*. He had no intention of making a bad decision, but Phil took determinism to an extreme at times. He figured that if *he* were in control, he would make the decision that was right, even if it wasn't necessarily his first choice. Besides, Michal had a great mind, never mind the great body. He imagined sitting up late nights and talking with her over drinks on their yacht as they sailed around the world. It sounded better and better the more he thought about it. School was a means to an end for him and being with Michal was a great, albeit different, end.

"I've already called the doctor," Michal said.

"When's the appointment?" Phil's heart sunk a bit.

Had Michal not misremembered the date of her appointment they might still be together. But instead she said, "The 15th." The appointment was actually on the morning of the 13th. Michal showed up at the clinic on the 13th, and when Phil didn't show, she went ahead with the procedure, scared and alone. Phil showed up on the 15th and found out after telling the receptionist that he was Michal's husband that her appointment had actually been two days before.

The next time Phil saw Michal, he laid into her about what a goddamned hypocrite she was to talk about equality and men having to take responsibility, then to take away his ability to be with her. He was all right with the decision but he had been making plans. He told her about yachts, and world travel, and tutors around the world, and how he had plenty of money, always would. For her part, Michal screamed at him about being such a selfish ass and that she was the one who had the biggest say. How could he be such a MAN as to think of this as only his decision? They both yelled a bit more—a lot more, actually. Phil called her an idiot girl who didn't know any better and Michal told him that his genes were defective as a male, not enough length and legs and all that implied. In the end, Phil stormed out of her apartment and spent the next two hours alone in his car, on the beach, crying in a manner most un-guy-like.

Both Michal and Phil were deeply saddened and angry. Neither talked to the other for weeks, until Max finally felt the need to intervene: "You two love each other," Max told them separately. Sure they did, they said, but it was over. Max finally got the two of them together but it was never the same. They'd be friends again, but never lovers.

Back to the RTSS

Michal looked at Phil. "You know, Richard Swinburne argues that Jesus' Resurrection is God's divine signature on His work, showing that He had become incarnate, which obviously involved the violation of natural laws and which could only have happened if natural laws depend for their operation on God. Of course God had good reasons to become incarnate, to identify with our suffering and to reveal truth.[96]—Anyway, if we take Jesus' words seriously, Phil, when He invoked the Hebrew conception of hell as 'Gehenna'—remember the burning garbage dump outside of Jerusalem?—then those who reject God truly *do* experience complete annihilation. Their souls are burned up like incinerated garbage. You'll be as dead as those materialists you claim to admire. Worm food. Period. No more of you anymore, Phil." Michal was becoming impatient. *Why am I saying this? I don't believe it, but Phil has to believe in something.*

Michal changed gears. She had to get Phil thinking. "Phil, what about near-death experiences?"

"Normal brain functions gone awry. Hallucinations brought on by physical or psychological stresses on the brain before death," Phil said. "Or, more precisely, abnormal levels of dopamine—or how about trauma activating the brain's opioid system? Want me to go on?"

"Maybe in some cases, but others seem to be real. I'll give you a famous example: denture man."

"Denture man?" Phil laughed. "You didn't just say 'denture man'?"

"I did. —An unconscious man, hypothermic and without a pulse, was brought to a Netherlands hospital by ambulance. The head nurse removed his dentures so that he could put a ventilator on the dying man. The man was resuscitated but no one knew where the dentures had been put. When the same nurse walked into the man's room about a week later, he said, '*You* know where my dentures are. You were there when I was brought in. You took my dentures out and put them in a sliding drawer on a cart.' Well, it turned out that's exactly where the man's dentures were.[97] But if that doesn't convince you, many nurses and other caregivers report seeing a bright and sometimes colored light surrounding the dying person, one which emanates a raw feeling of love. A number of studies show that one in three caregivers—and in other studies one in two caregivers—experience this. Family members who are present often experience it, too. One of my best friends, Shelby, is a children's oncology nurse. She told me that recently she was caring for an eight-year-old boy. His mother was in the room, too. The boy told his mother, 'I see Jesus, Mommy.' Then his mother said to him, 'Go on.' And the boy reached out his hand and died."

Phil was starting to get frustrated. "So let me get this straight. Somebody has a hallucination and we'll call it God's doing, or Jesus'? Then just as you have said to me in the past, 'What's good for the atheist is good for the believer. . . .'" Phil pointed at the young man in the pea-green Yukio tee, whose glass he had refilled earlier. His head was still down. One arm hung limply off the table. The other hand not so much gripped as loosely cupped his glass. Phil approached to within a couple of feet. Puffing out his chest, he took in a big gulp of air in an exaggerated inhale. He held out his arms and then clapped his hands together while yelling, "WAKE UP!" The man raised his head suddenly and looked directly at Phil. His eyes were bloodshot saucers.

"When did *you* show up? How did you get here?" Phil gestured menacingly.

The man's eyes raced around the room. He leapt from his chair, only to send his glass flying off the table as his arms flailed for balance. Whether because of the alcohol or the sudden, startling assault, his legs failed him and he collapsed onto the floor. His attempt to break his fall failed magnificently, and his shoulder struck the hardwood with a jarring thud.

Michal got up to help the man, but Max put a gentle hand on her shoulder. "Leave Phil to his theatrics. We'll help the poor man in a minute."

Phil brought the guy to his feet and he could hear the gurgling and bubbling of the man's stomach as it tried to process the liquor churning within. Phil grabbed his face. "Are you dizzy? Is the room spinning? Do you feel sick?" Pitifully, the man gurgled out a "yes" before falling over again and emptying the contents of his stomach all over the floor.

Phil turned and walked away, shooting back over his shoulder: "I'm charging you for clean-up. . . ."

The man looked up. With a diabolical grin and frightening eyes, he declared: "In some ways it is more troublesome to track and swat an evasive wasp than to shoot, at close range, a wild elephant. But the elephant is more troublesome if you miss." Then he burst into a strange little laugh.

Phil shook his head at the nonsense. The rumpus he'd just wrought gave him a strange, burning pleasure.

Phil's actions were so unexpected, so outrageous, that Michal convinced herself that she hadn't seen it all properly. She had watched the whole thing, but this behavior was well beyond the pale, even for Phil. She looked at the poor man lying on the floor, refusing to believe her eyes. But something in Max appreciated what Phil was doing, even though he couldn't quite condone it.

Phil held up his hand as they both began to protest. "*Making a point.* . . . That man there just had an experience. His adrenaline triggered and his fight-or-flight instinct kicked in. Looks like flight won out." Phil gave a sardonic smile. "I could say that his experience is proof that gravity temporarily failed, inertia disappeared, and that the little liquor fairies no longer wanted to stay in his stomach, so they grabbed whatever was nearest them to take for a snack and burst out. In fact, that is exactly what did happen because—well—just look at the proof." He pointed to the man, still trying to stand up amidst his own vomit.

Michal looked at Phil who had become a moustache-twirling villain. "He's drunk! AND YOU'RE AN ASS!" Her outburst took her by surprise.

Phil smiled. "You and Maxie choose to reject science and instead believe in possibilities. Well, I wholeheartedly believe in a possibility as well. Not unicorns this time, but liquor fairies. You know they live in alcohol? And I'm certain that I could get enough people to believe in this, if I just worked at it. . . ."

Michal just kept looking at the guy on the floor. She felt Max's hand on her shoulder. She heard a noise and realized that it was Phil's voice.

"Michal, Max. . . . Look, it's a herd mentality. Enough people believe in something and then it starts to become real. Watch the news today? —In their mad rush to be first, they invent all kinds of ridiculous though possible *bullshit.* Then other news agencies report on the spurious allegations as if they are fact. Before anyone can blink, much of the populace believes something completely false. It happens today on the Internet at a blinding pace. It happened on October 30, 1938, when Orson Welles so craftily retold *The War of the Worlds.* It happened with the Salem witch trials of 1692, the Leeds scare in 1806, *The Sun's* bat men on the moon, and even in Jesus' time with his so-called Resurrection and all of those supposed Resurrection appearances. . . . Up until I said 'Jesus,' you would tell me it's all mob mentality brought on by some kind of pseudo-Jungian mass hysteria. You, of course, reject that Jesus' Resurrection is anything but factual. But I would tell you that all of these hallucinations up to and including near-death experiences are nothing more than your brain tricking you. You know that things are grim, maybe you don't even understand what's going on any longer, but your brain starts grabbing for experiences to fill the void and, lo and behold, it reaches for images of the most common—or perhaps even the most fantastical—experiences you've had earlier in life. It's just like having a dream that seems so real, until you wake up and are presented with evidence to the contrary."

Michal sneered at him. "These people had real experiences, Phil. Your denial of their experiences is nothing more than your desperate attempt to validate your life and your conclusions. Especially since you only have a few months left, you stubborn son of a bitch!"

She regretted the words as soon as they flew out of her mouth. She wished she could take them back as she watched Phil's face fall. *But he wouldn't take his own words back because he thinks they're true. What's good for the atheist is good for the believer.*

Max, ever the peacemaker, redirected Phil's attention to himself.

"Phil, let's use the science that we all love so much." Max gestured to his friends, then brought his hands reverently to his chest. "You claim that we become nothing after we die, correct? If not, then you have to abandon materialism."

Phil sensed the set-up of an argument and cautiously replied, "All right, Huckleberry, let's see what you got."

"Let's consider this: Would you say that our universe as we know it is a closed system? That is, despite what science fiction would have us believe, wormholes aren't opening to other realities and flooding their energy into our universe?" Max raised his eyebrows, as his question hung in the air. Phil shook his head.

"Many scientists would agree with what you are saying, though there are also those who believe in an open or infinite universe, infinitely expanding. The Big Bang seems to imply a closed universe, though. There are, however, some exciting new theories that suggest alternate realities exist and furthermore—"

Max cut him off. "Ah yes, but currently those theories aren't even close to being provable—just like God. So according to *you* we must reject them."

"That's true, Phil. Max has a point there. What's good for the atheist is good for the believer."

"Fine, they're not provable, so I will, *at least for now*, allow that the universe is a closed system." Phil looked at Max, who was smiling.

"Exactly—and that only strengthens my argument. If the universe is a closed system, then the law of conservation of energy applies. . . ."

"Wait," Michal cut in. "How could the universe obey the energy conservation law during its evolution after the Big Bang? Did the universe have a constant mass during its evolution, or did the mass increase with its radius? If so, then the law of conservation doesn't seem to apply. —That is, if I'm understanding the science correctly."

"A lot of scientists hold that the universe started with zero radius and a set amount of matter-energy, and as it evolved its radius increased and the density of matter and energy fell, so that the total quantity of matter and energy is conserved," Max said.

"Fine, so you two can cite some examples from science. Congrats. Except that you didn't specifically state the first law of thermodynamics. You know, where it says that energy can neither be created nor destroyed but only transformed from one form to another." Phil attempted to regain some control over this argument, but felt it rapidly slipping away from him. He looked at his friends defiantly.

"Keep going, Phil, we're just playing out the rope." Michal looked at Max, her smile growing as she waited for Phil to follow the train of thought to its inevitable conclusion.

"So if energy is neither created nor destroyed"—Phil paused, thinking about the ramifications—"and matter is energy—" He stopped, then nodded his head. "Touché, Max—at the very least materialism fails. Of course, we haven't shown that souls exist. Just that they might."

Max and Michal beamed triumphantly. "You're actually forgetting about the Higgs-Boson, so you're still sunk," Max said, patting Phil's shoulder. "That's OK, great master, we're here for you when you fall down. Isn't that right, Michal?" He reached behind the bar, grabbed a bottle and poured Phil a drink.

"Well, I'm not too sure about all of the science we just spouted, though it was kinda fun," Michal said. "Of course, I'm way out of my element. But if it were this easy, then why aren't there more believers among scientists? There must be some hole in our argument. But then again— Anyway, I *have* read that quantum physics seems to prove that souls exist, so yet another dig from the science you so adore, Phil." She smiled broadly. "If science suggests you might just be wrong about materialism, then maybe you're wrong about some other things, too." She looked at Phil. She was beginning to brighten up. She entreated him: "Why is it so hard for you to accept that there *might* be a God, just as various theoretical objects *might* exist even though you've never seen them? Why do you have such a hard time with the former but not the latter?" She reached out and held his hand. "You believe in a God, too. You just call it 'Science.' And you rely upon testimony in the sciences, especially scientific theories, which we fumble to understand as we were just now. Even one of your frequently quoted philosophers, David Hume, said there is no species of reasoning more common, more useful, or more necessary to human life than testimony.[98] One misunderstands or misleads if one assumes that science doesn't rest on testimony. We *all* rely on testimony, which informs our beliefs, and often our most cherished or stubborn ones. And isn't it hubris, Phil, to believe that reality is only as big as your perception of it? Imagine how small reality was before seafaring, or prior to the invention of the telescope or microscope. Reality is much bigger than you can perceive."

THE NEXT DAY. *At the RTSS*

Michal walked through an unfamiliar hall toward a door opened just a crack. The room smelled like sunshine and lavender. She entered. It was a small, crooked room, empty except for an unplugged refrigerator full of CDs of various sorts, a big bathtub in the middle, a crystal bowl of bright red cherries (she could smell their sweet taste), and a bottle of champagne next to a fluted crystal glass. It reminded her a bit of the room on Great Jones Street, but it was warmer and far more inviting. It suited her just fine.

The room was bright orange, her favorite color. The bathtub was one of those old fashioned types with claw feet, just like Grandma had. It was bright red. There was a big window that opened up to a garden of color. She could hear birds in the nearby branches, gossiping in song.

Michal walked up to the refrigerator and peered inside. It was stocked with all of her favorite music: The Beatles, Bob Marley, Aretha Franklin, Etta James, tWicEbakED, David Ford, Ben Harper, Amos Lee, and of course, Cake. . . .

She grabbed a disc and looked around the room trying to find a CD player. She couldn't find one, but the music began to play anyway—in her head? In the room? It didn't matter. She ran a warm bath and poured herself a glass of champagne.

Stepping into the tub, she thought how perfect it all was. *If only there were someone to enjoy this with me.*

Just then, Michal heard a rustling from the garden.

"Michal," a familiar, friendly voice called out. It was one of Michal's favorite mentors, Falconer—the one who had set her straight about feminism. Falconer peeked through the window and smiled.

"I thought you were—" Michal began and smiled back.

Falconer put her elbows on the windowsill and rested her hands on her chin, in the way she always did. As she spoke to Michal, words escaped from her head in comic-strip bubbles. Michal noticed the tattoo on her arm.

"Your tattoo," Michal began, "Wittgenstein's duck-rabbit."

"What do *you* see, Michal?" Falconer asked in a cartoon bubble. Her head looked like an inflating balloon.

"Well, I've always seen a cuttlefish, but that would make me a bit. . . ." Michal took a sip of champagne and her heart warmed at once. "So what is it *really?*"

"You're not asking the right question, Michal. Wittgenstein was trying to show us that perception is fundamentally interpretive. We always see something *as something.* Our perceptions are filtered through our language, our culture, and our experience. Indeed, through our entire past.[99] If someone had never seen a rabbit, that person could never see this figure as a rabbit." She touched her tattoo. "Perception is an interpretive act."

"But then what is *really real?*" Michal asked.

Suddenly the room went dark. She set her champagne glass down and sunk neck deep into the tub.

Falconer began to speak again, a big bubble forming over her head. The room brightened once more.

"There's no real answer to that question, Michal. Philosophers have been trying to figure that out since at least Plato," Falconer said.

"I really miss you," Michal said.

"I never really left," Falconer said. Michal could have sworn the bubble turned heart-shaped. She sat back up in the tub and grabbed her champagne.

"Remind me about Plato and the rest—what they say about reality."

"You remember Plato's cave, of course.[100] Socrates is speaking with Glaucon. He asks Glaucon to imagine humans dwelling in an underground cave, their necks and legs fettered so they cannot move. They can only look forward."

"I remember," Michal said, "A fire is blazing behind them and people are standing between them and the fire, holding puppets in the shapes of various objects—trees, animals, and so on. The prisoners see the shadows from these puppets, which the fire casts on the wall of the cave."

"And, of course the prisoners conclude that there is no other reality than the shadows made by the puppets," Falconer said.

"So what happens next?" Michal knew the answer but she wanted to hear Falconer explain it.

"One of the prisoners is released. He turns around and sees the puppet-objects. He has come a bit closer to reality, but he's not there yet. Then he is dragged out of the cave and into the light of the sun. —Isn't that water getting a bit cold? In any case, you're wrinkling up like a prune." Falconer smiled. "Come out to the garden with me."

Michal took another sip of champagne, stood up, put on her clothes and crawled through the window. The sun was dazzling. She followed Falconer to a nearby bench, where they sat down. Michal held Falconer's hand.

"At first, the prisoner is blinded by the sun," Falconer began, "but then he gets used to it. Finally, he is able to look at the sun itself. —You know, this story would be much better if the prisoners were women. After all, we're the ones with the shackles on." She smiled.

"So this world that we inhabit is like the prisoners' cave-world," Michal said. "You know, Crazy Horse's vision, at least as Black Elk tells it, is like Plato's cave. Crazy Horse dreamed that he entered the spirit world, where the spirits of all things exist. The spirit world is the real world that lies behind this one. Everything we see here is a shadow from that world."[101]

"I imagine that if a time machine had taken Crazy Horse back to Socrates' Athens—well, they would have had quite a conversation," Falconer said. She bent down, plucked a single white lily and handed it to Michal. Michal lay down, resting her head on Falconer's lap. She held the lily against her chest, closed her eyes and smiled.

"You know, the *Upanishads* say that God—the Brahman or the True—is in reality identical to the true self, the Atman. The world and the false self that we mistakenly think ourselves to be are mere appearances of God. Adi Shankara, the eighth-century Indian philosopher and theologian, explained it well. He said that in the same way that those parts of ethereal space, which are limited by jars and water pots, are not really different from the universal ethereal space, so this manifold world with its objects of enjoyment, enjoyers, and so on, has no existence apart from Brahman."[102] Falconer touched Michal's hair as she spoke.

"Is this real right now? Am I really lying here on your lap, enjoying the warmth of this sun and this pleasant conversation?"

"Well, you know what Berkeley says: 'To be is to be perceived.' Reality consists only of ideas in the mind and what he calls 'spirits,' including the spirit of God who orders our experience," Falconer said. "Indeed the world of appearance *is* reality."[103]

Can all of this just be ideas in my mind?

"Berkeley was responding to Locke," Michal began. "Locke said that objects have primary and secondary qualities. Primary qualities are properties of objects independent of any observer, like solidity or extension. But secondary qualities are properties that produce sensations in observers, like color, taste, smell, sound, heat. . . ."[104]

"Of course, Berkeley disagreed," Falconer said. "He said that primary qualities are exactly like secondary qualities. For example, size is not a property of an object because size depends on the distance of the object from the observer."

"Descartes seemed to recognize this. He said that the sun appears very small, as if we could fit it into the palm of our hand. Only astronomical reasoning tells us that the sun is in fact very, very large.[105] —But come to think of it, Descartes was likely making a somewhat different point."

"Recall what Berkeley says—that if neither primary nor secondary qualities are actually 'in' the object, then nothing exists outside of our minds," Falconer said.

"Kant makes a similar move. He distinguishes between noumena and phenomena. The noumenon or 'thing in itself' is completely unknowable to humans. All we experience are appearances, not things in themselves."[106] Michal sat up and looked at Falconer. "I'm inclined to believe in philosophical or common-sense realism. Perceived objects really do exist in the way that they appear, independent of any observer. But then again"—she hesitated—"but then again, I've sometimes wondered about my experiences, whether they're real."

"What kind of experiences?" Falconer asked.

"Spiritual, religious, supernatural," Michal said.

"Like an oceanic feeling?"

"Remind me what that is."

"Freud's friend described a sensation of eternity—what Freud called an 'oceanic feeling.' He talks about it in *Civilization and its Discontents*. Freud said that such feelings are possible but they are mere fantasy, an ideological wish that gets interpreted as a religious state."

"But I don't think it's mere fantasy. I've *experienced* God."

"People in every faith tradition claim to have had religious experiences, Michal. Indian philosopher Sarvepalli Radhakrishnan does an excellent job of explaining this.[107] Buddhism centers on Buddha's enlightenment. Moses saw God in the burning bush. Jesus' experience of God at his baptism in the Jordan River was so vivid, so intense, that he felt the need to go for a time into absolute solitude to think about it. And what about the vision that came to Saul on the road to Damascus? It changed him from a persecutor of Christians to one of Christianity's greatest champions. And, of course, the life of Mohammed is full of mystical experiences. Even Socrates experienced the divine. The evidence is too massive to deny. —The experience of transcendence, of majesty, of timelessness, peace, and joy. And yet it's ineffable. Words fail to describe it, fail to capture it. But we must say *something*. It just is what it is and not anything else. . . ."

"But if this is true," Michal said, "then we're all right—or we're all wrong. If you shed all of the theology, all of the doctrine and the rituals, then the raw experience—the ineffable experience as you say—is the same. There is only one God, but we approach Him from different places and perspectives. —I'm just not sure I can accept this."

"Why not? We must distinguish the immediate, infallible experience of the divine from all the interpretation that gets mixed up with it. Think about it: as Radhakrishnan says, if Paul hadn't heard of Jesus, do you really think that he would have identified the voice that called out to him on the road to Damascus as belonging to Jesus? There is no such thing as pure unfiltered experience, Michal. Experience is always mixed up with layer upon layer of interpretation. You should know this from your own studies. Interpretations are cultural constructs and must be distinguished from the raw experience itself. Buddha recognized this."

"Maybe so. But I still believe that there is only one God and that He became a man in the person of Jesus. I can't be wrong about Jesus, can I? That would undermine my whole reality."

"What is the real meaning of faith, Michal? Certainly it isn't looking forward to a buttoned-up afterlife. When we live in this world outside of faith, we cling to the visible and disposable, to the transient. We give ourselves over to it. We make ourselves miserable slaves to it. We desperately try to secure and defend it, to cling to the perishable. This results in conflict with everybody else. And thus arise fear, envy, anger, jealousy, anxiety, strife and needless suffering. But when we surrender to God—however we understand God—we surrender this self-contrived security. We are freed from all that holds us in bondage. This is what is meant by 'faith'—turning our false security in the fleeting over to God. And this decision of faith is not made once and for all, but must be confirmed anew—a daily renewal of faith."[108]

Just then, Phil walked up to Michal and poked her with a pair of shears. "Wake up, Michal. Looks like you're getting a bit too much sun. . . ."

Michal stood up from the bench and walked back into the RTSS. She approached Phil who was snoozing in his bright red, overstuffed armchair. She bent over and kissed his forehead. "Wake up, Phil. I'd like you to get me another drink."

Michal's Grandma

Michal was nineteen when she learned to hate the smell of antiseptic and flowers. They commingled and created a dichotomy of smells at once both comforting and repulsive. The antiseptic lingered in her nose for hours, no matter how hard she tried to focus on the competing odors of burnt coffee or her Aunt Chloe's strong perfume. In later years, the smell brought back unpleasant memories. It would always remind her of hospitals. It would always remind her of the room where her grandma spent her last minutes on earth. It would always remind her of *terror*.

Michal stood in her dying grandmother's cramped hospital room. Her grandpa sat by the bedside, holding his wife's frail hand. He had been her beloved for almost seventy years. Michal stood squeezed between Uncle John, with the nicotine-stained teeth and Elvis hair, and Boone, her cousin visiting from Louisiana. The room was crowded with aunts and uncles, cousins, her parents, her brother Jack, and of course Grandpa—the only person in the room apart from Michal actually looking at Grandma. Everyone else in the room wore masks of smiles. The intern pushed Michal's family aside as he moved in to check Grandma's vitals. He looked at Grandpa and smiled. Grandpa smiled back and resumed holding his wife's hand. The intern looked over at Michal. He shook his head and cast his eyes downward. Then he walked out, past the many get-well cards and other well wishes adorning the room, pushing aside one balloon and walking past those damnable flowers.

They weren't damnable *then*. At the time they were comforting, even pleasant and pretty. Michal remembered looking at the petals, how they lifted upward, ever hopeful. She watched as each of the family came to the bed, leaning over

Grandma to say their final goodbyes, mostly mumbled words, scarcely intelligible. Grandma received their affections with dimmed eyes, her chest moving laboriously as she fought for every breath, her eyes fluttering from the effort. Nobody knew what to say.

Each time another relative pressed past her to sit with Grandpa, she would reach into her purse and rub at a folded piece of paper there. It was her talisman, a ward against the coming pain of losing her grandma. Finally when it was her turn, she pulled out the paper, unfolded it and read aloud, the way Grandma had taught her: " *here is the deepest secret nobody knows. . . .*'

"Remember this poem, Grandma? You would always read e. e. cummings to me. Remember? Remember Grandma?" Michal began to cry, then whispered the last verse of the poem:

"i carry your heart (i carry it in my heart).'

"I love you, Grandma." Michal gazed lovingly at her grandma, whose eyes were now fixed on the ceiling.

Grandpa was crying as well. "She loves you too, Michal," he managed to say.

The room was silent for what seemed to Michal an eternity. Grandma's labored breathing could no longer be heard. The machines said that she was still there, but they also foretold that she would soon be leaving them. As they watched her chest rise and fall ever more slowly, they all began to hug each other.

Suddenly her grandma's eyes went from empty to aflame with terror, as if she were witnessing some horrific event.

"Nooooooo!" Her grandma let out a loud piercing cry.

Everyone cried out at once: "What is it, Buttercup?" "What is it, Mom?" "Grandma, what's wong?" They were speaking over each other. Uncle John yelled into the hall for the nurse. Michal choked out, "Are you OK?"

"Noooooo!" Grandma repeated.

Michal's heart pounded before it leapt into her throat. She couldn't swallow. "Grandma!" she finally cried out.

Her grandma's arms began flailing wildly. It seemed as if she were being yanked from her bed by an invisible force.

"They're here to take me—to take me—TO TAKE ME!" She repeated the words again and again, each time more forcefully and more terrifying.

"What's wrong, Grandma? Please stop—please stop, Grandma. It will be OK," Michal said in a trembling voice. Uncle John called for the nurse again.

"She must be hallucinating, Michal." Aunt Chloe, dressed in a vintage 1960s-leopard-print jumpsuit, grabbed hold of Michal's shoulder.

Michal looked at her Grandma. She didn't look like she was hallucinating.

"Don't let them take me!" Grandma pleaded. She was thrashing in her bed with more strength than Michal had seen her exert in months. Grandpa gently and lovingly held her down.

"What is it, Grandma?" Michal tried to remain calm.

"Demons. De-e-e-emons. . . . Please don't take me. Nooooooo!" Her grandma let out another blood-curdling scream. Grandpa leaned over her and sobbed.

Aunt Chloe approached her mother. "You see *demons?*" she said, as if speaking to a child. "It's OK, Ma. There's no such thing as demons. —It's OK. Just calm down if you can. We're all here, Ma."

Michal's Aunt Vi walked up to her mother and placed a small cross in her hand. She looked at her sister and whispered loud enough for Michal to hear, "There *are* demons. There are demons *in this room*. It don't matter to demons that she's an atheist, Chloe. Demons are itchin' to grab at atheists' souls."

"Stop it, Aunt Vi!" Michal screamed. She was trembling.

Just then, Michal's grandmother gasped. Terror was fixed on her face as she took her last breath. Michal walked out of the room shaking as the nurses hurried by. She listened as they told everyone in their calm nurses' voices that her grandma was gone. Aunt Vi walked out into the hall, a pair of white Sunday gloves draped over her purse. She handed Michal a lace kerchief.

Michal's words tumbled out all at once. "She was a good woman, Aunt Vi. Grandma was a good woman. Grandma was just hallucinating. Demons don't exist. I love you, Aunt Vi, but demons don't exist. You shouldn't scare people like that. Think of Grandpa. Don't hurt Grandpa like this. Don't hurt *us* like this."

Aunt Vi held her close and hummed a little tune while she rocked her.

"Every knee shall bow, every tongue confess, that Jesus Christ is Lord. . . ."

Michal returned to the present, her body still reliving the stress of that hour.

Real life is scarier than monster movies.

She glanced over at Phil at a total loss for words. *What can I possibly say? How can I make it better? How can I comfort him? Aunt Vi was right. Demons do exist. Demons grabbed hold of my grandma, I know. I just know it. She was a good woman but she was an atheist. . . . Should I tell Phil? Should I tell Phil about Grandma's horrifying death? He'll think it's just a bunch of nonsense. . . . Unicorns, he'll say.* She directed her thoughts to God: *Do I tell him, God? I know that demons are real. You rescued me from demonic oppression. . . . I love Phil. . . . I never stopped. I can't help but love him. I don't want him to experience the kind of death Grandma did. If I tell him this story, maybe he will believe. —But he won't believe. Who am I kidding? This is Phil. God, I know you love Phil. Demons might take him to hell at his death, but I believe that my Savior Jesus is rescuing people from hell as I speak. I can imagine Jesus meeting Phil in hell. I can imagine Jesus saying the same words to Phil that he did to Peter, who denied Him three times before being reconciled to Him again: 'And whom do you say I am?' And Phil's eyes and heart will be opened and he will reply, 'My Lord and my God.' And Jesus will embrace Phil in his loving arms. . . .* Then Michal laughed to herself. *That's not likely to happen. Phil will reject Jesus. He will reject Jesus and be a smart ass, telling him that He's a lousy superior being. He'll say, 'Well, you should have given me more evidence.'* She couldn't help but laugh at Phil being defiant in the face of God Himself.

God, you have to save Phil. Jesus conquered Hell and Death. . . . Please, God, save Phil. We all have to leave this earth some time. Death is our price for this earthly life but death is also our one-way ticket to your Paradise. If you choose not to save Phil's body, then please, God, please save his soul. Anything short of saving all souls is not a complete victory and my Savior is completely victorious. Michal prayed fervently, while she watched Phil get another drink.

THIRTEEN
"The Infinite Omelet Scene"

Michal opened the cabin door and stepped outside. As she walked along the path to the main building, she approached a middle-aged woman sitting on a bench. Forty-five? Or fifty maybe? The woman wore a bright yellow dress which, with her bright yellow hair, perfectly complemented her flawlessly peachy-brown skin. She was holding a bright yellow umbrella to shield her from the morning sun. Michal smiled at her curiously.

"Oh, aren't you just something to behold! What a pretty girl you are. Sit with me for a few minutes. I haven't talked with anybody all morning," the woman said with a smile.

Michal sat down. "OK, I suppose I have a bit of time." She didn't want to be rude.

"You know," the woman began, "you know Gandhi himself once sat right where you're sitting. It was a few years before Mr. Phil bought the place, but I can tell you firsthand that his bottom snuggled that stone just like yours is right now."

Michal gave her a puzzled look.

"I know what you're going to say—he's dead. I thought so too. But he chased me here. Chased me right here to this very place. Do you want to hear the story?"

"Sure." Michal wanted to get away from this crazy woman, but she didn't want to appear impolite, especially if the woman was Phil's friend.

"You'll love this." The woman's excitement shone through her smile. "My dog and I were at the farmer's market in the village picking up some daikon root and Mr. Gandhi walked up and stood right next to us. I don't know Mr. Gandhi's first name—I'm sure his mother gave him a nice one—but there he was. Skinny little man with glasses wearing a long yellow robe. —My dog loves yellow just like I do. Well, when Gandhi wasn't looking, my dog bit his robe and ripped a piece off it. Then my dog went running, running right to this place. I caught up with him and told my Rusty, 'Naughty boy, naughty, naughty boy.' And there Gandhi was, demanding his piece of fabric back. It must have been expensive is all I can say. I offered to pay for it, but he told me he had some wisdom to share with me instead."

"Uh-huh." Michal looked down at her watch and then looked up and smiled at the woman.

"Oh, you're just so darn squeezable.... Let me give you a squeeze." The woman set down her umbrella and squeezed Michal tightly before letting her go. She continued with a smile: "In case you didn't know this about Gandhi, he led a peace movement. —A peace movement to free the Mongolesians. At the time they were under English rule, and then before that it was the Russkies. This would have been about 1972. Gandhi developed this philosophy of peace—"

"This is all very interesting, but I need to be going. My friends are waiting for me inside."

"Oh, they won't start without the pretty lady." She picked up her umbrella again to shade her face from the sun. "You should use an umbrella. It will keep that face pretty for years. —So Gandhi was trying to tell me about force, you see. Truth force, universal force, soul force, silent force—all these different forces. Actually, he seemed like he was very, very confused. Poor little man. Well, I listened politely, of course, but I was starting to get a little nervous. I think he wanted to be my ringmaster—if you know what I mean." She winked. "So what's your name?"

"Michal."

"What do you know! My ex-husband's name was Mikuni. That's pretty close. Close enough for us to be friends." She smiled. "My name is Saffron. Please don't tell Mr. Phil that you ran into me. He'll make a big fuss. Besides, I think he wants to be my lion tamer—if you know what I mean." She winked again. "So you probably want to hear about my ex-husband—why he would leave someone like me. I know—it doesn't make any sense."

Michal smiled at her politely, trying as hard as she could to wait patiently for the conclusion of her story.

"Mikuni told me that it was on account of Gandhi, but I think it was because of Mrs. Nagazumi. I think Mikuni liked her for her trapeze act—if you know what I mean." She winked a third time.

Michal stood up, trying to hold in laughter. "I really must be going, Saffron. It was very nice talking with you."

"Goodbye, Michal. Maybe we can do this another time. . . . Why don't you tell Mr. Phil that you ran into me? It looks like he could use a lady friend."

The scent of freshly brewed coffee wafted through the rice-paper screen that separated the kitchen from the bar. The aroma teased Michal's nose as she followed it to the kitchen.

She smiled at Phil as she entered. "Just ran into Miss Saffron. . . ."

He smirked.

"So how did you sleep last night?" she asked.

"I slept like the dead."

Michal didn't appreciate the joke, though she wasn't sure whether he was joking or just being nihilistic. "Are you having coffee with that Irish Cream?"

"Wanna join me?" He put a six-second pour in his black coffee.

"Ah, hell, why not," she said. He began pouring.

Just then, Max walked in, his hair tousled from sleep. He was still wearing his red-and-black plaid pajamas. He saw Phil pouring the liqueur into Michal's cup. "Starting a bit early, are we?"

"I don't think he ever stopped. . . . Nice pajamas." She raised an eyebrow.

Max ignored her and made a beeline for the coffee pot. He filled a Yellow Submarine mug (complete with cartoon John Lennon peeking out the porthole) to the brim before cautiously taking a sip.

The smell of melting butter wafted from Phil's omelet pan, the butter crackling a merry breakfast time tune. "Anyone want an omelet?" he asked, pointing the spatula at his friends. "I can add ham, cheese, onion, mushroom, *nattō*. . . . I might be able to find more ingredients in the fridge."

"All of the above but the ham, of course. Wait—not the *nattō* either. It's too sticky and slimy—YUCK—and in any case, who adds *that* to an omelet?" Michal said.

"Oh, and Max, I was using the liqueur for a sweet little treat. . . . Unfortunately you don't get any since you're so derisive of those of us who use liquor in our cooking." Phil did his best to look innocent as he sipped his coffee. "It just so happens that I also added it to the Irish-twisted angel-food cake I just baked. One of my grandmother's favorites. I decided it would be wise to take advantage of the proximity of the bottle and enhance my coffee." Phil motioned to the Irish Cream.

"I didn't know you could bake," Max said.

"It was on my little bucket list, y'know? Short time to live, a lot of things still to do." He smiled. Michal thought the smile looked a little more forced than usual.

"Angel-food cake—or would you prefer I say 'imaginary being cake,' Phil?" Max laughed.

Phil looked at Max, making a very big show of thinking long and hard about his friend's comment, finally offering, "Nope, angel-food cake is fine with me, along with deviled eggs and devil's food cake, even though devils don't exist either. . . . Jeez, just because I don't believe in supernatural beings doesn't mean that I don't believe in linguistic expressions." He laughed.

"Don't forget angel-hair pasta," Michal said. "I think that a conversation about angels would be appropriate here, Phil."

"Do tell." Phil closed his eyes as he sipped his coffee.

"Phil, you said you brought us here for a reason. We're not idiots, so we know what that reason is." She watched Phil's face for any sign he acknowledged what she was saying. He only blinked as the steam from his coffee reached his eyelids.

"Speaking of angels," Max began, trying to steer the conversation away from what he knew Phil would undoubtedly use as an excuse to upset Michal again, "we barely started our conversation about heaven last night."

"I have some awesome ideas about heaven and angels." Michal looked at Phil. He was smiling around his coffee cup. "Of course, a lot is just speculation."

"At last, breakfast for the mind." Phil set down his cup and rested his chin on his interlaced fingers as he batted his eyes.

"Or the soul," Michal said.

"Can't we discuss Frege's *Sense and Reference* instead? You know, real philosophy." Phil snickered.

"Come on, Phil," Michal pleaded. "Keep an open mind."

"OK, fine. A starving man takes what he can."

"Great," Max said, as he picked up a knife and cut himself a slice of cake. Phil handed him a plate. "We can learn a lot about angels and heaven in many passages in the Bible. But I can't rightly start off this discussion without giving at least a nod to Thomas Aquinas. Not that I'm all onboard with what he has to say, but he wrote extensively about angels, discussing both their nature and activity, in his *Summa Theologica*."

"How many angels are dancing on this spoon?" Phil held up his wooden stirring spoon and grinned widely. Max and Michal just shook their heads.

"Aquinas actually constructed an argument for the existence of angels meant for those who don't want to rely only on faith and what scripture says. Their existence is necessary, given God's perfection. The argument goes something like this: Because God is good, He created beings in His likeness, just as heat produces heat. Since God created beings through His intellect and His will, it follows that there must be intelligent creatures among his creations. But not merely intelligent creatures like humans, because pure intelligence, which God's perfect universe demands, cannot be a characteristic of embodied creatures like us, who are limited to the here-and-now. So incorporeal angels must exist, given the fact of God's perfection. —But again, that's according to Aquinas' logic. I'm sure you can find several holes in it, Phil." Max smiled.

By now the two friends should have been used to Phil huffing every time he heard something with which he disagreed. Maybe it was too early in the morning, or maybe they just never quite got over it, but it was still annoying.

"Max, let me get out just one big knitting needle to unravel that argument. The whole thing is based on the given that God exists. I won't even go into how it relies on His perfection, which neither Michal nor I accept, nor that He created all of the angels and didn't just happen to find them and co-opt them into His service." He smirked. "Oh wait, I just did. —But all of that aside, if I don't believe in God to begin with, then the entire argument is academic." He sipped his coffee. "Which is fine with me—something light with which to start the day." He tilted the pan to flip Michal's omelet.

"For the sake of argument, Phil," Max continued, "let's say there *is* a God. There *is* an afterlife. So we can discuss the nature of the denizens that occupy that God-space known as 'heaven.' There are all kinds of angel stories in the Bible and descriptions of different kinds of angels: the seraphim, cherubim, and the archangels—even guardian angels. Remember Jesus' words in Matthew? 'Do not despise these little ones, for their angels always behold the face of my Father in heaven.' At least one of the Psalms speaks about guardian angels, too."

"Our guardian angels are here right now—even yours, Phil," Michal interrupted. "They look on us as needy younger siblings. We are like little brothers or sisters under their charge. We're always getting lost, getting into trouble, getting into accidents. For this reason, we owe our angels our gratitude and respect."[109]

"I can't tell whether you're kidding." Phil looked a bit puzzled. "I certainly hope you are. But I'll let you believe in your invisible yes-men if you wish."

"Angels make up the heavenly host. They praise and serve God. They comfort, protect, intercede, instruct, and prophesy. Angels are messengers. The Greek word *angelos* actually means 'messenger,'" Max said.

"And the Hebrew word for angel is *malak*," Michal said.

"Are we in a competition here? OK—*tenshi*," Phil remarked. "Since we are in Japan."

Max rolled his eyes and went on: "Angels sometimes turn out to be the divine presence of God. The angel who appeared to Moses as a flame of fire in a bush turned out to be God just a few verses later."

Michal piped in, "Angels ministered to Jesus after Satan tempted him. —If we're to believe that story. There are all sorts of reasons not to. —But angels also destroy, inflict punishment, and kill. Think of all the shit they unleash on the earth in the Book of Revelation. Of course, I don't believe that Revelations is any more than a really good work of fiction—parody even—and perfect for the big screen. The author cribs all sorts of Old Testament writers and the Book of Enoch. What's really funny is that he lifts passages completely out of context. And he makes some pretty good jokes, too."

She momentarily lost her train of thought. —*Oh yeah, the Book of Revelation.*

"Take Revelations 17. The beast is described as the one who was, is not, and is to come. This is pretty funny—it's a parody of the description of God as the One who is, who was, and is to come.... Did you guys know that the beast is Nero? People expected that he would come back to life and resume power. The number of the beast, 666, is the sum of the Hebrew letters spelling 'Neron Caesar.' That is, Nero. The Hebrew letters, like the Greek, had numerical equivalents. The real proof for this is that some of the ancient texts read 616, instead of 666, which drops the 'n' in 'Neron.' I could go on and on about Revelations. It's such a weird book. —But I digress."

"Ah, but a fascinating digression." Phil smiled as Michal scanned the room. He wondered what she was looking for.

"I believe that the covenant of the New Testament prevents a repeat of Sodom and Gomorrah, where angels were tasked with the investigation and subsequent destruction of sinners. That whole reinforcing of free will and the completeness of God's love and all that.... Though it's not what I believe, many, many people think that the Book of Revelation speaks truth. The angels will punish the unbelievers on earth," Max said.

"And all at God's bidding. What a loving being you two worship. He sounds like he has dissociative identity disorder." Phil folded the omelet onto a plate, sprinkled it with some chives and a pinch of salt and handed it to Michal. "So your mad-scientist God, who doesn't give us enough information to actually believe in Him, is now going to send His heavenly thugs to punish us for not doing His will? What a charmer." He dropped a pat of butter into the pan and watched as it began to sizzle and melt. "I wonder if God sits and watches all of those people being tortured in hell with the same curiosity that I'm watching this butter?" Phil turned to Max, "Want one, too?"

Michal wrinkled her nose. She was starting to think that eternity would be sans Phil regardless of what she said, though this did conflict with her universalism. Maybe a different tack.

"Actually," Michal said, "a lot of the angel and demon stories, and especially the ones found in the New Testament, are taken from the Book of Enoch. Enoch had tremendous influence on the Bible. I don't think many people know that."

Phil and Max acted out a little pantomime while Michal was speaking. Phil pointed at foods on the counter and Max made hand-motions to select the ingredients of his omelet.

Having finished his order, Max began, "Don't forget that demons are said to be fallen angels. C.S. Lewis said that the sin of both men and angels is made possible because God gave us free will.[110] Also, Augustine explained that good and bad angels do not result from a difference in their nature or their origin, since God created them both. Most chose to continue their allegiance to God, but others—being enamored of their own power and inflated with pride—chose to rebel against God."[111] Max got a plate from a cabinet and set it within Phil's easy reach.

"Augustine," Max continued, "actually discusses the creation of angels and demons, which he claims only seems to be omitted from Genesis. He links their creation to the creation of the world. In his *City of God*, Augustine wonders why the angels were apparently not listed among the created works of God. But then he provides an interesting answer.[112] He claims that when God said, 'Let there be light, and there was light,' He was actually speaking of the creation of the angels. The angels, being illumined by the Light that created them, themselves became light and were called 'Day.'" Max grabbed a mushroom from the cutting board, popping it into his mouth before Phil tossed the rest in the omelet pan.

"So when God said, 'Let there be light,' the angels came into existence. Augustine's account of the creation of the angels answers a common objection: How could there be 'light' on the first day if the sun and stars didn't exist till the fourth day? The right answer, at least according to Augustine, is that the light was that of the angels.

"Augustine tells us that the fall of the angels also occurred on the first day," Max continued. "This is what Genesis means when it says, 'God divided the light from the darkness, and God called the light 'Day,' and the darkness He called 'Night.'" He watched Phil add some sort of weird, disagreeable spice to the pan, wrinkling his nose at the offense.

"So here we have Augustine, desperately straining to make sense of a fictitious account of creation, so that he can—what?—hold onto his faith? Of course, I know why he would do that. He's afraid the angelic good-fellas would bring him a horse head." Phil laughed at the imagery.

"There's a great deal of research on this subject. Jewish angelology and demonology have a long history, which includes several metamorphoses as a result of many cultural influences, including the Canaanites, the Babylonians, the Egyptians, the Persians, and the Greeks. Consider Isaiah 14:12," Michal said. "It supposedly describes the fall of Satan and his attempted overthrow of God. But the author is actually referring to an unnamed Babylonian king trying to overreach his power. The author draws on the Canaanite myth of the gods Helel and Shahar, who fall from heaven as a result of rebellion. The New Testament writers reinterpret this as the fall of Satan and his angels. Luke 10:18 actually has Jesus saying that he witnessed this event."

Phil laughed again. "Let me get this straight. The Bible—well, the Old Testament anyway—doesn't even talk about the fall of Satan, and the angels are, well, everything that you talked about—but you still think I should believe in them because you're paying protection money for me—praying for the salvation of my eternal soul?"

"Actually, in the Hebrew Bible—the Old Testament—Satan is not even a singular being. Satan, or better *Ha-Satan*, is a title bestowed on a class of being. It means 'The Adversary' or 'The Accuser.' Anyway, you should believe in angels because there have been innumerable testimonial accounts—first-hand experiences. Trust me on this one," Michal finished.

"Can we move on to heaven now?" Phil asked, noticing something in Michal's eyes that he didn't really want to explore. "Perhaps I'll be a bit more convinced—though notice how I'm not holding my breath."

"One more point about angels, which is actually related to heaven—" Michal began.

"If you must."

"Remember what I said the other day about how Christianity teaches that we will have real bodies in the afterlife?" Michal looked at Max for affirmation.

"Sure, but isn't this end-times stuff? You know, after Jesus returns we get new bodies? New heaven and earth?"

Michal began to answer, but Phil cut her off. "Wait, you can't believe that now, can you, since it comes from Revelations and you just said that Revelations is a load of crap." Phil was gaining steam again. "Sure, I'm paraphrasing you, but you can't use Revelations as the basis for your argument when you don't think it's anything more than an ancient lampoon."

"He's got you, Michal," Max said.

"Hang on, guys. I'm not basing my belief in a new heaven and earth on Revelations, which is a load of crap. I accept your paraphrase, Phil." He bowed with a flourish. "Jesus himself speaks of His return and initiating a kingdom. It could be this current earth, but since we humans have managed to so fantastically destroy the shit out of it—you know, global warming, extinction, warfare, overpopulation, fracking and Twinkies, which have a millennium-long shelf life—well, hanging out with Jesus on this earth wouldn't be so heavenly." Michal thought on her words and then continued: "You know, many of our problems could be solved if we wiped a lot of people off the face of this planet—the Rapture would take care of that. . . ." She smirked until she realized how offensive she sounded. "Anyway, so God has got to start over. This is also why I believe that Jesus is coming soon. If He doesn't come soon, He won't have a planet to return to."

"You mean the planet that God is going to remake in all of His power? Don't you believe that God can remake the planet from His mighty words alone, even a dung-heap of a planet, such as the one we're sitting on now?" Phil asked contemptuously.

"I'm going to ignore that. . . . I was trying to say something about our bodies in the afterlife. Of course we will have bodies. As Kreeft says, it is irrational to suppose that we will be an entirely new species. Remember Psalm 8? 'What is man, that you are mindful of him, or the son of man, that you visit him? You have made him a little lower than the angels.' But in the afterlife, our status will be elevated. In Luke, Jesus says that since we are the children of God and the children of the Resurrection, we will be equal to the angels. But, of course, this doesn't mean that we will become angels. We are an altogether different species. Humans become saints, not angels." Michal paused and handed her empty cup to Phil, eyes pleading for more coffee. "It seems like we're going to have three different kinds of bodies in successive order, at least if we follow Kreeft's scholarship here. Immediately after death, we will find ourselves out of our old bodies and into new ethereal ones. This seems so obviously true, especially if we take seriously the many accounts of out-of-body experiences as well as stories from premodern cultures, including the words of Paul himself, who claimed to have visited the third heaven and gazed upon the glory of God. This was the dwelling place of the blessed, according to mystical Judaism." She reached for the coffee cup, which had the perfect amount of room for a shot of Irish Cream. Phil teasingly refused to give it to her.

She continued, "The resurrection body, of which Paul also speaks and which Jesus assumed on earth between his Resurrection and Ascension, is a solid body. But like I said, we won't quite recognize each other at first, at least by sight—remember, Phil, Caravaggio's transgender Jesus? By the way, this reminds me of the *Odyssey*. The goddess Athena touches Odysseus with her golden wand and his appearance changes. He becomes lithe and young, ruddy with sun, jawline clean. His own son doesn't even recognize him and thinks him to be a god. . . ." She smiled. "In any case, it seems that we will get yet another body, a glorified body, of which both Paul and the author of First John speak. 'We shall be like Him, for we shall see Him.'" She reached out for the coffee cup. "I'm done now. Give me my coffee, you ass."

"Wow, Michal, I'm always amazed at your skill at making completely random connections. Anyway, we already spoke about out-of-body experiences." Phil playfully held onto the coffee cup, then added some Irish Cream and stirred. Handing it to Michal, he continued, "You need that drink if you think that I'm about to take the testimony of people whose chemical balance and electrical impulses are on the fritz to begin with, not to mention the shit-ton of drugs from the doctors. You know those docs who cruelly bring them back from Paradise, only to deposit them back into this wretched world?" He looked at Max. "What do you think, sir? You were at death's door at that rehab center, or so you keep saying. Any near-death experiences there?"

"Can't say that I did," Max said, matter-of-factly. Phil went on:

"I still think that if heaven exists or if there is a new heaven and earth as you say—and all of this is a big, big IF and highly unlikely, impossibly unlikely—then I *still* say that it will be incredibly boring. Why would God want to miss out on His endorphin buzz from watching us get it right? Of course, that can't happen, because, as we've already discussed, according to most accounts of heaven we won't be able to sin. It won't be any part of our makeup, so it will be as impossible as it is for me to defy gravity right now and fly. So why should I hope to go there?"

"We will not be bored because we will still not have perfect knowledge, so we will always be learning—and learning is extremely enjoyable. And we will be with God and we will never come to the end of exploring our understanding of Him," Max said.

Phil raised an eyebrow, "You go ahead and explore your understanding of God. I'm going to be exploring my understanding of a few thousand delicious succubi."

"Only if you can catch them. . . . We also get to hang out with our loved ones and have unending philosophical discussions." Max raised his coffee mug in salute.

"With the likes of Socrates!" Michal exclaimed. "This will be a huge pleasure."

"At bottom, we will enjoy being with God. We will not be playing harps and polishing halos, although I believe there will be music and dancing and we will be in the company of angels. —But not Socrates since he was neither a Christian nor a Jew, instead being a devout polytheist. In any case, that hardly sounds boring to me," Max said.

"Of course Socrates will be there, Max," Michal said, taking extreme exception. "Remember in Acts 17, I think, Paul tells the Athenians that the unknown god whom they worship is really our God. And he also says that God writes His laws in our hearts, so even those who have never encountered our God—like Socrates, who was born before Jesus—will still make it to heaven because they followed God's laws written in their hearts. Think about what an awesome man Socrates was, always trying to morally uplift the Athenian youth. Since Socrates was born centuries before Jesus, how can God hold that against him? —I have no doubt that Socrates will be there."

Phil raised his spatula, saw that Michal was gathering a head of steam, and lowered it. Any objections would have to come later, but he was pretty sure that this redemption relativism would not ring true in the pews of the churches.

Michal was looking up, thinking about visions of heaven. Then she saw Phil lowering his spatula and wondered whether he would be considered a good man. She thought about a passage from one of the Gnostic gospels, Phillip:

The pearl, which is thrown into the mud, is not worth less than it was before. So it is with the children of God. Whatever becomes of them, they are precious in their Father's eyes.

Phil is God's child, whether he recognizes this or not, she thought. *He's just a muddied-up little pearl, that's all.* The notion flittered from her mind and she thought about heaven again.

"I'm completely convinced that there will be animals there too, since we enjoy them so much here on earth, and, of course, we're getting a little taste of heaven right here—well, I'm getting a *big* taste of heaven, and if this is all the heaven that God ever offers me, I am quite all right with it. But back to animals: the psalms, if we appeal to them, confirm this. And remember Elijah was taken to heaven in a chariot pulled by horses. And don't forget Isaiah 11: 'The cow and the bear shall graze, their young ones shall lie down together, and the lion shall eat straw like the ox.' So there will be animals, because they are incredibly pleasurable to us.

Our pets will be there. And lions, tigers, and bears will rest their heads on my lap to be petted." Michal sounded dreamy.

"I'm not going to burst your bubble, but I'm pretty sure that only humans have souls, despite what Don Bluth thinks about doggie heaven." Max looked away from Michal and carefully inspected the golden brown veins in the Italian marble countertop.

"I need to rein you guys back in," Phil declared. "All of this is utter specula-tion—fabrication! And Michal, you have been guilty of invoking a lot of scripture to support your beliefs, when you already said that you are suspicious of the whole of it. . . . We could talk about Valhalla and Ragnarök next, but then I think you'll say that they're just mythological attempts to understand the physical world. So why privilege your mythology?"

"You know, Phil, the scholar Rudolf Bultmann notes that the entire world-picture of the New Testament is mythical, so you're right on that count," Michal said. "The world, as you know, is presented as a three-story structure with earth in the middle, heaven above and hell below. The Son of Man will come on the clouds of heaven and the faithful will be caught up to meet Him in the air. And earth itself is presented as a theater for the workings of supernatural powers—of God and his angels, Satan and his demons. —A world where humans are not their own masters, where demons can possess them, but God and the forces of good can also direct them and even give them the supernatural power of the Holy Spirit. But this particular mythological world is not unique to Christianity. Its roots can be found in Jewish apocalyptic literature and the Gnostic myth of redemption. Bultmann says that it would be a forced *sacrificium intellectus* to believe in this mythical world, but there can still be some truth to be had inde-pendent of this mythology.[113] Of course, I disagree with Bultmann that the entire New Testament world-picture is mythological, but you get what I'm saying."

"I like Bultmann," Phil said.

"Of course it's all speculation, Phil. Even Paul admitted we can't understand the afterlife when he says, 'Eye has not seen, nor ear heard, nor have entered into the heart of man, the things which God has prepared for those who love him.' Although Revelations does give us some elaborate descriptions of the New Jerusalem. But Michal's not going to accept any of it," Max added.

"Right," Michal said.

"Well, this is what sounds good to you." Phil passed a fresh-out-of-the-skillet omelet to Max and then tossed him a fork. Max masterfully caught it, as if he'd been catching forks his whole life. "But other cultures have different conceptions of heaven and the afterlife. How do we know which is right, if any?" Phil began making another omelet. "For example, consider the afterlife as the Qur'an describes it. As I've read, heaven is a garden paradise where the faithful lie on brocade couches in a climate-controlled environment, wearing green silk and silver bracelets, drinking from crystal goblets without fear of headaches or intoxi-cation, eating pomegranates and dates, and surrounded by 'bashful, dark-eyed virgins, chaste as the sheltered eggs of ostriches'—evidently all of the faithful are men." Phil leered at Michal. "Or lesbians"—then thought through the ramifications of that: "Whereupon they will be promptly buried up to their necks and stoned to death."

Michal frowned at Phil's joke. "No they don't, not according to the Qur'an. They go under house arrest until they die, or they get married off—still pretty bad."

"You're right, Phil," Max said, ignoring Michal's comment. "Buddhists believe that paradise comes when the body is free from suffering and rebirth—when it reaches nirvana. This earthly life is akin to hell, since the body is where pain is experienced, and so they advocate letting go in order to be released from our earthly suffering. Many pagans believe in the Summerlands, a warm-summer-meadow type of afterlife, which only serves as a resting place before one is re-incarnated." He watched Phil add more butter to the pan, crack a few eggs and throw in some crushed garlic and kale.

"Don't you both see the problem?" Phil added bacon and four different kinds of cheese. "These people wholeheartedly believe in their versions of heaven. The thing is, if any of them is right, then the rest of you are wrong." He pointed at Max. "Unless we assume that we each end up in our own version of heaven." He smirked and then looked very seriously at Michal. "Your version of heaven could not possibly include Republicans." She laughed while Phil continued, "Christians, Jews, Muslims, and—well, you're all pretty much screwed unless you're gonna go with some kind of relativism." Phil folded his omelet, slightly runny, and slid it onto his plate. "I don't know if you've been watching the news over the last few decades, but most Christians, Jews, and Muslims don't take kindly to relativism."

Michal pushed the remainder of her omelet around her plate. Her hand went numb from the motion and she dropped her fork. She didn't believe any of what Phil was saying. "But Phil, if you don't believe in the afterlife and you're wrong—and both Max and I think you are—then aren't you the least bit concerned about what's going to happen when—" Michal wasn't ready to say it just yet. She picked up her fork, put a cold piece of omelet in her mouth and immediately regretted it.

"Look, we've been over this ground already. I'll just be gone. I believe this because it makes sense and because it's more likely than a lot of fanciful stories. It's painful, because I can't find any evidence that we get to continue to enjoy ourselves with our best friends." Phil's voice caught in his throat. "I choose not to believe in some doctrine just because it comes from my culture and served the will of the priests from times past—or because it feels good, comfortable, and safe. I choose to believe in the only logical conclusion. There are no angels, no demons, no heaven and no afterlife." Phil balanced his plate on his coffee cup and walked out into the bar. A lone patron sat there studying the menu, then looked up at him expectantly as he approached from the kitchen. The man adjusted his tortoise-shell glasses and opened his mouth to speak.

Phil cut him off with broken Japanese, "My bar is closed. Go away."

He held the door for the man as he rose and left.

Max and Michal watched this exchange. Max held Michal as tears welled in her eyes.

§§§§§

FIVE YEARS EARLIER. *Room 320 in the Oxford Hotel*

Phil looked at the headboard. It read: *Come, gentle dreams, the hours of sleep beguile.*

Embossed letters on hammered copper rose above the heads of would-be sleepers in a room entirely too yellow for Phil's taste. He looked at the lace on top of his nightstand, the hardwood chest of drawers, and the chairs out in the sitting room. The room evoked feelings of times gone by, the turn of the century in the burgeoning town known as Denver. Phil placed his well-worn boots at the foot of the bed. He sat down and put his wallet on the nightstand. He stared at the digital clock, which seemed like an out-of-place alien in this antique room. It just didn't fit. If he were to have any supernatural experiences it would have to go— the rectangular chrome table lamp as well. Phil unplugged them and moved them to the bathroom. He went back into the bedroom. It looked every bit as authentic as he was hoping it would be. He had come here to experience—well—*something.* Death had been on his mind for the better part of the last several months. Ever since Crager had died.

He had even considered dressing the part to fully welcome any specters, anything that felt the need to come and pay him a visit. Maybe, if he were lucky, the lady spirit of Florence Montague would tug on his arms or steal his sheets. But he ended up wearing his usual: comfortable blue jeans, Stratford button-up, and trusty hiking boots.

It had been Crager's death that had motivated him to seek something that would confirm the existence of the spiritual realm. Since Crager had left—and left so . . . perplexingly—he had begun to think that maybe there was something to all of this afterlife nonsense. He had a hard time with it—with putting himself in situations like these—since it went against everything he believed in. But like everything else he did, he threw himself fully into the task.

His eyes fixed on the green- and yellow-striped wingback chair with the hand-embroidered pillow nestled in the seat. He looked past the chair to the lace-covered window, which was opened just a crack to let in some fresh air. He tried to tune out the noisy foot traffic and focus on the reason he was here in the first place.

"OK, Room 320, give me your best shot." Phil lay back on the bed and waited. He was a single male in a room allegedly haunted by a spirit whose favorite target was single males. It was his first stop on his world tour of haunted locales, but he hoped he would get lucky—even though he didn't believe in luck.

Hell, he didn't even believe in ghosts or the supernatural. Thinking back, though, he was reminded of Martin Crager, who quite obviously showed that whether one believed in the supernatural or not, the supernatural didn't seem to need your consent.

As his eyes began to close, he watched the lace curtains, which stood deathly still. Then he thought of Crager.

Phil remembered it well. Four of them occupied the room. There was Dr. Fontana, professor of psychology, Yves Clairborne, poet and philosopher, Phil, of course, with degrees in chemical engineering and geology, and bedridden Crager, with a Ph.D. in physics. Their common bond, besides friendship, was their staunch atheism.

Phil thought of the room buzzing with discussions of the afterlife—particularly the absurdity of the idea. Crager had joined in, on the edge of death but defiant to the end. He scoffed and challenged the powers that be to show him something. He all but dared them to convert him. He had declared, "I won't go running to comfort and ignorance, I'd rather have pain and truth."

Phil remembered that line: *Pain and truth.* . . .

Crager had been diagnosed with stage-three pancreatic cancer almost a year before. Phil was impressed by the fact that, even in this day and age, that single word—'cancer'—could cause such dread. There were cures for all kinds of cancer, although the word 'cure' was sometimes a stretch. Often life went on but at a terrible cost. Crager had stated what was already obvious to anyone who knew him: he would rather die than waste away. Although when he was first diagnosed he wasn't so willing to give up.

Crager pressed his friends to help him research alternative treatments and even the ridiculous notion of the afterlife. After five months, it was clear nothing was going to help him. No new research, no miracle cure, no fantastic technology straight out of a science-fiction movie. He was going to die. With that realization, Crager organized his affairs and set about preparing for the end at the tender age of fifty-three.

Of course, his version of preparing for the end turned out to be a madcap, almost desperately insane series of adventures. A man half his age would have been challenged to keep up. Martin Crager had regularly taken sabbaticals to go on various trips. Somehow he always ended up getting the university to pay, producing yet another book or series of papers. His trips always involved exploring the darkest and most dangerous places the world had to offer. Phil often joined him on his bungee-jumping, sky-diving, running-from-the bulls, "live-life-to-the-fullest" adventures. But as the end approached, Crager took still greater risks, pushing it too far even for Phil. And he was taking a monster concoction of brightly colored pills: to help him sleep, to keep him awake, to manage pain, to manage the side effects of other pills, and to fight the beast that was devouring his insides.

Now here he was hooked up to as few machines as possible. One to keep track of his vitals and transmit that information to the nurses' station, and one to give him peace in the form of a morphine at-will dispenser. The latter spent most of its time unused.

Crager elected for hospice after he had failed in his many adventures to "accidentally" kill himself. He had spent the last two months here, alternating between being bedridden and dragging himself to the toilet to vomit. In his lucid moments he was still a person. He was Martin Crager. But in the more unpleasant times—and they were occurring all the more frequently—he became something else—something alien to all four men. He was a chunk of meat, a stand-in for the real Martin Crager.

Phil's thoughts drifted to that final day. The nurses had told them it would be soon, his bowels no longer obeyed his wishes, he was in constant pain and he had been using the morphine more often. On hearing this last piece of information Phil immediately went to see him. Waiting there were Clairborne and Fontana. Clairborne looked every bit the poet-philosopher, with loose-fitting khakis and a turtleneck sweater adorned with his trademark woolen gray scarf. He carried a small notebook in which he wrote when the muse struck. Fontana appeared as though sleep were a friend with whom he had spent very little time—something to which his hastily tied tennis-shoes, well-worn jeans and rumpled shirt and jacket attested. Crager was no longer lucid, drifting in and out of consciousness, babbling like the very thing he had wished never to become.

When Phil entered the room, hearty handshakes and greetings all around gave the three friends something to distract themselves, giving way quickly to conversation. They talked for hours, watching helplessly as their friend slipped further and further away from the world of the living. They had all spoken coolly—almost coldly—about the inevitable and imminent event. Yves thought of the imagery, wondering about the great blackness in which Martin was no doubt enveloped. Phil recalled that he had rendered several verses about the unstoppable, inescapable, icy blue ocean of death that was swallowing Martin. Fontana remained nearby, a reliably sympathetic ear. He was sure to remind everyone present—himself included—of Kübler-Ross' stages of grief.

Five hours had passed. After reflecting on a dozen or so of Yves' verses, and much commiseration, they watched as Crager's body stirred for what they assumed would be the last time. His lips moved, though at first no sound issued from them. The three huddled around him, straining to listen. Although his whispers were barely audible, they hit like a cannonball to the chest. The nurse watched as they all reacted to Martin Crager's final words.

At first they dismissed it. Nonsense, Fontana had said. Their minds were projecting whatever it was they needed to hear onto poor Martin Crager—as if he were some kind of messenger from beyond, the ultimate authority on life after death. But it soon became impossible to dismiss it. He whispered over and over again about the light.

"The light—the light—everywhere—warmth—so inviting." Each word took several seconds to finish but it was unmistakable. He was talking about the light. How could he even utter this rubbish? It wasn't some deep genetic memory, or secret desire, or part of his upbringing. He had rejected these romantic notions of "the light"—going to it, hearing from it, believing in it.

Crager was the ultimate ambassador for skepticism and here he was sharing some metaphysical fluff. Phil stared in disbelief and wonder. Yves' poet's heart was secretly happy. Fontana dismissed it as some kind of hallucination, though he was having a hard time convincing even himself of the veracity of that claim in the face of raw experience. Finally, after about ten minutes, Crager's eyes fluttered open, lazily wandered to each of his companions and then closed one final time. He whispered the words "See—you—soon," exhaled, and was no more.

The three friends stared at Crager, trying to process what had happened, what it meant. The nurse who had been watching from the doorway walked casually into the room and shut off the monitor, marking the time on his notepad and then placing it in the pocket of his white jacket. As he went about removing the monitor and the IV, he saw that Crager had the faintest smile on his face.

"He's in a better place," the nurse said solemnly. Fontana was the first to reply—almost angrily—to this statement:

"He's not in a better place. There is no better place than the here-and-now. He doesn't believe in any of that nonsense. None of us does."

"I'm sorry. I didn't mean to offend you, but just look at his face. At the very least, he's no longer in pain and he's therefore in a better place than here."

"But he always said he would rather have pain and truth than comfort and ignorance," Yves responded.

The nurse looked down at Crager and shrugged. "I don't know that he kept to those values in his final moments. —Look at him." He gestured at the calm and peaceful face.

"His muscles went slack. It's natural," Phil said. "We shouldn't put any greater significance on it."

"I understand what you are saying, sir." The nurse's words held the barest hint of an apology. "I see here that he didn't note any religious affiliation. . . . Atheist, I assume? So I suppose you don't have anyone you wish for me to call?" He took out his notepad in preparation.

"No, he would not wish it," Yves replied. But he wasn't so sure anymore.

The nurse wrote something on his notepad. "I understand what you're saying, sir." He moved to leave the room, then paused. "But it does make you think, doesn't it? If a loved one who is so consistent in their beliefs and so adamant about them says something so different from anything that they believed—well, it makes you wonder whether they had some new experience. You know what I mean?"

Phil and his two friends sat silently in the room for some time. Yves wrote in his notebook like a man possessed. Fontana muttered quietly to himself, trying to make some sense of it all. Phil stared blankly out the window until they came and wheeled Crager's body away.

Three months later Yves Clairborne would be researching the supernatural and joining a church. Fontana began to explore the death process and commonalities between people's death experiences. Phil decided that he needed more data.

—Which brought him to Room 320 of the Oxford Hotel, waking with a start at something tickling his toes. When he opened his eyes, he could see a face with indistinct but feminine features hovering at the foot of his bed. He resisted the urge to scream, as small beads of sweat broke out on his brow. The face rocked to and fro. He could feel the ethereal fingers brushing on his feet. He looked again at the face. It seemed to beckon him, but Phil couldn't move. A light breeze disturbed the curtains. Phil managed to sit up and decided to try to make contact.

He adjusted himself to get a better look at the apparition. She seemed to follow his every move. Finally, when he screwed on his eyes, he saw that the ghost was nothing but the white-lace curtain. He let out a long breath. He got out of bed and walked toward the window. He closed it and tried to fall back to sleep. The remainder of his night was dreamless and lonely.

FOURTEEN

But who do you say that I am?
JESUS

LATER IN THE AFTERNOON. *At the RTSS*

Michal approached Phil and Max who were sitting at the bar.

"Did you enjoy your nap?" Max asked.

"I don't know why I got so tired. I guess arguing with the two of you is exhausting. But yes, I did."

"What would you like to drink?" Phil asked. "I've got an unopened bottle of Brunello di Montalcino Riserva. You love Brunello. Wanna try it?"

"I think I'll stick to some tea, Maxie-style." Michal smiled. "I can't keep up with the likes of you."

"I'll get you a cup."

"You know, Phil," Michal began hesitantly, "I've been wanting to talk to you about that comment you made about Jesus' Resurrection and mass hysteria. You upset me so much that I just wasn't up for the fight. But while I was in my room just now, I thought through what I want to say."

"Go ahead." Phil took a cup and placed it on a tray. He listened while Michal set up her argument.

"You dismissed Jesus' Resurrection as mass hysteria, but we have so many good reasons to believe that Jesus really did rise from the dead."

"I'm listening." *Sugar, cream, and a little napkin to complete the ensemble.*

"OK, but I don't want a lot of obnoxious interruptions."

"I can't promise you that. —Is this an argument, a statement, or a diatribe? I love a good argument, I'll listen to statements, and I'm usually amused by diatribes."

"Not interrupting would go against his very nature, Michal," Max said.

"Well, *try* at least, Phil. For my sake." Michal's eyes pleaded with Phil as he arranged the items on the tray.

"Go ahead. I'll try. Just nothing about the Shroud of Turin. You know they debunked that."

"You're already not trying and technically they 'rebunked' that," Max chided Phil.

"Sorry, Michal, the floor is yours." Phil brought her the tray and poured the tea.

"They've actually pushed the dates earlier on Turin, but no, I won't touch that. I've tried and failed with others. I'm taking another tack. Let's start with the first-century Roman-Jewish historian, Josephus. In his *Antiquities of the Jews,* we find three passages confirming not only the existence of Jesus but His historical significance. One passage notes the death by stoning of Jesus' brother, James, who was the head of the Jerusalem church and probably represented the so-called circumcision faction that Paul opposed. A second passage refers to John, called 'the Baptist,' who was executed. The final passage, the most interesting of all, discusses the life and death of Jesus, calling Him 'the Christ,' noting His miraculous deeds, observing that He won over both Jews and Greeks, that He was crucified, and that He appeared to others after His death. Significantly, Josephus was not a Christian. He was a historian."

Phil sat, listening to Michal. He looked at her expectantly as she finished her sentence. She took her tea and nodded. "You may speak now," she said with an air of mock royalty.

He bowed his head. "First, being a Christian and a historian are not mutually exclusive. One can be a historian and not a Christian or one can be a Christian historian. That said, it's a quibble so I'll let it pass for now."

"I was merely noting that since he was not a Christian, he had no reason to tinker with history. We should take his historical account to be accurate and not motivated by any Christian bias," Michal huffed.

"I do want to point out that the third passage you reference, the *Testimonium Flavianum*, is controversial.[114] Scholars suggest that some of it might not have been written by Josephus at all but added later to promote Christianity."

"I'm aware of that, but still much of it is credible. Anyway, if we look at the gospel accounts, we are also given almost incontrovertible evidence of His Resurrection. I won't go into all of the evidence, but highlight what I take to be the most significant. I'll first note that Jesus' tomb was found empty by a group of his *women* followers. That the gospels would note this is incredibly significant. We've talked a lot about the status of women in Jewish society, so hear me out on this. The testimony of women in Jewish society was considered to be so unreliable that women could not even serve as witnesses in a Jewish court of law. So the fact that women and not men discovered the empty tomb strongly suggests the historicity of that event."[115]

"It may suggest authenticity but it also suggests something else," Phil responded matter-of-factly. Michal waved him on:

"Go ahead, Phil, I'm drinking my tea."

"Well, the fact that women followers found the empty tomb is perfect politically. Think about it. If people accept it, then it can be used to show historicity. If, however, people don't believe it, then it can just be passed off as 'women's talk.'" Phil laughed. "See how much has changed in a couple of thousand years?"

"Phil, you're attributing modern behaviors to ancient peoples," Max said.

"Max, I'm just relying on human nature. I would like to say that human behavior has changed over time, but unfortunately I don't believe it has in any appreciable way."

Michal piped in: "Phil, the earliest known Jewish response to the announcement of Jesus' Resurrection—that the disciples came and stole the body—was a desperate attempt to explain why the women discovered that the tomb *was empty*."

"That actually supports my previous supposition. First, send in disposable witnesses, and then, if they aren't instantly dismissed, send in someone credible to hit the home run." He eyed his empty glass, thought that the ice cubes looked lonely, and grabbed for the whiskey bottle. "Barnum and other charlatans have done it for centuries."

"Phil, are you calling the writers of the Bible 'con men'?" Max asked straight-faced. He wasn't shocked—little shocked him any longer—he was just confirming what he thought he heard.

"Maybe not them, but definitely King James and his paid cronies," Phil said. "Sure, thieves of some sort took the body. It's the most logical explanation and doesn't require any supernatural chicanery. Many of Jesus' followers had motive and opportunity to do it. On the other hand, we have no evidence whatsoever that people's dead bodies are restored to life and rise into heaven." He paused. "I'll follow that logical fallacy with my own appeal to reason. *Any reasonable person* would conclude, then, that somebody stole the body."

"No one had any motive to steal the body," Michal responded. "Think about it. Let's consider everybody who might have stolen it. First, grave robbers. Grave robbers are interested in valuable stuff that is buried with bodies, jewelry and the like. They don't steal the corpse itself. But suppose they *were* interested in the corpse for whatever preposterous reason. They certainly wouldn't undress it and leave the burial clothes behind, carrying the body off naked with dangling limbs. This is completely ridiculous. The disciples would not have stolen the body. They sincerely believed that Jesus was resurrected, so much so that they were willing to die excruciating and degrading deaths for that belief. If the body were stolen, someone wanting to save his skin would have given up the details eventually. The Jewish authorities certainly didn't steal the body. If they had, they would have produced it as soon as the disciples started to preach the Resurrection. And why would ordinary Jews steal the body? There would be no reason. In any case, the theft would have eventually been exposed. The Jewish authorities would have paid a good chunk of money for information on the whereabouts of Jesus' body. But they got none. So they made up the completely lame and most unlikely rumor that Jesus' disciples stole the body."

Michal caught herself laughing out loud, seemingly out of nowhere. "Having said all that, I don't really believe much of any of it. . . . I don't think that Jesus' mangled corpse was literally raised to life. I agree with James Tabor here.[116] It wasn't as if His actual flesh-and-bones were resurrected. I know that the later gospel accounts have Jesus appearing in His physical body, eating fish and bread and showing His wounds to prove He's real. It's interesting that the earliest gospel, Mark, doesn't report any resurrected Jesus sightings. These were added to the text much later. Many Christians don't know that. Remember, Paul talks about 'leaving the old clothing behind.' His visions were of Jesus' *spiritual body* and he likens his encounters to others' experiences. Jesus' new resurrected body was most likely a spiritual one. —I guess I'm siding with some of the Gnostics here. How could Jesus' flesh-and-blood body have ascended into heaven anyway? Which leaves us with our original question: 'What happened to Jesus' corpse?' In my mind, the most likely suspect is Joseph of Arimathea. Remember, he found a *temporary* tomb for Jesus' body. Joseph of Arimathea likely moved the body at the bidding of Jesus' mother and sisters to complete Jesus' burial in a permanent tomb. . . . "

"WHAT?" Max and Phil gave disbelieving stares.

"Doesn't make me any less a Christian," Michal said.

FIFTEEN

"What if Jesus had a vagina?"
"Did you just say what I think you said?"

FOURTEEN YEARS EARLIER. *Santa Barbara*

Red and gold dappled the water as the surfers on dawn patrol caught the first waves of a sun-kissed Saturday morning. Half-a-mile or so offshore, Phil and Max sat in weathered Adirondack chairs on the deck of *The Gloria*. Michal sat on Phil's lap. He raised his glass of bourbon to Max and Michal.

"To the good life and college," Phil said. Michal and Max raised their glasses and smiled.

"To having rich friends," Max said.

"I'll drink to that," Michal said as she snuggled into Phil's chest. He caressed her neck, felt his grandmother's necklace, and smiled.

"I know," she began, trying to look innocent, like she had one-hundred-and-two times before. "I promise to put it back in your grandma's jewelry box."

Phil smiled again. "Is it too trite to say that it's five o'clock somewhere? Well, I guess it's about five o'clock here—in the a.m." He smirked.

In the distance, Phil noticed a red-striped cigarette boat approaching. He untangled himself from Michal and stood up. "Excuse me for a moment." He kissed her on the forehead.

Max got up and put on his boat shoes. "You need some help?"

Phil gave Max *the nod*.

The boat pulled up, as Max scanned the horizon with binoculars. Seeing no other boats around, he said, "We're clear."

Two men climbed up on deck, carrying four cellophane-wrapped cubes. Max noticed the muscles working on the beefy arms of the first man who boarded. He was wearing green trunks and a tribal tee. He had the kind of body that could only come from years of surfing and ocean living. Max took an extra long time to look him over.

"Keep an eye on the horizon, Romeo," Phil admonished him.

Max took one more look at the luscious eye candy and then resumed scanning. "Still clear."

"Not my flavor, man," Green Trunks announced. "However, I'd like to nail that tasty dish over there. She's hotter than hot sauce." He motioned to Michal, who was lounging in her electric-blue string bikini.

"Back off, that's mine," Phil said and instantly regretted it.

"I'm not a piece of meat for either of you pigs," Michal huffed as she got up. Phil watched her ass bounce as she disappeared below deck.

The four men finished their transaction in silence, except for Max's stifled laughter. "You're gonna get it, man. Or I should say, you're *not* going to get it."

"Shut up Max," Phil said with knitted brows.

Phil handed the two men a small box of unmarked twenties. They shook hands in a complex testosterone-fueled ritual and left.

Max and Phil watched them disappear into the blinding sun. After about five minutes of scanning the horizon for Coast Guard or other law enforcement, they went below deck to find Michal. She was making herself another Bloody Mary, mumbling inaudibly. She saw Max and Phil come down the ladder and launched into Phil with a kick to his shin. "Why do you men always have to be such pigs?" The question was obviously rhetorical, since she didn't seem to be willing to listen to an answer.

"Hey, I defended you." Phil was legitimately hurt. "Besides, it's the fault of those Judeo-Christian ethics that this guy is always on about." He motioned to Max.

Max looked incredulous. "What? You either need another drink or I need to cut you off. Honestly, I'm not sure which."

Michal struck at the opening in the conversation. "Phil's right, Max. America—indeed, most of the world—has labored under the yoke of patriarchal oppression for most of history. Especially during Biblical times, including when Jesus lived. I mean really, why did Jesus have to be a *man* anyway?" She spat the words at Max, as if he had been the one who made the decision in the first place.

"What? I— That doesn't even make any sense."

"Actually, Max, she's dead-on accurate. Jesus was a Jewish *male,* after all. I know that Jesus had to be a human to understand our suffering and all that rot, but why would he have to be a man?"

"YEAH, MAX—WHY?" Michal slapped Max's back.

"I didn't write the Bible. I'm not divinely inspired. But if we read the scriptures, then yes, Jesus did have to become human. Some people believe that God had become so disconnected from the reality of human experience—as we so clearly see in the Old Testament—that He became human in order to gain experiential knowledge of our condition. The God of the Old Testament is like a father who doesn't understand his son's fascination with hip-hop. He saw what was going on but didn't understand that it could possibly be of any value, so he took away his CDs and car keys to punish him for his preferences."

Phil smiled. "I'm amazed that you can come up with something quite so profound, when you're already a tumbler-and-a-half of rum and coke in at six-o-something in the morning." He punched Max on the shoulder.

"I'm just that good," Max smirked.

Michal glared at them, apparently not willing to let this conversation get too friendly. "Of course God would show up as a man in Jewish society. Why would He think to challenge Himself, to make Himself uncomfortable? He would have really had a challenge were He required to be under the thumb of a Jewish man!"

Max and Phil stared at her.

She erupted at them. "You two don't understand! It screwed up the whole Bible and any chance of having an egalitarian society. There would never have been a 1 Timothy 2:15, *if Jesus had a vagina!*"

Max and Phil stared at her again, even more incredulously. Phil leaned over to Michal. "I'd be a Christian then. —I mean Jesus was the perfect human. Just imagine God's incarnation of a woman?" He motioned the silhouette of a woman's curves. Seeing Michal's look of scorn, he tried to get back to the subject. "Which verse is that?"

"How women are saved through child-bearing. It's actually pretty universally held as something that shows that Paul—or someone writing in Paul's name—was a flaming misogynist."

"Ah, remind me never to use that verse in the bedroom."

Michal pushed past Phil and Max and went up into the sunshine.

Max looked at Phil. "So Paul's a flaming misogynist, Michal's a flaming feminist, and you're a flaming asshole. —I'm, well, just *flaming*."

Phil leaned into Max and they both laughed in a drunken stupor. They could hear Michal yelling vulgarities at the sky.

"Come on, bro. I need to go up and eat a shit-ton of crow in order to even be around her again."

Max laughed. "I'll help fit your bib."

Back at the RTSS

"Michal, I will completely ignore your comment denying Jesus' bodily Resurrection unless you want to rejoin forces with me. Now, I *somewhat* agree with your original suggestion. You said that there was no good reason to steal Jesus' body." Phil looked at Michal, waiting for confirmation.

"Yes. . . . However we think of Jesus' Resurrection, whether bodily or spiritual, there would have been no good reason to *steal* His body. I thought I made that very clear. I'll set aside Tabor's hypothesis that they reburied His body—just for the sake of argument—you know, to help Maxie out. . . ." She grinned. "Then again, I haven't *completely* convinced myself of this new hypothesis. After all, God, being God, can do whatever He damn well pleases, including a bodily resurrection and soaring up into the sky in oxygen-thin air." She chuckled. "So the fact that the tomb was empty is evidence for the risen Christ."

"I said that I 'somewhat' agree, since I certainly don't agree that the disciples had no interest in stealing the body," Phil said. "Certainly it could have been His own followers trying to make sure that His words came true. —Michal, what kind of nonsense are you talking about, saying Jesus went up into the sky? God doesn't live in the clouds. Heaven's not skyward, in the clouds." He shook his head disapprovingly. "I know that's what that Ascension story is all about, but really? As your man Bultmann said, no one who's old enough to think for themselves believes that God actually lives in the sky. . . .[117] Anyway, I doubt seriously that anyone raided Jesus' tomb to get gold and treasure. So the only people who would have taken His body would be His followers or someone of a similar mindset."

"No, I don't believe that heaven is in the clouds," Michal responded. "My main point was that His followers had no idea what Jesus was talking about. They were expecting a political messiah. The evidence for this is that when Jesus was arrested, all of his disciples abandoned Him to die alone. Even Peter. Remember, Peter denied Jesus three times. Jesus did not live up to *anybody's* understanding of the messiah. The Jews had definite expectations of what that meant. Jesus' words about dying and rising again were completely obscure to them, because they were contrary to what they expected. Look at the gospel accounts. They clearly did not understand what He was saying. Why would they take the body? Jesus died. But they had already abandoned Him at His arrest. Just another failed messiah. Let's wait for the next one.... But no, that's not what they did in the end. Jesus unexpectedly appeared to them—as I said, I'm now inclined to believe that it was a *spiritual* appearance—and then His followers came back in spades. A resurrected messiah? Now *that's* something to believe in. One who will rule a kingdom far more spectacular than any kingdom here on earth. Then they looked back on the course of events and Jesus' words made sense."

Phil looked at Michal and nodded as if he were seriously mulling this over, which encouraged her to continue:

"Many people experienced the resurrected Jesus. Paul was personally acquainted with many of them. Again, I'm inclined to think that they encountered an incorporeal Jesus, but I'll set that aside. Almost all scholars and historians note that people certainly *believed* that they'd had that experience. Why suppose it was mass hysteria? Consider this: The disciples *suddenly believed* that Jesus was raised from the dead despite that they weren't expecting this at all. Remember, they never understood what Jesus was trying to tell them about His death and Resurrection until *after* it happened. Think about it! Their leader was dead. Nobody expected the Jewish messiah to suffer such a shameful and humiliating death. The messiah was supposed to be another King David. He was supposed to be a political figure who would rule on earth, as foretold by Daniel. Even more importantly, Jewish belief precluded anybody rising from the dead until the general resurrection of the dead at the end of the world.[118] But Jesus' followers came to believe in the Resurrection because they had some sort of transformative experience. Perhaps the greatest transformative experience was Paul's. Remember, he was a vicious persecutor of Jews until he encountered the resurrected Jesus, and then his life was instantly and magnificently transformed. The best evidence for Jesus' Resurrection is a transformed life."

Phil shook his head. "Michal, don't you think that Jesus' supposed Resurrection might just be based on the myths of the dying and rising pagan deities Osiris and Adonis?"

"No, Phil. These deities were mythological symbols of the crop cycle. Crops die during the dry season and come back to life during the wet. That's not at all like the resurrected Jesus, who died once and came back to life for all eternity. Like I said, the best evidence for the resurrected Jesus—however we understand that Resurrection—is a changed life."

"*Your* changed life, Michal. Others have had similar experiences and—" Phil's voice was getting agitated.

Michal shot him a disagreeable look. "Just wait. I'm not finished. Paul and others immediately and directly experienced God as the resurrected Jesus. They didn't come to know God by argument but by direct experience, and nobody could convince them otherwise. Nobody can convince *me* otherwise."

"Are you done now? What about all those who claim to have religious experiences that run counter to Christianity?" Phil asked.

"This is precisely what Falconer—I knew you were going to say that. . . . Sure, people can *claim* such a thing, but what does that really prove? Suppose that you are in a room with a bunch of color-blind people—I read this example somewhere. You point out red and green objects and you ask them, 'Can you see a difference?' Well, since they *can't* see a difference when you claim that there *is* a difference, they will just dismiss your claim as nutty. In terms of *showing who's right* you're at a standoff, aren't you? But the fact you can't show them you're right doesn't invalidate *your* experience, does it? It doesn't mean that what you claim is false or that there is no truth of the matter. You, who see colors properly, are at a complete loss as to how to *show them* that you are right—and yet you undoubtedly *are* right. Now, don't go appealing to science and say that science can *prove* that red and green exist, because objects reflect or emit different wavelengths of light. I think you know what I'm getting at. When a person has such a firsthand experience of God, an experience that someone else hasn't shared, you're at a deadlock, aren't you? But that doesn't mean the person's experience isn't real. I don't mean hallucinatory, but, rather, a genuine encounter with God. Multiply such encounters many times over and I'd say that's damn good evidence for God's existence."

"I find it interesting that you insist on calling the experience 'real' and yet you offer no evidence to support it's *being* real on any scientific or even remotely verifiable level. You use scientific examples, but then you state that I am not allowed to appeal to science, that I should take it on faith that what you experience is real."

"My experiences are REAL." Michal didn't look defiant. She didn't look angry. She didn't look petulant. She looked confident and determined.

"I understand that your experience is real to *you*," Phil began, "but it's real because of your experience. In no way do I wish to invalidate that experience. The experience is as real as any buddy-bonding outing, sweat-lodge experience, or acid trip. Take your pick. They are all real. The brain will make whatever it wishes to be real."

Phil was trying to stay calm. The point was discussion. The point was, at least for him, to have the two people he loved and trusted the most provide a good—no, merely an *adequate*—argument. *And that hadn't happened yet.* "Remember some years back when God-loving suburban moms across America were convinced that a Fisher-Price doll was saying 'Satan is King' and 'Islam is the Light'?—I guess they were Islamophobic, too. This is a perfect example of mass hysteria and the power of suggestion. It also happened in the late nineties when those *gay* Teletubby dolls were supposedly saying 'Faggot, faggot, bite my butt.' —Power of suggestion. All of a sudden moms everywhere were hearing what they were primed to hear. . . ."

Max couldn't help but chuckle. Michal looked at Phil as he paused. "Go on."

"Once again, I will defer to the power of the cinema. In *Milk Money*, V tells Frank there's a place you can touch a woman to make her go crazy and that place is her heart. And of course Raquel Welch said that *the mind* can also be an erogenous zone."

Michal looked exasperated. "Phil, not everything is about sex, and besides I don't get where you're going with this."

"You're right, not everything's about sex, but it's one of the best examples. Sex is an experience where we can all pretty much agree on some of the effects. And most everyone beyond their teenage years—well, except for him, lately"—Phil jabbed at Max—"has had a sexual experience." Max stuck out his tongue. "Your mind tells your body how to behave. Your body has a real, verifiable response. Different stimuli affect different people, just as different experiences have varying effects. The same person who would arouse Max would not likely arouse a heterosexual male."

"Don't bring me into your argument, Phil. That's twice and I'm not sure I want to be your example," Max said and grinned.

"Sorry pal, you're fair game," Phil shot back. "Everyone is fair game and all of our experiences need to be called into question: my experiences, your experiences, Michal's experiences—everyone's experiences. Should we say that a peyote trip is less real than a religious experience? Some Native Americans use peyote to bring about a spiritual experience. The trick is to understand it, or at least attempt to understand it, in a rational manner."

"Phil, not everything is rational. Many of us have had experiences that are undeniable to us and have had a profound impact on our lives," Max said.

"I believe in those experiences on a personal level. They're real to the person experiencing them. But I can't subscribe to them in any universal sort of way." Phil shrugged. "Michal, I believe you had another point before I so rudely interrupted you with *facts*."

Michal's eyes shot daggers at Phil. "Yes, I did, and I would like to give you some *facts* to employ in your stubborn and closed-minded experiment. I, Max, early believers, the saints, ordinary people today—the *greatest evidence* that these experiences point to the truth of Jesus is *profoundly changed lives*. Paul had one, I had one and Max had one. My belief is grounded in my experience. Not in any argument. Most of the arguments are bad. Almost nobody comes to God through argument. We're not Data from *Star Trek*, you know. That's why I could never bring myself to believe until I had an undeniable experience." Michal watched Phil shake his head.

"So, are you willing to say that all of the pagans who have similar undeniable experiences from their patron deities have shown evidence of the Goddess? Or what about those who believe in spirit guides or ghosts? What about the Hindus and *their* undeniable experiences? Those who practice Candomblé would tell you that their religious understanding is based on a great number of *undeniable experiences*." Phil began to pace the floor as he spoke. "Michal, there are countless self-proclaimed religious believers who have experiences that they, too, provide as so-called evidence. But to be considered evidence, the experience must be repeatable. In that case, the religion with the most reliably repeatable experiences would be Haitian Vodoun. They have zombies. Real, observable, undeniable, religious experiences of *zombies*."

Max stopped stirring his tea mid-rotation. "Zombies? Really Phil, zombies? How can you even compare the two?"

Phil stopped his pacing in front of Max. "Not you, too? Vodoun, as a religion, is neither less nor more valid than yours. Neither is Hinduism or paganism. You can't use experience as evidence unless you are willing to allow for everyone else's experiences, too. To do otherwise would be extremely ethnocentric, not to mention arrogant. Aren't you begging the question?"

Michal slammed her cup down on the table. "Phil, Christian experiences of God are repeatable and numerous. We can trust the testimony here. But even more, my color-blind example shows that someone has to be right. The point is that no one is in a position to demonstrate that to the person lacking the experience, since the experience is theirs alone. But here is evidence that the other religions don't seem to have. Like I said, evidence of a changed life. I was a hate-filled, prescription-drug-addicted slut, and in an instant I was changed. Max has a similar story, don't you, Max? Well, if not by the power of Jesus, then what?"

"While I agree with you, Michal, Phil is right about one thing. Your argument does beg the question. We say God or Jesus changed our lives, gave us a miracle. But how do we know that it's a miracle? We say that it came from God. We are justifying our experiences with our beliefs and justifying our beliefs with our experiences." Max took a sip of tea. "I can offer a different example to make a similar point. Suppose I told you that I encountered a talking fish at the koi pond. I can describe him to you in extreme detail. He was three feet long. He was a brilliant turquoise with shimmering flecks of red, gold, and white. Suppose, further, that I told you that the fish spat a silver coin from his mouth. —Well, this is exactly what happened." Max pulled a coin out of his pocket and dropped it on the table. "Isn't the coin proof that I encountered a talking fish?"

"I love it, Maxie," Phil exclaimed. "You're taking lessons from me. Well done."

"But there's no reason to believe you, Max. Unless perhaps there was something weird in those omelets that Phil served us and you're seeing things. On the other hand, if thousands of people claimed to experience talking fish, and their lives were transformed because of those experiences, then yes, I'd pause and reconsider. The number of people who have had direct experience of God with no reason to lie or deceive is incredible."

"Hallucination or mass hysteria—or brain tumors," Phil responded. "I've said this before. It's yet another appeal to popularity, or more appropriately to the mob."

"It's still a circle no matter how you look at it, Michal," Max reiterated.

"I've got this one," Michal began. "William Alston noted the circle and argued that Christians should try to find common ground with nonbelievers by appealing to argument, since obviously nonbelievers would rail against the circle just as you two did. There seems to be no way for the believer to provide a noncircular proof. But the fact of circularity doesn't make it any less rational to believe, since this is the way that the believer formed her belief. And at bottom, it really isn't circular at all. The evidence for God's existence is the *experience*.[119] Suppose I told you I ran into a snake outside. Wouldn't you believe my experience? My testimony about my experience? Especially if I have no reason to lie? I experienced God with my full-blown senses, in the same way I would have experienced a snake in the grass. It was that real. Clearly Jesus' followers did, too. They *saw* the resurrected Jesus. —Ah, but I suppose now in your desperation, Phil, you will say that this was an imposter or a first-century version of a hologram."

"Let me offer two counter-examples, Michal. First and most obviously, *snakes exist.* Most everyone has seen them and many have studied and classified them. If we were in Antarctica, say, and you said you saw a snake outside, I might be less inclined to believe you. However, since you are someone I know and trust, I *might* still believe you. It's not beyond belief that you could have seen a snake in Antarctica. My other counter-example is this—" Phil got up from his chair and walked out of the bar. Max and Michal both looked at each other. Max stifled laughter.

"Now what? What do you think he's up to? We've both seen his antics. They can be pretty—" Michal searched for the words to convey Phil's various eccentricities.

"Insane?" Max offered. "Maybe we should just go with *interesting.* As in the Chinese sense."

Suddenly they heard yelling from outside. It was, of course, Phil.

"Kuso Kurae!" They heard him, but they didn't understand what he was saying. The tone, however, left no doubt that he was mad at someone. Finally, Phil walked back inside and grabbed his drink.

"Yes, Phil?" Max looked at him with smiling eyes.

"Can you believe the nerve of some people? I'm going outside to find my invisible pet unicorn to show the two of you, and *they* want to come in and get served a meal! I'm busy here. We're doing PHILOSOPHY. . . ." He walked over to the window and flung it open. Thrusting his head and arms out, he screamed and waved, "And tell your friends not to come around here either, especially when we're doing philosophy!" The sound of a car could be heard from outside. Phil slumped down on the window sill, seemingly exhausted from his tirade.

Max and Michal both looked at him.

"From the sound of it, you did succeed in showing them their error in judgment. They've got some nerve wanting to get a meal at a restaurant," Max jibed.

"Back to your train of thought, Michal. Before we were so rudely interrupted by actual customers." Max rested his elbow on the table and took another sip of tea.

"By what?" Phil asked. All anger vanished from his demeanor.

"By customers, Phil. Although it doesn't take too much experience to know that you are rude and customers would naturally flee from you." Michal's patience was wearing thread-thin.

Phil looked at Michal deadpan. "While that's ordinarily true, it's not this time. There weren't any customers out there." He walked over to Michal and took out his phone. He pressed the screen and the sound of a car could be heard.

"I tricked you. Plain and simple. It's a car ringtone. There were a dozen other explanations, but the most logical one was that what I was saying was true. Let it be known that I—*and Dogberry*—am an ass, so it's very likely that I would be yelling at a customer. It's also possible, though not likely, that my establishment would have a customer. Your experiential knowledge of me encouraged you to believe that it was so, and that I would send them away in favor of a philosophical discussion. But this all turned out *not* to be so, even though experience led you to believe otherwise." Phil put away his phone. "David Blaine, David Copperfield, Doug Henning, Houdini, and my favorites Penn and Teller, have been abusing people's perceptions to their own ends forever. I say 'forever,' because I believe that the first great magician was a religious leader. His first great trick was telling people that God existed, and that He cared about our meager lives."

Phil sat down at the table and took a sip of his whiskey before he continued:

"Experiential knowledge is not inherently trustworthy. Hume worked diligently to disprove the very miracles you claim that Jesus performed, including His Resurrection, which is arguably the greatest of all so-called miracles. Hume claimed that belief should be proportional to evidence. When all the evidence points to one conclusion, we should definitely believe it. But when it comes to miracles, our evidence is based on the testimony of others, which must be weighed against the laws of nature. Since a miracle is an event that violates the laws of nature, the testimony of witnesses has to outweigh those laws. But the laws of nature are constant and unchanging. And so the witnesses always lose. Their testimony has to be more compelling than the laws of nature that it contradicts, and so it is always outweighed by the evidence against it.[120] Hume has a great line in *Of Miracles*." Phil attempted his best Scottish accent: "'When anyone tells me that he saw a dead man restored to life, I immediately consider, within myself, whether it be more probable that this person should either deceive or be deceived, or that the fact, which he relates, should really have happened.'"[121]

"I imagine that you, like Hume, would find a naturalistic explanation for *anything*. I suppose that if Jesus were to return right now, right here, you would explain it away as some kind of CGI wizardry!" Michal shot back. "And Hume is begging the question in assuming that the laws of nature can't be broken. They can. *God can do it!*"

"The real question is what should we trust?" Phil first pointed at Michal, then at Max. "I trust your judgment, I trust your opinion, and unless I have something to convince me otherwise, then like the disciples I will fight to make whatever it is that you say true…" He lowered his head. "Especially when I so desperately need it to be true."

"Well, I pray that God blasts you with an undeniable experience, Phil. Then you'll understand what I've been talking about. You know how much of an atheist I was. Look at me now. You can throw everything at me. Anything and everything. But I won't change my mind. I simply *can't* change my mind, given my experience. It's as real as this cup of tea in my hands. So it seems that we are at a standstill, especially since you are so closed-minded. You want us to help, but you aren't receptive to any of it. You are just so frustrating!" Michal began to break down again, alternating between shouts and tears, exasperated at her friend. "I GIVE UP!"

Max sighed, walked over to Phil and rested a hand on his shoulder. He looked at Michal and began to speak in a calming voice.

"At some point guys, we need to let go of the actual argument. You can prove the worth of God's presence in your life, you can argue for the changes due to His grace. You can even argue the feelings you have about God. But at some point you have to let the argument go and accept one important thing on faith. —God's presence in your life. You will never convince anyone who hasn't had an experience, hasn't had *your specific experience*, hasn't had a similar life-changing experience, that your God is the right one. And, for the record, we shouldn't. That's not what we're called to do, either as Christians or decent human beings. We're to love God with all our heart, all our soul, and all our mind, and to love our neighbor as ourselves. Telling someone that their God is a sham and not the true God is not loving our neighbor as ourselves."

Nathan

The steady dripping sound had kept Max awake for hours. He sat in a tan upholstered high-back chair that would have been comfortable had he been there only a short while. Thirty-six hours, however, was an eternity, interrupted by only a few short breaks in the cafeteria. Nathan's mother had come and gone, her gray winter gloves lying forgotten on the side table next to a half-empty water pitcher. He glanced out the window and noted the same gray sky as yesterday, and the way the lines of the red-brick medical buildings across the courtyard contrasted sharply with the ominous slate-colored clouds. Max felt Nathan's fingers as they dug into the top of his hand. He snapped his focus back to Nathan's face, which was locked in a pained grimace.

Periodically, Nathan's face would constrict, brows drawn together and eyes clenched tight as if to ward off whatever kind of nightmares the medication inspired. His hands would grip the blankets or Max's hand, desperately clinging to the cliff that stood between life and death. Max gently squeezed the hand shrunken from lack of sustenance, the skin paper-thin, translucent, the veins a stark bluish purple against pasty white. He stared at the blanket drawn up to Nathan's neck and the heating pad placed over Nathan's stomach, which rose and fell with each labored breath.

Assorted bits of medical machinery cluttered the sterile room and connected in various ways to Nathan, their monitors turned away from the bed at Max's request. Max's attention wandered from the machines to the tubes and wires running to Nathan's body, finally settling on his IV tube. The nurses had a difficult time with the needles, struggling to find any usable veins. They finally settled on one in his neck. The robot-faced computerized morphine machine stared cruelly bedside. Max wanted so much to press the button that would ease Nathan's pain before it happened, but they had placed a locked clear case over it, since Nathan was unable to manage the pain on his own.

The white gauze wrapped around Nathan's head made him look almost mummy-like. The hiss of oxygen in the mask that covered his nose and mouth reminded Max of a riled-up rattler ready to strike.

Nathan's face finally went slack, this bout of pain or nightmare obviously over. Max lessened his grip on Nathan's hand and noticed the bracelet on his own wrist bearing Nathan's name, resting next to the only other piece of jewelry he ever wore: a black leather band with a steel plate that read "Take my will and my life. Guide me in my recovery. Show me how to live." The letters 'NA' and five hatch marks, both in black, decorated the sides of the small metal plate. Both bracelets were gifts from the man whose hand he now held.

Max leaned over to adjust Nathan's pillow. The smell of disinfectant over-powered Nathan's normally woodsy scent. Standing up, Max busied himself with straightening the newly formed creases in the bedclothes, before resuming his position in the chair next to his lover's bedside. As he sat down, a man with white hair pulled into a loose ponytail walked slowly by the opened door and looked directly at Max. His long legs were fitted in faded boot-cut denim that seemed ill-matched with his expensive-looking brown blazer. It wasn't the first time that Max had seen the strange man whose skin was the hue of an over-roasted turkey walk the hall. He had gone by three times yesterday afternoon and twice last night. He was somehow familiar, but Max couldn't remember where he'd seen him before. He shook his head and returned his attention to Nathan, who was finally sleeping peacefully as the drug took effect. Max curled his arm around Nathan's blanketed body and laid his head down on the bed, letting his eyes close for a few minutes.

"Ain't it hard when our loved ones are sufferin' and we are so powerless?" The man's words jarred Max from his catnap.

"What?" Max raised his head.

"May I?" A few strands of hair the color of fresh-picked cotton had escaped the man's ponytail, settling around his temples like bird's wings. Max heard a creak of metal and the scuff of the man's shoes on the hospital's tile floor, as he pulled up a chair and sat across the bed.

"This your brother?" The man looked at Max's hand, which held Nathan's tightly. He smiled.

"Um, yes—he's my brother." Max's voice went low with caution. "What can I do for you?" Max stood and busied his hands, straightening up the blankets around Nathan.

"It says on the boy's chart that you're 'is next of kin. I was wonderin' if you wanted me to say a prayer for the both of ya."

"I appreciate that, but we're fine right now. Thank you for your kind offer. Who did you say you were?" Max's body began to tense but the man's face broke into a smile that eased his misgivings. He sat back down in the chair and leaned toward the man, who started to speak.

"It's amaazin,' but you look nuttin' like 'im," The stranger began. "Are you stepbrothers or half-brothers?"

"What difference does it make? I'm here for him when no one else is. I'm the only family Nathan's got."

"That's nice. —It says here Nate's mother came for a visit." The man glanced at the trashcan. He raised his eyebrow at the many pairs of discarded white latex surgical gloves. Max followed the stranger's gaze, noting his piercing green eyes.

"She did. But they don't really get along. When she realized that he couldn't talk to her or listen to her constant litany of complaints, she left." Max stared at Nathan's face, willing him to wake up.

"It's not Christian-like to speak about one's mama so harshly. 'Honor thy father and mother'—so says the commandment." The stranger raised his eyebrows at Max. Max turned back to the man, eyes wide.

"My apologies." Max said as he rubbed his nose. "I haven't slept well in a long time. I meant no insult. You a pastor?" Max's eyes narrowed as he scrutinized the man's face. He noted the very pronounced scar on his cheek that marred the man's features.

"Sumpin' like that. I reach out to those sufferin' here and try to give 'em what they need. A measure of solace or redemption." The man's long tapered fingers tapped his chair in a haphazard rhythm. He crossed his legs, letting his foot dangle, the shine of the black shoes quite at odds with the frayed denim.

"That's a noble calling. What denomination are you, if you don't mind me asking?" Max turned back to Nathan and noted that his fingernails needed trimming. He reached into the side table drawer for Nathan's grooming kit and began to clip his nails.

"I'm what you call 'non-denominational.' God doesn't really care what religion we are, so long as we follow His commandments." The man got up and stood by Nathan's bedside.

"Want me to pray for him, son?"

Max finished with Nathan's right hand and looked up. There was something in the man's eyes that gave him pause but he said, "That would be nice. My priest is coming soon, but as they say, every prayer helps."

"It's good you believe in prayer, boy. But unless you stop and truly repent your unchristian behavior, God doesn't care so much."

Max's hand stilled. "What exactly do you mean by that, sir?" His face reddened and his hands began to tremble slightly. He dropped the nail clippers on the blanket and squeezed Nathan's hand, hoping that his touch would be calming.

"I only mean what's in the Good Book, son. You don't get to heaven unless you are ready to give up a life of sin and beg the Almighty for forgiveness. Our Lord sees all. And it don't exactly look like you're ready to do that just yet. Don' you think you should oughta have done that by now, boy?" Max's face froze as the man reached across the blanket and pulled Nathan's limp hand away.

"What right do you have comin' in here and talkin' to us like that?" Max stood up as he watched the man grasp Nathan's hand.

"Oh, I'm not talkin' to both ya'll—just you. Nate's in no position to listen to me now, is he? If he could hear me, I might be tryin' to convince him to give up *his* life of abomination and turn back to God." The man's voice was like fingernails on a chalkboard, causing the hairs on Max's arms and neck to stand up. He felt a chill.

"That's a buncha bunk. That's a buncha bunk from the very first word that came outta yer ugly mouth— Now get out," Max managed through gritted teeth.

"Hmmm. You would think someone on your path would show more manners. I'll go, but keep in mind, young sinner—as I done told you, God sees all. He knows what's in yer heart."

Max barely heard the door close before he collapsed in the chair. He picked up Nathan's hand and placed a gentle kiss on his palm.

"Don't listen to him, Nathan. Judge not. Remember? Let's get back to your favorite book, OK?" Max wiped away a tear from his face and then heard an alarm from one of the monitors.

Dazed, he felt himself being pushed out of the way as medical personnel flooded the room. His body went numb. He was still shaking his head "no" when the doctor said, "I'm sorry." Max collapsed to his knees.

Father Manganiello made the sign of the cross as he entered the now silent hospital room. He looked somberly at Max and then put his hand on Nathan's head and began to pray:

"O God, whose mercies cannot be numbered, accept our prayers on behalf of thy servant, Nathan. . . ."

EARLY EVENING. *At the RTSS*

Phil got up from his bright-red overstuffed armchair and wandered into the bar. Max was sitting at a table, sipping some tea and looking wistfully at a ticket stub that he'd pulled out of his wallet. Last season: Rangers versus the Oakland A's. The Rangers had finished the season just 5½ behind the A's. They'd just missed the playoffs. But he wasn't sad about *that*. He didn't go to the games to actually *watch*. He went for the crowds. They offered an occasional distraction from his studies. He was resistant to going at first, but Father M insisted that he give himself a break now and again. Max had a hard time giving himself a break with respect to this—or anything else.

Max was heavy-hearted—but those weren't quite the right words to describe his feelings—because he was missing *him*.

It was a ridiculous nachos fiasco. He saw Cary Grant—yes, Cary Grant—at the concession stand before the first pitch. Cary stood in line in front of him ordering nachos. But unbeknownst to Cary, he was giving his order to the hotdog and burger guy, who didn't know anything about nachos. He walked down the line and tried ordering again, but this time he gave his order to the pizza girl. She pointed out the nachos guy. Cary then asked the pubescent boy in the tidy blue-and-white uniform, "Are *you* the nachos guy?" (because he wasn't sure of anything anymore), and the boy said, "Yes, but I don't know how to make nachos. This is my first day." So Cary pointed out the various ingredients—the chips, the queso, the tomatoes and jalapeños—and told the poor confused boy how to put it all together. It was clear that Cary was at his wit's end, but Max couldn't help laughing inside.

Cary found his seat while Max ordered a couple of burgers. He knew who the burger guy was, thanks to Cary's confusion. Max's order was uneventful and after squirting some ketchup, mustard, and mayo on his burgers he found his seat: section 134, right along the first baseline. It turned out to be next to Cary's. Max smiled at Cary, whose name at this point he still didn't know. Cary smiled back. Until he took a bite of his nachos.

"Dammit!" Cary said. "There are hot-dog bits in the queso!" He put a nacho in Max's face. "Taste this. Do you taste hot dog? In my God-damned nachos!"

Max laughed as he grabbed the chip and took a bite. "Yep. That'd be hot dogs, all right. . . . Hot-dog nachos." He kept laughing.

"I'd go back and insist they make another order but I'm afraid I'd end up with peperoni in it next time," Cary said, then cracked a smile.

"How about if I eat the chips with the hot dogs on them," Max said. "My name's Max Cardin, by the way." He extended his hand and smiled.

"Cary Grant," Cary said.

Max couldn't help but laugh out loud. "Did you say *Cary Grant?* I think I saw you in *Philadelphia Story.*"

"Unfortunately, I've suffered my entire life as a result of my mother's insufferable movie star crush," Cary said.

"Well, Cary Grant was dreamy—and so are you." Max didn't mean to say that last bit out loud and he caught himself blushing.

"You are too," Cary said with a smile. Max didn't expect that. He smiled broadly.

Max and Cary shared the nachos. Max didn't mind the hot-dog chunks. He was completely captivated.

Max fell in love that afternoon at the Rangers' game. The two guys hung out for a few hours, sharing laughs and stories. They didn't even know the final score of the game. But Max was conflicted. Cary took Max's cellphone, put his number in it and handed it back to Max. Max promised to call. Max wanted to call. Once he picked up his phone to call, even rehearsing what he would say. He wanted to be charming. That wasn't hard for Max, but sometimes he lacked confidence. Especially when a love interest was involved. But he had his studies. And so he never called. Right now, sitting in Phil's bar looking at the ticket, Max's heart hurt.

Phil, who sat down next to Max, noticed.

"What have you got there, Maxie?"

Max looked at Phil, tears welling up in his eyes. "Nothing. It's nothing, really." He stuffed the ticket back in his wallet.

"Texas Rangers," Phil said, noting the stub. Max just nodded.

"This doesn't have anything to do with that guy—what was his name, Rock Hudson?" Phil cracked a smile.

"Cary Grant."

"Right. Wanna talk about it?"

"Nothing to say. I made a choice."

"Pretty stupid choice, my friend, especially since the Episcopal Church has ordained noncelibate gay clergy since—when? 2010? But you know that, Max. Didn't the Episcopal Church say that monogamous gay couples stand in sharp contrast to the many sinful patterns of sexuality that we see in the world today?" Max nodded. "So why do you do this to yourself? Don't you want somebody to love?" Phil sang out the question like the Beatles' tune.

"You're one to talk," Max said, trying to smile. "Speaking of which, is our beauty still sleeping?"

"That ship sailed long ago," Phil began. "Probably. . . . But back to you and *your* choice."

"I know my church's stance on gay clergy but my diocese is more conservative," Max said. "And I respect their choice."

"Easy fix. Let them have their conservatism. Go somewhere else."

"God led me to my church. I really believe that. I belong there."

"Even with that jerk, what's-his-face?"

"Gideon Morris."

"Think about what you're saying, Max. Do you really think that your God sent you Gideon? Wouldn't He rather send you Cary? Here God sends you Cary but you're so blinded by this calling of yours that you missed the opportunity for love altogether. . . . What more do you need, Max? A burning bush? I'm sure I've got some matches lying around somewhere."

"As much as you think you're all that, Phil, you're definitely not God. Nope, you lighting a little bonsai tree won't convince me."

"But Max, don't you see? You're like that story of the guy in the flood."

Max tried to remember whether there was somebody in the Flood that he'd forgotten. Nope. "Everyone except for Noah and his family died in the Flood," Max said.

"No, not *the* Flood story, Max. A story—a joke—about a guy caught in a flood. Someone comes in a big truck to rescue him, and he says, 'No, thank you, God will save me.' So the waters rise, and he goes to the second floor, and then up on the roof, while rescuers show up first with a boat and then a helicopter."

"Right, and each time the guy refuses to be rescued and says 'God will save me.' Finally he drowns, and when he shows up in heaven, he asks God why He didn't rescue him." Max chuckled. "And God says, 'Hey, I sent you a truck, a boat, and a helicopter. What more do you want?'"

"Exactly," Phil said.

"But you don't understand, Phil. God doesn't want me to abandon my deaconship."

"God's not asking you to abandon your deaconship, Maxie, God's just asking you to go on a date."

"I don't know." Max reached back into his wallet and grabbed the Rangers ticket. He put it up to his lips.

"My guess is that Cary's a better kisser than that piece of paper," Phil said and smiled. "Do I have to remind you of what you already know? You seem to make a habit of doing that to me. Now it's my turn." He smirked. "The Church has been using that Holy Book of yours, selectively interpreted and stripped of its historical context, to justify its own prejudices in the guise of strictly following God's word. —Well, that's fucked up."

"You're right, of course, but like I said, God sent me to *my* church and they're not exactly OK with noncelibate gay clergy."

"I thought you believed in free will, Max. You're acting like God's little puppet. Can't you wrap your head around the possibility that God wants you to be with somebody—with Cary?"

"Maybe so," Max said. "But it's probably too late at this point. With Cary, I mean."

"You still have his number?"

Max nodded.

"So call him. Worst case, he's no longer interested or available but if you don't call him you'll never know," Phil said.

Max smiled. "Maybe..."

"Max and Cary sitting in a tree. K-I-S-S-I-N-G. . . ." Phil laughed.

Max stood up from his chair and squeezed Phil's shoulder. "Come on, Cupid. Let's go wake up Michal."

SIXTEEN

The truth does not change according to our ability to stomach it.
FLANNERY O'CONNOR

EARLY THE NEXT MORNING. *At the RTSS*

Michal spent a long time thinking about getting up. Phil and Max were most certainly still asleep, and in any case she didn't think she could open her eyes. But then she heard a sound. It was the sound of pages turning. Someone was in her room. Michal sat up and unglued her eyelids. She saw a giant toad sitting in the corner, so tall that its head was bent over to avoid touching the ceiling. It was grayish-brownish-green and bumpy, with bulging eyes. It looked at her and closed the book.

"Good morning, Michal." It gave a friendly toady smile.

She reached for her pajamas, which were on the floor next to the futon.

"Would you mind turning away while I get dressed?" She wasn't as shocked as she should be. She addressed the toad matter-of-factly. Perhaps she was dreaming. In any case she was going along.

It lifted the book to cover its eyes.

She hastily dressed.

"My dear Michal," the visitor began.

"Who—I mean what—are you?"

"Don't you recognize me? I'm James—your advisor. Have you forgotten me already?"

"You certainly don't look like James."

It extended its skinny bumpy arms to have a look at itself. It dropped the book to the floor, startled.

"Oh dear," it responded in a panic. "Wrong script." Suddenly it transformed into the recognizable body of her old lover.

"James. . . ." Michal's heart skipped a beat. She was overjoyed. "Let me give you a hug. It's been so long."

She rolled off the mattress and approached James, who was still sitting in the corner.

"I have something for you." James stood up, reached into his hunter-green blazer and pulled out a bunch of red tulips—roots and all—as if he had just pulled them out of the garden. As he extended them to her, small chunks of dirt fell to the floor. "Your favorite." He smiled.

"You're supposed to cut off the roots, you idiot. You're supposed to give her tulips with stems. Tulip with stems!" a voice sounded inside James' head.

James felt like the very idiot he was accused of being. He dropped the tulips to the floor.

"Sorry, Michal. Those aren't for you. My mistake."

"You idiot." The voice inside James' head became increasingly impatient. "Who are you anyway? Is this your first assignment?"

James responded in thought: *My second. My first assignment was during the Great War.*

"The Great War? That was one hundred human years ago. What happened? Did you lose your charge to the Enemy?"

He fell on a grenade just a tad too soon. I almost had him. Our Father Below didn't understand evidently. He ordered my suspension. . . . Well, I'm back now. I'm just a little out of practice.

"James?" Michal looked at him strangely. "Are you OK?"

"I'm fine," James replied nervously. Suddenly his head began to change into a giant toad's head again.

"Stupid malfunction." He cursed a few times. Michal watched him metamorphosing from a toad to James and back to a toad again.

"Leave, you idiot!" The voice inside James' head screamed.

I've got this under control.

James resumed the shape of his familiar self.

"When did you get to Japan?" Michal asked. "Or, I should say, *how* did you get to Japan? I know you hate to fly."

"I took one of those—" James seemed not to be able to find the right word. "Flying contraptions."

"You mean an airplane?"

"Yes, an airplane," James said confidently.

I've got this now. No need to watch over me.

"Can I have that hug now?" Michal smiled warmly. She wasn't sure how James got here, or why he was behaving so strangely, or even whether he was just a figment of her imagination, but she was glad to see him.

"I've got a disease. You really shouldn't touch me."

"A disease? Are you OK?"

"Not a serious disease—a social disease. What do you call it? A socially transmitted disease."

James smiled at how well he was doing now.

"Redirect," the voice in James' head said.

You're still here?

"Ask her about her teaching appointment."

"Your teaching appointment. . . ." James said.

"What? What about my teaching appointment?" Michal asked curiously.

"How's it going there? Do you like it?" *Just start acting like a normal human being.*

"Remind her about her defense," the voice inside James' head urged.

James sat next to Michal, who had plopped comfortably back onto her mattress.

"I'm surprised they let you teach since you never earned your Ph.D.," James said.

Michal responded in a queasy voice, "What do you mean?" She strained to get the words out.

"You ran out of the defense. Remember? I asked you a question. I thought it was a soft ball, an easy pitch, but you freaked and ran out of the room. You never returned. I never saw you again," James said.

"Well played," the voice said in James' head.

"Thank you," James replied.

"Thank me for what?" Michal felt sickened by his words.

"That wasn't meant for you. . . . Sorry, I don't know why I said that."

"Does your university know that you are an imposter?" The voice prodded in James' head.

"Does your university know that you are an imposter?" James asked Michal.

"Imposter?" Michal asked incredulously. "What do you mean? I finished my defense. We broke open a bottle of champagne in your apartment later that night. Remember? Diego showed up stoned. We couldn't get him to leave."

"I'm sorry, Michal. But it didn't happen that way," James said blankly.

Michal grabbed hold of her comforter, clenching it tightly. She began choking with tears, then finally caught her breath and said, "No! This can't be. I finished—I finished my defense."

"Get out of there while you've got her," the voice said to James. "Nice work. Just get out of there NOW."

"James—" Michal reached out to try to hold him. She sobbed. James backed away. He smiled, satisfied at a job well done, when suddenly two imposing figures appeared beside Michal, standing over her.

"Get out of there, now!" the voice inside James' head repeated even more insistently.

The Enemy appears to have sent His forces. What do I do now? He began to panic. Michal was oblivious to all that was going on around her. She just sobbed.

Suddenly James turned into a tiny centipede. He crawled off the mattress and disappeared.

Just then, Phil slid open the door. "Michal? Are you all right? You're crying."

He looked down on the bamboo floor and noticed a tattered book.

"That's an interesting choice," he remarked. "I would have never thought you'd take interest in that."

He noticed the tulips scattered about the floor.

"I see you've been in my garden."

Michal's head was buried under the tear-soaked comforter. She hadn't really been paying attention, but she knew that someone was in the room. She was almost afraid to look for fear her sense of reality would be challenged yet again. Finally, however, she was confident that Phil was in her room. Phil had been talking with her. Phil was real. It was safe to look.

She opened her eyes to an empty room.

MID-AFTERNOON, THE SAME DAY

Michal sat on a stone bench next to a twisted old bonsai tree. It seemed to hold so many secrets. The tree was about five feet tall and nearly twice as wide, with a purplish black trunk. She studied all of the gnarls, the grain, every seeming imperfection. She could see evidence of years of changes—snips and cuts here and there—that had shaped it into what it was today.

How alike we all are to the bonsai. Michal looked around the Zen garden as she caressed her necklace, the afternoon sun warming her face. Like so many things with Phil, it was thoroughly kempt, immaculate in fact. Unfortunately, it was devoid of a soul. She was reasonably certain she had seen this pattern at the Hakone Gardens in Saratoga. Each furrow was raked to never cross itself, to never show any disturbance of the pattern. Yet it all seemed just a little too forced, too ordered. Michal wondered about the time Phil must have spent studying photographs, making sure that he got everything just right, making sure that every line was exactly where it needed to be. If it was just like the original photo, did it still retain the spirit that was captured in that photo?

She studied the mound of large rocks several yards in front of her that sat in the middle of gravel meticulously hand-raked to suggest ripples of water encircling a mountain. Or at least that was the intent of the original. She wondered whether Phil had any original thoughts at all.

She heard the crunch of gravel as Max and Phil approached.

"There you are. . . . We hate to disrupt your Zen experience." Max smiled.

"Oh, hi," Michal said, not quite present.

"Are we bothering you? Thinking deep thoughts?" Phil asked. He reached out to touch her shoulder and paused.

Michal continued to study the gravel and the flow of the suggested water. The ripples of the water all seemed to flow to the bench on which she sat, all flowed directly to her. Eyes still downcast, she replied, "About Jesus— You know what Max and I believe about Jesus, Phil, but what about you?" She looked up at Phil, whose hand was still hovering indecisively near her shoulder. She reached out and grasped it. "At the very least, you've got to believe that he was a historical figure and a good man. Every credible scholar of antiquity says that we can at least be certain of Jesus' baptism and crucifixion, and many scholars hold that we can also be confident that Jesus challenged the Jewish religious authorities, taught in parables and performed healings."

Phil fought the urge to roll his eyes at the words "performed healings." "I agree with scholars that he likely existed. It would be foolish to say that he didn't. I'd be as Looney Tunes as those who say that Socrates was only a fictionalized character in Plato's writings, or even the nutty-as-fruitcake Holocaust deniers. I'll grant that Jesus likely existed, but he was merely a charismatic religious leader who appeared on the scene at exactly the right time. A charismatic leader probably married to the 'demoniac' Mary Magdalene. Nothing more."

"Possibly married to the epileptic Mary Magdalene." Michal smiled. "Anyway, at least you're willing to accept that He probably existed." She winced. "Small victories, I guess."

"Emperor Tiberius, who reigned during Jesus' ministry, treated the Jews pretty brutally. Pilate was even crueler. And before the Romans, there was of course Antiochus IV of the Seleucids, who persecuted the shit out of them, including brazenly defiling their temple. As you know, this led to the Maccabean

Revolt. . . ." He looked at Michal. "This is really more your thing. I'm just a dabbler in history when it serves my purpose."

Max smacked him on the shoulder. "I'm right here. Deacon? Seminary? I know a thing or two about this history as well." He feigned offense.

"Yeah, but since you're a deacon that means you're part of the system. I can't trust you to be honest," Phil said.

Max shrugged. "I'm a deacon who doesn't represent the Bible to be absolutely, one-hundred-percent accurate. It's more of a metaphor in places, intended to teach us truths about God's love for us."

"Well, you still don't know nearly as much as our religious scholar over here," Phil motioned to Michal.

"Thank you, Phil," Michal said, waiting for the other shoe to drop.

"Even though most of her brain seems to have departed in favor of fanciful visions." Phil winked at her good-naturedly, hoping she didn't take his sarcasm too seriously.

She stuck out her tongue. "Since you have at least honored my qualifications, I'll say thank you again and reluctantly tell you that you are right."

Phil bowed deeply. "Arigato Gozaimashto."

Michal winced again. "Really—how have you managed to survive in Japan so long with your terrible Western diction?"

"I don't speak it very much. Have you seen many customers?"

"No, I haven't, but the ones I have seen have been pretty strange. —You're right about Antiochus IV. He appears in Daniel as the little horn that emerges from the beast with ten horns. That beast reappears in Revelations, by the way, in an end-of-days role. Of course, this isn't a surprise." She stared off at the mountainside. "As I told you guys before, the author of Revelations chooses weird, often fictional stuff from the Hebrew Bible and weaves it into an end-times narrative. . . . Sorry for that random fact, Phil. Please continue." She looked at Phil and Max, who were pretending to be students again, cribbing notes off each other's invisible papers.

Phil quickly put his "notebook" away and responded, "Always full of related facts, Michal. . . . As I was about to say, the time was ripe for someone like Jesus to start a movement, someone who would challenge the religious status quo and the authority figures. That said, I certainly don't believe that he was the Son of God, born of a virgin—"

Michal cut him off. "I don't believe that virgin part either."

"You're going to turn this into another translation thing, aren't you?" Max laughed. "I will never understand how you can challenge or reject just about every major tenet of the Christian faith, and still call yourself a Christian. How do you do that?" He smiled, shaking his head.

Michal smiled at him and then looked back down at the ground. She spotted a little jade stone amidst the gravel and fixated on it.

"While I agree that it's important to believe in something, you do seem to pick and choose your favorite bits. Either way, I respect you for believing." Max watched Michal as she continued to stare at the ground. "In any case, Michal, both Matthew and Luke include the virgin birth."

After some silence, Michal finally said, "But Mark, the earliest gospel, does not recount the story of a miraculous birth. Indeed, like I said, the original un-edited ending of Mark doesn't even mention the Resurrection appearances. The gospels become increasingly theologically embellished, ending with John, where Jesus is the divine, pre-existent Son of God. There's very good reason to reject the virgin birth story. First of all, it comes from Isaiah 7:14. Remember that the New Testament authors were reading the Septuagint, the Greek translation of the Hebrew Bible. Isaiah 7:14 uses the Greek word 'parthenos,' which means either 'young woman' or 'virgin.' However, if you look at the context of that pas-sage, it should rightly be translated 'young woman.' 'The young woman is with child.' There's nothing supernatural about that."

She looked at Max. "In an age when average life expectancy hovered around forty, there would be many young mothers. Indeed, if my memory serves me, Israelite girls were considered to be marriageable at age twelve. In any case, the 'young woman' of Isaiah 7:14 isn't the mother of Jesus at all, but, rather, the mother of Hezekiah, who, along with David, Solomon, and Josiah, was one of Israel's greatest kings. Remember, the gospels were written years after Jesus' death. Mark, the earliest gospel and the one from which Matthew and Luke draw, was written around the year 66 or even later—more than thirty years after Jesus' death. Mark doesn't mention the virgin birth, nor does Paul, who wrote even earlier. The writers of Matthew and Luke wanted to see earlier prophecies fulfilled by Jesus, and so they misapplied prophecies and mistranslated or misun-derstood passages. Most of those prophecies concerned immediate events, not ones several hundred years in the future. Just look at the context. I've said this before." She paused and then continued: "You know, many Greek and Roman heroes were children of gods. —Hercules, for example. Giving Jesus a virgin-birth narrative, then, makes Him even more exalted, more heavenly, than those Greco-Roman heroes with whom the Jews were so familiar. But the virgin-birth story could also be early Christianity's answer to accusations of Jesus' illegitimate birth. Tabor argues in this way. As he puts it, the pedigree of Jesus' mother was likely disparaged by the locals who knew the stories of his illegitimate birth.[122] We find evidence in Mark, John, and even the Gospel of Thomas that such accusations were floating around. Anyway, Jesus can still be God even if He were conceived in the old-fashioned way."

"Michal, I've got to ask—you're constantly saying how the Bible doesn't fit commonplace interpretations of it, yet in certain places you assert its literal truth. If the Bible as a whole isn't the word of God, how can we tell which parts are and which parts aren't? You seem to pick what you like and discard the rest to suit your prejudices." Phil had been curious about this for some time. He had already set his hopes in Michal's knowledge of the Bible, so this particular discussion was long overdue. "You've just set up a very interesting discussion about the authority of the Bible, Michal, whether you intended to or not. I've wanted to have this conversation since you two arrived. Why do you assume that the Bible is right concerning certain claims about Jesus—His divinity, the various miracles He per-formed, and so on—but not others? The Bible reflects many truths of life, just like the Qur'an, Lao Tse's *Tao Te Ching*, or even *Black Elk Speaks*. But you don't follow them. You follow the Bible. As Russell said, people choose the book considered sacred by the community in which they are born, and then go on to choose those parts within that book that they like, ignoring the others. At one point, the most influential part of the Bible was the injunction 'Thou shalt not suffer a witch to live.' This justified all the witch trials in early modern times. Now that part of the text is just passed over as so much archaic nonsense.[123] Can your so-called experience of the divine be that powerful that an academic such as yourself would choose the Bible over so many other supposedly holy books? On what possible grounds are you justified in doing so? You can't just pick and choose, you know. Truth is truth," Phil said.

You're committing the fallacy of composition. Just because parts of the Bible aren't true doesn't mean that the whole thing isn't true, Michal thought to herself. As she was getting ready make the point aloud, she heard the crunch of gravel and noticed a man, casually dressed and wearing a pale green straw fedora, approach along the path that led back to the bar. The man saw Phil and smiled as he approached. Michal was surprised to see another customer. She was beginning to think that Phil didn't own a bar at all, but a personal amusement park of sorts.

"I heard a rumor that you carry Juyondai." The stranger addressed Phil.

"I do. You have exquisite taste." Phil spent several extra seconds studying the man. He looked like an older version of someone he once knew, of someone who had died.

"It is well-known that you are rude and coarse, even for a *gaijin*, but it is impolite in almost any country to stare," the stranger said.

"Odd—you look just like a young man I once knew." Phil gave a short bow. "Forgive me for being rude. My name is Phil. I should have—"

The stranger returned the bow, cutting Phil off with a disarming smile. "I am told I look like a lot of people. A German tourist once told me that I looked like Rommel. I suppose I just have—how do you Americans say it?—'one of those faces.' Call me Gimon." He extended his hand to Phil, who shook it heartily. "By the way, your footwear, Phil-san—looks a bit rheumatic. Kind of like that character in the old children's stories—Uncle Wiggily." He chuckled, then addressed our three friends, "I am getting ready to celebrate a big event. I would love it if you would break open a bottle with me. Perhaps you'd all join me in a toast."

"Of course. What are we toasting?" Phil asked as he motioned toward the bar. He quickly glanced down at his slippers. "Hey—" They began walking.

"I am welcoming a new member of the family. —I couldn't help but hear your challenge to your friend about the authority of the Bible." Gimon turned and addressed Michal. "You know, Jesus believed in the inerrancy of scripture."

"You may not get many customers, but the ones you do seem to be amazingly well-versed in philosophy and theology," Max leaned into Phil's ear and whispered.

"I know. Strange, that," Phil whispered back.

"—And, of course, everything that Jesus believed must be true since He is the Son of God. Would your God believe falsehoods? You do claim that He is the Son of God, young lady? —Wouldn't God only speak truth?" Gimon asked.

"Not to be impolite, but we are challenging whether the gospel writers actually gave us the literal words of Jesus. Indeed, we're questioning whether God's hand was in it at all," Michal said.

"Well, I'm certainly not questioning that, Michal. Of course God's hand was in it," Max said. "The question is how much and which parts, isn't it? Old Testament, New Testament—or how about the Apocrypha—those Enoch portions that you love so well, or maybe even one of your favorites, the Gospel of Thomas? If we're being selective, then aren't we just choosing only those portions that suit us? Cherry-picking our examples, like Phil says."

"If we just focus on the canonical gospels for now, it's obvious that since the authors of Matthew and Luke were writing for different audiences—Matthew, after all, was addressing a Jewish audience and Luke, a Greek one—we would find them presenting Jesus' words and stories in different ways to appeal to their respective audiences," Michal said. She turned to Phil. "You should understand, my friend, that what we have in the Bible, what ended up in the canon, is the result of socio-political muscle-flexing."

"Give me an example."

Michal gazed off at the mountains beyond. Phil couldn't help but notice Gimon's fascination with her, nor how easily he had inserted himself into their conversation. Phil wondered whether his friends had hired this man, as he suspected they had the earlier stranger.

"Simple to do," Michal began, returning her attention to the group. "Take Matthew. Remember: Jewish audience. In Matthew, Jesus always heals Gentiles at a distance, never face-to-face. We see this with the centurion's beloved servant, whom Max mentioned before, and with a Canaanite woman's daughter. Consider Matthew 15, where the Canaanite woman begs Jesus to heal her daughter. Jesus responds, 'It is not fair to take the children's food and throw it to the dogs.' 'Dogs' was a very insulting term in Jesus' day, fitting for the despised Gentiles. The woman replies that even dogs must eat the crumbs that fall from their master's table. Jesus heals the woman because of her faith, but do you really think that Jesus called this woman and her daughter 'dogs'? Of course not. I think we're right to dismiss these supposed words of Jesus as not worthy of our loving Creator. God loves all of His creation. He's certainly not going to call Gentiles 'dogs.' I can multiply examples."

"True, Michal, but Jesus was not beyond an insult here and there," Gimon replied. "Think of the camel and the rich man. I would think it very rude to tell someone that a camel has a better chance of squeezing through the eye of a needle than he has of getting into heaven. Obviously, given that camels can't do that, there are no rich men in Jesus' heaven. This is quite insulting to the rich man, especially if he has faith."

"Well, Mr. Gimon, I believe that Jesus was trying to sympathize with the most vulnerable in society, those who are downtrodden and even exploited by the rich. That is, if He even said those words at all. I recently came across something interesting while reading the Qur'an. That camel-and-the-eye-of-the-needle story is a great example of a monster translation error, and it shows that we simply cannot trust the Bible to report exactly what Jesus really said."

"That book of the Devil?" Phil jibed. Michal gave him a stern look.

"I'm joking, of course," Phil said. "I couldn't resist, given all the shit you gave me earlier."

"As I was saying—" Michal shook her head. "In the Meccan sura 'The Height,' we find God declaring that even if a thick rope were to pass through the eye of a needle, unbelievers would not enter the Garden."

"That does sound a lot like Jesus' saying, 'It is easier for a camel to go through the eye of a needle than a rich man to enter the Kingdom of God,'" Max said.

"It should. I'm reading a recent and acclaimed translation of the Qur'an by M.A.S. Abdel Haleem. He cites the twelfth-century Muslim theologian and philosopher Fakhr al-Din al-Razi—or just Razi—who argued that the proper translation is not 'camel' but 'thick rope,' so Razi was obviously familiar with the Jesus saying. The root words in Arabic are the same. As you probably know, Jesus spoke Aramaic, and Aramaic is the ancestral language of Arabic. Well, 'thick rope' makes a hell of a lot more sense than 'camel.' Even in the fifth century, Cyril of Alexandria said that the Jesus saying is a mistranslation. But he focuses on a Greek, rather than Aramaic, mistranslation. He said that the Greek 'kamêlos' or 'camel' was a misprint of 'kamilos' or 'rope.' Somewhere, there was a screwy translation, or possibly a screwy translation of a translation."

"Did you find any Biblical scholars talking about this? I can't imagine that this would go unnoticed," Phil said.

"Plenty," Michal said. "They're all believers—literalists, I mean—so far as I can tell. I think it's easier for people to accept the ridiculousness of the camel statement than to believe that humans got the translation wrong. It seems that they want to maintain that God gave us the Bible without human error, or that He wouldn't have allowed an improper translation—something that our friend Maxie here might say." She patted Max's arm. "Some of them even cite the Qur'an in making their argument. Earlier English translations of the Qur'an use the word 'camel,' but, as Haleem suggests, these translations are pretty bad and some are even driven by Islamophobic attitudes. Haleem mentions Alexander Ross' seventeenth-century translation—the first translation into English—whose title includes the words, 'for the satisfaction of all that desire to look into the Turkish vanities.' —I remain unconvinced that Jesus meant 'camel.'"

"But you must know, Michal," Gimon said, "that the Jewish Talmudic literature offers a similar aphorism about an elephant passing through the eye of a needle as a figure of speech implying the impossible. It goes like this: 'They do not show a man a palm tree of gold, nor an elephant going through the eye of a needle.' If this is so, then it's completely reasonable that Jesus would use the word 'camel.' And camels were undoubtedly commonly seen in Jesus' time, certainly more familiar than elephants."

"I agree with our friend, here, Michal," Max said. Gimon smiled.

"You're right, Mr. Gimon. It's found in Berakhot 55b of the Talmud," Michal said. "The Talmud was put together between the third and fifth centuries, so it predates the Qur'an, which was compiled by Abu Bakr, Muhammad's companion, in the seventh century." She paused to consider what she would offer next. "You know, the third-century apocryphal work, *Acts of Peter and Andrew*, has Peter performing a miracle on a dare made by an enraged Onesiphorus. Peter takes a small needle and summons a camel. Calling upon the name of Jesus Christ, he commands the camel to walk through the eye of the needle. As it says, 'Then the eye of the needle was opened like a gate and the camel went through it, and all of the multitude saw it.' I doubt he's the same Christian Onesiphorus mentioned in Second Timothy. . . . This is all such a great big mess."

"I do agree with you that 'thick rope' makes a lot more sense than 'camel.' That's cool that you found this nugget in the Qur'an," said Phil. "But I doubt that we'll suddenly start seeing Bibles printed with this new translation. It might start a riot or a revolution—certainly one or the other—because it would be aligning the Qur'an with Christianity. Or rather, Christianity with the Qur'an—God forbid!" He smirked.

"So given all this, how can we possibly know what Jesus really said? Let's consider the Gospel of John—I've mentioned this before." Michal looked at Gimon. He smiled widely, encouraging her to continue. "Almost all of John should be taken as a reaction against the Gnostic Gospel of Thomas. Many Gnostics believed that Jesus was a divine spirit who appeared in human form but did not have a real physical body. He was a hologram, as my students like to say. Notice how in John we find the Doubting Thomas story, which disparages the Gnostic Thomasine sect by showing how Thomas doubted Jesus' Resurrection until he felt the marks from the nails in Jesus' hands and put his finger in Jesus' lacerated side. Until he feels Jesus' real resurrected body—*body*, not merely spirit."

"Isn't there ample evidence that many of Jesus' words were paraphrased from other Jewish beliefs?" Phil asked. "So if some of the sayings attributed to Jesus endorsed Kabbalistic tradition or numerology, would you dismiss those as sociopolitically influenced, or would you consider them the actual words of Jesus?"

"Well, some argue that Jesus did have Kabbalistic-type leanings, that He was a bit of a mystic. And if you know the Bible at all, numerology is present everywhere," Michal noted. "Almost all of the numbers mentioned throughout the Bible are symbolic and not actual. —Except for the 153 fish that Peter supposedly caught with Jesus' help. I don't know where that number comes from. Some church fathers have tried to figure it out."

"But you get the question, don't you, Michal? Which parts are you going to accept as Jesus' genuine words and which will you reject as politics or propaganda?" Max asked. "Haven't you already stated several times that such-and-such wasn't what Jesus actually said?"

"It may not be my place to ask, but this is such a lively debate. . . . What about those things that you *do* believe about Jesus, about what Jesus said and did?" Gimon cut in.

"Right. How can you accept the miracle stories we find in the Bible, for example, as you claim to?" Phil held up his hands in exasperation. "It seems to me that the gospel writers had to show that Jesus performed miracles, including multiplying food and restoring the dead to life. The Son of God could not be upstaged by Elijah, who was said to have done these things first. Jesus had to be a Super-Elijah. He had to be like a great movie sequel. He had to be better than the original. Given this, why consider any of these miracles to be true? The gospel writers made Jesus into the greatest one-up man of all time." Phil affected his best New York Jewish accent: "'I'm Elijah. I raised the dead.' 'Well, I am Jesus and I raised *myself* from the dead.'" Then he laughed. "'Well I'm Elijah and I put elephants on the moon.' 'I'm Jesus and I know that you're lying.'"

The three looked at Phil, and then Gimon gave a hearty laugh. "You have a reputation for a reason, my friend. I see this now."

"I don't take all the miracles that we find mentioned in the gospels to be genuine. Again, I can give many reasons why the writers were motivated to include and sometimes embellish, or fabricate, their accounts. But I do think that the statement 'Jesus performed miracles, healings and exorcisms' is true," Michal said a bit impatiently.

"What about the things that Jesus said?" Gimon asked. "Again, I do not wish to be rude, but you three seem to be committed to truth. So I must ask: How can you presume to know how to distinguish between what Jesus actually said and what He didn't? Did you know that many of Jesus' most famous messages, like those He delivered at His Sermon on the Mount, have close parallels with Lao Tzu's *Tao Te Ching?* Do you think that maybe Jesus traveled East on the Silk Road, studying and living in China and Kashmir? We really don't know what He did before He started His ministry. The temple in Ladakh, Kashmir, tells the story of 'Life of Saint Issa, Best of the Sons of Men.' 'Issa' means 'Jesus.' Is this story referring to *the* Jesus? —So what makes you such an authority on the words of Jesus?"

Michal gave a puzzled look.

"Right. What makes any of us any kind of authority on this?" Phil motioned to the group. "You weren't there. Neither were the gospel writers, as you rightly noted. How can you claim to know, Michal?"

"I *don't* claim to know what Jesus really said. God gave me a brain, though, and so I think I can do a pretty good job of figuring which passages accurately reflect the spirit of Jesus' words and actions, and the words and actions of God more generally." Michal thought about what she might say next. "I just compare what I read in the Bible to what I take to be the true nature of God. If it fits God's true nature, then I accept it. If it doesn't, I reject it."

Max turned to Michal. "Remember that bit earlier about circular logic and begging the question? We only know of God's true nature by reading the Bible. Seems like you're stuck, Michal. That is, if you insist on arriving at God from a rational point of view."

Michal closed her eyes. *But my experiences of God disclose His true nature—I know what I experienced. Isn't that rational enough?*

Gimon looked at Michal. "You wish to say something?"

"No."

"You should not be afraid to share the truth with your friends, Michal," Gimon said, and then gestured at Phil. "This one is so coarse that I doubt he possesses feelings, much less is able to have them damaged."

"The right word is 'hurt'—one 'hurts' another's feelings, not 'damages' them—and yes, they can be hurt, but I encourage truth at all times and I try not to take offense to it when it is spoken, and especially when it is disagreeable." Phil looked at Michal, who was obviously struggling with a thought. He reached out and touched her shoulder.

"Then let us continue. Let's take the whole of the Bible, Michal, as you seem now to be suggesting, and not restrict our discussion to the gospels," Gimon said. "You suggest that the Bible is riddled with errors, misinformation or just flat-out lies. Why, then, would you place any trust in anything the Bible says? Why trust the Bible when it comes to the fate of your soul?" He turned without waiting for an answer, his step light and whimsical as he proceeded along the gravel path.

Max looked at Gimon. "He makes a good point, Michal, though far more directly than I would to a friend."

Gimon turned around and smiled. "You hold so very little of the Bible to be true, so why believe any of it? Why read it for inspiration? You certainly can't read it—at least on your view—to discern truth. . . ."

Michal stared at Gimon. Her face flushed. A cloud of doubt enveloped her. *Well, I believe in Jesus, just not all the mythology*—but she couldn't quite find the strength to say it.

Max and Phil drew closer to Michal. "Are you OK?"

She stared at the gravel. The little spaces between the stones seemed dark and foreboding. Finally she spoke just above a whisper. "Maybe I don't know what I'm talking about." At first Michal felt humbled by her ignorance. But then she felt sickened by her heresy. She thought herself accursed by God. "My God, I don't know anything."

Gimon was leading the way but his pace slowed upon hearing her words.

"What did you say? Are you admitting defeat?" Phil's voice was soft as he grabbed hold of Michal, "That's not the strong, assertive woman I know." He looked into her clouded eyes. "Nor the woman whose strength and faith I need now in order to make my best decision."

Michal was his only hope.

Gimon spun around. His turn reminded Max of a military man on parade. "You think there are so many errors and contradictions in the Bible, Michal, but all of these tensions of which you speak are easy to resolve—and I don't mean in any grasping-at-straws sort of way. I mean resolved in an altogether plausible way."

Our three friends looked suspiciously at Gimon. Michal finally replied, "Maybe you're right. Who am I to presume to know truth? Maybe I have been reading the Bible in the wrong way—too skeptically. Jesus did say to approach the Kingdom like a little child. My Aunt Vi warns me about this all of the time. I just don't know what to believe any more."

"Don't lose heart, Michal. We all go through spiritual droughts of sorts." Max touched her shoulder. "Periods of time when we question and doubt. Remember what led you to our Savior. Hold onto that when all else fails. You've got your experiences, remember?"

Phil continued to scrutinize Gimon who—for his own part—continued to project all of the confidence of a learned man, enjoying a lively debate. Phil couldn't help but wonder why he'd had so many strange customers lately.

Michal was trying to cheer up. "Yeah, my experiences. . . ." She fastened her eyes on Gimon. "Mr. Gimon, what do you believe? Are you a Christian?"

"I am not a Christian, but I do believe that Jesus is the Son of God." He burst into the merriest laugh.

Gimon was the first to reach the door to the bar. Shapes could be seen through the opened windows as if a great throng moved about the room. Phil looked curiously at the figures as our three friends approached.

"I've never seen that much activity in there. Where did they all come from?" He turned to Max with furrowed brow.

They could hear people chortling, glasses clinking, the thud of the dartboard as a game seemed to be in progress. The smell of roasted meats and cigars wafted out of the bar, accompanied by the overpowering stench of beer cheese, kimchi, and salted fish. They could overhear one couple commenting on their menu choice: "This thigh is quite meaty, very juicy. Jonathan Swift was right," one said. "You should try the fricassee!" answered the other.

It was the nature of the conversations that struck our three friends most. The talk wasn't about hookups, near-misses, and dreadful pickup lines. It wasn't the chatter you'd expect from couples enjoying a rendezvous, friends who hadn't seen each other in years, or regulars indulging in idle talk about sports or YouTube videos. Phil strained to hear some of what was being said, finally making out a discussion about Donald Davidson's argument for anomalous monism. He nudged Michal.

"Do you hear that?" Phil pointed—as if pointing would somehow increase the volume and make clear what was going on.

"You mean the mind-body stuff? Sure I did, but did you just hear that?" A couple was discussing Kant's *Religion within the Boundaries of Bare Reason* and the injustice of infinite punishment in hell. Michal craned her neck to hear, unthinkingly cupping an ear.

Max watched quietly, but then he overheard a discussion about Aquinas' *Summa Contra Gentiles* on how God's essential goodness cannot contain any admixture of any foreign element, and so evil cannot be in God at all. He leaned toward Phil. "Your clientele continues to be amazingly well-informed."

"Come on in," Gimon welcomed as he opened the door. "Join the festivities. I gathered a bunch of the locals." He turned to face our friends. "Your reputation as an eccentric is plain to see, but your additional reputation as a thinking hermit, a priest of a kind in philosophical discussion, inspired me to encourage conversations of substance. . . . I hope you approve, Phil-san."

Phil nodded. He wanted to be more curious but the conversations were welcome.

"You do have that promised Juyondai, right?" Gimon asked.

Phil nodded again. "Absolutely. I have a case. Nothing but the best." He affected his best proprietor's smile. "First bottle is on the house."

"That is very generous of you, but only if you will join me."

Max responded, "You're the one who offered to toast with us. I'm assuming Phil had that in mind before he offered a free anything." Then more conspiratorially, he leaned forward and mock-whispered to Gimon, "He is a bit of a cheapskate—that is but one of his many reputes."

Gimon laughed heartily. "Of course, my newfound friends."

They followed Gimon into the bar, eyes popping. Several wait staff, dressed in white button-up shirts and skinny green ties, spoke with customers—taking their orders, serving drinks and food.

Michal was completely drawn in, enchanted even.

Max smiled at Gimon and tapped Phil on the shoulder. "You certainly do make up for being such an ass at times." He moved in to hug Phil but then slapped his back in that most masculine of gestures. He whispered, "This isn't normal, is it?"

Still wearing his proprietor's smile, Phil said, "Nope—ride it out, but let's stick close."

Phil and Max squeezed Michal between them. They all smiled, but only Michal's seemed genuine.

The stranger's name had been flitting about Phil's mind. He was trying to find the English translation. "You have an interesting name. What does it mean?"

"Another reputation confirmed!" Gimon smiled. "Your Japanese is quite lacking. Suffice it to say, it is a pleasure to meet you. We can stand here and talk about my name, or we can talk about my name while we have that promised drink." He smiled again.

Phil shrugged and walked arm-in-arm with his friends, following Gimon up to the bar.

"Hey there, Joe! What you want?" The face belonged to a mid-twenties man Phil had once hired for a week or two when he first acquired the RTSS.

"What's with the Tokyo Rose bit, Hiroshi? I thought you hated that old stereotype?"

"Hai, and I still do, Phil-san. But I thought I should play the part of bartender to the *gaijin*. . . . What can I get you, friends?"

Max held up his hand. "I think we're good right now. But we would like three cups for sake. Mr. Gimon has generously offered to share his first bottle of Juyondai with my friends." He gestured over at Gimon who was pressing the flesh and kibitzing with everyone in the room.

Michal thought she saw a few people she knew over at a corner window. They were looking outside at the baby pterodactylus perched in the tree. *Baby pterodactylus perched in the tree?* She tried to move to get a better look, but there were too many people in the way. Besides, her friends' hands on her shoulders kept her from moving closer. *Likely just seeing things.*

"Gimon-san is very generous. I like that quality in a person, don't you?" Hiroshi lined up the sake cups on the bar.

"Speaking of generous. . . ." Phil gestured at Hiroshi. "Did I hire you for the day and I just don't remember it?"

"No. Gimon-san is paying my fee. He's very excited about this celebration. I'm surprised he didn't call ahead, but then"—Hiroshi smiled at Phil—"but then there was very little chance that your bar would be anything other than completely empty."

Phil laughed at the joke. He looked around the bar, mentally counting the number of occupants. He laughed again when he realized that—if there were a fire—there weren't nearly enough exits. . . .

WINTER

The sweeping blast, the sky o'ercast,
The joyless winter-day,
Let others fear, to me more dear
Than all the pride of May:
The tempest's howl, it soothes my soul,
My griefs it seems to join;
The leafless trees my fancy please,
Their fate resembles mine!

ROBERT BURNS

§

SEVENTEEN

I cannot begin to explain to you. . . . This is not happening. Oh wait, it is, isn't it?
EMILY ANDREWS

"I have rather enjoyed this storytelling. You might wonder why I know so much about our three friends. I have been studying them ever since I was assigned to be the manager on this case. Gimon has done good work so far, but now it's time for me to make my appearance. Indeed, I am due to show up there any time now. I'm just waiting for the call. I'll be facing off with our three friends on a dusty street in a desolate Western ghost town with a few tumbleweeds scattered about to complete the effect.

"I'll be the Man with No Name. Oh, how I love Sergio Leone Westerns! If only the scene would go down that way, but alas, I'll be appearing in Japan. Hang on—

"I need to hand over my duties as narrator to someone else. Come here, Nysrogh. —He does take his time. . . . I think he's afraid I'm going to do something terrible to him.

"Ah, there you are, Nysrogh. Now, I'm going to take an assignment earthside, so I need you to keep telling the story. Do you think you can handle that? — Don't disappoint me."

"Um. . . . Master stands in office and is very good-looking as he gets green jacket. . . ."

"That was truly dreadful. Could you please channel somebody more appropriate? Balan maybe?"

"Ah, I—ah—please don't hurt me—OK, let me try again. . . ."

"'The manager of the demons rose from his desk and walked over to his chrome-metal coat rack. He paused and looked at the bust on his wall. Putting on his green jacket, he walked back to the goat and patted it gently between its eyes. For a moment he thought he could hear the delightful eternal cries of anguish. He smiled and turned to leave the room.'"

"Much better. You may continue."

"Thank you, me shall."

The manager looked disappointedly at his minion. He was such a buffoon. But he was too valuable as a storyteller to be disposed of—in this particular instance, anyway. . . . Feeling he had made an acceptable decision—definitely not a good one, nor one in which he had not been unduly influenced—the manager stayed his hand from striking the minion down.

"Oh, I just got the call. Look for me, won't you?" the manager said to the audience as he strode out of the room.

"Next stop, the Rashomon Tea and Sake Shop," he said with a hint of laughter and then disappeared.

Our three friends continued to survey the room. Phil's head snapped around as the loud bang of a fist striking a table sounded from the corner nearest them. Two men, one looking rather pig-like and clothed in a Greek *chiton*, the other dressed in an olive tweed jacket and an untucked white button-down shirt, argued in Greek and German—two men who looked suspiciously like Socrates and Wittgenstein. Phil rubbed his eyes and looked again. The men were still arguing, still punctuating their statements by fist-banging, but had changed clothing styles to more modern and fashionable attire. He nudged Michal with his elbow and leaned closer.

"What do you see at that table in the corner?" He pointed to the two men.

Michal looked where Phil was pointing. She saw a couple in their late thirties sitting side by side. The man, wearing round black eyeglasses slightly askew with a pipe clenched tightly between his teeth, was gesturing frantically to the woman, who calmly lit the cigarette held lightly between her pale lips. The woman, several inches taller than the man, wore a simple beige long-sleeved sweater. Her dark hair was up in a haphazard bun, the front held in place by a paisley headband, which clashed with her black-and-green plaid skirt.

Michal blinked, trying to chase away the vision of Sartre and Beauvoir sitting at a table not ten feet from where they stood. "Um. . . ." Michal looked at Phil and then back at the table. Two men now sat where the couple had been. Michal turned toward Max. "What do you see there?"

Max was flummoxed, wondering what had Phil and Michal staring so intently. He looked in that direction and burst out laughing.

"So what do *you* see?" Michal playfully jabbed Max, which caught him off balance. When he righted himself, the three people were still at the table. Running off the names in his head, it sounded like the beginning of a joke: *Pope Francis, Oscar Wilde and C.S. Lewis walk into a bar. . . .*

Phil looked around and noticed that Michal and Max were gone. Not even twenty minutes had passed and already they were separated. "'Stick together,' I said. 'Seems odd,' I said." He huffed. "Faith, see what it gets ya?" He turned and noticed a lawyer-type with a briefcase staring at him impatiently. On instinct, he reached behind the bar and fished for a bottle of whiskey.

"Just what are you doing?" the man asked in a British voice.

"Getting a drink of Yamazaki. They say it upstages the Scottish brands. You want one?" Phil grabbed a tumbler and slammed it down on the bar.

"No thank you, sir. I will wait for the barman." He opened his briefcase and took out a thin file. Phil couldn't quite make out the name on the weathered tab.

"Suit yourself." Phil poured himself a drink. His first thought had been to drink straight from the bottle. The day had gone from hopeful, to odd, to suspicious, to downright delusional. He could hear the admonishments from Michal and Max in his head. He turned to the man sitting next to him and smiled.

"God has a plan," Phil said.

The man looked at Phil, a bit startled. "What did you say?"

"God has a plan. That's what *they* would say."

"Who would say?" The man straightened his green tie.

"My friends. *They* would say that I shouldn't worry about all these strange goings-on, because God has a plan."

"Are they religious?"

"Deeply, completely, to the exclusion of reason." Phil shot back the liquor and immediately regretted it. His face pinched together as he gritted his teeth and swallowed. "Except that right now God's plan seems to be to get me to think that I'm taking acid at a prog-rock concert."

"Ah, I see. What ah—" He straightened his tie again—a futile task since it was quite fastidiously straight already. "So what do you think is so wonky here?"

Phil poured himself another drink. "This party. You're waiting for the bartender, but he probably doesn't know where half the stuff is around here." He pointed at the prepubescent-looking boy as he fumbled and dropped a glass of bourbon, soiling his pants. The youth looked around nervously while three bar patrons looking like the Good, the Bad, and the Ugly erupted in laughter and applause.

"See, he's not really used to working here. Nor is this place accustomed to this kind of traffic. Look at it." Phil waved at the crowd of people. "It's never this busy for me, but then let it be known that I am an ass. . . ."

"You seem to know your onions around here. You must be the proprietor?"

"At your service," Phil replied as he downed his drink.

"Ah, then it seems that God—or at least someone—does have a plan. This paperwork is for you." The man handed Phil the file. "I need your signature on this deposition you gave for the wrongful death suit several years back."

Phil reached for the file then stopped. "That was done and over years ago." He eyed the barrister suspiciously.

"Indeed it was, sir, but some appeals took a while longer. They have finally cleared."

"Don't you usually do business in a more formal setting, say your office? You do have an office, don't you?"

"Of course, sir." He produced a business card like some magician's secret card trick. "But multiple calls have gone unanswered. I was told that you cherished your privacy." He looked around. "That does not seem to be the case today, sir."

"No, not today." Phil ignored the man's business card and opened the file. His arm went weak from some unknown weight, some force that took him to the burning oil rig, as he saw the name: *William Duplanchier.*

Phil read through the legalese, skimming parts until he saw Billy's name. His hands trembled, thinking of the day. The stench of burning oil filled his nostrils. Terror took possession of him and he closed his eyes. Then he felt something goopy and wet on his shoulder.

Months of ghost-hunting had conditioned Phil not to be startled by the unexpected. He had trained himself to control his responses to unusual occurrences, sounds, and feelings. Though people who knew him thought otherwise, he liked to think it made him ordered, giving him an almost Zen-like calm in the face of any storm. But the touch on his shoulder held a different feel. This wasn't an errant breeze touching him, a bit of curtain or sheet blowing in a breezy room. He felt bones pushing through the jelly of what was once flesh, digging into his shoulder. He willed his eyes to open, but they didn't obey this simplest of requests.

"Good evenin', sihr." Phil's eyes were glad that they had disobeyed. The voice sounded like someone speaking through a pot of boiling water, but it was unmistakable.

"Ain'tcha gonna open yer eyes and see who comes to visit ya?" The voice was almost conversational, save for the tinge of insistence.

Phil could guess at the temperature at which flesh melted and bones burned. Coupled with his knowledge of the heat of a petroleum fire, he could imagine how Billy's body must now appear. He chanced to open his eyes. He expected that it would be all over, that the phantasm would have disappeared—but, alas, he could still feel Billy's breath on his neck. Phil's face went pale and he closed his eyes again.

"Is something wrong, sir? You're a bloody mess." He could hear the barrister's voice. "Sir?"

Phil opened his eyes.

Nothing—other than an overly concerned suit-and-tie man looking at him, and the room full of various people—nothing. Billy was not there. Likely never had been there.

"Likely—that's funny."

"What's that?"

"I was laughing at my use of the word 'likely.' Something I wouldn't generally say about what couldn't possibly be real." Phil smiled. "Allowing for the thought that something so patently unbelievable should even be entertained. . . ."

"I must remind you, sir, that if you are not able to sign these papers in sound mind, I cannot accept your signature. You must be able to discern fantasy from reality." The barrister looked at Phil with strained patience.

"I'm fine. If anyone can tell the difference between meaningless fluff and empirical data, it's me." Phil took a deep breath, "I can sign the—" He saw Billy across the room, walking between tables, mingling with the crowd. Then he lost him. He could feel something tugging at the file.

"I must reschedule, sir. You are obviously not of sound mind right now. I dare say, you seem to have lost the plot. As much as it will delay the final outcome and as much as I do not wish to drag this on for the families any longer, I would be remiss in accepting anything from you."

Phil held the file. "I'm fine. It's just been a trying day. I can sign. I *want* to sign." He wrested the file free from the barrister's grasp.

"Brilliant—but no more delays, sir. You have wasted quite enough of my time." Phil felt duly chastised.

"Of course. Can I borrow your pen?" The barrister extended a pen and Phil began to sign. He saw Billy again, over by the window and then talking to the bartender, reaching out his crispy, blackened arm to get a drink. Phil tried to ignore it and continued to sign. His own signature suddenly seemed a foreign thing. "How do I spell—?" He realized that he was talking out loud, as he saw Billy sitting at the table with the other oil-rig workers, their clothing melted onto their bodies by the intense heat. "I can spell—" The 'F' in 'Foster' defied him to write the 'o'. Billy and the oil-rig crew all stared at him and yelled unintelligibly. Screams crowded Phil's head, drowning out the other noises from the bar. He looked down at the paperwork.

"I know what is real—I believe—I—" Phil reached for his glass and knocked it over. "If I can see it, touch it, it's real, if I can see it—" His voice trembled. He reached into his pocket and grabbed hold of the leather pouch—the one that Max had been given by the traveling salesman. He squeezed it tightly—in the way Michal might—as if by magic this would all go away.

As if by magic?! . . . .

The paperwork was being gathered up. Phil watched as the barrister hastily placed the file back in the briefcase. Billy yelled at Phil, joined by the chorus of oil-rig workers. Phil couldn't hear anything else. The bar was full of Billy-types and roughnecks, all horribly, torturously burned. He covered his eyes in a futile attempt to extinguish the images. But he could hear them—undeniably, verifiably so. He felt his sanity slipping away like some supertanker disappearing into a dense fog. It was here one moment—undeniable, massive and solid—and then it vanished. Fog everywhere.

He felt a hand touch his shoulder again and recoiled. He looked up to see a very concerned Michal surrounded by several worried patrons looking on. Cautiously, he reached out and touched her shoulder. She felt real enough. He grabbed her and held her close.

"It seemed so real—so real, Michal. If my senses lie to me—then—then what?" His words tumbled out like a Yahtzee throw. "What do I know? What do I—? I don't know what to—to—to *believe* anymore."

Michal held him closer. "I believe you, Phil."

Michal led Phil by the arm to a bar stool by the window. She had to shoo away some little insect creatures who were arguing about who had first dibs on the ladybug with the sumptuous smile. They cursed her as they left. She sat Phil down and pointed out the window to the garden.

"Look, Phil, it's your garden. Something real for you to hold onto." She wasn't entirely sure that he could take this kind of trial. He just wasn't used to warped perceptions of this magnitude.

Michal stood beside him for several minutes as she looked about the brooding, red-lit bar. The sight of it called to mind Dante's *Inferno*—but the place felt *cold*. It was certainly not inviting, despite the seeming merriment. Gimon walked up and rested his hand on her shoulder to ease her discomfort.

"Follow me. I'd like you to meet Floyd."

"What about Phil?"

"Oh, he'll be just fine. Look, he's making friends already." Gimon pointed at Phil, who had already found his way to a nearby table bestrewn with scantily clad succubi. Their red skin glistened against the glowing orange light of the nearby fireplace.

"See, he's fine. Come on."

"Who's Floyd?" Michal wrinkled her nose.

"Only the best damn bartender from New York to Tokyo. He'll fix you something to quiet those nerves."

She noticed a woodcutter and a bandit-type arguing with a woman, while a Buddhist priest looked on. Then she thought she spotted Phil throwing darts with some of the red-skinned goddesses.

"What can I get you, beauty?" Floyd asked Michal when they approached the bar. He smelled like farts from the bowels of an outhouse. He stood barely taller than the counter. Michal could have sworn that Floyd was the one-armed man from the teahouse—but he was making her drink adeptly with both hands.

Floyd handed her the drink.

"Take a look around," Gimon invited. "I'm sure there are people you know."

Michal's eyes ranged over the place. It *was* Phil throwing darts. He seemed to be having a raucous time—beer in one hand, dart in another. In typical Phil style, he was playing badly. One dart bounced off a nearby mirror and he gave a hearty laugh.

She turned and noticed Max who seemed uncomfortably out of place. She began to walk toward him, making her way through the crowds, when a professor-type in a greenish-brown tweed jacket approached her, holding an oversized cat.

"Are you going somewhere?" he asked with a heavy Russian accent.

"I know you," Michal said suspiciously.

"We really should talk." He caressed the nape of his cat's neck. "I'm sitting over there." He motioned to a nearby table.

Michal looked over in Max's direction, but he was gone. She glanced at the dartboard. A fight had broken out. The mirror that had been hit by Phil's stray dart was now shattered. A man was looking at his bloodied hand. She strained to see Phil but she couldn't.

"OK, sure. Why not?" Michal followed the man to his table.

"As you can see, I've been playing chess—with my cat." He chuckled. "He's beating me." He laughed again. Michal sat down. The cat sat on his haunches and glared at her suspiciously.

The professor downed his shot of vodka, then placed the empty glass in front of the cat, who was now sitting comfortably atop the table. The cat licked the inside of the glass clean.

"You hold a lot of heretical views, Michal."

"How do you know my name?"

"I overheard your friends say it."

"I see. And you're right, I guess I do." Not so long ago, Michal would have said those words confidently, but now she was ashamed, disappointed in herself even.

"You know, heresy is the sixth circle of hell," the professor said.

"Yes, but Dante was just a poet."

"Poets speak to the reality of life, of existence. You do know that there are only nine circles of hell. Heretics go to hell."

"I'm not going to hell," Michal said.

"What makes you so sure?"

Michal didn't sound very sure of herself. "Because I find it extremely difficult—indeed, altogether reprehensible—to believe that at the Final Judgment Jesus will be sitting on His heavenly throne holding a list of doctrines and kicking people's asses all to hell for getting it wrong. Jesus himself was a heretic. Look at how He challenged the religious authorities of His day, the Pharisees and Sadducees."

"Jesus was the *last* heretic. Now He's the Rule Maker, and people who break the rules have got to pay the piper."

"I'm no different from any other Christian who engages in the exact same sort of theological speculations. Every believer is a heretic, depending on which doctrine we appeal to. Just because I arrive at different conclusions doesn't mean I'm damned to hell. I mean, really, what kind of barbarous God would condemn people to hell for all eternity because we got wrong things we won't even know about until we're dead?"

"People—especially some pastor-types—like to blow all that hell-fire stuff out of proportion. I doubt hell is as bad as all that. In fact, I'm sure some of your loved ones are there. No doubt you have some loving relatives, maybe a grandmother, perhaps, whom you'd like to see again?"

"How do you know about my grandmother?" Michal asked, looking away.

"I don't. I was just suggesting a loved one. Don't you want to see your loved ones again?"

Michal took a sip of her drink. The cat hissed at her. Evidently her movement had disrupted his sleep. "My loved ones aren't in hell. My grandma—my grandma was grabbed by demons at her death, true—" *Why am I sharing this with him?* "But I'm certain that Jesus rescued her from hell. That's the loving Jesus I know. Nobody stays in hell but the demons."

The professor squinted at her. "No, Michal, once in hell always in hell. *Forever.* Except for the demons, of course, who are granted the pleasure of visiting this earth at will. There might be *some* hope that your grandmother is in Dante's Limbo—you know, for the unbelievers?—which, by the way, is only the *first* circle of hell. But you—? You will definitely be assigned to the sixth circle—*of Hell.*"

"I just don't buy it, Professor. You're making the Final Judgment into some kind of celestial game show. If we fail to state our answer in the form of a theological question or—*God forbid*—we quote the wrong theologian, we're damned all to hell.[124] I don't buy it." Michal said the words, but she was losing confidence and in any case she was missing Grandma.

The professor started to respond, but she stopped paying attention. In the corner of the room she spotted her grandma. Or at least she thought she did.

"Excuse me, Professor, but I think I see somebody I know." Michal hopped out of her chair without waiting for the professor's response. She couldn't believe her eyes. Grandma was in a plain lime-green-and-white-striped housedress. She was wearing her favorite apron: bright yellow with big red letters that read 'He's with Me for My Cooking.' Grandpa would always laugh when he saw it. Grandma was a horrible cook. Her gray hair was tightly curled as if she'd just had it in her pink squishy rollers. She wore no makeup except for bright red lipstick.

That was definitely Grandma. Michal couldn't help but smile. She quickly made her way over, pushing through the crowds.

"Grandma?" Michal asked hesitantly as she approached. The lights in the bar turned from a foreboding red to an inviting carnation pink—Grandma's favorite color.

"Michal, dumpling! I haven't seen you for years. Sit down with me." Michal sat down and held Grandma's hand.

"Grandma, how is this possible? This doesn't make any sense. You died. I was there when you died in the hospital room." Michal was beginning to question her own reality. Nothing made sense anymore. More doubt clouded her mind. Perhaps Grandma hadn't died. She didn't know what to believe.

"Oh, Michal, I am living in such a wonderful place now. I have roommates. It's not like living with Grandpa, although my three roommates definitely get on my nerves. Boy, do they get on my nerves. . . . I guess your Grandpa did too, always telling me to turn up the baseball game, so I'm used to it. But I rather enjoy my new home, actually. I wouldn't have it any other way."

"Where are you living, Grandma?" Michal remembered her death. How could she forget? She imagined all of the instruments of torture in the place that Grandma *should* be calling her home: the racks and red-hot pincers and all the other paraphernalia. *Of course, hell isn't like that,* Michal thought, but the images popped into her mind.

"I am living in a little apartment. Furnished in the style of the Second French Empire, or so I am told. It's very modish. You would just love the claret-colored sofa. My roommate tends to lounge on it, but it's so exquisite."

"That sounds like quite a place, Grandma. But I don't understand. Did you get better? Did you leave the hospital? What about Grandpa? He was heartbroken. He died of a broken heart, Grandma. Did Grandpa know? Did you leave him?" Michal was full of questions.

"I left the hospital, Michal, but I never got better. Your grandpa, so I hear, is doing quite well. He shares an apartment on the second floor with Margaret. He always had a thing for Margaret. He'd squeeze her knee under the table whenever we played canasta. . . . Oh, I must tell you, Michal. You should really come visit. You can stay with me. We will make room. My roommates—I have three of them, did I tell you? They can be quite annoying. One is a high-society type. She gets on my nerves the most. You know how I hate high-society types. But boy, can they tell stories!" Grandma smiled.

Michal looked at her grandma, studying her. Suddenly Grandma transformed before her very eyes, becoming a familiar, bumpy-skinned, brownish-green, bull-like figure of enormous stature. But only for a moment. It happened so quickly that Michal wondered whether it had happened at all.

"Are you OK, dumpling?" Grandma's eyebrows drew together, the picture of familial concern.

"Me? Yeah, sure. I think I must have eaten something disagreeable. I've had a really difficult day. You wouldn't imagine."

Grandma squeezed Michal's hand. Then she looked beyond Michal and her face suddenly brightened.

"There's your Aunt Violet," Grandma exclaimed.

Impossible. But she turned around and there she was in a sleeveless avocado-knit dress, wrapped in her mink stole and carrying her purse and gloves.

"Hello, Michal. Hello, Mother," Aunt Vi said warmly and sat down in the empty chair next to them.

"Aunt Vi—how did you get here? Did I tell you that I would be in Japan?"

"You know me. I'm quite good at finding out these things," she replied, then addressed her mother: "Ma, you're looking well."

"Thank you, Violet. Would you like a drink? The bartender makes a wonderful mint julep. You love mint juleps. He's very generous with the bourbon. Michal, won't you have one too?"

"I would love that," Aunt Vi replied. Grandma motioned to a waiter who quickly arrived and took their order.

"Michal," Aunt Vi began very seriously, "I see that you're still confused." She rhythmically, mindlessly, folded and unfolded her white gloves. "It seems that you still don't know exactly what you believe. Maybe you could tell me."

"Aunt Vi, you know how I disappoint you all the time." She hesitated to continue.

"Disappoint me? You're right, Michal. You disappoint me in so many ways. In so many ways you *really* disappoint me. . . . I worked so hard to get you to read the Word for what it was and you spent all your energy trying to find out what you thought it meant." She reached out and tapped Michal's nose. The gesture held years of memories. Unbidden, Michal felt tears welling in her eyes. "It's as plain as the nose on your face."

"Aunt Vi, I was trained to study the Bible critically. I can't help but look at it this way. But that doesn't take away from my love of our Savior. Trust me on this one."

"Trust you? I don't trust you. I trust in our Lord, though really I must question whether He's *your* Lord. *My* Lord expects me to love Him enough not to question Him." Aunt Vi looked at Michal, who suddenly felt seven again.

"Remember that time that you jumped off the roof wearing the bedsheet?" Aunt Vi asked.

"As you know, Jack convinced me that I was Superman."

"*Jack* convinced you? You wouldn't listen to me but you listened to your younger brother," Aunt Vi said with a tsk-tsk. "That's just it. You believe in the wrong things. You believe in your own human ability to make any sense of the majesty and power of our Lord and Savior. You have always been headstrong and confident. While that can be a virtue, this thing that you are thinking now, this *pride*, it is *S-I-N*. . . ." Aunt Vi drew out the word, which pained Michal's ears. "You think you know? Tell me, what have you learned in all the time that you've tried to understand? *To lean on your own understanding?*"

"Proverbs 3:5. Really. I'm tired of people throwing this in my face. Look— God gave me a brain, Aunt Vi. God gave me a brain and I should use it."

"WHO gave you a brain?" She looked expectantly at Michal.

"*My God* gave me a brain—the same God as yours. We're not supposed to send our brains out to lunch."

"No, Michal, your god is knowledge, your own pride. We are supposed to use our brains to solve practical matters in this world. Not to figure out God's will or analyze His word. Who are you to question God, the Creator of our universe? Your god wants you to question him like a little girl who wants to break her leg. My God wants me to trust Him." Aunt Vi shook her head. "Your god is not *the God*. You should admit that." She took Michal's face in her hands and held her close, so close that Michal could smell the mix of mint and bourbon from Aunt Vi's favorite drink. "Use that great big brain of yours and know the Truth."

"My God *is* the true God, Aunt Vi. He knows my heart, just as much as He knows my skeptical brain. How can you say this to me?"

"Because, child, I taught you everything about God when you were just a lost little lamb. And look at you now." She pointed at her with a wrinkled finger. "Nothing's changed, Michal. My God is *not* your god. So which is it? Am I wrong? Or maybe"—Aunt Vi sipped her mint julep—"just maybe *you* are."

"What do you want me to believe? That the earth is only six thousand years old, despite all the evidence? That I was made from Adam's rib? Come on, Aunt Vi. I'm not that gullible little girl anymore."

"And you are still leaning on your own understanding. Look around you. Is Grandma here? Am I here? Who was that dreadful man who made such a mess out of trying to prove God? Descartes, I believe? Do you trust your own eyes now? *You* certainly couldn't bring this about. You don't have the ability. GOD DOES, but not *your* god. Not the god of knowledge, the god of rationality." Aunt Vi's voice increased in tempo and volume as she punctuated each word with ever-more-violent thrusts of her flabby arm.

Finally she looked at Michal directly. "You're not a Christian, Michal. You've been playing at it for a few years now, but you may as well embrace your god of knowledge, because he's no god of mine." Michal could all but hear the lower-case 'g' in Aunt Vi's voice.

Michal wondered at it all. *Can I be that wrong?* Then Michal looked around. Grandma was sitting next to her, smiling rapturously. Aunt Vi was here— impossibly here. Phil's dead friend was having a drink with the gardener across the room. None of this made any sense and none of it was even remotely within the realm of probability.

Michal looked at her hands. She thought about all the books she had picked up with those hands over her many years of education. The years of textual analysis—of reading line by line for contradiction and clarity—were written on every contour of those hands. What more could those hands—or for that matter, *her brain*—have done? How much better might they have served her, in revealing the *truth* of the Bible instead of the falsehoods? She saw Aunt Vi get up and walk away. Michal put her hands to her face. She began to weep.

For seconds—minutes, perhaps—she wept, until she felt Grandma's loving hand on her shoulder.

"It's OK, dumpling. It's OK. Your Aunt Violet doesn't know. She only repeats what she has heard." Michal sunk into Grandma's embrace, sobbing through the smell of brimstone on Grandma's apron.

Brimstone? Michal shook herself back to her senses and looked up into Grandma's piercing red eyes.

Grandma's grip was an iron vise. "It's not all a lake of fire and eternal torture, dumpling. In fact that rarely happens. Not even to the worst of them."

"Your nice apartment—" Michal said in a hollow voice. She tried to smile.

"You read, dumpling. But not everything you read is right. You've been walking away from the inconsistencies in the Bible for years now. And well you should." Grandma patted Michal's shoulder and then released her hold. Her eyes softened. "You know the truth. You've written about it, read it, you debate it. The Bible is nothing but a book of lies. You *should* trust in your own rationality. You are beautiful and brilliant—far more than anybody else in the family." She stared into Michal's eyes. "You know the truth."

"I *do* know the truth. You know, when I was entering this place, I heard a couple of people talking about Kant. How he thought that hell couldn't exist because it's so unjust to send people to an eternal punishment for finite sin. So I just can't bring myself to believe that Jesus really said anything about hell. It was probably inserted later as Christian scare-tactics to bring in more believers."

"*Who* supposedly talked about hell?" Grandma drew Michal's eyes again. "Who, dumpling?"

Michal thought on this. *Can that be false too?* Everything she had ever studied told her that Jesus was a historical figure, but everything she had ever studied—the scientific literature, anyway—told her that miracles didn't happen, miracles were perceptual miscues. One had to *believe* in miracles. And Michal could feel her belief slipping.

"There, there, Michal. Oh, my poor little dumpling. Hell isn't all that bad, really. Think about it. It's just a place that is *not heaven.* You don't think that this self-important God of yours will just suddenly start treating you like an individual, do you? Certainly not when He has you in His own home. I imagine you'll be mopping those streets of gold or cleaning all those stained glass windows. Think of all those robes you'll have to bleach. Oh, and don't forget to praise Him frequently.... On the other hand," Grandma said, sarcasm dripping from her voice, "you can go somewhere where you can be a *real* individual and not a housekeeper for the *Most High*."

Grandma continued: "Either God is the one true God and He has been lying to you all this time, in which case hell can't be anything other than *not heaven*, or God is just another more powerful being who has been kicking us around like little sock monkeys. If so, then hell is *freedom* from that Bully. There is plenty of room for you in my apartment." She looked at Michal sweetly. "If you would like to come live with Grandma?"

Michal began to pull away from Grandma. It sounded so inviting a moment ago: eternity with Grandma, or, if not eternity, then at least an afterlife. She looked at Grandma for a bit longer as a massive bull-creature walked right behind her. Michal turned away, but she could feel Grandma's hot breath on her neck in great, hot, fetid puffs. She looked up and there was Max standing over her. She got out of her chair and stood by him.

Max smiled at Grandma, not a hint of fear in his eyes. He must have seen her as the loving grandmother Michal knew. "Well there y'all are. You must be Michal's memaw." He extended his hand. "I'm Max. Can I borrow your—what is it that she calls you?" Max looked at Michal expectantly.

"Dumpling," Michal managed to say in a little voice.

"Dumpling! That's so darn cute. Y'know my *pa-paw*, when I was a young-un, used to call me a li'l spitfire. Of course, this was before I got *big*. I just love nicknames, love the names he used to come up with. Though he shore din't want to be showin' any love to us kids all the time. He was the one who brought out the belt." Max's smile continued, but Michal could feel his strong hands holding her. "Aw, but that's a kind of love, isn't it?"

Grandma giggled. "Indeed it is, young man. Michal felt my wooden spoon on more than one occasion."

"I'll bet she did. She's a stubborn one." Max held her a bit closer. "You mind if I borrow her for a bit? We have some business to look over—our flight back to the States, y'know?" Max made a sour face. "Planning—sometimes I just hate it." Max pulled Michal a small step away from Grandma.

"You go right ahead dear, you little spitfire. Michal and I have an eternity to catch up," Grandma said.

Max took Michal over to the bar and handed her a cup of tea. He held up a finger and the bartender brought him a shot. He slid it to Michal like a lifeguard throwing a safety line to a drowning victim.

"You looked like you could use a friend."

"So you're a demon. We all have our problems. You don't happen to know a guy by the name of Descartes, do you?" Phil looked at the man he had come to know as Tanaka over the past two years of his intermittent patronage.

"Funny mortal. Nice to see you haven't lost your sense of humor. Or is that desperate sarcasm?" Tanaka took a drink of his sake as he caressed the hair of a passing succubus.

"Desperate would imply I'm losing control. I don't think that's the case at all." Phil raised his glass in a toast. "Just because you're a demon doesn't mean there is a god. This is one primitive who has no intention to bow down to aliens just because they have a thunder stick and magic light." Phil drained his bourbon and refilled his glass.

"But, my friend, you aren't just facing a superior being, you are facing the supernatural. You *have* accepted that I am, yes?" Tanaka's voice had Middle Eastern swirls, sounding like the oboe solo in the Bacchanale from Saint-Saëns' *Samson and Delilah.* "How can you possibly deny the evidence of your own senses? These are the very faculties upon which you base the veracity of the empirical world. Do you now distrust even those?"

"Nice try, Tanaka, but that dog won't hunt. I have always distrusted my senses. I wait for them to be verified by both my body *and* my mind. But that's neither here nor there. Let's just say that I accept that you are a demon—a real, honest-to-the-God-for-which-I-have-no-evidence demon. Just because you're a superior being in the business of doing 'evil'"—Phil felt his fingers betray him by making air-quotes—"it still doesn't follow that there is a God."

"Oh, Phil, you are like a child crossing your arms and holding your breath. Really, you continue to deny your senses and even worse your logic."

"I know who I am, but what are you?" Phil stuck out his tongue, playing the child he was accused of being.

Tanaka rolled his eyes. "Very cute. That's even worse than your Shakespeare reference earlier."

"So that was you, eh? Or some incarnation thereof?" Phil swirled his whiskey. "Not a surprise. You *are* a more powerful being, anyway. But you're still not God, now, are you?"

Tanaka shuddered at the thought of it. "No, I am not."

"And that, my friend, is precisely the problem. You didn't make the universe, but you're more powerful than I am. Just as I am more powerful than those ants in my garden. You no more deserve my worship than those ants should worship me—though I might rather enjoy it."

"Your logic is elusive, Phil-san. And I think it's actually downright weak. Please try to defend your position. I have given you proof of my power, my ability. I, in fact, could have made the universe as far as you are concerned."

"Ah, you could have and I've never really argued that. Are you sure you believe in God? You are heralding my argument."

"Go on." Tanaka looked amused but impatient.

"Fine, I accept your power. I might even accept that the being that you call 'God' has enough power to create the universe. But did He create everything? Did

He create everything that ever was? Morality, laws of physics, the proboscis monkey?" Phil smirked.

"Let's just say He created you, and leave it at that."

"Sorry, Tanaka, that's not good enough. I can go to a petri dish and create life. That's no proof whatsoever. If God is not the OMNI GOD, then He is no God at all. He is just a more powerful being that we find hard to grasp." Phil began to sip his whiskey, then stopped. "Look, Daniel Dennett talks about Supermanism and I think it applies here.[125] As Dennett says, Superman is intelligent, on the side of good, capable of amazing feats and deeply interested in the inhabitants of planet earth. Superman shares these same characteristics with God, or God in the flesh—His boy, Jesus. Right?"

"I think that God would have something to say about your comparison of His Son to a comic book character."

"But that's the point. They and their abilities are beyond the ken of mortal man. Superman can save people from disease by using his heat vision and burning out cancer. He didn't, but he could have. In *Superman* #700 he is confronted—Never mind, you get the point. Jesus cured diseases, but the explanation we get is that it was through the power of God. Jesus died and rose from the dead. But Jesus is a piker in that He only rose once. Currently, Superman has been 'born again' at least ten times. When you look at it, a real Superman is just as plausible as Jesus or God." Phil aimed his glass at Tanaka. "So I'll start believing in Jesus, when you start believing in Superman."

"Ah, but Superman is a character that comes—"

"—from a comic book?" Phil smiled. "Yeah, comic books have gotten a bad rap for not being 'real' literature. Kind of like the Bible. Have you ever actually read *Numbers*? Shopping lists are more interesting."

Tanaka exhaled slowly. "So your point is that Jesus and Superman are equally plausible? How can that possibly lead you to your conclusion that God is not God?"

"Quite simply, really. If God did not make everything, if God didn't make all that is, including all laws, all morality—I mean absolutely *everything*—then He is nothing more than a more powerful super being à la Superman. A 'Q,' if you will accept the Roddenberry reference. The only difference between God and Q is that God claims to be God, whereas Q went out of his way to show that he wasn't anything of the kind." Phil raised his glass. "God is more Barnum than beatitude."

"Perhaps, Phil-san, but does it not make more credible the existence of an afterlife, something more than our earthly existence?"

"Mr. Demon-san, I have never ruled out the existence of an afterlife. I simply don't have any evidence for it. Bertrand Russell put it well. When he was asked what he would say to God when God asked why he didn't believe in Him, Russell said, 'Because, Sir, you never gave me enough evidence.' It's not that I don't want to believe in God. It's that I've never been given any proof. The Christian God 'might' exist, but so might the gods of Olympus, or of ancient Egypt or Babylon.

We have no way of knowing. It's not that I don't *want* to believe in the afterlife. There just isn't any proof. I have no problem with an afterlife or an existence beyond this one. The problem I have is with the *nature* of that afterlife, should it exist."

Tanaka raised an eyebrow, a smile curling his lips. "Then you are not an atheist, but an agnostic. By your own admission, if you are wrong in this could you not also be wrong in your agnosticism? Further, if you are wrong in this, could you not, Phil-san"—Tanaka swirled his sake—"be wrong in many other things, up to and including your judgment that there is no God, capital 'G'?" Tanaka downed his sake triumphantly. "I am looking forward to your company for all eternity!"

"Tanaka, my friend, if I am to accept that the rest of eternity will be spent in your company, then I can think of far worse hells." Phil went to refill his glass again only to find the bourbon bottle empty. He began to fish around behind the bar for another. "Or are you saying that I should take Pascal's wager and buy myself some fire insurance? I may never need it, but better to have it and not need it, than to need it and not have it, right? Have you heard of the nineteenth-century Spanish philosopher Miguel de Unamuno? —Of course you have. Man wants nothing of a god except immortality. Follow the heart, the heart that wants immortality, and with Pascal choose to believe. "'Tis a tragic fate, without a doubt, to have to base the affirmation of immortality upon the insecure and slippery foundation of the *desire* for immortality. . . .'"[126] Phil ogled a buxom succubus as she walked by. She gave him a wink.

"You know, my man Voltaire called the wager 'indecent' and 'childish.' But in any case, *which* God are you going to wager on? You want to put your money on the right God, after all. You want to go 'all in' on the right God? But suppose you do manage to wager on the right God. God knows the heart, Phil-san. There is truly no such thing as fire insurance, my friend."

"Ah, but according to which salvation myth? God may know the heart, but there are certain rules that even *He* has to follow, not least of which are His own. Does it not say in one of many verses in that Good Book, 'For whosoever shall call upon the name of the Lord shall be saved'? Or how about, 'Whosoever shall confess me before men, him will I confess also before my Father, which is in heaven'? Or what about that old trope we find on billboards at every American ball game, John 3:16: 'That whosoever believeth in Him, shall not perish but have eternal life'? I'm not making this up. It's in the Bible. Are we to have the argument again about picking and choosing which are the actual words of God and which aren't?"

"I remind you that the Bible also says, 'You say you believe in God? You do well. But even the demons believe and they shudder.' I myself don't find the Great Almighty particularly scary, mind you. But it takes more than mere belief or confession to secure your place in heaven. I'm already looking forward to showing you your room in hell, Phil-san. I've got to say, though, that His scare tactics—

that talk of weeping and gnashing of teeth— are overstated. One gets used to it in no time."

"Best keep that window treatment for the Lake of Fire on hold. Seriously, we're back to the same tired old argument. The Bible says one thing but then it says another. It says 'do this and you're good,' but then another writer says 'oh sorry, what that other guy meant to say was do this *and* this.' At what point do we say that we have the definitive, authoritative Word of God? How can we possibly know the original intent of the author—all the more so if the author is God Himself—if later authors come in and edit, add, and embellish? And who's to say that there isn't another author waiting to jump in and write even more? What will *that* author say? 'Sorry, all the previously written stuff is just exaggerated fiction but what *I* have is the *real* Word of God. You see, I have this new interpretation. . . .' Please, that argument never ends."

Phil found another bottle of liquor back behind his trusty EW 23. He dusted it off and placed it on the bar.

"This is a very old and very special bottle of liquor. I have been saving it for a special occasion. I think this occasion qualifies. But before I pop the cork, I want to find my friends. You know, the friends who aren't demons or trying to trick me into saying or believing one thing or another. . . . Well, at least mostly." Phil looked around the crowded bar. He finally spotted Michal and Max speaking to an older woman who looked a lot like Michal's grandma—at least from the photos he'd seen. "Looks like they're currently engaged."

He reached behind the bar and retrieved a much more ordinary bottle of his trusty EW 23. He looked at the remaining bottle. At one-twenty-five a pop, he figured it was a small price to pay for a little solace. All the more since he'd let this demon know that he would not go gentle into that good night. After he cracked the seal, he spun the top off with a flourish and poured a small glass.

"But I *would* wager that if God Himself showed up, I wouldn't want to share this bottle with Him. You see, I think He's pretty much a dick."

"I'll raise my glass to that. . . . But you know, Phil-san, we've yet to invoke the tired old free-will argument that so many Christians make. A world with free will is better than a world without, and free will necessarily introduces at least *moral* evil. I'm not sure we want to tackle that now, however, my friend. You haven't enough spirits to carry us through that one!"

"My friends and I have drawn daggers over that topic. If free will necessitates evil, that means that God built it that way. Which means that God wants us to struggle."

"Sure He did. He'd rather have creatures with free will than beings that robotically follow Him. The Egomaniac demands praise, worship, love. Robots can't give him that," Tanaka said.

"But Tanaka, you're missing the point. God has the power to make the universe however He wishes. Why not make it so that we can have free will without the evil? Or is your argument that free will doesn't actually exist without evil? The ol' trope of light and dark?"

"To have free will means to have the ability to choose and one can always choose wrongly. Many wrong choices have led to evil."

"But this is the system that God chose to set up. Couldn't He, being all-powerful, have chosen a different system, one in which we would always choose the good? He set it up so that we do, in fact, choose evil, but choosing evil obviously results in a lot of pain and suffering. What is the point of this life, then? Is it just a journey or is the destination to become a good person, a good *soul*? If so, there is no such thing as evil *per se*. Instead, we should merely call such unfortunate happenings 'opportunities' to become wiser, more knowledgeable or whatever-you-want-to-call-it. Am I going to have to extol the virtues of Stalin again?—I'd say 'Hitler,' but that seems to be more offensive—well, maybe not recently."

"You know, the Buddhists say there would be far less pain and suffering if we just let go of our attachment to the impermanent—and it turns out that *everything, everyone, every experience,* is impermanent. In any case, evil is merely a social construct, as I've heard you argue before. What's evil to you might not look so bad to me. And if evil is just a social construct and not something real in the world, then God is off the hook," Tanaka said. "Of course, as my man Morrow once put it, my boss really had a *boom period* between '37 and '45. You might be impressed to know that he stitched 4,328,713 yellow stars inscribed with the word 'Jude.'"[127] He grinned.

"Good one," Phil said with a wink, but then felt more than a tinge of disgust. "I think I've demonstrated enough times to my friends that my perceptions of right and wrong could challenge even the demons themselves."

"So, Mortal Who Thinks He Knows the Mind of God," Tanaka jibed, "then God *is* off the hook."

"Assuming, Dweller of the Abyss, that there *is* a God—and I dare say that you haven't come remotely close to convincing me."

"Phil, I agree that God's a dick, as you so eloquently put it, since He has *lorded* over our kind for eons." Tanaka winked. "See what I did just there?"

"You amuse yourself and I must admit me too." Phil watched the dim light play on the ice cubes in his whiskey.

"Phil, why exactly do you believe that God is a dick? You're one of the humans He dotes on. You owe him your very existence."

Phil sipped his whiskey with eyes closed, savoring the burning sensation. "Let's say that I do owe God my existence. Let's even say that I accept that God created humanity. If I were to bow down to Him, I would be going against the very values that I have come to embrace from my own experiences. In the Bible, God tells us to be kind, loving, and forgiving, but *the Creator Himself* ignores these values. Are we going to say that God doesn't have to follow His own rules?

Fine, let's allow that for just a moment, and I mean just for a moment, and ask the obvious question. . . ."

"Hang on. You are invoking the very thing you claimed ought not be invoked. The so-called Word of God!"

"My apologies, are you going to burst into flames? I've only introduced it, as it's central to your argument that God exists and that there is truth in His Bible. If I can counter that argument using your own material, or in fact God's own material, then my argument would be that much stronger. Suffer through my argument, if you will."

"Fine. I'll suffer through your Bible-invoking argument, if you insist—you know how our kind loves suffering. But we both know from past experience that it doesn't get us anywhere. I just reference the Bible now and again because that's what you humans like to do. I'm right there with you about the so-called truth of the Word of God. But please continue, my friend."

"Thank you," said Phil. "It's nice to have friends in high *and* low places." Phil lifted the glass to his lips and then paused. "Let's put it another way. What do you call a being that doesn't follow its own rules? —At best insincere, right? Downright hypocritical?"

"I think I can accept that," Tanaka said.

"So if a being who doesn't follow its own rules is insincere, then can't we say that it doesn't believe that it should have to follow those rules? Are we on the same page?"

"I think I see where you are going."

"Indeed you probably do, since you can see more than my mere mortal perceptions." Phil raised his glass in the air in a silent toast to his companion. "That said—why doesn't God have to follow His own rules? Is He too good for them? And if God doesn't need to follow His own rules, then how do we know that He isn't breaking them even now? He promises us a path to salvation, but what's stopping Him from saying at the end of our slavish existence, 'Changed the rules on you!' Maybe we're *supposed* to be cruel to each other. Maybe we're *supposed* to question authority, God's authority, and only by doing so will we transcend being mere followers of God's will to actually understanding it."

"Why should God have to follow His own rules? A parent has rules for his child to follow. 'Do not cross the street.' 'Do not talk to strangers.' Stuff like that. Of course a parent shouldn't follow these rules. They're for the child's good, not his own. But you are anticipating a deeper problem with the Almighty. If God made up the rules about right and wrong, good and bad, then God Himself has *created* goodness and badness and He could have made different rules. God says adultery is wrong but He could have said otherwise. 'Go screw thy neighbor,' He could have said. If you say that God could *not* have made His rules differently, then God must be appealing to something outside of Himself to know what good and bad *are*. But then He is not God! You know, Plato made this type of argument long ago. My friend Horpyna, the old witch of Devil's Gulch, helped him construct it. She's one bad ass, I tell you. Has white teeth so strong she could chew up a breastplate."

"Michal has shared this argument with me —well, back before she got sucked into all of this believer's crap. But, Tanaka, you strike at the very core of the atheist argument." Phil looked at him suspiciously, wondering why he would take his side. *Where are you going with this?* Wary of his responses, Phil continued, "If God created good and bad, then God could have created them differently, and, more importantly, God could have made it easier to be good rather than bad. Is it better to make the beings of a world such as ours appreciate good, or is it better to actually *make* them good? Why create us like He did?"

"I'm not sure I agree with your statement. Or perhaps I don't understand it. Maybe you could elaborate," Tanaka said.

Phil felt a tinge of triumph but feared the consequences of winning this argument. "Consider it like this. If God made us, then God could have made us however He wished, right?"

"Of course, Phil, including making some of us evil—at least what most would consider to be evil. Curious, right?" Tanaka leered at Phil.

"You're distracting me again." Phil waggled his finger. Tanaka smiled.

"So if God could have made us in any way, why make us flawed? Before you get on the 'so that we could become better' bandwagon, let me explain why that doesn't hold water. Let's say you are in the business of building cars. You would want the car to be popular, utilizing all the best parts. Let's say that it's a muscle car like a '72 Ford Gran Torino. You know, the kind that Walt Kowalski tinkered with in the Clint Eastwood film. You would want it to have the most powerful engine, the best interior, a great paint job—" Phil paused.

"I've heard this argument before. Philo makes it in Hume's *Dialogues*. Only he doesn't use a muscle car." Tanaka waved him on.

"You mean Philo wasn't a time-travelling muscle-car fan?" Phil winked. "So you wouldn't make it out of alignment, the timing off, the interior ragged, the body half Bondo-and-primer. That kind of car only appeals to a very select few, the wrench-turning crowd. And it would *only* appeal if it were a steal—something one might pick up from the junkyard."

"So God made an imperfect car. Why not? Better for those mechanics to work on, right? To make it better."

"You're missing the point, Tanaka. This isn't GM, or Chrysler, or some other cash-strapped company. It's God, Creator of time and space. Do you think His store of power is finite? I think not. So God did not have to economize in His creation. He should have been able to make His creatures, *us,* in the best possible way. I just don't agree with Leibniz that we live in the best of all possible worlds." Phil took a sip of his drink. "But then, Leibniz was trying desperately to prove that God exists."

"Phil, I dare say you are acting quite arrogantly here, presuming to understand the Almighty's reasons for His creation. Remember what He told Job? Do you know more than God? Were you there at the time of His creation? Do you know God's plans? This *is* the best of all possible worlds. A world with less evil would have less goodness. But you are also being very narrow-sighted. For this universe is only one among many universes. Sure, there might be evil in this itty-bitty universe of ours, but there is tremendous goodness in the rest of His creation and it far outweighs the evil here. Perhaps you will disagree? But then have you traveled outside of our little universe, or even outside of this meager little planet of ours? I see that you've gotten as far as Japan. . . ." He smiled, quite pleased with himself.

"No, I haven't traveled outside of our universe, though I might sell my soul to do so." Phil grinned. "But before you take me up on that offer—that I have a soul or that you're in the market for it—I need to address your proposition. It could be that we are not the chosen of God. It could be that we are part of some greater plan. I might accept that, since you are stating with some authority that we are not the only universe and not the only rational life. It still proves a previous point I made: at least so far as we're concerned, God's a dick."

"Again, I agree, but I think you need to back that up with a better argument. Currently, you have only suggested that God wants you humans to be better and to arrive there by your own power. Beyond that, your argument is still struggling."

"Struggling? Hmmm, it seems more like you are struggling to ignore the obvious. Maybe you are part of His grand plan to get me to become this better being. I'll play along, then. Let's consider two hypotheses. The first is that we humans aren't the ultimate design and the other is that God is playing with fire when He doesn't have to. Care to follow me, Neo? Or do you prefer Thomas Anderson?"

"I'm a demon, my favorite place is Hollywood. I will, however, have some difficulty in accepting that you are Morpheus, my teacher." Tanaka looked sideways at Phil.

"I'll be your teacher, all right, but first you have to follow along. So to begin, we humans are not the ultimate design. This should go quickly unless you want to be deliberately obtuse." Phil crossed his arms and then quickly dropped them to his side.

"I'll let that pass. Convince me, sensei," Tanaka said.

"If we humans are the subjects of God's experimental design, then we are not the end-all-be-all, the final product. We are merely some point along the way. All of our decisions, all of our mistakes, all of our learning, all of this exercise of our free will—we are not the benefactors of this earthly education. The most likely answer is that we are benefitting some future being. Take you demons, for example. Do you not enjoy torturing us humans? Is not your purpose to try to tempt us away from the Light, the Good, God, or whatever? Isn't your purpose, your goal, to test us? Indeed to test our resolve to do good?"

"Let's say that it is."

"Then what about this: Do *you* benefit from our improvement? To be specific, I'm not asking whether you benefit from those who fail, but from those who resist your temptations and become better beings?"

"Sure we do. We become cleverer. We've got to, right? We find other ways to woo and entice. We become more cunning, more devious. You can't resist forever. You are weak. We just need to find a way to exploit that weakness. So, indeed, we do become better beings."

"You speak with such frightening accuracy, Tanaka. But even in leading us to sin, you can do much good. A man kidnaps, rapes, tortures, and murders a young girl. The parents are devastated beyond belief. Their lives are crushed, changed, completely transformed. But they decide to start a foundation, write books, go on talk shows, and in the end they manage to prevent thousands of other girls from enduring a similar fate. Overall, they do more good than the evil done to their daughter. But their poor daughter— What about her? She is dead. She in no way benefits from the ensuing acts. She is forced to take an entirely different journey. She will never be the benefactor of all this good. And if you asked her, she'd be generous in saying that God is a dick."

Tanaka looked at Phil. "But as you said, the overall good is improved. You are working against yourself. And in any case, the girl *is* in a better place, or so it's been said. So she does benefit."

"I am *not* working against myself. Think about it. We humans are the experimental subjects in God's grand experiment. We will not enjoy the benefits. Indeed, we are obviously the result of some great experimental error. Systematic? Random? Outright blunder? Hell, I don't know. Someone—some other being— will enjoy the fruits of our suffering. The parameters will be adjusted, the experiment will be run again, and God will keep trying to get it all right. But just like that little girl—or you demons—we will look up at God and say 'you're a dick,' because it doesn't matter to the dead and discarded whether something good comes after them. They are still cast aside as so much mistaken clay and they're still *fucking dead.*"

Tanaka played with his glass, watching as the liquid began to boil then as the tumbler turned to slag and melted. The temperature in the room climbed to a sauna. "I don't think I like being put in the same group as mortals. Please make your second point before I burn your pleasant little bar to the ground."

Phil could well believe that the temperature had risen. He could sense it, though he had no idea how Tanaka pulled it off. It defied all logic and scientific principle—except when you included in that logic the fact that there was a demon in the room and apparently an increasingly angry and fiery one. *Well, if I'm going to die anyway, might as well be pissing off a demon and getting burned alive for my trouble.* He mulled over the words. When he died, was he going to burn in some lake of fire? Could he really stick with his logic in the face of an actual demon? He thought about Pascal's wager again.

"Phil, I believe you were going somewhere else with your 'God is a dick' argument. Or are you rethinking your position?" Tanaka chuckled. It was a dry, crackling sound, like coal in a paper bag.

Phil came back from his brooding. "So do we accept, at least provisionally, that God is a dick to those who end up on the wrong side of His grand experiment?"

"Again, I agree with you. Do go on." It was more of a command than a polite request.

"In that case, let's move onto my second point. I showed, in my previous example, that we are not likely the benefactors of this experiment. I would further add that not only are we not the benefactors but God doesn't even care much about His experimental subjects. There is no heavenly institutional review board overseeing His research. In the meantime, whatever horrible things befall us, it's not His problem because ultimately He has bigger goals—the greater good and all that."

"Go on."

"God has no concern for us. He has no concern for those who fail. In order for other beings to become better, most of us fail in droves. How is it that this loving God can so easily sacrifice us for the sole purpose of getting to a better 'something else'? Do we have to know the mind of God or travel to other universes in order to be able to transcend our limited understanding and know that in both the macro and the micro schemes of things, God is not a loving god, but a faker?" Phil finished his drink and threw the glass triumphantly into the fire. "He *says* that He loves us, but in reality He only loves *some* of us. The rest? We're just little steppingstones on which others tread on their path to greatness. We're like a young man helping to put out an oil-rig fire so that someone can have another"—the room began to spin as Phil looked at the ceiling and watched the smoke waft hither and yon—"another box of books."

With that, Phil collapsed, striking his head on the table. Tanaka walked up to him, brimstone footprints in his wake, and leaned over Phil's unconscious body.

"Well done. You managed to argue and drink yourself into unconsciousness. Sleep well and dream of smart women."

Tanaka gave a wink and then vanished.

Max found the cacophony in the bar dizzying. The smoke from the cigars, cigarettes, even the roasted meats, stung his eyes and throat.

He looked around, not really focusing on any one particular gathering or person. Something kept moving just out of his sight, something in his peripheral vision. Dozens of people relaxed in the bar—sitting at tables, standing by the pillars. They all had some sort of libation in their hands. A young man stood behind the counter serving drinks—if you could call his actions that. He seemed not to know where anything was, and he struggled to fill even the simplest of orders. Max reached behind the bar only to find the space where he kept the tea kettle empty.

As he scoured the bar for the kettle, he caught a glimpse of familiar cotton-white hair. The person passed behind a group of disaffected youth—looking a lot like *The Mod Squad*—and then disappeared into the crowd. Max spun around, causing a pretty young woman to nearly spill her drink.

"I'm sorry, miss." The woman looked at Max and smiled sweetly, trying to catch his eye, but he had already turned toward the kitchen to continue his search. Winding his way through the throng of people, he almost walked right into an older man dressed in dirty flannel and denim overalls. A look of disgust passed over the man's lined features. Max thought he looked a bit too much like Gideon. He ignored the man and made his way to the kitchen.

Shaking his head, Max walked to the cabinet and began searching. He heard the screen slide open.

"Hey, Phil, where did you put the teapot?" He took a cup out of the cabinet, shut the cabinet door and opened the drawer to find a spoon.

"Ah'm afraid I have no idea, son, where the teapot is, and ah'm not Phil. He's otherwise—engaged at the moment." His words were direct, despite his seemingly lackadaisical demeanor.

Max's blood froze at the voice's deep tone and familiar Southern cadence. Slowly, he turned around, his movements almost comically exaggerated. When his eyes locked on the mane of cotton-white hair and brown blazer, he dropped the cup. Shards of blue porcelain shattered on the *tatami* mat, little razors cutting the tops of Max's feet uncovered by the bands of his *zoris*.

"What a mess. Here, let me help you." The white-haired man began to approach Max, his hands extending toward the broken cup on the mat.

Before Max could stop himself his hand balled into a fist. All of the rage he felt the day that Nathan died erupted from within and ended in his fist crashing into the man's jaw. Max's eyes widened in horror as a loud crack sounded. The man's body slammed hard against the refrigerator door. Max stared at his still-clenched fist, now throbbing in pain.

Max's adversary chuckled as he righted himself. He straightened his blazer and flicked a dust mote from his collar. He smiled a serpent's grin.

"I do believe you have me at a disadvantage, boy. Least yer only packin' yer fist. What on earth possessed you to take a swing at me like that? Where have your manners gone?" The man's grin spread across his face, displaying a sinister joy.

"*My* manners? What about *your* manners? You cost me the last moments of someone very dear to me, with your judgmental preaching and useless moralizing."

"Did I now? I don't quite recollect it like that, but that'd be the way of things, right, boy?"

Max watched as the man pulled down on his shirt, straightening out the wrinkles and tucking the shirttails back into the waistband of his denim. Though the blazer wasn't identical, this was definitely the same man from Nathan's hospital room.

Max straightened his shoulders and stubbornly thrust out his jaw before speaking. "What on God's green earth did you hope to gain by doing what you did, talkin' so ugly? What was your point in making me so miserable—trying to bring me closer to God? How can you justify your behavior?" Max leaned forward just a bit, daring the man to challenge him.

"Remember the Duchess in *Alice in Wonderland*? 'Tut, tut, child! . . . Everything's got a moral if only you can find it.' You've heard the Lord works in mysterious ways, haven't ya, boy? Look at the path you're on now. Would ya be there, if not for what happened to Nathan?"

"What in the name of all that is holy are you spewing about, charlatan? I know you. Don't think I don't." Max pointed his finger at the man. "Path? I'm fully aware of how God works in my life so you need to stay the hell out of it." Max gave a cold stare as the man began to laugh.

"Boy, you need to get your priorities straight. That's *blasphemy* thinkin' you know the mind of God. Wouldn't ya say, *Deacon*? Or is that heresy? I tend to get them all mixed up."

Max stared coldly at the man, willing him to leave. It didn't work.

"In any case, my boy, I'm just a rock along your path. Sort of like that story about being stuck between Scylla and Charybdis. You made a choice—now stick with it."

"What are you blathering about now?" Max bent down and picked up the shards, trying to ignore the man's insinuations.

"That whole argument about being a homosexual and walking the path of righteousness by being celibate. We both know that's a load of hogwash. I know your secret, what you won't even tell those heretical friends of yours for fear they would tar-and-feather your lily-white ass and defrock you."

"What secret are you squawking about?"

"You could've told 'em what you really felt, right? All that logic and philosophical bullpucky you're always spoutin' just disguises what you really want to say, what is truly in that heart of yours."

"And what would that be?" Max gritted his teeth and made a tight fist.

"Oh, you know. How you don't really have the courage of your convictions. How you don't believe your own assertions about God accepting homosexuality, because if He did He would send you someone who loved you, who wanted you. All of that absurd, pathetic bunk. Like somehow you *deserve* to be given that person, like Adam was given Eve. Somebody especially for *you*. Who are you to think that God would provide someone for *you*? You have the nerve to call *me* a charlatan. Pot. Kettle. Son." The man smiled diabolically. His eyes were a vivid, verdant green, like transparent emeralds. He sniggered.

Doubts slithered their way into Max's soul and his face went white. He could hardly breathe. The man was right. For all of his apparent certainty, he still felt, deep down, that if God loved him, if homosexuality were really acceptable to God, he would not be alone, he would have someone in his life. Max thought about all of the sleepless nights, the despair, the pain of insecurity and indecision about his chosen calling that he'd felt over the past couple of years. All of his regrets, all of his second guesses, crashed down on him like a two-ton brick. His knees buckled. Tears spilled from his eyes at the thought of being shut out from God's love. All of the struggles he'd faced with his faith and his chosen path now weighed down upon him.

The decision to pursue the priesthood that led to the mother-of-all-arguments with his father, the hours of denial and study locked in his room as he pored over texts trying to understand God's will, the sleepless nights spent in loneliness, the conviction that he didn't deserve God's grace because he desired men—all this because he had felt compelled to become a man of God. Max shook his head trying to joggle the demons out, but Gideon's face flitted through his mind—sneering at him, mocking him, the word 'faggot' reverberating through his head like the ringing of a giant bell. It would be so easy to let go of all of this and go back to forgetting, floating high in euphoric denial. He hadn't had these doubts when he was using and he'd had plenty of company. No loneliness there.

Max reached for the counter as the man continued to laugh derisively. His hand came down on a shard of the broken teacup, which he had just placed on the counter. A blaze of pain traveled through his now bloodied hand and up his arm. A memory—just as sharp and jagged—burst through his consciousness: the last counseling session he facilitated where he'd met Tyler, a friend of one of his clients, and the six-hour conversation they'd had over pots of coffee. Max regretted having to cancel a subsequent coffee engagement to get on the plane.

The man finally stopped laughing.

Max's eyes narrowed. He reached for the olivewood cross that his mother had given him, which hung around his neck. Peace flooded him, vanquishing the uncertainty and hopelessness. He closed his eyes, refusing to look at the man.

"I know who you are and it's not going to work. Nice try—you almost had me for a second." Max grabbed a towel, wrapped it around his hand and walked confidently out of the kitchen door, not looking back. He moved into the bar to search for Michal and Phil. He wandered around the bar twice before he finally spotted Michal talking with some seven-something-foot-tall amphibious creature. He blinked and rubbed his eyes but the curious thing remained. Putting on his best Southern smile and turning up the charm, he clutched his cross, keeping a close eye on Michal and her odd companion.

Michal walked across the bar taking in the bizarre sights. It was obvious by now that the whole thing was a demonic manipulation, perhaps even a trap. Apparently, now that the jig was up, the demons weren't even trying to hide their true forms—although it was weird to see her former student selling weed to Descartes. Obviously Descartes needed something to help him write his *Meditations* and it wasn't really a surprise that he'd know the one guy who could get him the best smoke. She looked through the window at the pond. She caught sight of a shadowy figure, a giant sea serpent looking like Leviathan under the bluish disk of the moon. She focused her attention back on the bar. Over here was a four-headed dog having a genial chat with a red-skinned sphere adorned with spikes. Sitting next to the window was a Minotaur-like creature chatting with a drunken samurai and a woodcutter. And over there was a curvy succubus having a drink with some kind of glowing green ooze creature and a bandit from feudal Japan. The ooze kept falling in sizzling plops from the seat on which it was attempting to perch, while the bandit kept trying to win the succubus' complete attention. The succubus looked familiar to Michal. The smile and that luscious golden hair reminded her of Gretchen. In fact, the succubus looked a bit too much like Gretchen. She turned and blew Michal a kiss.

Before Michal could walk across the room to talk to her, she spotted what looked to be James sitting at a small table in the corner, wearing an olive-green woolen turtleneck sweater. He was reading what appeared to be his favorite leatherbound book, ever so carefully turning each page. Yep, that was definitely James and definitely his prized 1917 *Book of Enoch.* Occasionally he would pause, lift his head, remove his glasses and take a sip of his drink. After watching James with intense curiosity for several minutes, Michal chose to ignore the Gretchen-succubus—tempting as she was. She walked up to James, gaining confidence with every step.

"James, sweetheart. It's you! Let's go into Phil's office where we can have a bit of privacy." She motioned him to a closed door adjacent to the bar. "I've got words to speak with you." She grabbed hold of his arm, pulling at it with a sense of urgency. "Come on. Let's go."

James closed his book and smiled widely. "Oh, you want to *sex* with me?" He followed her into Phil's office. The office was stark, bare of any embellishments save for a little bonsai on a shelf and a picture of a much younger Michal, Max and Phil on the beach in Santa Barbara. James strutted in front of her to the cherrywood desk and casually lounged against its edge. He licked his fingers and smoothed back his hair. Michal shut the door behind them and leaned against it. Sizing him up and down, she finally shook her head in disbelief, "OK, now I *know* you're not James because you can't even articulate a sentence, you *idiot.* So who are you? *What* are you?"

"I'm James. Don't I look like James?"

"The last time I saw you, you were a toad."

He pushed his glasses up against the bridge of his nose and walked right up to her. Michal reached behind her and grabbed the door as if planning an escape. James leaned into her. "You often see things in a kooky way," he said just above a whisper and then smiled lasciviously.

"Kooky way? Did you just say 'kooky'? James doesn't even have that ridiculous word in his vocabulary."

James placed one hand firmly on the door to the left of Michal and the other to the right, boxing her in, and then he leaned in even more. "Let me kiss you."

"Will you turn into a prince?"

"Huh?"

"Never mind." Michal pushed James' chest and he backed off a few steps. She gave him a stern stare. "Look. You think you destroyed me by suggesting I have no credentials?"

"You don't. You're a fraud," he jeered.

"You know I've gone through all of this before and without your help. *Imposter syndrome.* Heard of it? I'm a fake. I'm a phony. But you know something? I'm not. And I don't need your validation. Perhaps you are a lousy projection of my insecurities. Or perhaps you are one of these demon-types I've encountered all-too-often and in heavy doses lately. Or maybe you've been sent by God to humble me. Well, *fuck you,* James Imposter. *You* are the real imposter. In the name of Jesus and by the power of His blood, I demand that you leave!"

Suddenly James turned into a little toad. Michal smiled victoriously and opened the door. James the toad hopped out of Phil's office and right into the mouth of the professor's cat.

The window was open at the small table where Max, Michal, and Phil finally gathered. They had struggled across the bar through a press of patrons welcoming them to "their" party. Phil had wondered just exactly that meant since the first time he'd heard it.

"Do you suppose they mean the party for them, or the party we'll soon be joining—maybe forever?" He looked at Michal. "You're experienced in this sort of thing. What's going on? I'm way out of my depth. . . ." What had been happening had finally sunk in. Phil's eyes glazed over and he sat transfixed, as if made of wax.

Michal stared zombie-like out the window at the garden. She had heard Phil speak, but his words were nothing but meaningless noises. The only thing that she could think of right now was that Grandma was in hell. James was in the belly of a cat, but that was just desserts.

"Michal— Michal—?" Max looked at her, waving his hand in front of her face. "Come back to us." He moved her around on the seat to face him. Seeing her blank expression, he spoke in a soothing voice. "We are here. We are real. Come back."

Michal didn't respond. She only hazily comprehended that Max was talking. She felt herself spiral downward into the darkness.

"We've got to get her out of here." Max turned to Phil and noticed that he too was unresponsive. He kept repeating the same question in a mechanical way:

"What do I know?—What do I know?—What do I—"

Max scanned the bar. Everyone seemed to be having a grand time. Then he looked down at the table. There was still that half-empty martini sitting there—the same one that he'd been eyeing since they sat down, left behind no doubt by an earlier guest. Max loved martinis and the thought of forgetting all that had transpired by drinking this magical elixir was all too tempting. His hand moved toward the inviting drink. But then he thought better of it.

He opened the *shōji* and ushered his two catatonic friends out to the garden. New partygoers were still arriving. "Is this where Gimon's bash is?" The voice, which had an enticing British lilt, came from a strikingly dapper gentleman who was walking arm-in-arm with another man. They were both impeccably tailored and looked like twins. But they obviously weren't, judging by their overly flirtatious conduct. The second man looked at Max and his two friends.

"Are they OK? They look knackered. Either that or mad as a bag of ferrets. Let us help you bring them back into the bar." He took out a silk handkerchief the shade of absinthe and mopped lovingly at Phil's sweating brow.

"They're OK, I'm just getting them some fresh air. Thank you for your offer." Max so wanted to join the twins. It would be so easy.

"Well, all right, but then do come in and join us for a chin-wag. My friend and I would like to buy you a drink. Do you like martinis?" The first man looked at Max, his teasing smile suggesting more than a drink and conversation.

"Thank you, I will." Max feigned politeness. His mind was focused back on his friends.

"Smashing! I'm peckish, and my friend here could murder a sandwich. We best go in before all the food goes manky. We'll look for you inside."

"Fan-bloody-tastic," Max said, playing along. He led Phil and Michal to a nearby bench. Several minutes passed as Max kept watch. Many things went through his head, not the least of which was the irony of praying that Phil—of all people—would be granted God-given peace and strength. He repeated John 14:27: *"Peace I leave with you. My peace I give you. I do not give to you as the world gives. Do not let your hearts be troubled and do not be afraid."*

At the sound of Max's soothing voice, Phil came out of his trance-like state and looked at Michal. He extended a quivering hand toward her.

"Michal, Michal. Are you—?"

Michal felt the warmth of Phil's voice. She heard the words. They made sense. Images of Cyclops picking at her brain like an hors d'oeuvre quickly vanished from her mind.

"Phil, Max—I—you guys wouldn't believe what I experienced—especially you, Phil." She looked at Phil and noted the absence of his usual condescension. "Or maybe you would—" Suddenly she realized that they *all* had shared the experience. "So it wasn't just me then. . . ."

Max touched her shoulder again. "Nope, not this time, darlin'. This time I'm pretty sure that Phil and I both got a double-dose of your—"

Phil cut in: "This is not normal. We all suspected that something was—*amiss,* but this is well beyond amiss. I know what *I* saw. What did you two see?"

For the next several minutes they each related their encounters. At first they considered the possibility that the extremely eerie—even terrifying—situation in the bar was some elaborate magic trick cooked up by who-knows-who, one which altered their perceptions of reality in the most fantastical of ways. But no one was willing to say that their friends' tales were too strange to believe. It would have been completely disingenuous.

"So we've all had encounters that have shaken our faith to its very foundation. —Yes, Phil, *our faith.* Even you—" Max came across as matter-of-fact and not the least bit patronizing. "The question we all need to ask ourselves is—did it work?"

Phil spoke first. "I'm worried about the obviously supernatural party going on. Who is it for?"

"So *now* you're willing to believe?" Michal tried to wrap her head around Phil actually talking about demons and the supernatural. She reached out and pinched him.

"Reality check, Michal?" He smiled.

"Had to see. Everything else was so real, but the thought of you entertaining the supernatural was just a bit too much."

Max laughed. "Considering all we've seen, Phil's willingness to contemplate the supernatural seems pretty *rational.*" He punched Phil's shoulder affectionately.

Phil looked at his two friends. "I'm so happy that I can be a shimmer of amusement in this storm of insanity. It just so happens that I've never had a problem with the supernatural. It's just that I've never had any empirically verifiable data to confirm it—until now evidently. God knows, I've tried. *'God knows.'* —I guess I might have to rethink that phrase."

Michal moved to hug Phil, gathering in Max as well. "I have hope for you, Phil."

"Well, let's not fit me for a halo or horns just yet. What are we going to do about"—he waved at the crowded bar—"about that?"

Max stood up, keeping his arms on his friends. "*Count it all joy when ye fall into divers temptations.*" He let the words hang in the air.

"Really, Max, hitting me when I'm down? That's just not fair." Phil tried to sound sarcastic.

"No, Phil, he's right. *Count it all joy.* Obviously we're being tested. You're going to die and yet we're *all* being tested. Where will *you* spend eternity?"

"Wait a minute—whoa, whoa, hold your horses. *Tested? Last Temptation of Christ* kind of tested?" Phil smiled. "Am I now Christ? Or maybe Willem Dafoe? I like the thought, I have to admit, but—"

"No, Phil, you ass, but thank you so much for bringing us back to reality. You can't be Christ so put that thought away, you egomaniac. —Or Willem Dafoe for that matter, though you do share that same thin-lipped smile." Max smiled. "But Michal may be onto something here. All of us are having our faith tested." He chewed over the thought.

"Let's just pretend that I accept what you're saying—for the sake of argument. Shouldn't we just *leave?* The gate is right over there." Phil pointed at the gate that led out to the parking lot and his horribly maintained road. "I'm sure we could hotwire one of those ghost-cars."

"No, Phil, as scary as it seems, we are being tested, and we should man up and take this challenge." Michal flexed her little muscles as she was speaking and then looked at Phil confidently. "Thanks to the steady calm of our friend, here"—she motioned to Max—"it seems that you and I passed. —Well, at least the initial test."

"Hey, I didn't do it on my own. I kept clinging to our friendship. That kept me centered. Oh, and a jagged piece of porcelain in my hand."

"So let's leave then. We passed. Game over. In any case *I'm awful tired now, boss. Dog tired.*" Phil's voice tried to boom like John Coffey's as he kept eyeing the gate.

"This is not anything like that. . . . No, I still have too many questions. Why? How? You of all people—the science-minded guy—should appreciate that, Phil," Max playfully jabbed him.

"He's right. There are too many unanswered questions. Besides, I've got something that will work," Michal said.

Phil looked at his friends, eyes determined, jaw resolute. "Then we're decided. Let's go back in and find out. I'm sure there's more in store for us." He held out his arm for Michal. She took it and moved next to him.

"Once more unto the breach, dear friends." Michal took hold of Max's arm. Our three friends—now arm-in-arm—seemed to Michal like Dorothy, the Scarecrow, and the Cowardly Lion getting ready to confront the All-Powerful Wizard. She had to chuckle at the thought.

They stood there for a moment—smiling at each other, drumming up confidence. Phil finally broke the mood:

"If anyone starts singing *Kumbaya*, I'm heading for the gate."

Max and Michal laughed and our three friends walked back into the bar.

Philosophical discourse tends to fall into two types. The first type most people find approachable and tends toward great bar conversations. This includes, but is not limited to, how celebrities—say Brad Pitt and Angelina Jolie—might deal with the problem of world hunger. It is usually not anything substantive, and handy for impressing a potential companion, be it a one-night-stand or otherwise. In the grand scheme of things, it tends to be looked upon as more cerebral than, say, comparative analyses of sports performances or inquiry into the veracity of reality shows.

Then there's the second kind—the kind that makes most people run quickly and politely away. This variety can most often be found in upper-level philosophy classes or coffee houses with a preponderance of turtlenecks and tweed jackets. These discussions often sound—at least to the untrained ear—more like a string of words put randomly together in garbled fashion. You might know many of the words, but somehow they aren't arranged in quite the way to which you're accustomed. Topics such as whether the problem of mind/body dualism is indeed resolved by John Searle's assertion that the mind is merely a part of the body and thus is no more problematic than the banal proposition that micro- and macroeconomics both describe the same system. Or perhaps Davidson's postulation concerning strict laws, that for any causal relationship between events E1 and E2, there must be a hypothetical law of the form (C1 & D1) that directly implies D2, where C1 states a set of standing conditions and D1 is a description of E1. . . .

Generally, this is the moment in the conversation when the average person suddenly becomes aware of temporal passage and realizes that they need to attend to their domesticated feline's dietary needs—more commonly expressed as "Oh, look at the time! I just forgot that I left the cat out and I need to feed her." It is worth noting that when our three friends re-entered the bar, the melodious song of the nightingale still trilling in their heads, the patrons seemed to be engaged in conversations entirely of the second sort, even though few were wearing turtlenecks or tweed jackets. Most strikingly, nobody seemed to be excusing themselves to take care of their cat. Daylight was just breaking and yet the party was still in full swing. Time stretched out like pulled taffy.

Something drew Max back outside. Ordinarily he wouldn't think to leave his friends—especially after all that they had gone through—but he just wasn't his usual self. Transfixed, he walked out to the koi pond.

He looked up at the sky. There was still the faintest hint of the moon. The water was cold and clear. Max sat on the edge of a large flat rock that extended into the pond by several feet, water up past his ankles. Koi, with vibrant orange and ghostly white scales, darted between and under his feet—oblivious and untroubled. A soft fog enveloped the trees, making the pine needles appear shrouded in thin silk.

A muffled plop sounded as he tossed a rock into the water. He marveled at the little waves created by that one tiny disturbance. He knew that if he tossed another rock, it would impact the first set of waves but not stop them, just effect a change until they finally cancelled each other out. That reminded him of Phil and Michal. Sometimes he felt like the rock and other times he felt like the point where the waves would meet.

Strange things happened last night.

"What strange things, Max?" The voice behind him was familiar and instantly brought a smile to Max's face. He turned his head. Rory O'Connor, his roommate from seminary, looked down at him with an infectious smile. Max stood up.

"What?" Confusion set in as Max looked at his surroundings: still in the garden, still foggy, still first light.

"I asked you, what strange things happened last night? Do you need to repent something?" Rory's smile turned into a leer. He wiggled his eyebrows up and down. His trademark three-day scruff darkened his face, making the white of his teeth stand out. His eyes sparkled.

"What are you doing here?" Max looked around again, but his eyes were drawn back to Rory as he sat back down on the flat rock. Rory pulled off his shiny black shoes, followed by his black-and-white checkered socks.

"You're asleep now, idiot. You lay down on the rock and closed your heavy eyes. You stayed up all night. You're not as young as you used to be, you know." Rory laughed as he dunked his feet into the water. "These don't bite, do they?" He eyed the koi suspiciously before looking back at Max.

"They don't bite, and I'm well aware that I'm not as young as I used to be. So I'm dreaming?"

"Looks like you need to work a few things out. Talk to a fellow man of the cloth." Rory tapped the white collar at his throat, causing his gold-and-emerald shamrock pin to strike the fabric of his black lapel. "It might put things into perspective." Rory smiled wider, his eyes crinkling at the corners.

"It's damn good to see you, Rory. Are you still in the Dominican Republic?"

"So far as you know." Rory laughed. "What's so strange?"

"If what we experienced was real, then we were all being tempted by demons. But it could also have been a shared hallucination brought about by bad food, or at least in my case, bad tea." Max kicked the water, causing the koi to swim away.

"What do *you* think it was?" Rory began arranging little pebbles in rows along the edge of the large flat rock on which he and Max were sitting.

"I'm not sure. I know I'd like to *think* it was a hallucination." Max looked at the distant trees, which he could just make out through the fog.

"Why? Wouldn't the reality of demons bolster our belief in God?" Rory continued to add pebbles to his rows, methodically arranging them in three rows of six pebbles each.

"I don't need demons to prove to me that God exists—I know He does. I have faith in His existence and in His grace. You know I do." Rory added the last pebble and turned toward Max.

"Sure, but wouldn't it be nice to have proof?"

"Irrelevant, Rory. I made the choice to believe in Him, trust in His mercy and guidance. Didn't you?"

"Of course. But I can't help but think that having a demon appear before my very eyes might just make me feel a bit more justified."

"I don't feel any different one way or the other. I just worry about Michal and Phil. I've felt God's presence in my life walking with me since I left rehab. No demons, no angels, just His ever-present peace."

"Why worry about them? Michal's been talking about demons for years."

"If that's true, shouldn't I have felt something? Tried to help her? I never put much stock in it *really* being demons, you know? I never really believed any of that bunk. Just her subconscious trying to get her to choose one path over another." Max toed a few of the larger rocks under the water.

"Ah, but God already chose for her, Max. God chooses for all of us. He sets us on His path and we follow His footsteps." Rory picked up a pebble from one of the rows and tossed it into the water.

"Hogwash, Rory. We aren't going to get into this again, are we?" Max's eyebrows drew together in a scowl.

"Seems appropriate, don't you think?" Rory threw another pebble into the water.

"I've already been over this with Phil and Michal. I don't subscribe to all that determinism or predestination bunk. The most important and sacred gift God gave us is free will. We all have to choose our path. 'Enter the narrow gate, for wide is the gate and broad is the road that leads to destruction, and many enter.' Demons or no demons, it's as simple as that," Max said and crossed his arms.

"I don't know, Max. Do you think you *really* choose? You might *think* that you are doing the choosing when you claim to choose God. But we do what God willed beforehand. Says so in His Word." Rory waggled his finger at Max, admonishing him. He threw another pebble into the water.

"No, just the opposite. By making my own choices I do exactly what God wants. I follow in the footsteps of all of His children who find their way to Him of their own volition, to be in His presence, accept His peace and guidance, use Him as our sounding board, give Him our trials, our problems, and even our anger, if need be." Max smiled. Rory's eyes went wide.

"Anger? So now you think you can yell at God? How is that reverent?"

"Reverent? Well, maybe not reverent. But it's what He's offering. He, more than anyone, can handle our fears, anger, doubt, grief, dissatisfaction, questioning. . . . Hell, we can even give Him a tongue-lashing with shaking fist." Max watched as Rory threw in another pebble. As if by magic, the number of pebbles in each row remained the same. *No matter, magic can happen in dreams.* The ripples in the water made it difficult to see the koi. They had likely scattered anyway.

"Whoa, criticize God? Who are we to criticize Him? He's perfect."

"We're His creation, His children. Look at Psalms 62:8, 'Trust in Him at all times . . . pour out your hearts to Him, for God is our refuge.' And remember poor Job? He got really pissed at God but God didn't punish him for it. Job's rant to God was purgative. It was necessary for Job to get all of that suffering off his chest."

"So you think it's OK to give God a piece of your mind?" Rory continued to toss pebbles.

"Sure. Who do you think gave me that mind in the first place? God is our Father, and like any father, He knows that we, His children, are going to get angry. But like any loving father, He'll be there to help us pick up the pieces. If we call on Him we will never be alone. He'll give us a big heavenly hug. But we don't just follow blindly. We actively choose Him at each step along the path."

"That's the story you're going to stick to, huh, Deacon?"

"It's not a story, it's the truth." Max stood up.

Rory stood up and kicked the pebbles into the pond in one fell swoop. The water remained still. Not a ripple to be seen.

Max stared at the pond, then looked at his friend, watching Rory's lips as he spoke.

"Well, I tried to set you straight, Max. It's always the ones from rehab. . . ."

A sound coming from the bar drew Max's attention. When he looked back, Rory was gone. Floating in the pond were dozens of paper pages. He peered into the water and saw that they were written in either Hebrew or Greek: pages from all sixty-six books of the Bible. As the ink began to smear on the pages, Max heard Phil call his name from the door. He looked at his friend and then at the glassy water of the pond. One page remained unsmeared as if encased in glass. Ecclesiastes 3:1: "*To everything there is a season, and a time to every purpose under the heaven.*"

Max shook his head. *Was this a dream? Was everything a dream? Even last night? But then where had these pages come from?* Max knelt on the flat rock and stared at the Ecclesiastes. *Why this passage? 'To everything there is a season.' There is a reason, a purpose, for everything—even for the strange events of last night.*

"Max, come on!" He looked at Phil and then at the water, but the pages were gone. The Byrds' song *Turn, Turn, Turn* played in his head as he thought about trying to fish for Ecclesiastes in the now-murky water. He thought about what the oracle had told Neo: "As soon as you step outside, you'll start feeling better. You'll remember you don't believe in any of this fate crap. You're in control of your own life, remember?"

"Free will," Max whispered to himself but loud enough for the koi to hear. "I believe. I choose to believe. I walk this path of my own free will. . . ." Max looked up to see Phil and Michal standing by the water's edge, curious looks on their faces.

"Come on, Max. No more wandering off. . . . There might be more surprises. Strength in numbers, y'know?"

EIGHTEEN

Blond! You know what you are? Just a dirty Son-of-a-Bitch.
TUCO, *THE GOOD, THE BAD, AND THE UGLY*

Reunited, our three friends returned to the bar. The fog had lifted and sunlight filtered through the pine trees, casting shadows all around the courtyard. When they walked through the door, Phil noted the relative lack of activity. Some patrons were moving sluggishly about, feeling the effects of the previous night's festivities. Others rested their heads on the tables, trying to sleep off their Bacchanalia. Phil could see Wittgenstein dozing next to Socrates, the latter's arm draped over Wittgenstein's chest. Michal saw Sartre and Beauvoir snuggling up on a bench, and Max, of course, observed the unlikely trio of C.S. Lewis, Pope Francis and Oscar Wilde, asleep in a huddle against the wall. An oil-rig worker, flesh charred and crisped, busied himself by cleaning off tables, while an over-sized toad licked out the dregs of some rather large beer steins.

"We're not in Kansas anymore, Toto," Max said.

"At least they're not challenging us anymore," Phil began. "And besides I'm not Toto, I'm the Cowardly Lion. I was the one who wanted to leave." He winked at Michal. "I guess that makes you Dorothy—sorry, apparently this isn't a contemporary tale."

"We're not challenging you anymore? —No, I think you've just gotten past the first round. It's now time for the showdown." A voice, dark and powerful, emanated from the other side of the bar. The sunlight, shining through the door behind them, stretched across the floor to stop right at the stranger's feet. Ennio Morricone's music was playing in the background.

A pair of feet in *geta* advanced into the light, making a scraping sound. The stranger took off his *kabuto* and shook it till it resembled a wide-brimmed cowboy hat.

"If your goal is to challenge our sense of reality, then mission accomplished," Michal said. She couldn't help but laugh.

"This is no laughing matter, mortals." Smoldering red eyes burned beneath the brim of the hat. They were facing The Man with No Name. A shot glass fell off one of the tables. It rolled across the floor, coming to a stop between our three friends and the poncho-wearing man who stood before them. He strode forward, the spurs on his *geta*-turned-fancy-cowboy-boots jingling with every step. He stopped and leaned against a barstool.

"Please, theatrics aside, come join me. Gimon seems to have failed in his task. I am delighted to inform you that he is sitting in a cauldron of boiling tar as we speak. Given his epic failure, the assignment was escalated to upper management." He produced a dusty bottle of amber liquid, brushed it off and placed it on the bar. "My name is Azazel. You may have heard of me."

"Oooo-K." Phil turned and looked at his companions. "Come what may?"

Michal looked at the stranger now sitting at the barstool. "Did he just say Azazel, like the Book-of-Enoch Azazel?"

"Yep, I think he did." Max shook his head. "Well, let's not keep our destiny waiting." He stepped forward, encouraging his friends to follow.

They approached Azazel. A few tense moments passed. Azazel finally opened the bottle and poured them each a drink in upturned shot glasses. He ignored Max's protesting hand and poured one for him anyway.

"I'll start this show as I believe introductions are in order. I know all of you *intimately*, one might say, as I have watched your travails, your failures and your so-called triumphs in your pitifully short lives. You have all read of me, but I'll tell you anyway." His voice was strangely peaceful and alluring. "I am Azazel. I gave man the glorious art of war, metals from the earth, adornments for the body, tricks for beautifying the eyelids—but I think we all know that I'm into much, much more than eyelids...." He looked salaciously at all three, not discriminating in his lust. "All measure of evil, corruption and seduction issue from my breath. I'm the King of Sinful Sots."

His words slammed into them like a big surfer wave, yet caressed them like a tender lover.

"Your life's accomplishments pale in significance compared to what I have achieved over many millennia, so I can appreciate that you may feel more than a little overwhelmed. Before we begin, I offer one chance for you to denounce your beliefs and I will be less harsh. But tax me"—his eyes flared and our three friends could hear the screams of the damned—"and I will make sure that your eternal torment rivals that of Pope Boniface VIII who occupies a very special place in hell—and one I make a habit of visiting...." He paused to let the impact of his words sink in. "Now would anyone like to take me up on my offer?"

Michal stood up. Facing Azazel, she pointed an accusing, confident, seemingly powerful finger directly at him. "You are an abomination and you have no power over me. In the name of Jesus Christ, our Lord and Savior, and by the power of His blood, I command you to LEAVE." She smiled smugly.

Azazel's eyes went wide. He covered his face with his hands. He began to wail. The sound of teeth, grinding uncontrollably, echoed throughout the bar. Suddenly he threw up his arms, sending his hat flying. His face was a contorted mass, roiling like molten metal. The fire in his eyes went cold and his head suddenly dropped down to his chest. His entire body wracked with spasms. Michal stood triumphantly before him. Even Phil was speechless.

Azazel continued to wail but something was off. His wails sounded different now—far more sinister. His cries of pain turned to fiendish laughter as he lifted his head. The flaming red eyes returned and stared Michal down to the floor. Now it was her turn to feel fear—only she was pretty certain that it wouldn't turn to laughter. She watched with horror as he knelt to pick up his hat and dust it off. Placing it back on his head, he walked up to Michal.

"That isn't going to work any more for you, young miss. I got permission to test you and that can't happen if you keep cheating." He smiled. "Cheating is my domain. Now"—he held the stool for her—"have a seat. We are going to have a discussion about your opinion of Jesus Christ, whom you so boldly invoked."

Michal cautiously sat down, confusion and fear playing across her face. Azazel's presence made no sense.

Max leaned over and held her shoulders, speaking loudly enough for Azazel to hear. "Don't worry, Michal. He may be all that, but Leviticus says he's also the goat of departure—you know, the scapegoat that the priest casts into the wilderness, Michal." He repeated her name, trying to restore her confidence.

"You would bring that up, sissy boy," Azazel shot at Max. "Nobody wants to hear your opinion."

"Hey." Max made noises of feigned insult. "Sticks and stones may break my bones. . . ." He smirked and pulled a speechless Michal closer to him.

Michal responded to Max in a little voice, eyebrows drawn together in thought. "It didn't work. I don't understand. Why didn't it work—?"

"Your superpowers won't work with me, young miss, so you'd better come up with a back-up plan and quick."

"Count it all joy, Michal," Max said.

"Look, you're impressive," Phil said, "but I can't see you coming at us with anything more than what your failed underlings attempted. So let's hear it Lord of Lies, of Filth, of Putrescence. . . . BOOOO!"

"Brave words coming from a man who has been told by the science he loves so dearly that he is dying—and without your eternal affairs in order. Tsk. Tsk." Azazel shook his head. "Let's deal with you first. Your argument should be the easiest to refute."

"My affairs are in order. My two most important affairs are right here with me." He smiled at Max and Michal.

"So you say." Azazel eyed Michal and Max before returning to Phil. "Well, don't go shouting down Saint Peter when he won't let you in." He snickered.

"Oh, don't you worry. I'll be showing him my middle finger. Anyway, I know what I believe. It doesn't matter whether there is an afterlife that involves you and Yahweh and all of His angels and demons. I figure that there are so many loopholes in all of the translations that I can argue my way out of anything." Phil raised his glass of whiskey. "To an eternity of argument. Hell for some but quite an appealing proposition for me." He held his glass suspended in the air waiting for Azazel to join him. "I've been waiting to enjoy this whiskey for quite some time."

Azazel raised his glass. "To your health—or lack thereof."

Phil went to sip the whiskey. The usual slight notes of oak and vanilla were altogether absent, drowned out by the not-at-all-subtle vapors of turpentine and rubbing alcohol. Forging ahead, he took a sip. The taste was toxic. He swished the burning liquid around in his mouth, then worked it down through repeated swallows. His face flushed.

Azazel shook his head. "You're a stubborn one." He looked at Michal. "He's looking a bit g-r-e-e-e-n around the gills, isn't he?" He stretched the vowels in 'green,' then doubled up in laughter.

Phil held up his finger as he continued to swallow the vile drink. Michal looked at Phil and then at Azazel. "You have no idea how stubborn. . . ."

Phil finally got most of the liquid down. He knew that he would regret it eventually.

"So, Phil, it seems that you were wrong in your choice of liquor. Something so simple and yet you got that wrong. Let me remind you of your words earlier: What if you're wrong about everything else? What if your ever-so-scrupulous analysis is missing some vital details and you turn out to be wrong about the afterlife? The soul? Can your arrogance pull you through?" Azazel's words cut at Phil's confidence.

"Azazel, are you suggesting that I'm not actually an empiricist, that I don't actually believe in my credo?"

"You have indeed stated my position. You are *not* an empiricist, Phil. You don't act on your beliefs as if they were true. You act on your beliefs as if they were only sometimes true, which according to your own assessment makes them false. You are a hypocrite and a liar."

Azazel's words crashed into Phil's skull. What right do I have to pass judgment on anyone else with my exacting logic when I can't even follow it myself? What does that make me? —It's a simple thing, really. All I would have to do is admit that I believed in one thing but acted in another way altogether. Simple. As simple as saying "I'm going to die," or "I have cancer," or "I'm a hypocr—"

Phil could feel his liar's heart pounding in his miserable useless chest. Far away, a boy who died because Phil couldn't compromise yelled at him in a deafening pitch, cheered on by a chorus of roughnecks.

Max and Michal moved forward as Phil began to sway.

Azazel cast a glance in their direction. "I wouldn't if I were you. Just think how he would feel if you helped him at this point. Even at the precipice he would reject your help, wouldn't he?"

It doesn't matter. I'm a fraud. I killed those men. . . . And I treated Max like a little boy. I hired someone else to watch after him. I wouldn't even do it myself. What kind of friend am I?

Phil heard Max screaming: "You are a terrible friend! —Humanist? You're not even human!" Phil looked over at Max, whose hands were held out accusingly, reaching for his throat.

His thoughts sent him further into the abyss. He thought of Italy, of Santa Barbara and that fateful Monday with Michal. *I could have had a life with Michal, but my hurt pride wouldn't let go of the fact that she excluded me. I gave her freedom to choose, but I wanted to be a part of her decisions. Did I want to be the leading part?* Phil imagined coming home to the same woman every day—a woman he could love, a woman he never had to cajole, purchase or con to be with him. He looked at Michal. She was pointing an angry finger in his direction.

Azazel smiled triumphantly, "Ah, the perks of this job!" He gave a shriek and laughed.

Max and Michal moved to prop Phil up.

Phil considered his life and his choices. Choices. Choices. Choices. The word played again and again, like a scratched CD. He thought of CDs, and vinyls, and zoetropes, and—CHOICES.

He had made choices. Were they his choices? Who knew? But he believed they were. He thought about ten coins in his pocket, barns that weren't there, missing shades of blue. All manner of other perceptual questions wandered around his mind like diaphanous pink elephants. He shooed them away, leaving only the word 'CHOICES.' He reached for the edge of the counter only to find his friends' hands waiting patiently.

He smiled at Max and Michal. "Choices. You assholes are my choices."

"Damn straight we're your choices, but don't forget who's the real asshole." Max smiled.

"We're your asshole choices, Phil. And we think they're pretty good choices." Michal held Phil's gaze for several moments.

Azazel stomped like a boy who wasn't getting his way. "But you're a fraud now, Phil. You're a fake. You'd lose an argument with yourself. You are the worst of what you envision in people. All your words are suspect now. Why not tell me that the moon is made of Gruyere? —It might be. I won't believe you anyway."

"Who cares? Guess what, Azazel? I don't have all of the answers. I never claimed to." Phil stood a bit taller. "I don't know what it's like to be a bat so I can't really discuss the truth of that, either. But I can hang upside down on a monkey bar and get an approximation. Without you and your entourage here, I, at least, wouldn't have any proof of the supernatural. Now that you're here, I've got a reason to believe. But guess what, oh demonic one?" Phil picked up his glass and poured a tall drink. "I don't care. . . . I'll keep arguing. I'll keep believing what I believe because I think it's right, just like my friends here think their beliefs are right. . . . They could be wrong. I could be wrong. But it doesn't matter. We'll keep enjoying each other in this life, because right now this is all we've got." He held up his glass in toast. "It's better to be damned to hell and have integrity than to be a fake with fire insurance." He swirled the liquor in his glass—"I believe this is yours"—and threw it at the demon.

"Fine, have it your way," Azazel said, glaring at Phil. "I've already claimed your soul so I'll just bide my time. You'll be dying soon enough, but you"—he turned to Max—"would be a much tastier treat."

Max turned his head, looked out the window toward the pond and then smiled at his friends. He held Michal's hand and put the other on Phil's shoulder. "As these friends are my witnesses, I lower my head before You, my Father, and confess that too often I have forgotten that I am Yours. Sometimes I carry on in my life as if there is no God and I fall short of being a credible witness to You. For these and other shortcomings, I ask Your forgiveness and I ask for Your strength. Give me a clear mind and an open heart so that I may remember the things I have learned from Your grace. Remind me—as You have always done when I've listened—to be the person You would have me be, regardless of what I am doing, or who"— Max paused and glanced at the demon—"or WHAT—I am with. Hold me close to You and continue to build my relationship with You, and with those whom You have given me—my greatest friends and mirrors on earth. Amen." Max looked Azazel squarely in the eyes and leaned forward just a bit. "OK, give me your best shot. It won't be any worse than what I've put myself through already."

"That was sweet—touching, really. Do you feel energized, boy?" Azazel raised an eyebrow and leaned back. "Don't bother answering, I know you do. Interesting, too, because you don't really need God to accomplish your—what is it you say nowadays?—ah, 'power-up' in the face of your foe."

"Don't they make demons smarter? That wasn't for *me* to power up. According to a few friends in the exorcism business, it's always wise to confess one's sins and ask for forgiveness before taking on a demon. That being said—" Max stepped forward and put up his fists, boxing style. Then he smiled and extended his left hand forward, palm up, and gestured for the demon to "come get some."

"So it's a fight you want? Let's establish some ground rules, then. We know who and what I am, but who and what are you, Max?"

"Surely you can do better than a bit of soul-searching, demon," Max said, stiff-necked.

"Humor me. I've got a simple question for you. What do you believe? In simple Sunday-school terms so we don't get all lost in the details."

"No one has put it more eloquently than the Nicene Fathers. I'm sure you know their creed but I'll repeat it for you in keeping with the Sunday-school reference. I believe in one God, the Father Almighty, Maker of heaven and earth, and of all things visible and invisible. And in one Lord Jesus Christ, the only begotten Son of God, begotten of the Father before all worlds. God of God, Light of Light, very God of very God. Begotten, not made, being of one substance with the Father, by whom all things were made."

"Well stated. It is rewarding to see that the church continues to brainwash—errr—*teach* their followers well. So you believe in God, then?"

"Of course I do. Just what are you getting at?"

"And where exactly do you get your image of God?" Azazel pointed at Max's Bible, which was sitting atop the counter.

"Quite a few places actually, including all those times people cite mysterious ways. Considering that I think God is in all things—even you—my image of God is pretty expansive. I do not try to put God in a box." Max's right eyebrow shot up, the same expression he wore when arguing with Phil.

"You dodge well. I can see why Phil enjoys your company. Since you're avoiding the obvious answer, I'll lead you there. Do you believe in Shiva, six-armed or otherwise?"

"No, I don't."

"Do you believe in Zeus—you know, the guy with the lightning bolts and star of recent major motion pictures?"

"No."

"Odin, maybe?"

"No."

"How about the Flying Spaghetti Monster? Are you and Phil brothers in the fold?"

"You're getting tedious."

"The great juju of the mountain top—?"

"Enough!"

"Oh wait, I get it—you must believe in Gaia, the Mother Earth. She's very popular with people these days, especially those of alternate persuasion."

"No, Azazel, I don't. Do I need to recite the Creed again?"

"No, not at all. I'm just making a point. You believe in the God of the Bible. The book that has been edited and redacted, translated and mistranslated, over and over again, over many centuries, often by men with political agendas, certainly not all of them divinely inspired. —I'm sounding like your friend over there." He motioned to Michal with batting eyes. "And still you believe in the Father-figure, the Son coming down and dying on a tree. Or even the brown-haired, blue-eyed Jesus from your picture Bible?" Azazel paused, waiting for Max to respond. As soon as Max opened his mouth, Azazel cut him off, "So at the very least, the authority of the Bible is suspect. I'm sure you must be able to agree with that. Didn't I hear you saying something earlier about books that ended up on the cutting-room floor?"

"Yes, I believe in the Bible," Max said.

"That was easy. So your foundation in the Bible is suspect. What about your teachers?"

"Like my Bible teachers? Seminary? I believe that God delivered His message through those people, yes. I believe He worked through them to bring me the knowledge and wisdom that He wanted to impart." Max tilted his head. "Just what are you getting at?"

Azazel smiled the oily smile with which Max was growing increasingly bored. "I think you get my point quite well. You believe that the messages you are getting are from God, from people who glean bits of truth from that flawed book."

"I believe that God uses people to deliver His message and that in spite of man's imperfections the message gets through."

"But what if—and this is just hypothetical—what if that message didn't come from God?" Azazel paced around the bar. "In war, it's called misinformation or counter-espionage. You plant little messages to get the enemy to think that they are getting the truth, but in fact they aren't. What if I could show you, definitively, that at least one of your great teachers wasn't from God at all?"

"That wouldn't be possible. It would just be another one of your damn tricks."

"I'm only giving you what you already suspect." He pointed behind Max's shoulder. Max could hear the slow measured walk of someone approaching from behind. He turned as he heard a familiar voice.

"Ah, Maxwell. You always were one of my best students." Father Manganiello walked up to Max, palms raised. Max stood frozen, eyes wide, mouth slack.

Father M stood straight and tall next to the bar. He wore his usual priestly black garb and white collar as if he were going out to visit the sick and the shut-in. Uncharacteristically, however, he wore a green stole—one that he might wear to deliver last rites in a hospital or give communion at mass. Max looked around for someone who was about to die. His heart sunk when he turned to Phil.

"Oh, Max, you look disappointed, surprised even. Could it be that you thought I had messages from God?" Father M asked with a sickening smile.

"This is obviously some trick of yours, Azazel. Father M is a good man, a godly man." Max stared into the face of his mentor. Father M smiled back with hell-fire in his eyes.

"No, Max, it's me, Father M. I remember our first meeting at rehab. Oh, you were such a mess then. Do you remember your ordination just weeks ago? I do. One to remember. A really nice ceremony except, of course, for that interruption by—what was his name—?" Father M tapped his chin and stared off into space.

"Gideon," Max answered dryly.

"Yes, Gideon. Some of my best work, I should say. Just enough to get the congregation to not only accept a fag but to defend and embrace him. Not bad, indeed," Father M gloated.

Max imagined the people in his life—all the leaders he had counted on for spiritual guidance. Could it be possible that some of them were influenced by demons? Gideon was an obvious choice. Any of the ass-hats who killed Jayden could have been under demonic influence. Or the politicians who want to deny gays equal rights. But Father M? That was impossible.

"It's possible, Max. It's the truth. Servant of Azazel for lo! these many years." Father M winked at Max.

Michal moved forward to hold Max, but Phil held her back.

"He's got this. He doesn't need our help just yet."

"How many other influences from your so-called God and His so-called Word do you think were also demonic? Look around this room. Some might even be your close friends." Father M gave a little laugh at the thought.

Max smiled at Phil. Could Phil be demonic, too? It seemed even more impossible than Father M's being a demon, but doubt had started to worm its way into his thoughts.

"So you're noticing your friend—that he's wearing green too? Have you noticed a pattern? We tend to be quite fond of green."

"But he's not even wearing green. And besides, Devil, sometimes green is just green."

"My bad. I've always been color-blind."

"So, what are you getting at, Fath—demon?"

"Quite simply this. Your faith is based on lies. Your rule book is flawed and your teachers aren't genuine." Leaning forward conspiratorially, he whispered loudly, "But we tried so hard to look that way, didn't we?" He leaned back against the bar smugly, then continued:

"If that's the case, then you gave Phil the wrong answer when he asked why you believe. You should have said you believe because of convenience—because of where and when you were born. Not because of any of that other hogwash." Father M reached behind the bar, grabbed a bottle of scotch and poured himself a drink. He tilted the bottle toward Phil. "You have good taste, my friend. I'm guessing hell will be sans alcohol for you. I imagine we'll keep the succubi away too, just to give you—what do you say?—blue balls." He leered.

Max stared at the back of an empty chair at a nearby table. It was all so natural growing up. Before he could remember much else, he could remember feeling reverence for nature, even praying after a fashion to the wind. At that moment he felt God in the world. Then, when he started going to church in his early teens, he believed God had been speaking to him through all of His other incarnations: the sand dunes, grasslands, and salt marshes. He thought of Romans 1:20: "For since the creation of the world, His invisible attributes, His eternal power and divine nature, have been clearly seen, being understood through what has been made, so that they are without excuse." God made himself known through nature, through love, through relationships.

"But if the Bible has flaws, then maybe Phil's right and none of it can be trusted," Max thought out loud.

"That is correct, Max. None of it can be trusted. Worse still, you were lazy. You chose convenience. You went with what was right in front of you. If you had decided to read Sun Tzu's *Art of War* instead, you might have ended up following Buddhism, or at least something more Eastern. So you're not only a liar, you're slothful. . . ."

Max began to lose his mental footing. He had stood defiantly at the edge and dared Azazel to push him. Now he realized that Azazel had pushed him far harder than he imagined possible.

He tried to run to constant truths. Those things he clung to in his darkest hours. One in particular rose to the top as it so frequently did: *God loves me.* The thought bolstered him momentarily. "God loves me and He wants me. . . ."

"Who loves you, Maxwell?" Father M asked, seemingly offended by his student being so obtuse. He took a drink.

God loves me played through Max's head only to be thoroughly quashed by doubt. "If my conception of God comes from the Bible and my teachers, and both of those are suspect, then my conception of God and His desires is suspect." A far darker thought crept into his mind. "If God loves me He would. . . ."

"Remember what you said before, Max? If God loves you, He would have given you someone to love on this miserable rock as you wait to pass through those Pearly Gates. But since it seems that you are still alone and will likely die alone, then God must not love you. Which means—?" Father M's eyes blazed with delight.

"If what you are saying is true, then I don't know anything about God." Max turned back to the window facing the pond. The words "pearly gates" rattled around in his head. Max squeezed his eyes shut for several seconds. He opened them and stared at the demon.

"Pearly gates? But God doesn't want us to wait for heaven to live our lives. We are called to live our lives choosing to walk the path toward God, to live our lives to the fullest, not—" Max shook his head, recognizing one of Phil's debate tactics. His thoughts ran in circles, trying to find the way out. The word 'choice' rang in his head. "Choosing God—" He stopped, trying to find the right words.

No. Max believed in God. He had chosen that belief and he would keep choosing it. The weight of sorrow and self-loathing began to lift. "Look, demon, I'm not waiting for heaven. I might not ever get there. You are forgetting the most important thing: free will. You've heard of John Piper? —I imagine you have. Remember what John Piper said: 'The gospel is not a way to get people to heaven. It is a way to get people to God.'[128] You are trying to obstruct my path, to guide me down a spiraling road of self-doubt. Very crafty."

Max glanced back at Phil. "But for many years, Phil has been trying to lead me toward his truth and away from my belief in God by using his God-given gifts of logic and debate." He smiled at Phil before turning back toward the demon. "It hasn't worked. If someone I call my friend can't do it—and in fact has turned me into a better Christian because of it—then you"—Max gestured at the demons— "certainly aren't going to do it." Max squared his shoulders and backed up a few steps until he was next to Phil and Michal. Michal reached out her hand and touched Max's arm. "We three have been hashing out arguments for, against, and about God throughout our entire friendship." Michal and Phil nodded.

"Ah, but Max, the Bible clearly states. . . ." Father M pointed to Max's Bible again.

Max's hands began to shake. The doubts were still there, the conflict, the desire to give up. Heroin was an easier demon to defeat than these.

"To quote something you apparently say"—Phil put his hand on Max's shoulder and interrupted the demon—"'don't miss the meaning for the words.' He doesn't read the Bible. He reads the Word of his God. —I get it, Max. I may not agree with it, but I get what you're saying." Phil glanced at his friends, then back at the demons, noting their glowering expressions. "C'mon, I got him to admit that the Bible was fallible and full of inconsistencies. I owe him a bone."

Michal nudged Phil on the shoulder and smiled.

Azazel looked at our three friends and gestured with both his clawed hands. He reached forward to clasp Max's shoulder.

"Max," Azazel's voice softened, "you know what? You're right. I can't convince you and that's good. You're on the path to salvation and who could fault you for a few doubts? Job had doubts, too." He pulled Max closer, away from his friends.

"You turned your life around and walk with Jesus now. I feel for you in those dark moments, not feeling God's love, wondering whether you need to renounce your 'orientation' to be fully loved by God." Azazel guided Max back to the bar, where a needle sat forlorn and pristine against the dark wood of the counter. Inside, a familiar liquid glittered in the low light. Max knew it would be light brown. His arm itched and tingled at the inner elbow. His face twitched slightly as he ground his teeth together, clenching his jaw. His eyes squeezed shut. He pushed Azazel away.

"I know you want it. I can feel it. When you and this syringe were friends, you had no doubts, everything was clear, shining even. I merely want to help you regain that clarity." Azazel extended his hand, syringe steady in his palm. "Remember, Max, there is a time for everything. A time to be strong, a time to be weak, a time for feeling the darkness and hopelessness of doubt, and a time to gain that elusive clarity."

"I forgive you," Max whispered through gritted teeth.

"What?" Azazel took a couple of steps back.

Max stayed where he stood, hands balled into fists at his sides.

"I asked you, boy, what you just said." Azazel's eyes narrowed as he leaned toward Max.

"I—forgive—you," Max whispered again as he backed away. His right hand clasped his left arm at the inner elbow. His fingertips dug into his flesh as he willed himself to forget the syringe.

"Hmph." Azazel's gaze turned from Max to Michal. He slowly circled her, inspecting her, as if peering deeply into her soul. She knew it was her turn and she had been silently bracing herself for his attack.

Remember what happens to Azazel in Enoch. Raphael binds him hand and foot. The desert splits open and he is cast there, covered in rough and jagged rocks and in total darkness, until the Day of Judgment, when he is cast into fire for all of eternity.

Azazel has already lost. He's acting desperately. He's failed with Phil and Max. I can handle this.

Remember the great, powerful Wizard of Oz is exposed as a small, harmless, ordinary middle-aged man. A hoaxer.

Put on the full armor of God, so that you can stand against the devil's schemes.

Neither death nor life, neither angels nor demons, can separate us from the love of God that is in Christ Jesus our Lord.

Azazel stepped back from Michal. He spoke to her with piercing eyes, "You find comfort in quoting the Bible, do you?"

"What?"

"You've been quoting scripture. In your head. Don't think that I can't get into your head. What comfort does this Bible give you when you don't believe a word of it?"

"It's not that I don't believe a word of it. I believe its overall message—that God exists and that He came into the world in the person of Jesus because He loves us."

"So you believe that God exists?"

"I do."

"Well, even the demons believe . . ." Azazel began.

Michal finished his sentence: ". . . and they shudder."

"You don't see me shuddering much now, do you?" He smirked.

"Is this all you've got for me, Mister Azazel, because I'd much rather be spending my time with my friends. You're free to leave. Really. Don't you think you've overstayed your welcome?" Michal was growing impatient.

"Cocky little hellcat, you are." Azazel extended his hand and gently stroked her hair. "I really like you, my little she-devil. We will get along just fine. Ah yes, you are exciting me already. I've prepared a bedroom for us in the Second Circle of Hell."

Michal felt herself getting aroused and felt disgusted at the thought.

Azazel moved his hand to her cheek, gently caressing it. "You like me too, don't you? I can feel it, just as you can feel it." He looked at her seductively. Michal turned away.

Max and Phil smiled at Michal, trying to encourage her. Gaining confidence, she pushed Azazel away. "Back off, demon!"

Azazel smiled widely. "Fine. Let's get back to that Bible of yours, Michal. You reject most of it because there is so much disagreement about it, so many contradictions and difficulties, as you yourself have so skillfully pointed out."

"Right. I can't accept the Bible as literally true and I don't think that any thinking person can."

"If there is so much disagreement about the Bible, as you rightly point out, don't you think that Jesus would be the most reliable authority? He was a good teacher, wasn't He? As a good teacher, wouldn't He communicate the truth clearly?"

"I suppose you're right, if the Bible records Jesus' actual words."

"Wouldn't it? Jesus wrote nothing down, but His followers collected His sayings in codices. You know, little notebooks. Wouldn't they have accurately recorded what Jesus said?"

"I guess you're right again." Michal felt her confidence slip. She grabbed hold of Max's strong arm.

"So Jesus did communicate truth clearly and so the disagreement is not because we don't understand His words, but because we pick and choose what to accept and reject. You say that you can't accept the Bible as literally true, but Jesus Himself did. You see it clearly when He quotes the Hebrew Bible authoritatively. Jesus was a fundamentalist[129]—you know, those fundamentalists you delight in deriding all of the time?"

"Jesus was not a fundamentalist." Michal tried to sound unruffled.

"Sure He was. Do I need to point out all of the ways? Aren't you the one with the Ph.D.? —What do fundamentalists believe, Michal? Come on, you know the answer. Gretchen was a fundamentalist. You remember, your lover Gretchen? I could always count on you and Gretchen to give me a good show. I get excited just thinking about it." Azazel deliberately, brazenly, rubbed his crotch.

Michal felt exposed again and covered her chest with her arms. Her face flushed.

"You turned Gretchen into a porn-addicted, atheistic sex kitten. Did you know that she died last year? Killed in a car accident. She's ours, thanks to you." Azazel beamed in delight.

After a long pause, Michal finally said, "I didn't know that." She felt sickened. How many other souls would she have to answer for?

Azazel egged her on. "Come on, Michal. What do fundamentalists believe?"

Michal began, "They quote Jesus, 'No one can get to the Father except through me.' 'Unless you are born again, you cannot see the kingdom of God.' 'The way to heaven is narrow and hard and few will find it.' Do I have to go on?"

"And that God will separate the sheep from the goats, the wheat from the chaff. So, my little chaffy goat, what does your Jesus believe?"

"The same." Michal felt deflated. Max hugged her and whispered, "You'll be all right."

"So Jesus is a fundamentalist. And as the Son of God, wouldn't He hold true beliefs?"

"He would."

"So fundamentalism is true."

Michal surrendered the words. "You are right."

Max leaned over to Phil and whispered, "She must be throwing him a bone."

"So you can't freely interpret the Bible according to your whims or prejudices. You must believe it to the letter."

"Maybe I am wrong. Maybe, when I die, I will find out that everything in the Bible is true to the letter, as you say. Even that the earth is six thousand years old. The whole of it. I don't really know what to believe anymore." She lowered her head.

"Jesus is Lord, correct? You know what the fundamentalists like to say? 'Lord, liar, or lunatic?'"

"Yes, Jesus is Lord. But I don't believe that Jesus is Lord because of the Bible. I believe it because of my experiences."

"Ah yes, your experiences." Azazel relished the words.

"You seem to know all about me. So you know what I've experienced—angels, demons, even Jesus Himself."

"Well, you say that you've experienced angels and demons and all of the rest. And I suppose that you can't deny what's in front of you right now." He beamed. "But weren't you *inclined* to believe such things? You always were one to believe in imaginary friends. Remember Thomas, your stuffed tiger that Grandma gave you on your eighth birthday? You claimed that he was magical and even told you secrets at night. He's why you love Phil's stone-tiger bench so much—and why you have that tattoo. Ah, those childhood memories. . . ."

"That's just kid's stuff."

"Just like the angel who visited you on your bed—kid's stuff."

"That was different."

"Was it, Michal? Was it really? Look at all of the people in your life who got you thinking this way—Aunt Vi, Maria, Gretchen. You were primed for this kind of thinking. So you wove dreams, nightmares, and wishful thinking into the fabric of your reality. But it's *all* just kid's stuff. Your whole life has been kid's stuff. You just happen to have been exposed to angel and demon talk. But it could have been *tennin* and *oni*."

"Kid's stuff." Michal started. "Perhaps, but no less real." She felt her confidence restored. "You might be right, Mister Azazel. It might all just be kid's stuff, but I love my life now. My changed life. I love myself and I love others, most of all my two friends here." Michal grabbed Phil and Max's hands and squeezed tightly. "And all this because I love my God. And I choose to love Him. You can never take that away from me."

Phil and Max leaned against each other, brothers in arms, much as they had in countless bars as they sized up the patrons or the conversations around them. They smiled. Michal was finished. She turned toward Max and Phil, eyes bright. Our three friends stared down Azazel, ignoring Father M.

"Seriously. . . ." Max dropped his hands to his sides and relaxed. "Just what did you hope to accomplish with this farce? Are we all hopelessly flawed? Yes. Are we all sinners in desperate need of a Savior? Of course. What exactly were you going to throw at us that could be worse than what we've already heaped on ourselves? We've all been at the bottom. I have skated the thin ice that lies between everlasting life and eternal isolation. I have heard God's voice in both a whisper and a deafening fury. I choose to listen to the voice of God."

Michal replied, "I choose the same. I will stand against you in His name."

Phil looked at the demon, "Amen! —Wait, that's not my voice. I will stand against you, too, but because it's the logical and rational thing to do—God or no God. You, sir, are no gentleman. You are—"

"Hmmm. Curious, that." Azazel wiped his face with his hands. His cowboy garb changed into an impeccably tailored navy-blue suit, crisp, white tab-collared shirt, and emerald-green tie. "That's not how I thought it would end." He picked an imaginary piece of lint from his lapel. "And I was so looking forward to that naked hot-tub scene. No matter. You creatures are always a source of amusement and surprises. This isn't the first time it's turned out unexpectedly. I wager it won't be the last." Azazel straightened his tie. He bowed his head.

"Devil, just come on back if you ever wanna try again," Phil said.

Michal gave a frown. "I think we've had enough. In the name of—"

Azazel held up his hand. "You can stop right there, luscious. We're going. Besides, as you've already found out, that doesn't work with me." He extended his hand to Father M and they headed toward the door. "It's been—interesting." He paused and looked back at our three friends. "I'm off to another appointment."

"Go back to your *boss*, demon," Michal said, "And just so you know: I wouldn't touch you with a thirty-nine-and-a-half-foot pole!" Max and Phil held her back as she tried to pursue them with swinging arms. Azazel turned and winked. "If you only knew what I know. No, your human brain couldn't take it. His could." He gestured at Phil. "And maybe his." He motioned to Max. "But not yours."

Azazel and Father M reached the door. "One piece of advice: stay on the path."

Phil chuckled. "And keep clear of the moors?"

Max laughed. "And beware the moon!"

Phil looked at Azazel with a smirk. "Come back anytime. The bar's always open."

"Don't worry, I'll be around. I'm sure I'll see each of you again—one of you sooner rather than later." With that, Azazel and Father M vanished.

Phil stared at the suitcases waiting to be loaded into the car that hadn't yet arrived. He swore he could hear a little voice coming from inside Michal's suitcase, squeaking "California, here I come!" He laughed at the thought. A breeze blew in from the open *shōji* screens and brought with it a damp chill. So much changed so quickly. How the time had passed. He waited for Max and Michal to come back into the bar, waited beside Max's teacup and Michal's wine glass.

Max checked the room for the last time and caught his reflection in the mirror as he reached for the door. His eyes looked tired—tired from staying up night after night, talking till the Japanese roosters crowed. He wouldn't trade that for all the sleep in the world. He smiled. They would still argue about free will and the afterlife, but there were new topics now, including whatever other kinds of supernatural creatures might exist. Even Phil's unicorns were a possibility, in Max's mind, anyway.

Michal picked up her purse and sunglasses and gave Kwan Yin one last glance before she shut the screen to her room. Her eyebrows knit together, a common expression since their confrontation with Azazel. She walked across the gravel path, opened the door to the bar and ran into Max.

"Ready?" Max asked.

"I think so. What time did we go to bed?"

"Around three, I think. Then I stayed up a bit longer thinking. You?"

"The same. At least I haven't had any more nightmares." They walked up to Phil, who was holding out a wine glass in one hand and a teacup in the other.

"I still think you both need to stay. We can go to Mount Fuji or Jigokudani Monkey Park. Maybe we can visit Himeji Castle. I hear that's really nice. What about Australia or New Zealand? The plane I have on reserve can go almost anywhere, except maybe Russia right now. We wouldn't want to make Max uncomfortable. . . ." Phil kept talking while Max and Michal sipped their drinks.

"Phil, we've both got to get back for a little while. We can figure out our schedules and take that trip." Max laughed and grasped Phil by the shoulder. "We won't leave you hanging for long."

"We'll make that trip happen soon, Phil. I promise." Michal put her wine glass on the bar and hugged him.

"C'mon, let's just leave now. It'll be fun." Phil knew what the answer would be. Michal and Max glanced at each other. Worry flitted across their features.

"We promise, Phil." Michal patted his shoulder. "As soon as we can, we'll meet up."

"Yeah, some of us actually have to work for a living, you bum." Max smiled.

"How much for you guys to stay, then? Ten? Fifteen thousand? What's money for, if you can't spend it on your friends?" Phil tried to hide the need he felt, the need to keep his friends close.

"When did you turn into a drama queen? That's my job." Max laughed. "I love you, my friend. We'll be back." He gave Phil a big hug.

"Get a room!" Michal laughed.

A horn honked. Michal and Max looked at the door. Phil frowned.

"We'll meet up—a month, tops." Max set the teacup on the counter and opened his arms. "Come on, give us a kiss." He puckered his lips and got a wet towel in the face.

"One month. I'm holding you two to that. One month or I'm coming to get you. I'll air all of your dirty laundry in front of the people who mistakenly respect your godly ways." Phil waved a pointed finger at his friends before picking up the wet towel that had fallen with a squishy plop in front of Max.

Phil tossed the towel in the sink behind the bar and used his long legs to beat Michal to her luggage. Max shook his head and picked up his suitcase, following Phil and Michal to the SUV. Max pointed at Phil. "Now look who's wearing high heels?" He smiled.

Phil looked down at his worn bunny slippers and looked back up at Max. "High heels?"

"Never mind. We'll tell you about it some other time." Max and Michal laughed.

Our three friends embraced once more and then Michal and Max got in the SUV.

Phil watched them head down the road, then chuckled as they hit a monster pothole. He turned back, entered the empty bar and looked around. He imagined the bar full of life—demonic or otherwise—and spun in a little circle, listening to the dreamt-up commotion. He closed his eyes and smiled. Eventually he opened his eyes, very much alone, lonely. Forlorn, he walked behind the bar, picked up the towel in the sink and began to clean. He bent over to rinse it out, and when he straightened up he saw an American-looking couple entering the bar, looking lost.

"Um, hello?" The woman began.

"Hi. I mean, uh, *koneechiwa yokoso*. Are you looking for a drink or some food? Maybe a room?" Phil asked.

They looked at him. "How much is a room? We just walked up here from the village. My wife was buying a little snow globe and we saw this place from the shop. We have a limited budget—" The man sounded almost apologetic.

"You're in luck. Today only, the first two nights are free whether you stay more than two nights or not." For the first time since buying the bar, Phil's smile reached his eyes.

Azazel walked through an uncharacteristically green meadow—a green so sharp it was painful even to him. Squinting, he approached the blizzard-white wall and turned the blizzard-white door knob of the pristine, almost invisible door. The familiar room loomed before him with its blazing fireplace and all-white decor. Defiantly, he pulled out his Cuban cigar, lit it, and pulled out a glass ashtray from his green suit coat pocket. The chair creaked as he got comfortable and waited.

"Oh, there you are, Sir." Azazel puffed on the cigar and exhaled the smoke, away from his employer. "Thank you, thank you. I lost faith—no pun intended—for a while there. I wasn't sure it was going to go according to—" Azazel shook his head. "Of course not. I look nothing like Thomas. But I don't have your faith, Sir. I wasn't built that way. The only faith I hold is—" He swallowed and paused, blanching at the look on his employer's face. "Oh." He laughed a full belly laugh and took another puff on his cigar. "You almost had me there. I don't understand why people are always saying you have no sense of humor. It's sharp, Sir, wicked sharp."

Azazel listened to his employer's evaluation and his eyes went wide. "Ah," he laughed, "you got me there again." His eyes shot to the fireplace while he pulled himself together. "I agree completely. They just don't make them like they used to. Well, maybe in the cinema—like those guys Sam and Dean. There's a pair who've always kept their faith no matter what screwed-up path they've chosen. Why can't we have more of that?" Azazel hoped that his diversion was working.

"Ah, touché, Sir. Speaking of that, I've got new recruits to torture and belittle as well as new files to look over. Would it be all right with you if I looked in on the boys from time to time?"

Azazel took another puff and tapped the white ash into his ashtray. He brought the cigar up to his lips and took a long drag before speaking again. Smoke puffed out with each word. "No, no—hands on only if it's warranted. You know those humans, always exercising that pesky free will—why that was a good idea, I'll never know." Azazel choked on the last of the smoke as he felt invisible fingers wrap around his throat—ironic, because he didn't need to breathe.

"Sorry, Sir," his words came out in a squeak. He exhaled the rest of the smoke. His eyebrow lifted, voice dripping with incredulity. "You've got to be kidding. Really? But these are my favorites." Azazel took the box of cigars and began to ingest them until nothing remained. "Happy?"

Despite having eaten his cigars, Azazel walked out of the house smiling. As he stepped through the door, the green meadow was gone, replaced by the bright neon lights and dingy streets of Vegas, off-strip. Azazel rubbed his palms together and took out a fresh box of cigars. He adjusted his emerald tie and walked into the casino, a smirk chiseled on his features.

NINETEEN

She was their Ammu and their Baba and she had loved them Double.
ARUNDHATI ROY, *THE GOD OF SMALL THINGS*

ONE YEAR LATER, JUNE 15, 2015

A black stretch limousine pulled up.

Rain fell steadily, partially obscuring the panoramic view of the Pacific Ocean from the corner of the Santa Barbara Cemetery. Dozens of people, mostly clad in black, walked quickly to their cars, black umbrellas shielding them from the downpour. One couple—a woman decked out in snow-leopard print and a faux fur stole, and a tall man in a charcoal suit and shamrock tie—strolled along the sidewalk, making their way past the mourners. Their umbrella, green as a black cat's eyes, stood out amidst those who had gathered.

Max and Phil rose from the chairs ringing the fresh grave. The scents of jasmine, orchid, magnolia and gladiolus hung like a ghostly mist. The rain, which had begun the moment Max had finished his prayer to the mourners, ran down the backs of both men's overcoats. Max glanced at his umbrella lying at the legs of his chair. He put his hands in his pockets and let the water cling to his eyelashes.

Phil buried his face in the spray of peach Juliet roses, white orchids, and Michal's favorite—red tulips. His fist closed around the stems, thorns piercing his skin. He pulled his hand back and stared at the red droplets as they mixed with the rain in the upturned palm of his hand. He turned to Max, wondering whether the water on his face was just rain or a mix of pain and nature.

"What do you really believe, Max? In light of everything we've been through, what do you really believe?" Phil let his hand drop, the pink water falling on the freshly turned dirt.

"Nothing's changed for me, other than continued clarity—and a boyfriend. I've been studying Job, though. The testing, the tempting. . . ." Max's voice sounded hollow even to himself. "I do think her soul is with God if that helps." Max looked at Phil's hand and reached inside his coat pocket for a handkerchief. He took the hand, wrapped the cloth around the palm and closed his fingers around it, before tying a knot in the fabric. He noticed that Phil's other hand was clutching the necklace. Max raised his face to the clouds, letting the water spatter on his cheeks. "I think she's probably giving Him hell, though." They chuckled.

"This all feels so surreal." Phil glanced around. The mist had begun to roll in from the ocean, the salty droplets clinging to his eyelashes and beard. It looked as if the clouds had descended to the tops of the trees that divided this corner of the cemetery from the church next door. If he reached out far enough, he could touch them. *As close to the heavens as I can get, short of a space shuttle,* Phil mused. He bowed his head.

Words echoed in Max's mind. *Weeping may last for the night, but a shout of joy comes in the morning.* But just how long does the night last? He looked at Phil and wondered at the sight—Phil's chin lowered and eyes closed. Maybe the night won't last that long after all.

Phil raised his head and looked at the gravestone that he and Max had purchased:

BRILLIANT WOMAN, STUBBORN HUMAN BEING, FAITHFUL FRIEND

He thought of how Michal's Aunt Vi had reacted when she saw it. No reference to God. He smiled.

"So what did the doctors say?" Phil jumped at the sound of Max's voice.

"Doc says everything is fine. It was all a mistake." Phil turned his back to the gravestone.

"That's irony for you. I hate irony. Irony's a bitch." Max pushed the toe of his black loafers into the mud, making a shallow indentation that quickly filled with water.

"Nope, irony is one of three male characters in ancient Greek comedy," Phil said.

Max grimaced.

"Never mind, let's go get a drink. I know this great bar. . . ." They began to walk toward the laneway leading to the cemetery entrance, where the limo waited.

"Shut up, Phil." Max poked at him good-naturedly. "As usual, you're ruining the moment."

A GLOSSARY OF JAPANESE TERMS USED IN THE NOVEL

gaijin a foreigner.

geta a Japanese wooden shoe with an elevated base and a fabric thong that passes between the big toe and the second toe.

kabuto a type of Japanese helmet first used by ancient Japanese warriors and in later periods worn as part of the traditional Japanese armor of the samurai class.

kakebuton the comforter or quilt portion of a Japanese futon set.

kami a divine being in the Shinto religion.

kappa a yōkai found in Japanese folklore.

kappamaki a cucumber sushi roll.

kasagi the horizontal beam of a torii.

koshihikari a popular variety of rice, cultivated in Japan.

kuraokami a legendary Japanese dragon and Shinto deity of rain and snow.

makura a traditional Japanese pillow, often made of buckwheat.

nattō a traditional Japanese food made from fermented soybeans, with a powerful smell, strong flavor, and slimy texture.

nori an edible seaweed eaten either fresh or dried in sheets.

oni demons or ghosts of Japanese folklore.

ryokan a traditional Japanese inn.

shikibuton the mattress portion of a Japanese futon.

shōji a sliding outer or inner door, made of a latticed screen covered with paper.

sugegasa an Asian conical hat used primarily as protection from the sun and rain.

tatami a rush-covered straw mat often used as traditional Japanese floor covering.

tennin spiritual beings found in Japanese Buddhism, similar to Western angels.

tōrō a traditional Japanese lantern made of stone, wood, or metal.

torii a traditional Japanese gate often found at the entrance of a Shinto shrine.

tsunokakushi a traditional headwear worn by the bride in Shinto wedding ceremonies.

yōkai supernatural monsters and spirits found in Japanese folklore.

zori a traditional Japanese-style sandal similar to a flip-flop.

NOTES AND REFERENCES

[1] See René Descartes (1641), Meditation 1, *Meditations on First Philosophy.*

[2] "The Butterfly Dream" is found in the *Zhuangzi*, a third century BCE Chinese text, named after its traditional author, Zhuang Zhou.

[3] See Gilbert Harman, *Thought* (1973).

[4] Professor Martin Luther makes this point in David Davalos' 2008 play *Wittenberg.*

[5] See "Time," *Stanford Encyclopedia of Philosophy* at plato.stanford.edu.

[6] See J.M.E. McTaggart's "The Unreality of Time" (1908), *Mind* 17, 457–474.

[7] See Maurice Merleau-Ponty's *Phenomenology of Perception* (1945).

[8] Komarine Romdenh-Romluc provides a similar example in *Routledge Philosophy Guidebook to Merleau-Ponty and Phenomenology of Perception* (2011).

[9] This view is often called "Reductionism with Respect to Time," which is opposed to the view offered by Plato and Newton, often called "Platonism with Respect to Time." Aristotle's view on time is found in his *Physics* (4th century BCE). Plato's conception is found in his *Timaeus* (4th century BCE).

[10] See Sidney Shoemaker's "Time Without Change" (1969) *Journal of Philosophy* 66, 363–381.

[11] See Immanuel Kant (1781), *Critique of Pure Reason.*

[12] Plato's aesthetics is found in several of his dialogues, including the *Symposium, Republic, Parmenides, Phaedo, Phaedrus, and Philebus.*

[13] See Ivan Panin (1891), *The Structure of the Bible: A Proof of the Verbal Inspiration of Scripture.*

[14] See Denis Dutton, "Aesthetics and Evolutionary Psychology," *The Oxford Handbook for Aesthetics,* ed. Jerrold Levinson (2003).

[15] See David Hume (1738), *A Treatise of Human Nature.*

[16] See Immanuel Kant (1790), *Critique of Judgment.*

[17] See Michal Rosen (2012), *Dignity: Its History and Meaning.*

[18] Thanks to Randall Sunshine for educating us about veterinarians and suicide.

[19] See Michael Coogan (2011), *God and Sex: What the Bible Really Says.*

[20] See Gail Corrington Streete (1998), *The Strange Woman: Power and Sex in the Bible.*

[21] See Jennifer Wright Knust (2012), *Unprotected Texts: The Bible's Surprising Contradictions about Sex and Desire.*

[22] Many of Max's arguments are presented in Daniel Helminiak's book, *What the Bible Really Says about Homosexuality* (2000).

[23] For a good discussion about mixings, confusions, and boundary crossings, see Jerome T. Walsh (2001) "Leviticus 18:22 and 20:13: Who is Doing What to Whom?" *Journal of Biblical Literature,* 120:2.

[24] Edith M. Humphrey makes this argument in "The New Testament Speaks on Same-Sex Eroticism" (2003) at edithhumphrey.net.

[25] See Karl Heinrich Ulrichs (1862) *The Riddle of Man-Manly Love.*

[26] This type of argument is discussed by blogger Dan Herrick in his post "Is Christianity Anti-Gay?" found at danherrickphilosophy.com.

[27] Max's argument can be found in Macrina Cooper-White's "Homosexuality May Have Evolved in Humans Because it Helps us Bond, Scientists Say," *Huffington Post* (November 26, 2014).

[28] See Aristotle's *On Interpretation.*

[29] See Alan Patten (2002), *Hegel's Idea of Freedom* (Oxford Philosophical Monographs) and Georg Wilhelm Friedrich Hegel (1820), *Philosophy of Right.*

[30] See Immanuel Kant's *Groundwork of the Metaphysics of Morals* (1785) and *Critique of Practical Reason* (1788).

[31] See Simone De Beauvoir (1949) *The Second Sex,* and Jean-Paul Sartre's *Being and Nothingness* (1943).

[32] See A.J. Ayer (1954), "Freedom and Necessity."

[33] See Susan Wolf (1980), "Asymmetrical Freedom," *The Journal of Philosophy* 77(3), 151–166.

[34] See Gottfried Leibniz's *Théodicée* (1710), and Voltaire's *Candide* (1759).

[35] See Peter Tse (2013), *The Neural Basis of Freewill: Criterial Causation.*

[36] See Anselm's *Proslogion* (1078), and Descartes' Meditation 5, *Meditations on First Philosophy* (1641).

[37] See Richard Taylor (1963), *Metaphysics.*

[38] See Ray Bradford, "Moral Responsibility in a Deterministic Universe," at westminstercollege.edu.

[39] See P.F. Strawson (1962) "Freedom and Resentment," *Proceedings of the British Academy* 48, 1–25.

[40] Michal is referring to the moral theories of Immanuel Kant, Aristotle, and Jeremy Bentham and John Stuart Mill.

[41] See James D. Tabor (2013), *Paul and Jesus: How the Apostle Transformed Christianity.*

[42] See Roger E. Olson, "How serious a heresy is universalism?" at patheos.com.

[43] For a similar discussion, see Peter Kreeft (1990), *Everything You Ever Wanted to Know About Heaven But Never Dreamed of Asking.*

[44] See Bertrand Russell (1927), "Why I am Not a Christian."

[45] See James A. Fowler, "Universalism: Forms and Fallacies" at christinyou.net.

[46] See Peter Kreeft (1995), *Angels and Demons: What Do We Really Know About Them?*

[47] A version of Max's argument can be found in Peter Kreeft (1990), *Everything You Ever Wanted to Know about Heaven But Never Dreamed of Asking.*

[48] See Susan Wolf (2015), "The Meanings of Lives" in her *The Variety of Values: Essays on Morality, Meaning, and Love.*

[49] See John Stuart Mill (1863), Chapter 2, *Utilitarianism.*

[50] David Wiggins (1976), "Truth, Invention, and the Meaning of Life," *Proceedings of the British Academy* LXII.

[51] See Lewis Richmond (2013), "Emptiness: The Most Misunderstood Word in Buddhism," *Huffington Post* at huffingtonpost.com.

[52] See M.E. Waithe, *A History of Women Philosophers*, in four volumes (1987, 1989, 1991, 1994) and "Feminist History of Philosophy," *Stanford Encyclopedia of Philosophy* at plato.stanford.edu.

[53] See Genevieve Lloyd (1993), *Man of Reason: Male and Female in Western Philosophy*, and Susan Bordo (1987), *The Flight to Objectivity: Essays on Cartesianism and Culture.*

[54] See Alejandro Korn, "Values are Subjective," in *Latin American Philosophy in the Twentieth Century* (1980) ed. Jorge Garcia and trans. Francis Myers.

[55] See Robert Gnuse (2011), *No Tolerance for Tyrants: The Biblical Assault on Kings and Kingship.*

[56] See A.J. Ayer (1936), *Language, Truth, and Logic.*

[57] Augustine (5th century CE), *On the Trinity.*

[58] A respondent, "Philotheia," makes a similar argument to the question: Can you prove that the invisible pink unicorn doesn't exist? *Yahoo! Answers.*

[59] See Anthony Flew (2000), "Theology and Falsification: A Golden Jubilee Celebration" at infidels.org.

[60] See Claudia Card (2005), *The Atrocity Paradigm.*

[61] See Charlotte Delbo (1985), *Auschwitz and After.*

[62] See, for example, Kant (1790), *Critique of Judgment.*

[63] See Eric Michael Johnson (2012), "Ayn Rand vs. the Pygmies: Did Human Evolution Favor Individualists or Altruists?" at slate.com.

[64] See Friedrich Nietzsche (1887), *On the Genealogy of Morals.*

[65] See David Hume (1751), *An Enquiry Concerning the Principles of Morals.*

[66] See Richard Dawkins (1976), *The Selfish Gene.*

[67] Joshua May, "Psychological Egoism," *Internet Encyclopedia of Philosophy.*

[68] See Richard Rorty (1989), *Contingency, Irony, and Solidarity* and Porty (1994), "Human Rights, Rationality, and Sentimentality," in *On Human Rights* (Oxford Amnesty Lectures), eds. Stephen Shute and Susan Hurley. See also John Dewey (1960), *The Quest for Certainty: A Study of the Relation of Knowledge and Action* (Gifford Lectures 1929).

[69] For similar examples, see "Duck God is Best," at r/atheism reddit.com.

[70] See Philippa Foot (2003), *Moral Dilemmas: And Other Topics in Moral Philosophy*

[71] Thanks to Carrol Miller for sharing the story of the Peng and the dove.

[72] Thanks to Jordan Quinn whose Facebook post inspired this comment.

[73] See Okot p'Bitek, "On Culture, Man, and Freedom," in *Philosophy and Cultures* (1983) eds. H. Odera Oruka and D.A. Masolo.

[74] See John Locke (1690), *An Essay Concerning Human Understanding.*

[75] See Susan James, "Feminism in Philosophy of Mind: The Question of Personal Identity," in *The Cambridge Companion to Feminism in Philosophy* (2000) eds. Miranda Fricker and Jennifer Hornsby, and Rae Langton, "Feminism in Philosophy," *The Oxford Handbook of Contemporary Philosophy* (2008), eds. Frank Jackson and Michael Smith.

[76] For a similar example, see the *Stanford Encyclopedia of Philosophy*, "Personal Identity," at plato.stanford.edu.

[77] See Ted Sider, "Temporal Parts," in *Contemporary Debates in Metaphysics* (2007), eds. T. Sider and J. Hawthorne.

[78] See John Searle, "The Chinese Room," in *The MIT Encyclopedia of the Cognitive Sciences* (2001), eds. R. A. Wilson and F. Keil.

[79] See Sandra Harding, ed. (2004), *The Feminist Standpoint Reader: Intellectual and Political Controversies.*

[80] Sandra Harding (2004), "Comment on Heckman's 'Truth and Method: Feminist Standpoint Revisited': Whose Standpoint Needs the Regimes of Truth and Reality?" in *The Feminist Standpoint Theory Reader: Intellectual and Political Controversies*, ed. Sandra Harding.

[81] Much of this discussion draws on "Truth," *Internet Encyclopedia of Philosophy* at iep.utm.edu.

[82] Sigmund Freud (1927), *The Future of an Illusion.*

[83] See William James (1907), *Pragmatism: A New Name for Some Old Ways of Thinking*, and *The Meaning of Truth* (1909). See Michel Foucault (1980), "Truth and Power," in *Power/Knowledge: Selected Interviews and Other Writings, 1972–1977*, ed. C. Gordon.

[84] See José Medina (2012), *The Epistemology of Resistance: Gender and Racial Oppression, Epistemic Injustice, and Resistant Imaginations.*

[85] See Baudouin Dupret (2011), *Practices of Truth: An Ethnomethodological Inquiry into Arab Contexts.*

[86] See Plato's *Apology.*

[87] Jeff Mason, "Death and Its Concept," philosophersmag.com, January 31, 2015.

[88] See Peter Kreeft (1990), *Everything You Ever Wanted to Know About Heaven.*

[89] See Thomas Hobbes, *Leviathan* (1651) and *De Corpore* (1655).

[90] See P.M. Churchland (1981), "Eliminative Materialism and the Propositional Attitudes," *Journal of Philosophy* 78, 67-90, and P. S. Churchland (1989), *Neurophysiology: Toward a Unified Science of Mind/Brain.*

[91] T.H. Huxley (1904), "On the Hypothesis that Animals are Automata, and Its History," in *Methods and Results: Essays by Thomas H. Huxley.*

[92] See John Hawthorne, "Cartesian Dualism," *Persons Human and Divine* (2007), eds. P. van Inwagen and D. Zimmerman.

[93] See for example "Human Evolution and Souls," *Philosophy Forums* at forums.philosophyforums.com.

[94] See Peter Kreeft (1990), *Everything You Ever Wanted to Know about Heaven But Never Dreamed of Asking,* which discusses the various possibilities of life after death.

[95] See the entry on the soul in *The Catholic Encyclopedia,* Volume 14, Charles George Herbermann, ed.

[96] Richard Swinburne (2003), *The Resurrection of God Incarnate.*

[97] G.M. Woerlee, "The Denture Man NDE," on the site *Near Death Experiences: Is There a Life after Death?,* at neardth.com

[98] See David Hume (1748), *An Enquiry Concerning Human Understanding.*

[99] See Ludwig Wittgenstein (1953), *Philosophical Investigations.*

[100] See Plato, Book VII, *The Republic.*

[101] See John G. Neilhardt (1988), *Black Elk Speaks.*

[102] See Adi Shankara, "A Commentary on the Upanishads," in George Thibaut, trans., *The Vendata Sutras of Badarayana with the Commentary by Shankara, Part I.*

[103] See George Berkeley's *Principles* and *Dialogues,* found in *The Works of George Berkeley, Bishop of Cloyne* (1967), eds. A. A. Luce and T. E. Jessop.

[104] See John Locke (1690), *An Essay Concerning Human Understanding.*

[105] See René Descartes (1641), Meditation 3, *Meditations on First Philosophy.*

[106] See Immanuel Kant (1781), *Critique of Pure Reason.*

[107] Sarvepalli Radhakrishnan (2009), *An Idealist View of Life.*

[108] Rudolf Bultmann makes a similar point in *New Testament and Mythology and Other Basic Writings* (1984), ed. and trans. Schubert M. Ogden.

[109] Many of Max and Michal's points are found in Joan Carroll Cruz (1999), *Angels and Devils.*

[110] See C.S. Lewis (1952), *Mere Christianity* and Lewis (1940), *The Problem of Pain.*

[111] See Augustine, *City of God.*

[112] See Taylor Marshall, "When were the Angels Created? (Saint Augustine)" at taylormarshall.com.

[113] Rudolf Bultmann (1984), *New Testament and Mythology and Other Basic Writings,* ed. and trans. Schubert M. Ogden.

[114] The *Testimonium Flavianum* (or Testimony of Flavius Josephus) is the name given to the passage at Book 18, chapter 3, 3, of Josephus' *Antiquities of the Jews.*

[115] Many of Michal's arguments here are given in William Lane Craig and Walter Sinnott-Armstrong (2004), *God? A Debate between a Christian and an Atheist.*

[116] See James D. Tabor (2013), *Paul and Jesus: How the Apostle Transformed Christianity.*

[117] See Rudolf Bultmann (1984), *New Testament and Mythology and Other Basic Writings*, ed. and trans. Schubert M. Ogden.

[118] See William Lane Craig and Walter Sinnott-Armstrong (2004), *God? A Debate between a Christian and an Atheist.*

[119] See William Alston (1993), *Perceiving God: The Epistemology of Religious Experience.*

[120] David Hume (1748), "Of Miracles," Section X, *An Enquiry Concerning Human Understanding.*

[121] *Ibid.*

[122] James D. Tabor (2007), *The Jesus Dynasty: The Hidden History of Jesus, His Royal Family, and the Birth of Christianity.*

[123] See Bertrand Russell, "An Outline of Intellectual Rubbish" in Russell (2009), *The Basic Writings of Bertrand Russell.*

[124] See, for example, "Can Good People Go to Hell," at www.dailycatholic.org.

[125] Daniel C. Dennett and Alvin Plantinga (2011), *Science and Religion: Are They Compatible?*

[126] See Miguel de Unamuno (1954), "The Hunger of Immortality," in *The Tragic Sense of Life*, trans. J. Crawford Fitch.

[127] See James Morrow (1997), *Blameless in Abaddon*, where Jonathan Sarkos, aka the Devil, makes this point.

[128] John Piper (2011), *God is the Gospel: Meditations on God' Love as the Gift of Himself.*

[129] We find this argument in Peter Kreeft's book, *Socrates Meets Jesus: History's Greatest Questioner Confronts the Claims of Christ* (2002).

INDEX OF PHILOSOPHERS, THEOLOGIANS, WRITERS, AND OTHER THINKERS

Made in the USA
San Bernardino, CA
30 June 2016